Corruption, Fraud, Organized Crime, and the Shadow Economy

Advances in Police Theory and Practice Series

Series Editor: Dilip K. Das

Civilian Oversight of Police: Advancing Accountability in Law Enforcement
Tim Prenzler and Garth den Heyer

Collaborative Policing: Police, Academics, Professionals, and Communities Working Together for Education, Training, and Program Implementation
Peter C. Kratcoski and Maximilian Edelbacher

Corruption, Fraud, Organized Crime, and the Shadow Economy
Maximilian Edelbacher, Peter C. Kratcoski, and Bojan Dobovšek

Policing in Israel: Studying Crime Control, Community Policing, and Counter-Terrorism
Tal Jonathan-Zamir, David Weisburd, and Badi Hasisi

Policing Terrorism: Research Studies into Police Counterterrorism Investigations
David Lowe

Policing in Hong Kong: History and Reform
Kam C. Wong

Cold Cases: Evaluation Models with Follow-up Strategies for Investigators, Second Edition
James M. Adcock and Sarah L. Stein

Crime Linkage: Theory, Research, and Practice
Jessica Woodhams and Craig Bennell

Police Investigative Interviews and Interpreting: Context, Challenges, and Strategies
Sedat Mulayim, Miranda Lai, and Caroline Norma

Policing White Collar Crime: Characteristics of White Collar Criminals
Petter Gottschalk

Honor-Based Violence: Policing and Prevention
Karl Anton Roberts, Gerry Campbell, and Glen Lloyd

Policing and the Mentally Ill: International Perspectives
Duncan Chappell

Security Governance, Policing, and Local Capacity
Jan Froestad with Clifford D. Shearing

Policing in Hong Kong: History and Reform
Kam C. Wong

Police Performance Appraisals: A Comparative Perspective
Serdar Kenan Gul and Paul O'Connell

Los Angeles Police Department Meltdown: The Fall of the Professional-Reform Model of Policing
James Lasley

Financial Crimes: A Global Threat
Maximilian Edelbacher, Peter Kratcoski, and Michael Theil

Police Integrity Management in Australia: Global Lessons for Combating Police Misconduct
Louise Porter and Tim Prenzler

The Crime Numbers Game: Management by Manipulation
John A. Eterno and Eli B. Silverman

The International Trafficking of Human Organs: A Multidisciplinary Perspective
Leonard Territo and Rande Matteson

Police Reform in China
Kam C. Wong

Mission-Based Policing
John P. Crank, Dawn M. Irlbeck, Rebecca K. Murray, and Mark Sundermeier

The New Khaki: The Evolving Nature of Policing in India
Arvind Verma

Cold Cases: An Evaluation Model with Follow-up Strategies for Investigators
James M. Adcock and Sarah L. Stein

Policing Organized Crime: Intelligence Strategy Implementation
Petter Gottschalk

Security in Post-Conflict Africa: The Role of Nonstate Policing
Bruce Baker

Community Policing and Peacekeeping
Peter Grabosky

Community Policing: International Patterns and Comparative Perspectives
Dominique Wisler and Ihekwoaba D. Onwudiwe

Police Corruption: Preventing Misconduct and Maintaining Integrity
Tim Prenzler

FORTHCOMING

Women in Policing: An International Perspective
Venessa Garcia and Patrick F. McManimon, Jr.

Stalking: Policing, Investigation, and Prevention
Karl Roberts and Michelle M. Garcia

Police Reform in The New Democratic South Africa
Moses Montesh and Vinesh Basdeo

Corruption, Fraud, Organized Crime, and the Shadow Economy

Edited by
Maximilian Edelbacher
Peter C. Kratcoski
Bojan Dobovšek

CRC Press
Taylor & Francis Group
Boca Raton London New York

CRC Press is an imprint of the
Taylor & Francis Group, an **informa** business

CRC Press
Taylor & Francis Group
6000 Broken Sound Parkway NW, Suite 300
Boca Raton, FL 33487-2742

Printed on acid-free paper
Version Date: 20150909

International Standard Book Number-13: 978-1-4822-5531-7 (Hardback)

Visit the Taylor & Francis Web site at
http://www.taylorandfrancis.com

and the CRC Press Web site at
http://www.crcpress.com

This book is dedicated to Maxmilian Edelbacher, son of Maximilian Edelbacher.

Contents

Series Editor's Preface

While the literature on police and allied subjects is growing exponentially, its impact upon day-to-day policing remains small. The two worlds of research and practice of policing remain disconnected even though cooperation between the two is growing. One of the major reasons is that the two groups speak in different languages. The research work is often published in hard-to-access journals and presented in a manner that is difficult to comprehend for a layperson. On the other hand, police practitioners tend not to mix with researchers and remain secretive about their work. Consequently, there is little dialog between the two and almost no attempt to learn from one another. Dialog across the globe, among researchers and practitioners situated in different continents, is of course even more limited.

I attempted to address this problem by starting the International Police Executive Symposium (IPES: www.ipes.info), where a common platform has brought the two together. IPES is now in its 22nd year. The annual meetings that constitute most of the major annual events of the organization have been hosted in all parts of the world. Several publications have come out of these deliberations and a new collaborative community of scholars and police officers has been created whose membership runs into the several hundreds.

Another attempt was to begin a new journal, aptly called *Police Practice and Research: An International Journal* (PPR) that has opened the gate for practitioners to share their work and experiences. The journal has attempted to focus on issues that help bring the two onto a single platform. PPR is completing its 16 years in 2015. It is certainly an evidence of the growing collaboration between police research and practice that PPR, which began with four issues a year, expanded into five issues in its fourth year and, now, it is issued six times a year.

Clearly, these attempts, despite their success, remain limited. Conferences and journal publications do help create a body of knowledge and an association of police activists but cannot address substantial issues in depth. The limitations of time and space preclude larger discussions and more authoritative expositions that can provide stronger and broader linkages between the two worlds.

It is this realization of the increasing dialog between police research and practice that has encouraged many of us—my close colleagues and I connected closely with IPES and PPR across the world—to conceive and implement a new attempt in this direction. This led to the book series, Advances in Police Theory and Practice, that seeks to attract writers from all parts of the world. Further, the attempt is to find practitioner contributors. The objective is to make the series a serious contribution to our knowledge of the police and to improve police practices. The focus is not only on work that describes the best and successful police practices but also one that challenges current paradigms and breaks new ground to prepare the police for the twenty-first century. The series seeks a comparative analysis that highlights achievements in distant parts of the world and one that encourages an in-depth examination of specific problems confronting a particular police force.

Corruption, Fraud, Organized Crime, and the Shadow Economy examines the interconnections of the formal economy, the informal economy, corruption, fraud, financial crimes, and organized crime in various countries throughout the world.

The meaning of the term *shadow (informal) economy* is generally not fully understood, even by those who study economics and the relationship of economics to crime. In this book, the various meanings of the term are explained to illustrate how the shadow economy is manifested.

While every country will have some form of a shadow (informal) economy, the extent and manner in which the informal economy is manifested by each country depends on a number of factors, including the stability of the government, the stability of the laws governing the people, the amount of internal and external conflict the country is experiencing, the resources available for the country to develop and prosper, and the quality of the leadership. To this extent, financial crime, fraud, corruption, and organized crime can prosper in countries that have weak leaders and insufficient crime control mechanisms.

It is hoped that through this series it will be possible to accelerate the process of building knowledge about policing and help bridge the gap between the two worlds—the world of police research and police practice. This is an invitation to police scholars and practitioners across the world to come and join in this venture.

Dilip K. Das, PhD
Founding President
International Police Executive Symposium (IPES)
www.ipes.info

Founding Editor-in-Chief
Police Practice and Research: An International Journal (PPR)
www.tandf.co.uk/journals

Prologue

This edited book, *Corruption, Fraud, Organized Crime, and the Shadow Economy*, was the outcome of the discussions of a small working group of researchers and practitioners who were interested and specialized in the fields of organized crime, fraud, and corruption. The members of this working group cooperate in different combinations with other experts, such as Dr. Wolfgang Hetzer, former advisor to the Director of OLAF; Dr. Alexander Seger, Head of the Economic Crime Division at the Council of Europe; Professor Alexander Siedschlag, University of Homeland Security in Washington; and Professor Friedrich Schneider from the Johann Kepler University in Linz, Austria. Dr. Schneider is the expert on the shadow economy in Austria and is also well-recognized worldwide since he has been researching and writing about the shadow economy and its effects on the formal economies of Austria and other countries of Europe for more than 20 years. He has contributed an important chapter to this book. The members of our working group and coauthors include

Univ. Prof. Dr. Arije Antinori, Sapienzia University, Rome, Italy
Univ. Prof. Dr. Bojan Dobovšek, Maribor University, Ljubjana, Slovenia
Univ. Prof. Dr. Branislav Simonović, Kragujevac University, Kragujevac, Serbia
Univ. Prof. Dr. Peter C. Kratcoski, Kent State University, Kent, Ohio
Univ. Prof. Dr. Michael Theil, Vienna University of Economics, Wien, Austria
Univ. Prof. Dr. Gilbert Norden, Department of Sociology, Vienna University, Wein, Austria
Docent Christian Felsenreich, Human-Factors and System-Safety Scientist and Trainer, Psychotherapy-Scientist, Counselor and Coach, Austria
Hofrat Mag. Maximilian Edelbacher, ACUNS, Vienna, Austria

The editors and many of the authors of the chapters have attended many international conferences, congresses, and forums at which they either presented papers or led round table discussions on the topics addressed in this book. These meetings include the meeting of the Crime Commission held yearly at the United Nations in Vienna and the meeting of the Academic Council on the United Nations System (ACUNS), which is connected to the UN Liaison Office and is also held annually at the United Nations in Vienna. The editors and authors have also presented papers on the subjects of fraud, organized crime, corruption, financial crimes, international crime, and other related topics at a number of other international conferences, including the International Police Executive Symposium (IPES), the Academy of Criminal Justice Sciences (ACJS), the American Society of Criminology (ASC), the European Society of Criminology (ESC), and the Society for Police and Criminal Psychology. The presentations and round table discussions by the editors and several of the authors on the relationship between the worldwide financial crisis of 2008 and organized crime, financial crime, fraud, and corruption were discussed at the European Society of Criminology conference held in Ljubljana, Slovenia, and also at a United Nations conference held in Vienna. These discussions led to an edited book titled *Financial Crimes: A Threat to Global Security*, published by CRC Press in 2012.

The discussion of this topic was continued during a round table session at the Crime Commission Meeting held at the United Nations Center in Vienna in 2014. Several of the sessions at this meeting that dealt with organized crime were organized by the Academic Council on the United Nations, Vienna Liaison Office. The speakers in our group included Bojan Dobovšek from Slovenia; Arije Antinori from Italy; Branislav Simonović from Serbia; Roland Worner, head of the Zurich Insurance Group, Department of Risk Management; and Michael Theil and Maximilian Edelbacher, both from Austria. The importance of the topic and the information given at the session by the participants caught the interest of the director of UNODC, Fodotov, who asked the round table group to present an official position that UNODC could take in regard to the relationship of organized crime and the informal economy. At this time, we did not have an inspiring answer, so we took a rather diplomatic position by stating, "Take care of the threats." In short, the participants agreed that there is a need for more research on the relationship between crime and the economy. However, a positive outcome of the meeting was that the participants of the workshop were determined to continue researching and writing on the topic and thus the idea for a book on the subject emerged.

This book, *Corruption, Fraud, Organized Crime, and the Shadow Economy*, is closely related to the book mentioned above. The basic idea and proposal to publish this book came from Bojan Dobovšek and Maximilian Edelbacher. They discussed the topic with many of the people mentioned earlier and, through correspondence with many of the authors, motivated them to complete research and write chapters for the proposed book. As the conversations and exchanges of information continued, the working group began to understand more clearly how financial crimes and organized crimes are related to the informal economy through the use of fraud and corruption and how the effects of this relationship can jeopardize the financial security of a country. To understand the effects of financial crimes, there is a need to analyze and understand more deeply the relationship of organized crime and the informal economy, since they are based on fraud and corruption. Furthermore, these corrupt activities are often committed by high-level government officials and executives of large corporations.

The financial crisis has still not ended. Corruption is still a major problem in most countries of the world. The goals, strategies, and activities of successful organized criminal groups are more than ever based on economic crimes, financial crimes, fraud, and corruption to gain maximum income.

When trying to understand the essence of the relationship of the informal economy and organized crime, a definition is very useful. Although both subjects, the informal economy and organized crime, cannot be clearly defined by only one definition, it is a necessary starting point for our work. Not all activities and exchanges falling under the umbrella of the informal economy are necessarily harmful or illegal. Bojan Dobovšek noted that some economists defend the view that all money, even if it is dirty money, stimulates the economy. As we know, the economies of Thailand, Singapore, and Hong Kong back in their earlier histories experienced their boom while under the influence of money from an illegal economy.

Maximilian Edelbacher

Acknowledgments

This book presents the experiences of academics and practitioners who deal with or conduct research on matters related to the informal economy and its links to organized crime, financial crime, white collar crime, and corruption. We thank the authors for their efforts to create awareness about the challenges and dangers that exist for all of us in democratic societies. Bojan Dobovšek, Peter C. Kratcoski, and I want to acknowledge the expertise of all our coauthors and colleagues on panels and round tables at various meetings with whom we discussed the problems and dangers of today's societies and what can be done against them. In this book, we examine the links between crime and deviant behavior and reveal that what is new is the fact that there exist dense links between the behavior of each of us and the strong intensity of professional criminals. Organized crime gang members abuse the potential for criminal, deviant behavior in each of us for their own purposes and create danger for our societies. But how can we avoid being victimized in this matter?

We want to thank all of the individuals who contributed to this publication. Bojan Dobovšek developed the idea of exploring the links between the informal economy and organized crime. We are indebted to Friedrich Schneider, a long time expert in the field of shadow economy, for showing us, through his empirical investigations, the financial flows of organized crime and tax fraud in developed countries. Arije Antinory, an expert in the field of Mafia organizations, makes us aware of the changes in Mafia operations, reporting that, instead of murder, the Mafia is focusing more on white collar crime and corruption. Michael Theil analyzes the effects of the shadow economy on the insurance industry as an important part of the world economy. Petter Gottschalk adds the dimension of defense strategies against the activities of Hells Angels in Norway. Benjamin Potz, Dominik Sporer, Christian Zirgoi, and Birgit Gusenbauer have contributed their fresh ideas by discussing falsified prospect theory in the context of corruption and the links between social fraud and organized crime, using Austria as an example. Martin Meissnitzer describes organized crime and fraud in the construction industry. Country perspectives of Austria, the Balkans and Serbia, Canada, China, Japan, Romania, Norway, Slovenia, and the United States are delivered by Maximilian Edelbacher, Branislav Simonović, Goran Bošković, Minoru Yokoyama, Sorina-Maria Cofan, Peter Gottschalk, Katja Eman, Tine Furdi, Rok Hacin, Bojan Dobovšek, Li Ziangxia, and David G. Baker. All these examples deepen our understanding of the links between the informal economy and organized crime, white collar crime, fraud, and especially corruption. The chapter by Christian Felsenreich on the topic of human risk factors and compliance to norms summarizes the dimensions of the dangers. In addition, this book would not have been possible without the networking skills of the president of IPES, Professor Dr. Dilip K. Das. He opened areas of wisdom, power, and contacts to us that made it possible to meet experts, important academics, and practitioners dealing with all these issues. At his yearly conferences of IPES and by information published in *Police Practice & Research: An International Journal*, of which Dr. Das is editor-in-chief, we gathered a wealth of important information. Without his contacts at CRC Press/Taylor & Francis Group, this book would not have been possible. Finally, we express our thanks to our partners at CRC Press/Taylor & Francis Group, especially to Carolyn Spence and the editorial staff, for their support and guidance.

Maximilian Edelbacher
Peter C. Kratcoski
Bojan Dobovšek

Editors

Maximilian Edelbacher graduated from Vienna University (Mag. Jur.) and was Hofrat of the Federal Police of Austria. He served as the chief of the Major Crime Bureau, and as an international expert for the Council of Europe, OSCE, and UNO. He also chaired the Austrian Antifraud Insurance Bureau and has lectured at several universities, including the Vienna University of Economics and Business Administration, Danube University in Krems, and Vienna University, Department of Sociology. Edelbacher was also appointed as special investigator of the AVUS Group on white collar crime cases, as vice president of the Vienna Liaison Office, of the Academic Council on the United Nations, and as director IPES. He is the author of a number of books and journal articles.

Peter C. Kratcoski earned a PhD in sociology from the Pennsylvania State University (University Park, Pennsylvania); an MA in sociology from the University of Notre Dame (Notre Dame, Indiana); and a BA in sociology from King's College (London, United Kingdom). He has been selected for several postdoctoral grants by the National Science Foundation. He taught at the College of St. Thomas (St. Paul, Minnesota) and the Pennsylvania State University prior to assuming the position of assistant professor of sociology at Kent State University in 1969. He retired as professor of criminal justice studies and chairman of the Department of Criminal Justice Studies at Kent State University in 1997. He is currently a professor emeritus and adjunct professor at Kent State University. He has published many books, book chapters, and journal articles in the areas of juvenile delinquency, juvenile justice, international policing, and crime prevention. He is a member of the International Police Executive Symposium, the Society for Police and Criminal Psychology, and the Academy of Criminal Justice Sciences.

Bojan Dobovšek earned a PhD in criminology from the University of Ljubjana (Ljubjana, Slovenia) and became an associate professor of criminal investigation and is now a vice dean of the Faculty of Criminal Justice and Security at the University of Maribor (Slovenia). He is the author of a book about organized crime and editor of several publications on corruption and organized crime. His ongoing research projects focus on corruption in state institutions, corruption networks, organized crime and terrorism, methodological obstacles in measuring corruption, analyses of conventions on corruption, and art crime investigation. He has served on the Commission for the Prevention of Corruption and is on the board of trustees of the Association for Research into Crime against Arts. He is the author of draft recommendations for a number of Organization for Economic Cooperation and Development (OECD) projects, including Anti-Corruption Networks for Transition Economies; the Anti-Corruption Action Plan for Armenia, Azerbaijan, Georgia, Kazakhstan, the Kyrgyz Republic, the Russian Federation, Tajikistan, and Ukraine; and Ecological Crime. He is a partner of the Institute for Politikwissenschaft und Sozialforschung, University of Wurzburg, Germany, and visiting professor on faculties in Ghent, Sarajevo, Belgrade, and Zagreb. He is running for the Minister of the Interior in Slovenia.

Contributors

Arije Antinori, PhD, earned a PhD in criminology from the University of Bologna in consortium with the University of Rome La Sapienza, Rome, Italy. Dr. Antinori has worked as a sociologist, criminologist, and geopolitics analyst. He also earned a master's in theories and methods of criminal investigations. He is currently a research area coordinator at the Criminology, Crisis Communication and Media Laboratory at La Sapienzia. He is a member of the Italian Society of Criminology, the Italian Society of Victimology, the Academic Council on the United Nations System (ACUNS), the Italian National Security Watch, and the International Police Executive Symposium (IPES). He is a qualified researcher at the Centre for Military and Strategic Studies (CEMISS) and an election observer for the European Union. Dr. Antinori researches and teaches several master's level subjects, including terrorism and media, crisis management and communication, counter-terrorism, communication and rime, and Islam and terrorism. In these fields of expertise, he is working on his second PhD.

David G. Baker, PhD, earned a BA in political science and history from Manchester College (Manchester, United Kingdom), an MA in political science from the University of Illinois, Champaign, and a PhD in political science from the University of Illinois, Champaign, in 1976. He served as a faculty member, chair of the Political Science Department, and associate dean at Hartwick College in Oneonta, New York, before assuming the position of associate professor of political science and associate dean at Kent State University (Kent, Ohio), in 1994. He served as the interim dean at the Kent State University Stark Campus during the 2004–2005 academic year and as associate professor of political science until his retirement from Kent State University.

Goran Boskovic, PhD, is an associate professor in the Department of Criminalistics, Academy of Criminalistic and Police Studies, Belgrade, Serbia. His research interests are focused on criminal investigation of organized crime, criminal intelligence analysis, special investigation methods, money laundering, and financial investigation. He is the author of two books and over 50 scientific papers published in journals and presented at scientific and professional conferences.

Briget Burbeck, PhD (formerly Gusenbauer) earned her doctorate from Vienna University of Economics and Business in 2010. Prior to joining the faculty at FH Joanneum University of Applied Sciences in Graz, Austria, she worked in the financial industry for five years. Her research activities are focused on various aspects of behavioral economics. Dr. Burbeck serves on the editorial boards of several international journals as well as a reviewer for Sage Publications and Springer Publications.

Soria-Maria Cofan graduated from the Faculty of Physics, University of Bucharest (Bucharest, Romania), and went on to earn an MSc in physics and a post-university degree in public relations from the University of Bucharest. Chief Superintendent Cofan joined the Romanian National Police Force in 2002 as a public relations officer and spokesperson and also served as a strategic analyst and as chief of the Crime Intelligence Analysis Unit. Currently, she works as a crime intelligence analysis police trainer at the Institute of Studies on Public Order, the main training provider for the personnel of the Romanian Ministry of Internal Affairs. She coordinated for the first Romanian Manual for the Crime Intelligence Analysis and has published in various specialized journals. She has also written several chapters for books related to intelligence analysis. Her main focus is on the conceptualization of the intelligence analysis field in Romania and the use of the latest technologies in the professional training of intelligence analysts.

Katja Eman, PhD, is an assistant professor of criminology at the Faculty of Criminal Justice and Security, University of Maribor (Maribor, Slovenia). She was a junior researcher during 2009–2012. Her PhD dissertation focused on environmental crime. Dr. Eman coedited a monograph titled Environmental Crime and Environmental Protection: Multidisciplinary Perspectives (2012). Her research interests span green criminology, environmental crime, organized crime, corporate crime, crime prevention, crime mapping, and legitimacy.

Christian Felsenreich studied engineering and earned a BA and an MSc from the Technical Engineering School for Mechanics and Production Engineering. He also studied psychotherapy science at the Sigmund Freud Private University in Vienna (Austria) and earned another BA. He earned a second MSc in human factors and system safety from the Lund University School for Aviation in Sweden. He is a trainer in the fields of human factors and system safety and teaches courses in high-risk environments, lectures at Sigmund Freud Private University, and is an active member of Plattform—Menschen in komplexen Arbeitswelten (www.plattform-ev.de). He maintains a private counseling practice and has written several books and articles.

Tine Furdi is a student of the Faculty of Criminal Justice and Security, University of Maribor (Maribor Slovenia). He is currently completing a master's study program. His main areas of study and research include criminal investigation, organized crime, white collar crime, and police techniques.

Petter Gottschalk studied at the Technical University of Berlin, Germany, and finished his master of business administration, continued at the Thayer School of Engineering, Dartmouth College, and Sloan School of Management, MIT, Cambridge, Massachusetts, and earned a master of science in 1998. He finished his studies at the Henley Management College, Brunel University (United Kingdom), earning his doctor of business administration. Since 2000, he has been professor at the BI Norwegian Business School for strategy, knowledge management, outsourcing, IT planning, police leadership, organized crime, financial crime, and law firm management. He was an associate professor and industrial professor at BI, CEO for the Norwegian Computer Center (1990–1995), CEO for ABB Datacables, vice president and CIO for the Computer Center, ABB Norway, and research scientist for the Resource Police Group in the field of systems dynamics simulations and operations research. He teaches on the characteristics of white collar criminals, policing white collar crime, policing organized crime, knowledge management in policing, knowledge management in law firms, knowledge management systems, information management strategy, and information technology strategy.

Rok Hacin is a junior researcher and PhD student at the Faculty of Criminal Justice and Security, University of Maribor (Maribor, Slovenia). He holds a master's degree in crime mapping and fear of crime. His research interests include penology, crime mapping, legitimacy, and fear of crime.

Martin Meissnitzer, PhD, studied law and Arabic studies in Vienna, where he earned a PhD in 2013, while working for the Department for Criminal Law and Criminology at the University of Vienna (Wien, Austria). Currently, he works as a legal expert for the Main Association of Austrian Social Security Institutions, mostly dealing with fraud-related aspects of social security. He also teaches at the University of Vienna. His main areas of research focus on the legal aspects of white collar crime, especially undeclared work, social fraud, and wage dumping, as well as the European Social Security and Labor Law.

Benjamin Potz received a master of arts degree in business in emerging markets from the FH Joanneum University of Applied Sciences (Graz, Austria). His research interests include international management, market entry strategies, management in emerging markets, corruption, decision support systems, and software project risk management.

Friedrich Schneider earned a bachelor of economics and bachelor of political science in 1972, and a master of economics in 1973. In 1976, he became Dr. rer.soc. (PhD in economics). All his academic degrees were earned from the University of Konstanz, Germany. In 1983, he earned his habilitation—promotion of being able to compete for a full professor (chair in Europe) at the University of Zürich. He earned several honorary degrees of doctorate: University of Lima, Peru, January 2003; University of Stuttgart, Germany, in February 2003; University of Trujillo, Peru, October 2006; and University of Macedonia, Thessaloniki, September 2012. His employment started in 1983, and until 1984, he was visiting associate professor, GSIA at Carnegie-Mellon University (Pittsburgh, Pennsylvania). He was associate professor of economics (tenured position), Institute of Economics, Aarhus University, Aarhus, Denmark (1984–1985); visiting professor, La Trobe University, Melbourne, Australia (1986–1987); and visiting professor, at the University of Saarbrücken, Saarbrücken, Germany (1994–1995). He acted as dean of the Social Science and Economic Faculty at the Johannes Kepler University, Linz, Austria (between 1991 and 1996), where he was a professor of economics since 1986 (chair in economic policy and public finance, tenured position). He was president of the Austrian

Economic Association between 1997 and 1999, vice president for foreign affairs at the Johann Kepler University of Linz, and president of the German Economic Association between 2005 and 2008. Since May 2013, he has been a visiting professor at Otago University in New Zealand, and from June 2013 until June 2016, he was chairman of the Academic Advisory Board of the Zeppelin University, Friedrichshafen, Germany. His research fields are general economic policy, public finance, shadow economy, organized crime, environmental economics, privatization and deregulation policies, and public choice. He has consulting experience and has worked on projects for Austrian industries, the Federal Austrian Chamber of Commerce, the Federal Austrian Ministry of Economics, the Federal Austrian Ministry of Finance, the National Central Bank of Germany, Bank Austria, and the Brussels EU Commission. Between 1974 to December 2013, he published 70 books, 206 articles in scientific journals, and 178 chapters in edited books.

Branislav Simonović, PhD, is a professor at the Faculty of Law at the University of Kragujevac, Serbia. He is a full-time professor of criminalistics (criminal investigation). He has written on the informal economy in Serbia and the relationship between the informal economy and corruption (and political corruption) in Serbia.

Bostjan Slak serves on the Faculty of Criminal Justice and Security, University of Maribor (Maribor, Slovenia).

Dominik Sporer completed an undergraduate degree and a master's degree in business in emerging markets at the FH Joanneum University of Applied Sciences, Graz, Austria. He also completed a master's degree from the National Kaohsiunh Rorst University of Science and Technology, Taiwan. His research has gained national recognition and he was honored with the Economy Meets Science—Wirshaft trifft auf Sinnenschaft—Award presented by the Austrian Federal Economic Chapter. He gained professional experience in the marketing department of the Austrian newspaper *Kleine Zeitung* and currently serves as the sales manager for Brigi and Bergmeister.

Michael Theil earned an MBA with honors with a major in transport, logistics, management, insurance, and information management in 1994. In 2001, he finished habilitation and became a university docent at the Vienna University of Economics and Business Administration. He is a member of the Board Governors of the Association of University Professors, a member of the Senate and Works Council of University Professors, and a cooperation delegate for partnership with different universities. Currently, he is an associate professor at the Institute of Risk Management and Insurance at Vienna University. He has published numerous articles, reviews, and book chapters and is the author of *Crimes against Insurances*. His specialty areas include accounting, general management, insurance, marketing, and quality management. He cooperates with the Institute of Finance and Management Science, the Norwegian School of Economics at Bergen, and Bradley University, Peoria, Illinois.

Minoru Yokoyama, PhD, completed his BA in law and MA in both criminal law and sociology at Chuo University in Tokyo. He finished his doctorate at Chuo University. He is a professor emeritus and former dean of the Faculty of Law, and a former vice president of Kokugakuin University in Tokyo. He is a former second vice president of the Research Committee for the Sociology of Deviance and Social Control of the International Sociological Association. He is a president of the Japanese Association of Social Problems, a former president of the Japanese Association of Sociological Criminology, and a president of the Tokyo Study Group of Sociological Criminology. He is a member of Presidium of General Assembly of the Asian Criminological Society. He worked as a vice chair of the Local Arrangement Committee, International Congress for Criminology held in Japan, International Society for Criminology, held in August, 2011. He has presented numerous papers at national and international conferences and symposia and has published numerous articles in professional journals.

Li Xiangxia began studying Chinese law in 2002 at the Chinese University. She finished her bachelor's degree in 2006 at the Zhenghou Institute of Aeronautical Industry Management Law, and her master's in political sciences and law in 2011 at the Chinese University of Political Science and Law, Changping, Beijing, People's Republic of China. At the end of 2011, she continued to carry out her doctoral research subject at the University in Vienna on the subject of organized crime. She worked as a lawyer's assistant for one year in China, as an assistant for a summer program between China University, Department of Political Science and Law. She has attended many seminars and workshops of different academic institutions. She speaks Chinese, English, and German.

Christian Zirgoi completed a master's degree program in business in emerging markets at FH Joanneum University of Applied Sciences, Graz, Austria. His master's thesis was titled Analyzing the Impact of Corruption Distance on Foreign Direct Investment with the Characteristics of the Prospect Theory. He is currently employed with Mayr-Melnhof Packaging UK Limited.

1. Introduction

The Relationship of the Informal Economy to Corruption, Fraud, and Organized Crime

Maximilian Edelbacher, Bojan Dobovšek, and Peter C. Kratcoski

Definitions of the Informal (Shadow) Economy

The informal economy is emerging worldwide as an antipode to the formal economy. Although only partially visible and parallel to the formal economic system, it is manifested in social and cultural activities in European cities in the tourist trade, in the form of vendors in the streets and squares or those selling flowers in restaurants. It has links to drug trafficking and prostitution, but also provides economic opportunities for immigrants, young people, and students. It has links with the formal economy, contributes to the forces of formal and informal social control, and is an important factor in the economies of European countries (Shapeland, 2003). The importance of the informal economy can be seen in three different forms of formal policy: the financial or economic order (formal economy), the social order (state and urban policy), and the criminal justice system. However, in some areas there is no clear dividing line between the formal and informal economies. Work in the fields of hospitality, tourism, and construction that is usually performed by students, young people, migrants, and tourists operates mostly in the context of the formal economy for low pay. In some cases, the employer pays taxes and health insurance (formal economy), in other cases, the employer's contribution is not paid per employee (informal economy). There are two different definitions of the informal economy, the economic definition, which defines the informal sector as a sector that does not contribute to the national tax revenue and the economy; and the legal definition, which defines the black or forbidden economy (penalized by the law). Politicians provide us with a third definition, a gray economy, which is a slippery slope. They usually try to hide its existence under the carpet to maintain social stability and peace. We should also point out that, in times of financial crises, financial income (even criminal) is as important as political motivation, since it contributes to generating a more positive image of the economy to the public. An analysis of the definitions shows that there are attempts to merge these concepts and blur the distinctions between the *white* (legal, formal economic activity, not protected from paying taxes), the *gray* (legal, informal economic activity, with the services completed off the record), and the *black* (illegal, informal economic activity) economies.

The fiscal and economic factors that define the differences in the economic definitions in trying to distinguish whether a particular activity falls in the formal or informal sector are not necessarily in step with the social and political factors that influence the decision whether an offense is punishable or not, as defined in criminal law. The differences between the formal and informal sectors and between the legal and illegal sectors have been created on the basis of history, culture, and time and space, and may differ between various parts of Europe and other parts of the world. In an analysis of the Belgian experience, it was concluded that the black economy and related fraud will not usually appear in a national economic assessment, so they were regrouped in terms of the national economy. The activities that defined the informal economy in a broad sense are more heterogeneous than those attributed to the underground economy. The informal economy has become an artificial construct that exists primarily due to the efforts of countries to regulate the taxation of such economies (Shapeland, 2003).

Paoli (2003) describes the informal economy as an essentiality that can only exist if there is a formal economy. If there were not a formal economy, which is a national regulatory framework for economic activities, there would be no informal economy. The ideal market economy, without regulation or any discrimination between formal and informal, would lose its meaning. The essence of the informal economy therefore is the relationship between government and economic activity. The government is the body that governs taxes and defines the boundaries that distinguish between formal and informal, between legal and illegal activities. Despite the fact that the boundaries of the informal economy are regularly crossed by many operators, we can confirm that some criminal organizations are able to be active, simultaneously and continuously, in various sectors of the informal economy as well as in the sectors of the formal economy (Paoli, 2003).

The informal economy is increasingly encouraged by many economists, because in some instances the survival of national and regional economies depends on the informal economy. Countries are looking for different sources of income, and these sources can be found in the informal economy. One of the reasons is the high tax burden on legitimate entrepreneurs who often are tempted to acquire services through the informal economy, which includes the black market and informal employment (Shapland and Ponsaers, 2009). A high level of the informal economy can be the assistance a country needs to adjust its economy, become a modern society, and achieve economic and political globalization, even though its involvement in the informal economy and tax evasion poses a serious threat to the individual and to society (Dobovšek et al., 2008).

Undeclared work includes all paid activities that are principally legal but are not subject to social security contributions and paying income tax to the tax authorities, not the activities that are not legitimate, such as smuggling, drug trafficking, or other criminal activities. Undeclared work is not limited to work performed for money. The person completing the work can receive payment in other ways, such as being given expensive gifts or property. Payments may also comprise goods, equipment, or an exchange of service or services. For example, a plumber may insert the plumbing in a house owned by an electrician, who in return installs the electric wiring in the plumber's house. In most countries, these types of transactions must be reported if the providers of the work expect payment, or if the value of exchanged goods or services exceeds a certain threshold. Illegal work activities are those activities that should be reported, but remain unreported to the income tax authorities and institutions responsible for collecting social security taxes. In some countries, it is not necessary to report to the authorities income from work that falls below a certain threshold, while in other countries, almost every cent earned must be reported (such as *masters* in England). In general, the tax systems and the rules vary greatly among countries. In some countries, such as Sweden and Denmark, almost any labor is income taxable, while in the other countries there are some limits set on what income is liable for taxation. The second example is one of the side incomes a country can use to increase its tax base (European Commission, 2007). The more one discovers the large amount of hidden work that is completed outside the labor market, the more it becomes clear that this work is being completed by the poor and unemployed people of the society (Pahl, 1987).

Trafficking in Humans and the Informal Economy

Trafficking in human beings is a good example of an illegal activity that involves its victims in different forms of undeclared work. Evidence of the growth of human trafficking on the black market comes from different countries. This evidence confirms that more and more people are being pushed into forms of work based on the scheme of human trafficking, especially women and children, which almost constitutes modern slavery. These workers are taken advantage of by operators of the *black market* by being forced to provide sexually oriented services, such as engaging in prostitution, pornography, sex tourism, and other sex-related activities. Others become victims of labor exploitation, such as production, construction, and agricultural work (Ivakhnyuk, 2005).

Labor exploitation in the black economy is one of the most harsh abuses, since these laborers are rarely regarded as victims of trafficking and receive little assistance, compared to those who are trafficked for the sex trade, who often are eligible for aid and assistance from social service agencies. Those who are trafficked for the purpose of providing labor for construction and agricultural work are generally treated as illegal immigrants and thus as criminals (Global Alliance Against Traffic in Women, 2007). There are several reasons for employers to use *illegal* workers and not to report them to the authorities and for *illegals* to be willing to work for low wages often under very poor working conditions. One of the main reasons is that employers, employees, and the self-employed can increase their income and reduce their costs by avoiding the payment of tax and social security contributions. Another important reason is inadequate control over private activities when labor regulations are not clearly defined (Daza, 2005). The cornerstone of the prevalence of undeclared work is the search for a less expensive labor force, since the high cost of labor is the dominant element determining competitiveness in the market, particularly in labor-intensive areas of work, such as cleaning, agriculture, and the construction sector. These are some of the areas where, in some countries, the majority of the employers rely on migrants who are considered an alternative cheap labor source in comparison with the more expensive local workforce. Employers are looking for a cheap labor force that will in turn reduce the cost of production and the sale price. In such situations, exploitation of workers often results (Ollus and Jokinen, 2011).

Informal employment is considered to be illegal, undeclared work and it is common in developed countries as well as undeveloped countries, although the transit situation is quite different, due to the specific historical development of the countries. Industrialized countries are gradually expanding their informal sector, which includes visual activity (asylum seekers) and invisible activities (hidden workshops, which take advantage of the labor force) in order to solve the problem of unemployment and the need for seasonal workers. Informal employment includes all types of paid work. For example, seasonal work in agriculture might include picking fruit or planting and harvesting crops. This work is not recognized, regulated, or protected by laws and regulations in some countries. As a result, some of the workers have social security, paid sick leaves, holidays, or bargaining power granted by their employers, while others do not. There are several categories of recruitment of workers involved in the informal–formal economy situation. First, there are employers who are owners of commercial enterprises and owner operators of informal enterprises and self-employed workers, including self-employed workers who are heads of household enterprises that use unpaid family members as workers. Second, there are salaried workers, such as employees of informal enterprises, and ordinary workers who have no fixed employer (subcontractors, household workers, temporary and part-time workers, and undocumented workers) (Ruiz, 2004).

Informal employment is associated with certain activities, including paid domestic services, agriculture, hospitality, retail, certain companies, and construction (Barnable, 2002). Because of irregularity of the worker situation, there is pressure for the development of a hard policy toward the regulation of employment. However, some employers want to avoid the regulatory requirements for obvious reasons. Some employers provide wages and working hours, that in most cases, constitutes low wages and long working hours, unpaid food and transportation, and relatively loose labor discipline. Informally employed workers accept the conditions mainly due to a lack of opportunities in the formal economy labor market (Ram et al., 2004). Potential laborers are often misled about the pay and working conditions of a job, which allows those involved in the trafficking of human beings to entice workers to these jobs in the informal economy. Individuals are initially presented information on jobs that turn out to have quite different working conditions than those presented. The individuals decide to accept the jobs based on the faulty information provided by the employer and afterward discover that the work situation is far below what was expected. However they are now trapped and soon become victims of human trafficking on the black market employment (Shapland and Ponsaers, 2009).

Organized Crime and the Informal Economy

The definition of organized crime presented at the Convention on Organized Crime, the so-called Palermo Convention in 1990, is used in this chapter. Since this definition is well known, it is not cited in this introduction to the relationship of organized crime to the informal economy. At a round table presentation held in the United Nations Complex in Vienna, in 2014, moderated by the German Ambassador to the United Nations, his Excellency Mr. Konrad Max Scharinger, it was mentioned by Bojan Dobovšek that generally there are three areas of an economy, which are different in structure as well as in the way they affect the national economy and lives of the people of a country. These three areas include the white economy, the gray economy, and the black economy.

The "white economy" can be seen as the legal economy, that is, all the products and services that are produced in this field. The "gray economy" is the production and services that are not criminal or forbidden, but which are hidden to avoid the paying of taxes. The "black economy" encompasses all activities that are based on crime, such as trafficking of human beings, weapons, or drugs. These are the types of illegal activities that are handled by the organized crime gang members all around the world. Some of these organizations are well-known famous groups such as the Italian Mafia, Russian Mafia, and Chinese Mafia. Of course there also exist a number of other famous groups that are not mentioned here, but these criminal organizations are well known to international police organizations, such as Interpol and Europol. These criminal groups all want to penetrate legal markets, some through informal economic activities. Until now, an efficient strategy to overcome such modus operandi of criminal organizations has not been implemented by local, regional, international, or specialized and nonspecialized police organizations.

Austrian Meeting on Crime and the Informal Economy

In Austria, we began to discuss for the first time the relationship of organized crime and the informal economy after the "Fall of the Iron Curtain" in 1989. After the Soviet Union was dismantled, so much damage was caused by imported crime in Austria, because of the open borders with surrounding countries, that the high-level administrators of large insurance companies started to assess how much damage was done by this large influx of crime and what can be done to prevent it. This starting point led to an understanding of "where deviant behavior really starts." During the meetings, the whole spectrum of deviant behavior, starting with avoiding taxes and the shadow economy and ending with the damage insurances and the Austrian economy had to suffer by all kinds of crimes like robbery, burglary, theft, and fraud, were discussed.

The impact of organized crime by investing in a legitimate enterprise or by creating their businesses has an impact on the overall economy. It creates the black market as a parallel system market, which is not controlled by the state with its policy. From what has been stated, it follows that those who created the economic policy cannot ignore the fact that in addition to the legal markets there are also illegal markets in which regulatory measures are ineffective. Since such markets are making vast profits that cannot be accurately registered, it calls into question all comparable statistics based on official data obtained. Since the statistics on the gross domestic product are seen as unreliable, we must focus on what is happening in the illegal market. If the gross domestic product increases, the country is considered to be economically healthy, but we should view other indicators, such as unemployment, inflation, real output growth, productivity growth, and the standard of living as measures of the country's economy. If we compare the analog effects that organized crime has, that is, its activities in the economies of countries, we can see that it would be necessary to consider the influence of organized crime as one of the indicators that is directly related to the assessment of international economic efficiency. A particular problem is the increase in economic crime in countries in transition, because these countries have no tradition of a stable market economy, as well as not having adequate legislation dealing with the market economy and no measures against the informal economy.

Corruption by the Elite

Today, we are not only confronted with the crimes caused by common criminals or by organized crime, but we are also confronted with an enormous increase of *elite corruption*, that is, financial crimes, ongoing speculations by financial institutions that lead us to fear that the economic system, the euro and the dollar, may crash. Today, the question is: "Have we learned something from the experiences of 1930s worldwide economic depression?" On the one side, "the rich become more and more wealthy" and the "poor become more and more poor." The idea of an ideal distribution of all wealth that even started with the French Revolution and was repeated by the Revolution in 1848 is completely neglected by neoliberalism. Even the European Union seems to support the economic ideas of the rich much more than the *social care* for the weaker parts of the European society ideas. Lobbyism and market strategies are dominating the national economies. The pull and push factors of the economy, mainly those that bring in refugees to Europe for economic reasons, which is because they hope to find much better living conditions in Europe than in Africa or Asia, are closely tied in with both organized crime and financial crime. The criminal exploitation of men and women is a consequence of criminal groups and employers who offer *good jobs* and living conditions to immigrants but end up only providing below-standard living quarters, low wages, and very poor working conditions.

Conclusion

In conclusion, we must focus on employers who stimulate the informal market by exploiting workers in order to make higher profits, as well as on closing the doors for the organized crime groups that use all the opportunities offered by the financial systems to maximize their profits. In this regard, the contributors to the chapters of this book offer some insight into the reasons for the development of an informal economy in various countries and the ways the negative effects of corruption, fraud, and organized crime on the economy and standard of living of the people of these countries can be reduced.

References

Albrecht, J. and Godfroy, T. (ur.) (2003). *The Informal Economy: Threat and Opportunity in the City* (str. 133–173). Freiburg, Germany: Br: Luscrim.

Barnable, S. (2002). *Informal Employment in Countries in Transition: A Conceptual Framework.* London, UK: School for Economies.

Centre for Equal Opportunities and Opposition to Racism (CEOOR). (2009). Trafficking in and smuggling of human beings: Annual report. Brussels, Belgium: CEOOR.

Daza, J. L. (2005). *Informal Economy, Undeclared Work and Labour Administration.* Geneva, Switzerland: International Labour Office.

Dobovšek, B. (2009). *Transnacionalna Kriminaliteta.* Ljubljana, Slovenia: Fakulteta za varnostne vede.

Dobovšek, B., Žibert, F., and Pirnat, A. J. (2008). Ekonomski vidiki trgovine z ljudmi na zahodnem Balkanu. *Varstvoslovje*, 10(4), 633–665.

European Commission. (2007). Undeclared work in the European Union. Pridobljeno na http://ec.europa.eu/public_opinion/archives/ebs/ebs_284_eu.pdf. (Accessed May 10, 2013.)

European Commission. (2011). Fight against trafficking in human beings Belgium. Pridobljeno na http://ec.europa.eu/anti-trafficking/section.action?sectionId=ee0a97c9-c36f-4075-9c15-823c947f4aab&sectionType=TAG&page=1&breadCrumbReset=true.

Europol. (2009a). EU organized crime threat assessment. Pridobljeno na https://www. europol.europa.eu/sites/default/files/publications/octa2009_0.pdf.

Europol. (2009b). Trafficking in human beings in the European Union: A Europol perspective. Pridobljeno na http://ec.europa.eu/anti-trafficking/entity;jsessioni289 Bojan Dobovšek, Leja Drobnak NZDKy5zcpFh44YXNPhRTPS2mQZY7GrhGGyXnGN0nJvJlR7Gy!1145937442?id=b50db72c-6434-41c4-9c50-5fa9166e7df5.

Global Alliance against Traffic in Women. (1999). Human right standards for the treatment of trafficked persons. Pridobljeno na www.globalrights.org/site/.../IHRLGTraffickin_tsStandards.pdf.

Global Alliance against Traffic in Women. (2007). GAATW organisations and friends in Europe jointly call for effective human rights protection of persons affected by human trafficking. Pridobljeno na ww.gaatw.org/UNAdvocacy/CoE_GAATW_statement07.pdf.

Ivakhnyuk, I. (2005). The significance of the informal sector in attracting illegal migration including trafficking in human beings: Exchange of information, experience and best practices. *Predstavitevna Thirteenth OSCE Economic Forum Demographic Trends, Migration and Integrating Persons belonging to National Minorities: Ensuring Security and Sustainable Development in the OSCE Area Prague*, Prague, Czech Republic, May 23–27, 2005.

Kara, S. (2009). *Sex Trafficking: Inside the Business of Modern Slavery.* New York: Columbia University.

Kazenski zakonik, R. S. (2008). Uradni list RS (55/08).

Naim, M. (2005). *Nedovoljeno: kako tihotapci, prekupčevalci in posnemovalci uporabljajo globalno gospodarstvo.* Ljubljana, Slovenia: Založba Gnostica.

OkvirnisklepSveta Evropskeunije z dne 19. Julija 2002 o boju proti trgovini zljudmi. (2002). Pridobljeno http://eur-lex.europa.eu/LexUriServ/LexUriServ. do?uri=CELEX:32002F0629:SL:NOT.

Ollus, N. and Jokinen, A. (2011). *Trafficking for Labour and Labour Exploitation—Setting the Scene.* Helsinki, Finland: HEUNI.

Pahl, R. (1987). Does jobless mean workless? Unemployment and informal work. *The Annals of the American Academy of Political and Social Science*, 493(1), 36–46.

Paoli, L. (2003). The informal economy and organized crime. In V. J. Shapland, M. Ram, P. Edwards, and T. Jones (eds.) (2004). *Informal Employment, Small Firms and the National Minimum Wage.* Coventry, UK: University of Warwick. Pridobljeno na www.lowpay. gov.uk/lowpay/research/pdf/t0NTAVZ4.pdf.

Ram, M. and Edwards, P. (2004). In T. Jones. *Informal employment, small firms and the national minimum wage.* Warwick: University of Warwick. http://www.lowpay.gov.uk/lowpay/research/pdf/tONTAVZ.pdf, www.lowpay.gov.uk/lowpay/research/pdf/tONTAVZ.pdf. (Accessed May 18, 2014.)

Ruiz, M. (2004). *Informal Economy*. Brussels, Belgium: Eurodad.
Shapland, J. (2003). Looking at opportunities in the informal economy of cities. In J. Shapland, H.-J. Albrecht, J. Ditton, and T. Godefroy (ur.). *The Informal Economy: Threat and Opportunity in the City* (str. 1–25). Freiburg, Germany: Br. Iuscrim.
Shapland, J. and Ponsaers, P. (2009). Potential effects of national policies on the informal economy. In V J. Shapland and P. Ponsaers (ur.). *The Informal Economy and Connections with Organized Crime*. The Hague, the Netherlands: Bju Legal Publishers.
Shelley, L. (2010). *Human Trafficking: A Global Perspective*. New York: Cambridge University Press.
Vlada Republike Slovenije. (2011). Boj proti trgovini z ljudmi. Pridobljeno na http://www.vlada.si/si/teme_in_projekti/boj_proti_trgovini_z_ljudmi/Trgovinaz ljudmi in eformalna ekonomija – analiza belgijskih izkušenj.
Weyembergh, S. (2009). *The Evaluation of European Criminal Law*. Brussels, Belgium: Editions de I'Universitete de Bruxelles.

2. The Informal Economy and Organized Crime

Bojan Dobovšek and Boštjan Slak

Introduction

This chapter aims to serve as an introduction into the complex issues of the informal economy from a more criminological standpoint. We feel that criminological standpoints with regard to the informal economy are often neglected and unheard. The informal economy (especially in times of economic crises) presents a great hindrance to the official bodies of the states, mainly because they see the informal economy as a hidden funds reserve. Funds desperately needed to repay the debt accumulated under the neoliberal way of doing business are not available. Unfortunately, politicians and policy makers tackle the problems of the informal economy with the usual approaches of repression and the creation of complex legislation, which on top of its complexity is out of touch with reality, as common people do not engage in complex economic reflection on how bad tax morale or the informal economy is linked to defunding of public services. They engage in simple cost–benefit behavior and thus the state, with its tax burdens, is considered the enemy. Contrary to the policy makers' approach, general public common sense also tells them that for every burden that the state will impose on the shoulders of companies and financial institutions, these companies and institutions will defer this cost on the consumers. The informal economy is and will even more become a luring place where, due to the austerity and heavy burden under which the companies and financial institutions must operate, these policies of the government are causing an even bigger loss of yield in the state budget.

When a state fails to provide jobs and goods or any other services or does so with extremely high prices, organized crime, with its cheap alternatives, is there to step in place (Allum and Siebert, 2003; Clinard and Meier, 2011) by providing fake designer clothes, medicine, tools, or any other faked product known to man. This is especially true in times of economic crisis (European Police Office, 2013). Untaxed tobacco or alcohol products are also cheaper. Organized crime can also provide loans and credit or questionable services for troubled businesses fairly cheap in comparison to legitimate businesses, services to legitimate companies such as *waste management*. Organized crime thus becomes somewhat of a "Robin Hood" (Dobovšek, 2012), gaining public support even though its intentions are not the slightest bit altruistic. Many, but thankfully not all, state, academic, or even hobby economists fail to acknowledge this criminological knowledge and regard criminal activities and profits of crimes as completely separate and not a bit connected to the informal economy, let alone to the formal economy, besides recognizing how much damage crime causes to the society.

In this chapter, rather than arguing why it is wrong to engage in the informal economy, we wish to present the idea that legitimate economic actors as well as illegitimate economic actors engage in informal practices. They do so because a lack of regulation (or regulation without enforcement) allows them to do so (see discussions in Snider, 2008; Tombs, 2008; Edelbacher and Theil, 2012). But this also means that such regulation enables organized crime to enter the legitimate economy as well. If we dare to be a bit provocative, such legitimate businesses engaged in questionable activities behave in the same manner as organized crime. We will now take a closer look at organized crime, what it is and how it is connected to the informal economy.

Defining Organized Crime

Defining organized crime is a task undertaken by many scholars, institutions, organizations, and agencies. As the number of definitions is increasing daily, one must be even more cautious in his or her academic and research undertakings when choosing and arguing his or her working definition of organized crime. Definitions gathered on the *Organized Crime Research* web page, by von Lampe (2014), show this flood of definitions. Unfortunately, this means that one can easily choose (or coin) a definition most useful for his or her scholastic or research undertaking. Of course, there are definitions that are more dominating than others. These are mostly the ones of international organizations as they have greater impact and are in most cases required to be transplanted into the national legislations. Countries are usually included in several different international bodies, however in this sense, the common organizational denominator is the United Nations. The latter defines organized crime groups as a "structured group* of three or more persons, existing for a period of time and acting in concert with the aim of committing one or more serious crimes† or offenses established in accordance with [United Nations Convention against Transnational Organized Crime Convention], in order to obtain, directly or indirectly, a financial or other material benefit" (United Nations Convention against Transnational Organized Crime and the Protocols Thereto, 2004, p. 5).

The activities that organized crime groups undertake are vast and diverse. Clinard and Meier (2011, p. 162) list seven predominating activities. These are illegal gambling, racketeering, distributing illegal drugs, usury or loan sharking, illicit sex, reselling stolen or hijacked goods, and controlling legitimate businesses. The latter activity is only engaged by the organized crime group that has already developed its reach to this degree. There are three stages of development of an organized crime group (Dobovšek, 2008). The first stage is the development of street gangs, where groups dominate one limited territory. These groups often conduct the *classical* crimes, such as racketeering, thefts, extortions, and usury. Their acts are not very organized and they often use violence. In the second stage, the group begins to dominate a larger area, crimes are more organized, and they also try to get informally (through corruption or threats) connected with local politicians and businessmen. In the third stage, an organized crime group has so much informal influence that it can influence state bodies and amend legalistic or economic matters in the way that it will benefit them (Dobovšek, 2008). Such influence and power over the state power players (firms, business elite, organized crime) can influence the creation and implementation of national legislation, and when such legislation is usually shaped to their benefit, it is also often named *state capture* (Hellman et al., 2000). Organized crime as state capturers is appearing in Latin America and in some ex-soviet countries, where state capture type of behaviors is exercised by oligarchs as well (Iwasaki and Suzuki, 2007). In countries where the captor is a member of the political or business elite, there is the so-called captured economy, where "public officials and politicians privately sell underprovided public goods and a range of rent-generating advantages *à la carte* to individual firms" (Hellman et al., 2000). While organized crime groups can also gain such

* "Structured group shall mean a group that is not randomly formed for the immediate commission of an offense and that does not need to have formally defined roles for its members, continuity of its membership or a developed structure, p. 2" (United Nations Convention against Transnational Organized Crime and the Protocols Thereto, 2004, p. 5).

† "Serious crime shall mean conduct constituting an offense punishable by a maximum deprivation of liberty of at least 4 years or a more serious penalty" (United Nations Convention against Transnational Organized Crime and the Protocols Thereto, 2004, p. 5).

influence over the formal economy, there is also a possibility that the informal economy, by extensively thriving on the criminal activities of organized crimes, overgrows and replaces the formal one. Something of this kind happened in the post-1980s in Bolivia due to the drug trade.

Due to various factors, namely, media representation, which is fueled by the political debate of "monstrously evil" organized crime, most people imagine organized crime groups as a Mafia or cartel-like structure composed of Italians, Russians, Albanians, and other ethnic or racial groups and with their activities including illicit trade in arms, drugs, and human trafficking and the involvement in the sex trade, while economic or corporate crimes are not viewed as part of their domain (van Duyne, 2010; Woodiwiss, 2003). However as some scholars have argued, such a perception is flawed. Sutherland was one the earliest scholar who successful warned about such misperception (Sutherland, 1940). Others following and redeveloping his ideas created the scholastic thought that some organized crime groups behave as rational economic businessmen that are similar to their legitimate counterparts who strive to the maximization of profits with minimum cost (Allum and Sands, 2004; Broude and Teichman, 2009; D'Andria, 2011; Sellin, 1963; Vaknin, 2000). Combining the Sutherland thought of white collar crime or business crimes as organized with the notions that some organized crime groups besides their classical undertaking engage in economic criminal activity, one comes to the notion of organized business crime (Pečar, 1993). Infiltrating legitimate spheres, informal arrangement, exploiting people and opportunities, having monopolistic stand ground, and mostly operating in the gray area are some of its characteristics (Pečar, 1993). In this way the informal economy is a crucial operating field, and though in some way the informal economy shares its basic traits with organized crime, organized crime and the informal economy should not be equated.

Defining Informal Economy

In the broadest sense economy can be divided in two main groups: formal (regulated economy) and informal (unregulated) economy (Shapland and Ponsaers, 2009b), with its numerous *aliases*—the unofficial economy, the hidden economy, the subterranean economy, the shadow economy, the parallel economy, the irregular economy, the social economy, the underground economy, and the criminal economy (and in Europe, also the "black economy" and the "second economy") (Henry and Sills, 2006, p. 263). It is also called the "invisible, unrecorded and shadow economy or moonlighting" (Frey and Schneider, 2000, pp. 1–2) or "undeclared" and "cash in hand" (Williams, 2005, p. 38). Added to this are also language-specific names, such as *lavoro nero* in Italy and *Schwarzarbeit* in Germany (Frey and Pommerehne, 1984, p. 1). Also, similarly diverse are definitions of informal economy. Smith (1994, p. 4) offers the following four alternative definitions of an informal economy:

1. Market-based production* of legal goods and services that escapes detection in the official estimates of GDP.
2. Market-based production of goods and services, whether legal or illegal, that escapes detection in the official estimates of GDP.
3. Market-based production of goods and services, whether legal or illegal, that escapes detection by the tax authorities.
4. Market- and nonmarket-based production of goods and services, whether legal or illegal, that escapes detection or is intentionally excluded from the official estimates of GDP.

Webb et al. (2009) define informal economy as "the set of illegal yet legitimate (to some large groups) activities through which actors recognize and exploit opportunities" (p. 492). Equally broad is Sassen's (1994) definition, where "[informal economy] refers to those income-generating activities occurring outside the state's regulatory framework that have analogs within that framework" (p. 2289). Also broad is the definition used by the International Labor Organization (ILO): "The term 'informal economy' refers to all economic activities by workers and economic units that are—in law or in practice—not covered or insufficiently covered by formal arrangements" (Resource Guide on the Informal Economy, 2012). Buehn and Schneider (2007) state that one of the more frequently used definitions is the one that defines informal economy as "all currently unregistered economic activities that contribute to the officially

* The market-based production means that produced goods or offered services (legal or illegal) will be offered on the market, while nonmarketed will not be. Smith (1994, p. 3) lists "Household cooking and cleaning, imputed rent on owner occupied dwellings" as legal nonmarketed-based production activity and "Growing marijuana for own use" (for illegal nonmarketed-based production activity) as examples.

calculated (or observed) Gross National Product" (p. 2), excluding do-it-yourself activities. Ponsaers et al. (2008) have noticed that these various definitions fall mainly into one of the following groups: enterprise-based definitions, which focus on "the organization of the work and the links between different actors [e.g., Is this transnational criminality? How do goods travel across borders? Is it a form of exploitation or not?])", job-based definitions, which "highlight the potential of the informal economy to provide income for marginalized groups"; and activity-based definitions, which "offer an examination of whether the activity itself is criminal (drug taking normally is; selling medicines not—except when the goods are not what they seem, or have arrived in the seller's hands in an unorthodox, unregulated way)" (pp. 645–646). So it seems that "no single definition exists but it depends on the purpose" (Frey and Schneider, 2000, pp. 1–2). Definitions vary from researcher to researcher and from occupation to occupation. This of course, also applies to the actual meaning of informal economy (Gërxhani and Feige, 1999). This variety of meanings has certain shortcomings as the views of economists differ from those of politicians, jurists, and criminologists, yet they all engage in activities aimed in managing the informal economy.

It is clear that authors use two different sets of informal economy definitions (Fleming et al., 2000). The first set includes definitions where profit is gained from legal activities but workers, the scope of work, the product of work, or profit from work/product is in whole or in part unregistered (concealed) from state supervisors (see discussions in Buehn and Schneider, 2007; Chen, 2005; Nastav and Bojnec, 2007; Williams, 2005, 2006). The second (a more criminological view) also includes all those prelisted legal activities but also includes what many authors (Chen, 2005; Fleming et al., 2000; Henry and Sills, 2006; Hočevar, 2007; Ruggiero, 2000) refer to as the *criminal economy*, which constitutes illegal activities, and therefore the whole profit is logically concealed from state supervisors as well. Yet this informal and illegal profit still enters the legal economic sphere through simple everyday activities (like buying up supplies, paying for food, car repair services) or through complex money laundering schemes (see discussions in Feige, 1994; Ruggiero, 2000; van Duyne, 1996). This is perhaps the reason why the informal economy triggers association with criminal activity (Ruggiero, 2000). Yet this negative, even criminal-like overtone, is somewhat strange, as in narrations of Chen (2005) about the "discovery" [quotation in original] of the informal economy in Africa in the 1970s, it becomes very clear that the informal economy at first is not seen as a bad thing, despite the fact that it incorporates illegal activities as well as legal (see Hart, 2005). This notion of the informal economy is similar to that of Henry and Sills (2006), who were the first to describe research about the informal economy completed around 1958, and where it was not seen as negative but as a form of a survival mechanism. This also indicates that the informal economy is not a new phenomenon and studies of it can be found as early as the 1860s (Alderslade et al., 2006).

New readers into the informal economy perhaps could get the wrong image about the scope and traits of the informal economy, because in the works that deal with this subject, there is a domination of studies where the informal economy is studied in under- or nondeveloped regions (see Alderslade et al., 2006; Sassen, 1994). Yet this is far from reality as even highly developed countries can have a great share of the informal economy (Buehn and Schneider, 2007; Sassen, 1994; Schneider, 2011).*

* See Gërxhani and Feige (1999) for a discussion about the differences and approaches used in studies about the informal economy in developed versus nondeveloped, transitional, or third world countries.

The Connection between the Informal and Formal Economy

The informal economy is intangibly connected to the formal economy (Chen, 2005; see also Alderslade et al., 2006; Blunch et al., 2001; Henry and Sills, 2006; Sassen, 1994) and should not be so easily identified with illegality (Frey and Schneider, 2000), perhaps not even discouraged (Fleming et al., 2000). As mentioned, both illegal and legal segments of the informal economy influence the formal (and legal) economy (see Chen, 2005; Walle, 2008; Williams, 2005). Formal economies' every movement and factor, ranging from (the slightest) increases in taxation or social security contributions (Schneider, 2008) to most notably global crises, have its countereffect in the informal economy (see Chen, 2005; Ponsaers et al., 2008), and as scholars (Chen, 2005; Nastav and Bojnec, 2007; Williams, 2005, 2009; Williams and Nadin, 2011) have noticed, the informal economy has both social and economic (Williams and Nadin, 2011), positive and/or negative sides (Gërxhani and Feige, 1999). Negative being low standards of work conditions and job safety, lack of health insurance, fewer collected taxes, the latter affects the state budget; the informal economy also causes unfair competitive advantages, lack of records, foul claiming warranty, or insurance; the informal economy is distorting the official statistical economic reality, heavy (often poisonous) burden on the environment, and other negatives (Biswas et al., 2012; Chen, 2005; Gërxhani and Feige, 1999; Nastav and Bojnec, 2007, pp. 195–196; Williams, 2005, p. 40, 2009; Williams and Nadin, 2011, 2012). While the positive sides of the informal economy are lower operational costs and more people being employed, flexibility, and the great share of unofficial earnings entering the official economy, consumers pay less since no value-added tax is charged; the informal economy presents a safety net or means of survival, an improved standard of living, and other benefits (Gërxhani and Feige, 1999; Nastav and Bojnec, 2007; Williams, 2005, 2009; Williams and Nadin, 2011). Such effects are seen on the micro (personal) level as well as on the macro (having influence on the formal state) level (Frey and Schneider, 2000, p. 8).

Causes of the Informal Economy

While the basic reason for the existence of the informal economy is the existence of the demand for informal services and goods, the previously mentioned list of positive benefits of the informal economy represents sprouting causes for the existence of the informal economy. Other causes include increases in taxes and social security contributions (Buehn and Schneider, 2007), evading (intense) regulation and restrictions (Buehn and Schneider, 2007; Williams and Nadin, 2011),* and ill-functioning public sector, which is underfunded due to lack of funding from formal economy due to the informal economy (Schneider, 2011). Table 2.1 summarizes some of the empirical research about the causes of the development of an informal economy.

The roles of state institutions and their quality of performance is recognized in several factors contributing to (the rise of) the informal economy. As mentioned, there is a certain paradox—the greater the size of the informal economy, the less taxes are collected. The poorer are in frequency and performance the state services, the greater is the initiative to participate in the informal economy (Schneider, 2011). This all weakens the state, causing it to lose a grip on security and governance-related matters.

Works of Thießen (2010) and Gërxhani and Feige (1999) also offer a well-developed presentation of how much various factors (taxes, labor restrictions, social factors, etc.) are connected and can influence the informal economy. Logically, these factors reflect differently in a different form of governance and development (nondeveloped, transitional, developed). These intakes also to some extent confirm Webb et al.'s (2009) view about the importance of social and group elements and the informal economy.† In the end, we can see that an informal economy can be "a calculated strategy, a sign of solidarity or an indicator of cultural uniqueness" (Walle, 2008, p. 654). This also results in a frequent desire for subcomponentization and subdividing the informal economy.

* Or as Walle (2008) well exposed—in this intense consumerism in which we live—the informal economy with its lack of interest for the social or physical security of workers, deregulated work schemes, and development of questionable products, and overall lack of state supervisors is well desired. Or as neoliberals put it more "nicely," entrepreneurs get involved in the informal economy as a result of stringent and burdensome state regulations. On this, see also Blunch et al. (2001), Chen (2005), Fleming et al. (2000), Gërxhani and Feige (1999), Hart (2005), Henry and Sills (2006), Losby et al. (2002), McElwee et al. (2011), Ponsaers et al. (2008), Sassen (1994), Schneider (2008), Shapland and Ponsaers (2009b), Webb et al. (2009), and Williams and Nadin (2012).

† See Gërxhani and Feige (1999) and Webb et al. (2009) for more about social and demographical matters in connection with the informal economy. See also Blunch et al. (2001), Buehn and Schneider (2007), Chen (2005), Schneider and Enste (2000), Smith (1994), and Thießen (2010) for more detailed discussions about general issues related to the informal economy.

Is There More Than One (Sub) Type of Informal Economy?

The previously mentioned description of the division of the informal economy between legal but unregulated, unreported and illegal, and nonregulated and unreported is one of the more frequently used componentizations. Thomas (2001, p. 2) offers a broader structure of the informal economy, respectively, its activities:

> This notion that the informal economy can have different levels of (il)legality is similar to Sassen's (1994) three components view, that is, criminal, unreported profit, and unreported activities. Similarly, after close analyses, we propose a model of an informal economy that consists of white, gray, and black segments of informal economy.

The White Informal Economy

The *white* segment of the *informal economy* consists of activities in which a profit or a profit itself is seen

Table 2.1 The Main Causes for the Increase of the Shadow Economy

Factors Influencing the Shadow Economy[a]	Influence on the Shadow Economy (in %)	
	Average Values of 12 Studies	Average Values of Empirical Results of 22 Studies
Increase of tax and social security contribution burdens	35–38	45–52
Quality of state institutions	10–12	12–17
Transfers	5–7	7–9
Specific labor market regulations	7–9	7–9
Public sector services	5–7	7–9
Tax morale	22–25	
Influence of all factors	84–98	78–96

Source: Schneider, F., The shadow economy and shadow economy labor force: What do we (not) know? (No. 5769), Discussion paper series, Forschungsinstitut zur Zukunft der Arbeit, Bonn, Germany, retrieved from http://www.econstor.eu/handle/10419/51986, 2011.

[a] "The overview is based on the studies in which the size of the shadow economy is measured by the MIMIC (Multiple Indicators Multiple Causes) or Currency Demand Approach. As there is no evidence on deterrence using these approaches—at least with respect to the broad panel database on which this table draws—the most central policy variable does not show up. This is an obvious shortcoming of the studies, but one that cannot be coped with easily due to the lack of internationally comparable deterrence data" (Schneider, 2011, pp. 12–13).

as legitimate on all accounts, yet is protected from taxes or enriched with various forms of interest with questionable creative financial (accounting) measures. Cases of various forms of capital flight would serve as the best example. This is somewhat similar to what Henry and Sills (2006) name "informal unofficial economic activity," this being activities with an aim "to get around rules and processes typically not using money but favors, privileges and perks as a means of exchange. They are not parasitic, nor illegal, but not a formal part of policy or practices of an organization" (p. 264). We grant that such a definition of this subsegment of the informal economy is slippery, however, when considering the notion exposed by Walle (2008), when she questions where to draw the line between unregulated informal economy and neoliberal (un)regulated formal economy. The white economy becomes a label that could be used for common day standard practices of big businesses. The cost of such practices and the importance of moral (ir)responsibility (of 13 European countries) was well exposed in an international report about tax evasion and capital flight, coordinated by the European network on debt and development (Eurodad), who stated that the amount of taxes that must be paid by corporations has everywhere, but in Africa, decreased, but there was an expansion of tax burden increment on the common people (Eurodad, 2013). Similarly irresponsible are the behavior of the European governing bodies that have, by failing to establish a secure labor environment for otherwise legally employed immigrant workers, created formal settings, which in nature resemble the informal economy (Williams, 2009). On the positive side, the white informal economy can be used to categorize what Henry and Sills (2006, p. 264) name the *informal social economy*, and this being a free or minimally paid execution of services among neighbors or friends, neighboring help, do-it-yourself, and household activities. The question that remains is where to draw the line among neighboring or friendly help and economic activity. Some economic activity can be repaid with such ways as bartering or swapping (Losby et al., 2002), which is also used among friends and family. Many authors of the informal economy, a priori, exclude do-it-yourself (Losby et al., 2002), neighboring, and similar quid pro quo activities from the informal economy. Our opinion is that as soon as activities are paid with cash in hand, such activities should be listed under the gray segment of the informal economy.

The Gray Informal Economy

The gray subcategory includes legitimate activities, however done or paid off the record. It also includes activities that are not complied with work-related regulation (see Shapland and Ponsaers, 2009a). This is the broadest category, and the most unregulated economic activities fall in here. It ranges from off-the-record (with cash-in-hand payment) house or car repairs and tutoring to off-the-record production of goods or services (Losby et al., 2002). It also includes cash-in-hand methods of payment of wages for the formally employed. Williams (2009) noticed occurrences of such practices throughout all 27 EU member states (though the occurring percentage varies from state to state; he based his notes on 2007 Eurobarometer data). He also writes that not so small a number of entrepreneurs engage in the informal economy, especially at the early stages of business (Williams and Nadin, 2012). The key notion here is the fact that as long the provided services and goods are legal, the state occasionally turns a blind eye. These *alegal* activities (Blunch et al., 2001, p. 15) are being tolerated by the state as long as these activities are done by those that are hard to employ as this presents a form of a safety net (Gërxhani and Feige, 1999; Losby et al., 2002; Thomas, 2001).

The Black Informal Economy

The black segment could be most easily described as that segment of the informal economy that most authors (Chen, 2005; Henry and Sills, 2006; Hočevar, 2007; Ruggiero, 2000) name criminal economy. The latter is in most cases seen as provisions of goods and/or services that are against the criminal law (Shapland and Ponsaers, 2009a, p. viii). Some divide illegal trade in three different forms: mainly the trade in forbidden goods and services (drugs, arms, prostitution), trade in legal goods but made illegal due to intentional avoidance of taxation or payment of duties, and trade using illegal practices to gain certain competitive advantage or by making profit from unrealized sales, transports, and other transactions (these are mainly practices of various tax evasion schemes, tax carousel frauds, and insider trading) (Fadahunsi and Rosa, 2002; McElwee et al., 2011; Tičar and Bernik, 2012). All this is similar to a (division of) the informal economy. Though perhaps most hidden from all three segments of the informal economy, the profits and activity from the black informal economy still influence the formal economy (McElwee et al., 2011). Cannabis cultivations provide demands that legitimate hydroponics shops can satisfy (Bouchard and Dion, 2009). Sometimes the untainted organized crime or corruption force people to engage in illicit entrepreneurship practices (Fadahunsi and Rosa, 2002) or the informal economy is funded from criminal activities to the extent that they outstage the formal one (Jiménez, 1989).

Notes on Measuring the Three-Segmented Informal Economy

None of the empirical literature relating to the informal economy reviewed by the authors of this chapter included all three segments of the informal economy. Considering the elusiveness of the economic behavior described under the white informal economy, perhaps this complete analysis has never been completed. Most of the empirically based studies used the bipartial categorization, meaning that the empirical studies of the informal economy excluded criminal markets and illegal goods (like drugs), even though some measuring methods could be used (like the methods of currency demand). For those who are interested in the findings of these classical studies, see the works of Friedrich Schneider.*

* Friedrich Schneider has also written exhaustively about different methods used to measure the informal economy, about their benefits and weaknesses. For instance, see Buehn and Schneider (2007), Frey and Schneider (2000), Schneider and Enste (2000), and Schneider (2008, 2011).

The Informal Economy and (Organized) Crime

Though the informal economy and organized crime share some factorial and behavioral traits (Shapland and Ponsaers, 2009b), the relationship that we wish to enlighten is the mutual connection and roles of (organized) crime in the informal economy and vice versa. But which acts in the whole pallet of (un)regulated

Table 2.2 The Structure of Informal Economic Activity

Sector	Market Transactions	Output	Production/ Distribution
Household	No	Legal	Legal
Informal	Yes	Legal	Quasi-legal
Underground	Yes	Legal	Illegal
Criminal	Yes	Illegal	Illegal

Source: Thomas, J., *SAIS Rev.*, 21(1), 1, p. 2, 2001, doi:10.1353/sais.2001.0025.

activities unrecognizably connected to (il)legal markets are/could/should be regarded as crime? Is it a crime if an "average Joe" performs a legal and reported activity (e.g., car repair), but part of his or her reports to financial authorities are misleading? What if a big company employs unregistered workers that perform legal and registered activities? Scholars that research the informal economy (Chen, 2005; Heber, 2009; Losby et al., 2002; Sassen, 1994; Webb et al., 2009) list even more examples of a mixture of legal and illegal elements in the (in)formal economy (see also Table 2.2). Yet such acts can only be labeled as crime if provisions of criminal code were violated. Also, "some activities taking place in the informal economy fall within informal institutional boundaries (i.e., norms, values, and beliefs of large groups in a society) but outside formal institutional boundaries (i.e., laws and regulations)" (Webb et al., 2009, p. 493). Such activities are, with respect to state policies regarding the informal economy, treated as illegal, but the state then either turns a blind eye to them (Blunch et al., 2001; Williams, 2009) or harshly prosecutes them, deciding what is best for the state.

One would think that the whole story is far less complex when the products of crime are sold on the illegal or black market(s), and perhaps that is true in the cases of illegal drugs and human body parts. However, although stolen jewelry, cars, and car parts are usually sold in such markets, they are also sold in legally operating shops and firms. Crimes against the environment are done by legal business entities (Eman et al., 2013). Drugs are sold in legally managed bars, owned by drug dealers, sometimes funded from illegally gained drug funds. These sorts of money laundering schemes should also be listed under the informal economy, since they are basically no different from legitimate firms being funded by profits of undeclared work, done by unregistered workers, or with funds remaining from the nonpayment of taxes from undeclared profit. In addition to money laundering, there are two more ways in which illegal (criminal) capital can enter the legitimate economy. The first is through basic everyday consumerism (van Duyne, 1996). This also often happens with much of the earning from informal economy (Schneider and Enste, 2000). The second way is through rational economic investment in shares, buyouts, crediting, or funding the establishment of legitimate business. Of course, the control over business can also be gained through violence and/or corruption. There are different roles of corruption in the (in)formal economy (Buehn and Schneider, 2007; Fadahunsi and Rosa, 2002; Schneider, 2008; Thießen, 2010), from "greasing the bureaucratic wheels," to gaining control over important managerial or procedural matters, buying permits, gaining questionable interest, or political influence. And as Thießen (2010) notes, corruption and the informal economy are complementary in both low and high income countries. But here it must be noted that it is not only organized crime that uses corruption to gain advantages; legitimate businesses use it too. Also, other illegal practices that are often attributed to the criminal world are knowingly and intentionally employed by legal businesses (Beetham, 2003; Naím, 2008; Ruggiero, 2000). Sometimes they simply help criminal(s) organizations for some mutual benefit (European Police Office, 2013). This questionable mutual cooperation varies in size and ranges from low-scale acts, when, for instance, taxi drivers drive prostitutes and their clients from or to the brothel, to large-scale acts like illegal waste dumping performed by organized crime groups (Naím, 2008; Walle, 2008) or helping with the employment of unregistered workers (Heber, 2009).

Of course, some businesses and (business) environments are more vulnerable to exploitation or manipulation from organized crime than others (Vander Beken and Van Daele, 2008). The level of connection of organized crime and legitimate business also depends upon the level or state of organized crime group(s). The most important thing that must be realized here is the fact that formal business (deregulated) settings that legal businesses help shape through lobbying, political activities, or consulting groups are (ab)used by organized crime. Every economic development, especially liberalization (Broude and Teichman, 2009), in some way or another helps (organized) crime in either easing their activities (Forde and Patterson, 1998) or providing help in transportation of illegal goods and people (criminal, illegal immigrants) (Mitsilegas et al., 2003). Global financial markets and financial services help with money laundering (Hočevar, 2007).

Conclusion

First, we must emphasize that we agree with scholars and thinkers that see the informal economy as a permanent occurrence. As it is historically told; it is not a trait of a single system (Gërxhani and Feige, 1999). It can be found in (post) socialist regimes (Polese and Rodgers, 2011) or in capitalist societies (Blunch et al., 2001; Buehn and Schneider, 2007; Henry and Sills, 2006).* Perhaps capitalist regimes even fuel it more as they strive to minimize costs and taxation (Chen, 2005; Walle, 2008). Therefore, a shift of perception about the informal economy is needed. Instead of fighting it and seeing it as an anomaly (see Sassen, 1994), we should curb it to minimize the risks that it brings, especially since deterrence as the mostly used method to fight the informal economy has weak or even counterproductive results (Thießen, 2010). This can be seen most notably in regard to drugs, prostitution, and alcohol prohibition (Frey and Schneider, 2000). Fragmented approaches such as described by Williams (2005) as the UK approach, where several different institutions are dealing with the informal economy by targeting different segments of the informal economy and thus applying different working definitions of it,† with limitedly successful end results, are also very frequent. While several authors (Shapland and Ponsaers, 2009b; Webb et al., 2009) emphasize that it is more effective for governments to improve implementation of laws rather than increase their number. Proper social, labor, economic, and security policies toward an informal economy and its composing subjects (which are unemployed or self-employed) should be developed (Chen, 2005; Schneider, 2008; Webb et al., 2009). Improvements in anticorruption measures and fostering *better* rule of law decreases the informal economy (Buehn and Schneider, 2007).

We can conclude that the informal economy in some countries escapes state control and it is hard to control. As we can see, the formal and informal economies are closely linked. Changes dictated by the policy on the formal economy are de facto reflected in the informal economy, segments of which are sometimes controlled by criminal organizations. Thus, the activities of criminal organizations depend on those who create policy in the country. Some economists can also defend the view that the money, even if it is dirty money, stimulates the economy. But we saw that such money encourages speculative investment and creates a climate of violence in the country, which has a negative impact on formal markets. Investing only in repressive measures (fiscal and regulatory policies in a formal economy), creates greater incentives for companies to relocate their assets to the informal economy and thus increase investment for corruption. It seems that corruption is appearing as a fill rouge of all the problems analyzed, so curbing corruption will also have a positive impact in controlling organized crime and the informal economy. This is why we should shed more light on these problems and in the future analyze the dynamics and characteristics of the rule of law that are subjected to the adverse influences of corruption in the world.

* See Blunch et al. (2001) for discussion about some other misperceptions of the informal economy.

† See also Feige (1994).

References

Alderslade, J., Talmadge, J., and Freeman, Y. (2006). Measuring the informal economy: One neighborhood at a time. Brookings Institution, Metropolitan Policy Program, Washington, DC. Retrieved from http://www.brookings.org/metro/umi/pubs/20060905_informaleconomy.pdf. (Accessed February 13, 2014.)

Allum, F. and Sands, J. (2004). Explaining organized crime in Europe: Are economists always right? *Crime, Law and Social Change*, *41*(2), 133–160. doi:10.1023/B:CRIS.0000016223.49968.17.

Allum, F. and Siebert, R. (2003). Organized crime: A threat to democracy? In F. Allum and R. Siebert (Eds.), *Organized Crime and the Challenge to Democracy* (pp. 1–22). London, UK: Routledge. Retrieved from http://www.tandfebooks.com/isbn/9780203426418.

Beetham, D. (2003). Foreword. In F. Allum and R. Siebert (Eds.), *Organized Crime and the Challenge to Democracy* (pp. xii–xiv). London, UK: Routledge. Retrieved from http://www.tandfebooks.com/isbn/9780203426418.

Biswas, A. K., Farzanegan, M. R., and Thum, M. (2012). Pollution, shadow economy and corruption: Theory and evidence. *Ecological Economics*, *75*, 114–125. doi:10.1016/j.ecolecon.2012.01.007.

Blunch, N.-H., Canagarajah, S., and Raju, D. (2001). The informal sector revisited: A synthesis across space and time (Social Protection Discussion Paper Series No. 0119). Retrieved from http://www-wds.worldbank.org/servlet/WDSContentServer/WDSP/IB/2002/01/17/000094946_01120804004891/Rendered/PDF/multi0page.pdf. (Accessed February 12, 2014.)

Chapter 2

Bouchard, M. and Dion, C. B. (2009). Growers and facilitators: Probing the role of entrepreneurs in the development of the cannabis cultivation industry. *Journal of Small Business and Entrepreneurship, 22*(1), 25–37. doi:10.1080/08276331.2009.10593440.

Broude, T. and Teichman, D. (2009). Outsourcing and insourcing crime: The political economy of globalized criminal activity. *Vanderbilt Law Review, 62*(3), 795–848.

Buehn, A. and Schneider, F. (2007). Shadow economies and corruption all over the world: Revised estimates for 120 countries. *Economics: The Pen-Access, Open-Assessment E-Journal, 1*, 1–53. doi:10.5018/economics-ejournal.ja.2007–9.

Chen, M. (2005). *Rethinking the Informal Economy: Linkages with the Formal Economy and the Formal Regulatory Environment.* Helsinki, Finland: United Nations University WIDER. Retrieved from http://www.wider.unu.edu/publications/rps/rps2005/rp200510.pdf.

Clinard, M. B. and Meier, R. F. (2011). *Sociology of Deviant Behavior* (14th ed.). Belmont, CA: Wadsworth Cengage Learning.

D'Andria, D. (2011). Investment strategies of criminal organisations. *Policy Studies, 32*(1), 1–19. doi:10.1080/01442872.2010.520558.

Dobovšek, B. (2008). Economic organized crime networks in emerging democracies. *International Journal of Social Economics, 35*(9), 679–690. doi:10.1108/03068290810896307.

Dobovšek, B. (2012). Marxist economy versus economic crime. In E. Devroe, L. Pauwels, A. Verhage, M. Easton, and M. Cools (Eds.), *Tegendraadse Criminologie: Liber Amicorum Paul Ponsaers* (pp. 437–448). Antwerpen, Belgium: Maklu.

Edelbacher, M. and Theil, M. (2012). White collar crime. In M. Edelbacher, P. C. Kratcoski, and M. Theil (Eds.), *Financial Crimes: A Threat to Global Security* (pp. 81–116). Boca Raton, FL: CRC Press.

Eman, K., Meško, G., Dobovšek, B., and Sotlar, A. (2013). Environmental crime and green criminology in South Eastern Europe—Practice and research. *Crime, Law and Social Change, 59*(3), 341–358. doi:10.1007/s10611-013-9419-0.

Eurodad. (2013). Giving with one hand and taking with the other—Europe's role in tax-related capital flight from developing countries. Retrieved from http://www.eurodad.org/takingwithonehand2013. (Accessed January 20, 2014.)

European Police Office. (2013). *SOCTA 2013: EU Serious and Organised Crime Threat Assessment.* The Hague, the Netherlands: Europol.

Fadahunsi, A. and Rosa, P. (2002). Entrepreneurship and Illegality: Insights from the Nigerian cross-border trade. *Journal of Business Venturing, 17*(5), 397–429. doi:10.1016/S0883-9026(01)00073-8.

Feige, E. L. (1994). The underground economy and the currency enigma. *Public Finance = Finances Publiques, 49*(Supplement), 119–136.

Fleming, M. H., Roman, J., and Farrell, G. (2000). The shadow economy. *Journal of International Affairs, 53*(2), 387–409.

Forde, P. and Patterson, A. (1998). Paedophile internet activity. *Trends and Issues in Crime and Criminal Justice, 97*(1), 1–6.

Frey, B. S. and Pommerehne, W. W. (1984). The hidden economy: State and prospects for measurement. *Review of Income and Wealth, 30*(1), 1–23. doi:10.1111/j.1475-4991.1984.tb00474.x.

Frey, B. S. and Schneider, F. (2000). Informal and underground economy. Working Paper, Department of Economics, Johannes Kepler University of Linz, No. 0004, Linz, Austria.

Gërxhani, K. and Feige, E. L. (1999). Informal sector in developed and less developed countries: A literature survey. Retrieved from http://citeseerx.ist.psu.edu/viewdoc/summary?doi=10.1.1.17.2818. (Accessed April 2, 2014.)

Hart, K. (2005). *Formal Bureaucracy and the Emergent Forms of the Informal Economy.* Helsinki, Finland: United Nations University WIDER. Retrieved from http://www.wider.unu.edu/publications/rps/rps2005/rp200511.pdf.

Heber, A. (2009). Networks of organised black market labour in the building trade. *Trends in Organized Crime, 12*(2), 122–144. doi:10.1007/s12117-008-9060-y.

Hellman, S. J., Jones, G., and Kaufmann, D. (2000). Seize the state, seize the day: State capture, corruption, and influence in transition. World Bank Publications. Retrieved from http://www.worldbank.icebox.ingenta.com/content/wb/wps4301/2000/00000001/00000001/art02444. (Accessed December 14, 2010.)

Henry, S. and Sills, S. (2006). Informal economic activity: Early thinking, conceptual shifts, continuing patterns and persistent issues—A Michigan study. *Crime, Law and Social Change, 45*(4–5), 263–284. doi:10.1007/s10611-006-9036-2.

Hočevar, V. S. (2007). *Pranje denarja: učinkovito odkrivanje in preprečevanje* (1. natis.). Ljubljana, Slovenia: GV Založba.

Iwasaki, I. and Suzuki, T. (2007). Transition strategy, corporate exploitation, and state capture: An empirical analysis of the former Soviet states. *Communist and Post-communist Studies, 40*(4), 393–422. doi:10.1016/j.postcomstud.2007.10.001.

Jiménez, J. (1989). Cocaine, informality, and the urban economy in La Paz, Bolivia. In A. Portes, M. Castells, and L. A. Benton (Eds.), *The Informal Economy: Studies in Advanced and Less Developed Countries* (pp. 135–149). Baltimore, MD: Johns Hopkins University Press.

Losby, J., Else, J., Kingslow, M., Edgcomb, E., Malm, E., and Kao, V. (2002). Informal economy literature review. ISED Consulting and Research. Retrieved from http://www.kingslow-assoc.com/images/Informal_Economy_Lit_Review.pdf. (Accessed April 2, 2014.)

McElwee, G., Smith, R., and Somerville, P. (2011). Theorising illegal rural enterprise: Is everyone at it? *International Journal of Rural Criminology, 1*(1), 40–62.

Mitsilegas, V., Monar, J., and Rees, G. W. (2003). *The European Union and Internal Security: Guardian of the People?* Hampshire, UK: Palgrave Macmillan.

Naím, M. (2008). *Nedovoljeno: kako tihotapci, prekupčevalci in posnemovalci ugrabljajo globalno gospodarstvo.* Ljubljana, Slovenia: Gnostica.

Nastav, B. and Bojnec, Š. (2007). Shadow economy in Slovenia: The labour approach. *Managing Global Transitions, 5*(2), 193–208.

Pečar, J. (1993). Združevanje v kriminalne organizacije—kriminal kot podjetništvo. *Revija Za Kriminalistiko in Kriminologijo, 44*(4), 327–337.

Polese, A. and Rodgers, P. (2011). Surviving post-socialism: the role of informal economic practices. *International Journal of Sociology and Social Policy, 31*(11/12), 612–618. doi:10.1108/01443331111177896.

Ponsaers, P., Shapland, J., and Williams, C. C. (2008). Does the informal economy link to organised crime? *International Journal of Social Economics, 35*(9), 644–650. doi:10.1108/03068290810896262.

Resource Guide on the Informal Economy. (September 3, 2012). International labour organization (ILO). Retrieved from http://www.ilo.org/public/english/support/lib/resource/subject/informal.htm. (Accessed February 24, 2014.)
Ruggiero, V. (2000). *Crime and Markets: Essays in Anti-Criminology.* New York: Oxford University Press.
Sassen, S. (1994). The informal economy: Between new developments and old regulations. *The Yale Law Journal, 103*(8), 2289–2304. doi:10.2307/797048.
Schneider, F. (2008). Shadow economy. In C. Rowley and F. Schneider (Eds.), *Readings in Public Choice and Constitutional Political Economy* (pp. 511–532). Boston, MA: Springer. Retrieved from http://link.springer.com/10.1007/978-0-387-75870-1_28.
Schneider, F. (2011). The shadow economy and shadow economy labor force: What do we (not) know? (No. 5769). Discussion paper series, Forschungsinstitut zur Zukunft der Arbeit, Bonn, Germany. Retrieved from http://www.econstor.eu/handle/10419/51986.
Schneider, F. and Enste, D. (2000). Shadow economies around the world—Size, causes, and consequences (IMF Working Paper No. 00/26). Retrieved from http://www.imf.org/external/pubs/cat/longres.aspx?sk=3435.0. (Accessed February 6, 2014.)
Sellin, T. (1963). Organized crime: A business enterprise. *The Annals of the American Academy of Political and Social Science, 347*(1), 12–19. doi:10.1177/000271626334700103.
Shapland, J. and Ponsaers, P. (2009a). Introduction. In J. Shapland and P. Ponsaers (Eds.), *The Informal Economy and Connections with Organised Crime: The Impact of National Social and Economic Policies* (pp. i–x). The Hague, the Netherlands: BJu Legal Publishers.
Shapland, J. and Ponsaers, P. (2009b). Potential effects of national policies on the informal economy. In J. Shapland and P. Ponsaers (Eds.), *The Informal Economy and Connections with Organised Crime: The Impact of National Social and Economic Policies* (pp. 1–22). The Hague, the Netherlands: BJu Legal Publishers.
Smith, P. (1994). *Assessing the Size of the Underground Economy: The Statistics Canada Perspective.* Ottawa, Ontario, Canada: National Accounts and Environment Division, Statistics Canada = Division des comptes nationaux et de l'environnement, Statistique Canada. Retrieved from http://publications.gc.ca/collections/Collection/Statcan/13-604-M/13-604-MIB1994028.pdf.
Snider, L. (2008). Corporate economic crimes. In J. Minkes and L. Minkes (Eds.), *Corporate and White-Collar Crime* (pp. 39–61). London, UK: SAGE Publications.
Sutherland, E. (1940). White-collar criminality. *American Sociological Review, 5*(1), 1–12.
Thießen, U. (2010). The shadow economy in international comparison: Options for economic policy derived from an OECD panel analysis. *International Economic Journal, 24*(4), 481–509. doi:10.1080/10168737.2010.525986.
Thomas, J. (2001). What is the informal economy, anyway? *SAIS Review, 21*(1), 1–11. doi:10.1353/sais.2001.0025.
Tičar, B. and Bernik, D. (2012). Omejevanje davčnih vrtiljakov kot posebne oblike organizirane kriminalitete v EU in Sloveniji [Fight against carousel fraud as a specific form of organised crime in the EU and the Republic of Slovenia]. *Revija Za Kriminalistiko in Kriminologijo [Journal of Criminalistics and Criminology], 63*(2), 103–111.
Tombs, S. (2008). Corporations and health and safety. In J. Minkes and L. Minkes (Eds.), *Corporate and White-Collar Crime* (pp. 18–28). London, UK: SAGE Publications.
United Nations Convention against Transnational Organized Crime and the Protocols Thereto. (2004). United Nations. Retrieved from http://www.unodc.org/unodc/treaties/CTOC/. (Accessed October 25, 2013.)
Vaknin. (2000). The criminality of transition. In M. Pagon (Ed.), *Policing in Central and Eastern Europe: Ethics, Integrity and Human Rights* (pp. 61–70). Ljubljana, Slovenia: Fakulteta za policijsko-varnostne vede [College of Police and Security Studies].
van Duyne, P. (1996). *Organized Crime in Europe.* Commack, NY: Nova Science Publishers.
van Duyne, P. (2010). Organised crime (threat) as a policy challenge: A tautology. *Varstvoslovje [Journal of Criminal Justice and Security], 12*(4), 355–366.
Vander Beken, T. and Van Daele, S. (2008). Legitimate businesses and crime vulnerabilities. *International Journal of Social Economics, 35*(10), 739–750. doi:10.1108/03068290810898954.
Von Lampe, K. (2014, Spring). Definitions of organized crime. Retrieved from www.organized-crime.de/organizedcrimedefinitions.htm. (Accessed January 29, 2014.)
Walle, G. (2008). A matrix approach to informal markets: Towards a dynamic conceptualisation. *International Journal of Social Economics, 35*(9), 651–665. doi:10.1108/03068290810896271.
Webb, J., Tihanyi, L., Ireland, R., and Sirmon, D. (2009). You say illegal, I say legitimate: Entrepreneurship in the informal economy. *Academy of Management Review, 34*(3), 492–510. doi:10.5465/AMR.2009.40632826.
Williams, C. (2005). Tackling the informal economy: Towards a coordinated public policy approach? *Public Policy and Administration, 20*(2), 38–53. doi:10.1177/095207670502000203.
Williams, C. (2006). *The Hidden Enterprise Culture: Entrepreneurship in the Underground Economy.* Cheltenham, UK: Edward Elgar.
Williams, C. (2009). Formal and informal employment in Europe: Beyond dualistic representations. *European Urban and Regional Studies, 16*(2), 147–159. doi:10.1177/0969776408101686.
Williams, C. and Nadin, S. (2011). Entrepreneurship in the informal economy: Commercial or social entrepreneurs? *International Entrepreneurship and Management Journal, 8*(3), 309–324. doi:10.1007/s11365-011-0169-0.
Williams, C. and Nadin, S. (2012). Tackling entrepreneurship in the informal economy: Evaluating the policy options. *Journal of Entrepreneurship and Public Policy, 1*(2), 111–124. doi:10.1108/20452101211261408.
Woodiwiss, M. (2003). Transnational organized crime: The strange career of an American concept. In M. E. Beare (Ed.), *Critical Reflections on Transnational Organized Crime, Money Laundering and Corruption* (pp. 3–34). Toronto, Ontario, Canada: University of Toronto Press. Retrieved from http://site.ebrary.com/id/10219213.

3. Financial Flow of Organized Crime and Tax Fraud in Developed Countries

An Empirical Investigation*

Friedrich Schneider

* An earlier and extended version of this chapter was published in Schneider, F., *Public Finance Rev.*, 41(5), 677, September 2013.

Introduction

Over the last decade, the growth of the world economy was quite high and improved economic well-being all over the globe, but this development was accompanied by some risks. Among them are proceeds from international organized crime and from financial and tax fraud,† which both rose remarkably in the last 20 years. This raises two questions:

1. From where do international crime organizations get their proceeds, and what do we know about their size and development?
2. How large are the proceeds from financial and tax fraud?

In this chapter, the main focus lies on providing a more detailed answer on the size and development of the proceeds of international crime and the ones from financial and tax fraud. An attempt is also made to give a preliminary answer to the origin of both types of criminal proceeds (questions 1 and 2). A detailed analysis of the financial proceeds and their sources is crucial in order to reduce their possibilities, so that the basis of their operations is at least limited. Hence, their review will meet two objectives: to widen the knowledge of this subject and the understanding of the main issues under debate and to focus on the literature closely related to the research topic. The body of literature on transnational crime financing is huge and diverse and quite often descriptive; hence in this chapter only those contributions that contain the latest and (hopefully) reliable figures are summarized.

This chapter is structured as follows. "Transnational Crime Proceeds and Money Laundering" provides a review of the empirical findings and on the kinds of transnational crime (including cyber crime) proceeds. "National Crime Proceeds and Money Laundering" makes some remarks about the Hawala banking system. In "Cost and Proceeds of Cybercrime: The Latest Development in International Organized Crime," some conclusions and policy recommendations are drawn.

† See for example Unger (2007), Walker and Unger (2009), Masciandaro (2004, 2005, 2006), Schneider (2010a, 2011), UNO DC (2010), Souza (2012), and Pickhardt and Prinz (2012).

Chapter 3

Transnational Crime Proceeds and Money Laundering*

Worldwide Figures

* For a detailed analysis, see Schneider (2008a,b, 2009, 2011), Schneider and Windischbauer (2008), Schneider et al. (2006), and Takats (2007).

Dirty money from crime is earned through various underground activities, like drug, weapons, and human trafficking. How much illicit crime money in all its forms can be observed?† The most widely quoted figure for the extent of money laundering criminal proceeds has been the International Monetary Fund (IMF) consensus range of 2.0%–5.0% of global gross domestic product (GDP) made public by the IMF in 1998 (compare IMF, 2001a,b).

Table 3.1 Financial Action Task Force (FATF) Estimates of Worldwide Money Laundering (1988–2005)

Amounts Estimated to Have Been Laundered (in Billions of USD)		As a Percentage of Global GDP (%)
1988	340.00	2.0
1996	1100.00	3.5
2005	2300.00	3.0

Sources: International Monetary Fund, Financial system abuse, financial crime and money laundering—Background paper, February 12, 2001; FATF, Financial system abuse, Report, Paris, France, 2007.

Table 3.2 International Monetary Fund (IMF) Estimates of Money Laundered Worldwide (1996–2009)

Estimation	Minimum	Maximum	Mid-point	Increase in %
IMF estimates of money laundered as a percentage of global GDP	2%	5%	3.5%	—
Estimate for 1996 in billion USD	600	1500	1100	—
Estimate for 2005 in billion USD	900	2300	1500	36.0
Estimate for 2009 in billion USD	1200	2900	2000	33.0

Source: OECD, Observer, Paris, France, various years, 1999–2010.

Tables 3.1 and 3.2 show the Financial Action Task Force (FATF) estimates and the IMF estimates of money laundered worldwide for a similar period of time (FATF 1988–2005; IMF 1996–2009). Considering first the FATF estimate, the amount of worldwide money laundering is 2.0% in 1988, increased to 3.5% in 1996, and decreased to 3.0% in 2005. The IMF estimate has a range of between 2.0% and 5.0% over the period 1996 to 2009. In absolute terms, money laundered worldwide increased by 36.0% from 1996 to 2005, and by 33.0% from 2005 to 2009, which is quite a dramatic increase. These FATF or IMF figures are more or less in a similar range.

In Table 3.3, the FATF estimates of global amounts of laundered money up to the year 2009 are shown. Here, the key focus lies on drugs and for this a calculation of the total amounts laundered from all criminal proceeds. In the year 2000, it was estimated that laundered money was $0.6 trillion USD, which doubled up to the year 2009 to $1.2 trillion USD.

Table 3.3 Financial Action Task Force (FATF) Estimates of Global Amounts of Laundered Money from 1988 to 2009

Estimate of Drug Sales in Key Markets (1988)	$124 Billion USD
As a percentage of global GDP (1988)	0.8%
Assumed proportion that is laundered	2/3%–70%
Estimate of amounts laundered related to drugs	$85 billion
Proportion in % of global GDP (1988)	0.5%
Estimated proportion of drugs in total amounts laundered	25.0%
Estimated total amounts laundered in 1988	$340 billion
As a percentage of global GDP	2.0%
Extrapolated to global GDP in 2000	$0.6 trillion
Extrapolated to global GDP in 2009	$1.2 trillion

Sources: Organisation for Economic Co-operation and Development, Financial Action Task Force on Money Laundering, Paris, France, 1990, p. 6, quoted in UNDCP, *Economic and Social Consequences of Drug Abuse and Illicit Trafficking*, UNDCP Technical Series No. 6, Vienna, Austria, 1998, p. 26; International Monetary Fund, Financial system abuse, financial crime and money laundering—Background paper, February 2010.

† Smith (2011) estimates that this amount is $1.5 trillion USD/year. However, these estimates are more guesstimates, because no clear sources are given and even more importantly, the procedure of calculation is not shown and critically discussed.

Table 3.4 Updated Financial Action Task Force (FATF) Model of Global Amounts of Money Laundered

Estimates of Drug Sales in Key Markets (UNODC Estimate for 2003)	$322 Billion USD
As a percentage of the world GDP	0.9%
Assumed proportion that is laundered (initial FATF estimate)	2/3%–70%
Estimate of amounts laundered related to drugs	$220 billion
Proportion in % of global GDP (2003)	0.6%
Estimated proportion of drugs in total amounts laundered (initial FATF estimate)	25.0%
Estimated total amounts laundered in 2003	$880 billion
As a percentage of GDP	2.4%
Extrapolated to global GDP in 2009	$1.4 trillion

Sources: International Monetary Fund, Financial system abuse, financial crime and money laundering—Background paper, February 2010; UNODC, World Drug Report, Vol. 1, Analysis, Vienna, Austria, 2005, p. 127.

Table 3.4 shows some newer FATF data, again for the drug market for the year 2003. For the year 2003, the FATF estimate of the total amounts laundered (from all criminal proceeds) is 880 billion or 2.4% of world GDP. Extrapolated to the year 2009, the calculation reaches $1.4 trillion USD.

In Table 3.5 money laundering by region is shown over the period 2000–2005. North and South America have by far the largest share with 37.8% in 2000, which remains more or less constant up to 2005, with 37.7%. Then Asia Pacific follows with a modest increase from 29.7% in 2000 to 31.5% in 2005. Europe slightly decreased; it was 27.8% in 2000 (of all money laundered proceeds) and declined to 26.0% in 2005.

In Table 3.6, the cross-border flows of global "dirty money" in trillion U.S. dollars are shown over the period 2000–2005 on a worldwide basis. This includes tax fraud money and all the money that leaves a country for criminal reasons. One can clearly see from Table 3.6 that the overall amount of dirty money laundered is between $1.1 and $1.6 trillion USD and increases to $1.7–$2.5 trillion USD in the year 2009. This is quite a large sum, which means between 2.9% and 4.3% of the world GDP. The classic criminal component lies only between 27.0% and 31.0% of the total dirty money. Hence, one clearly sees that capital flight and tax fraud money is by far the biggest proportion of dirty money.*

In Table 3.7, the proceeds from transnational crime (time range 2003–2009) is shown. Here we have a clear-cut result. Drugs are the biggest contributors with 50.0%, followed by counterfeiting with 39.0%, human trafficking with 5.0%, and oil with 2.0%. The proceeds from all other crime are much lower. In total, we have here a sum of $650 billion USD, which amounts to 1.1% of global GDP.

Finally, in Table 3.8, the estimates of worldwide turnover of organized crime in trillion U.S. dollars are shown. Table 3.8 clearly shows a huge range and it is left to the reader judgment to make his or her evaluation of

Table 3.5 Annual Money Laundering by Region, Billion USD (2000–2005)

Region	2000		2002		2005[a]	
America	313	37.8%	328	38.3%	350	37.7%
Asia-Pacific	246	29.7%	254	29.7%	292	31.5%
Europe	230	27.8%	234	27.3%	241	26.0%
Middle East/ Africa	38	4.6%	40	4.7%	44	4.7%
Total	827	100.0%	856	100.0%	927	100.0%
In % of GDP	2.7%		2.6%		2.0%	

Source: Katkov. N., Anti-money laundering: A brave new world for financial institutions, September 2002.

[a] Projection.

Table 3.6 Cross-Border Flow of Global "Dirty Money" (Including Tax Evasion!) in Trillion USD, Shown as a Percentage of Average GDP over the Period 2000–2005

	2000–2005			Extrapolated to 2009		
Variable	Low	High	In % of GDP 2000–2005	Low	High	Mid-point
Overall amounts laundered	1.1	1.6	2.9–4.3	1.7	2.5	2.1
of which criminal component	0.3	0.5	0.9–1.5	0.5	0.9	0.7

Sources: Baker, R.W., *Capitalism's Achilles Heel: Dirty Money and How to Renew the Free-Market System*, NJ, 2005, p. 172; World Bank, Macroeconomic indicators, Washington, DC, various years.

* Compare also Pickhardt and Prinz (2012).

Table 3.7 Proceeds of Transnational Crime (2003–2009)

Types of Crime	Billion USD	In % of Total Proceeds	Sources
(1) Drugs	320	50	UNO DC, World Drug Report 2005 (data refer to 2003)
(2) Counterfeiting	250	39	OECD, Magnitude of Counterfeiting and Piracy of Tangible Products (2009)
(3) Human trafficking	31.6	5	P. Belser (ILO), Forced Labor and Human Trafficking: Estimating the Profits (2005)
(4) Oil	10.8	2	GFI estimate based on Baker (2005) (quantities) and U.S. Energy Information Administration (prices: 2003–2010)
(5) Wildlife	7.8–10	1.4	GFI estimate based on Francesco Colombo, Animal Trafficking—A Cruel Billion-Dollar Business, Inter Press Service, September 6, 2003; Coalition Against Wildlife Trafficking, World Wildlife Fund
(6) Timber	7.0	1.1	GFI estimate for 2009 based on Seneca Creek and Wood Resources International, OECD
(7) Fish	4.2–9.5	1.1	GFI estimate for 2010, based on Norwegian national advisory group against organized IUU-fishing (FFA) and United Nations Food and Agriculture Organization
(8) Art and cultural property	3.4–6.3	0.8	GFI estimate based on Interpol, International Scientific and Professional Advisory Council of the United Nations Crime Prevention and Criminal Justice Programme
(9) Gold	2.3	0.4	GFI estimate based on estimates from UNO DC (2010) and other sources on illegal gold trade in DRC, South Africa and Peru
(10) Human organs	0.6–1.2	0.1	GFI estimate based on WHO, Council of Europe, United Nations
(11) Small arms and light weapons	0.3–1.0	0.1	GFI estimate based on Small Arms Survey and UNODC
(12) Diamonds and colored gemstones	0.9	0.1	GFI estimate for 2009 based on UN, Kimberley Process: Rough Diamond Statistics and U.S. Geological Survey
Total (1–12) (midpoint estimates)	645	100.0	
Total (1–12) rounded	650		
In % of global GDP in 2009	1.1%		
In % of average global GDP, 2000–2009	1.5%		

Sources: Global Financial Integrity, Transnational crime in the developing world, February 2011; World Bank, Macroeconomic indicators, Washington, DC, various years.

plausibility. A median of all estimates is $1.9 trillion USD for the year 2009 and the average is $2.1 trillion USD in 2009 or 3.6% of world GDP. The confidence interval lies between $1.6 and $2.6 trillion USD or 2.7%–4.4%. In general, we see that there is a huge variation and all figures should be handled with great care.

National Crime Proceeds and Money Laundering

Table 3.9 shows the estimated earnings from criminal activities in the United States over the period 1965–2010. Here we have two series: estimated criminal income including financial and tax fraud proceeds, and estimated criminal income excluding financial and tax fraud proceeds. In absolute figures, we have a strong increase from $49 billion USD in 1965 to $1043 billion USD in 2010. If we standardize these figures in percent of GDP, we have a modest increase up to the year 2000; it was 6.8% in 1965 and 8.0% in 2000, then it decreased to 7.0% in 2010. If we consider the ratio of criminal income in percent of total illicit income (criminal plus financial and tax fraud income), we see

Table 3.8 Estimates of Worldwide Turnover of Organized Crime, Billion USD, as a Percentage of GDP

Origin/Study	Year(s)	Volume in Billion USD (Worldwide)	As a Percentage of Global GDP
M. Schuster	1994	500–800	0.9–3.0
International Monetary Fund and Interpol	1996	500	1.6
UN estimates	1994/1998	700–1000	2.4–3.4
S. Kerry	1997	420–1000	1.4–3.3
J. Walker	1998	2850	9.5
National Criminal Intelligence Service	1998	1300	4.3
	2001	1900	5.9
	2003	2100	5.6
Takats (2007)	2005	600–1500	1.3–3.3
Agarwal and Agarwal (2006)	2005	2000–2500	4.4–5.5
Global Financial Integrity (2011) (estimate for transnational crime)	2000–2009	650	1.5
J. Walker (based on Walker and Unger) (2009)	2001	1000	3.4
Schneider (2008a)	2001	800	2.5
	2002	960	2.9
	2003	1200	3.2
	2004	1400	3.3
	2005	1500	3.3
	2006	1700	3.4
Tentative estimate[a]	2009[a]	2000	3.4
Median of all estimates	2009[b]	1900	3.3
Interquartile range of all estimates	2009[b]	1500–2400	2.6–4.1
Average of all estimates	2009[b]	2100	3.6
Confidence interval of mean (95%)	2009[b]	1600–2600	2.7–4.4

Sources: UNODC calculations, based on Schneider, F., *Public Choice*, 144, 473, 2010b; Walker, J., *J. Money Launder. Control*, 3(1), 64, 1999; Takats, I., A theory of "crying wolf": The economics of money laundering enforcement, Paper presented at the *Conference "Tackling Money Laundering*," University of Utrecht, Utrecht, the Netherlands, November 2–3, 2007; Agarwal, J.D. and Agarwal, A., *Finance India*, 19, 65, 2004; Agarwal, J.D. and Agarwal, A., Money laundering: New forms of crime, and victimization, Paper presented at the *National Workshop on New Forms of Crime, and Victimization*, with reference to Money Laundering, Indian Society of Victimology, Department of Criminology, University of Madras, Chennai, India, 2006; Global Financial Integrity, Transnational crime in the developing world, February 2011; Walker, J. and Unger, B., *Rev. Law Econ.*, 5(2), 821, 2009, the Berkeley Electronic Press; Schneider, F., Money laundering: Some preliminary empirical findings, University of Linz, Linz, Austria, November 2007, Paper presented at the *Conference "Tackling Money Laundering*," University of Utrecht, Utrecht, the Netherlands, November 2–3, 2007 and World Bank, Indicators (current GDP).

[a] Tentative estimate, assuming that Schneider's proportion of the turnover of organized crime expressed as a percentage of GDP remained unchanged over 2006–2009 period.

[b] Extrapolated to global GDP in 2009.

that classical criminal income ranges between 29.0% in 2000 and a maximum of 49.0% in 1985. This clearly shows that financial and tax fraud is again by far the largest crime figure in the United States.*

Table 3.10 shows the figures for Australia. Here we clearly see that fraud, drugs, and shoplifting are the three biggest types of crime. In total, the criminal proceeds in Australia reached 10.9 billion USD (in Australian dollars) or $7.1 billion USD or are in a range between 1.5% and 2.8% of Australian GDP.

* See also Pickhardt and Prinz (2012).

Table 3.9 Estimated Earnings from Criminal Activity[a] in the United States, Billions of Current USD (1965–2010)

	Tax Evasion Included		Criminal Income (Tax Evasion Excluded)		
Year	Estimated Criminal Income	In % of GDP	Estimated Criminal Income	In % of GDP	Ratio of Criminal Income In Total Illicit Income %
1965	49	6.8	18	2.5	37
1970	74	7.1	26	2.5	35
1975	118	7.2	45	2.7	38
1980	196	7.0	78	2.8	40
1985	342	8.1	166	4.0	49
1990	471	8.1	209	3.6	44
1995	595	8.0	206	2.8	35
2000	779	8.0	224	2.3	29
2010[b]	1043	7.0	300 (235–350)	2.0 (1.6–2.3)	29

[a] Criminal activities included trafficking in illicit drugs, human trafficking, burglary, larceny-theft, motor vehicle theft, robbery, fraud, arson, nonarson fraud, counterfeiting, illegal gambling, loan sharking, and prostitution. Tax evasion crimes included federal income, federal profits, and excise tax evasion.

[b] Tentative UNODC estimate based on previous estimates and trends derived from new drug and crime data.

Table 3.11 shows the crime proceeds for The Netherlands. Again, we have the remarkable result that 73.0% of all crime proceeds come from financial, social security, and tax fraud, followed by drugs with 12.4% and illegal workers with 3.1%. In sum, The Netherlands, between 11.0 and 19.0 billion USD euros, are the range of the crime proceeds, which amounts to between 2.6% and 4.3% of the country's official GDP.

Finally, in Table 3.12 the crime proceeds of Italy are shown. Crime proceeds from drugs are by far the largest with 60.0 billion euros, followed by ecomafia/agromafia with 16.0 billion euros and loan sharking with 15.0 billion euros. The total income of crime proceeds is 135.0 billion euros or 8.9% of the Italian GDP, which is a quite high figure.

Money Laundering: Some Methodical Remarks

That "crime" money is laundered has the purpose to make dirty money appear legal (compare Walker, 1999, 2000, 2004, 2007).* There are many methods of money laundering. Table 3.13 shows the 12 most common methods according to Unger (2007) and Walker (2007). Which of these methods is chosen depends on the type of criminal activity and on the specific institutional arrangements in a country where the criminal money is "earned." For example, in the drug business, method 8, business ownership, is quite often used.† In big cities, smaller amounts of cash are earned by drug dealers in a lot of different places, which they infiltrate into cash-intensive operations such as restaurants, which are especially well suited for money laundering purposes.

With the help of the MIMIC estimation procedure,‡ Schneider (2008a,b) and Buehn and Schneider (2011, 2013) estimate that money laundering and/or financial turnover from transnational crime has increased from $273 billion USD (1.33% of the total official GDP) in 1995 to $603 billion USD (or 1.74% of the official GDP) in 2006 for 20 OECD countries (Australia, Austria, Belgium, Canada, Denmark, Germany, Finland, France, Greece, Great Britain, Ireland, Italy, Japan, The Netherlands, New Zealand, Norway, Portugal, Switzerland, Spain, and the United States). These figures show a steady increase of the volume of laundered money over the period 1995–2006.

* Step one is the earning and collection of the crime money. Step two is to become as rich and influential as possible in the underground and legal world.

† Compare Schneider (2004) and Masciandaro (2004).

‡ The MIMIC (Multiple Indicators Multiple Causes) procedure is a latent estimation method where the dependent variable is unknown. Hence an attempt is made to model the unknown variable (amount of money laundering) with the help of causes (various types of crime and their proceeds) and indicators like the development of cash). For further explanations, see Schneider (2008a,b) and Buehn and Schneider (2011, 2013).

Table 3.10 Estimated Criminal Proceeds in Australia, Million AUD (1998 and 2003)

	2003 (Revised Estimates)		Midpoint Estimates in % of GDP	
Illegal Activities	**Min**	**Max**	**1998**	**2003 (Rev.)**
(1) Fraud	3000	3500	1.8	0.4
(2) Drugs	2000		0.2	0.3
(3) Theft			0.3	
(4) Shoplifting	1020	2460		0.2
(5) Car theft	654			0.1
(6) Stealing from persons	545			0.1
(7) Other theft	659			0.1
(8) Burglaries (breaking and entering)	1193		0.2	0.2
(9) Assaults	979		0.1	0.1
(10) Homicide	323		0.0	0.0
(11) Property damage	510		0.2	0.1
(12) Robbery and extortion	37		0.0	0.0
Total (1–12) in million AUD	10,920	12,860	2.8	1.5
Total (1–12) in million USD	7100	8300		
In % of GDP	1.4%	1.6%		

Sources: Data based on John Walker (AUSTRAC, RMIT University), 1998 and 2003 (updates from an original paper undertaken by the same author for the Australian Institute of Criminology in 1992), quoted in Unger, B., *The Scale and Impacts of Money Laundering*, Edward Elgar Publishing Company, Cheltenham, UK, 2007, p. 62; John Walker (AUSTRAC, RMIT University), The Extent of Money Laundering in and through Australia in 2004, Australian Institute of Criminology, 2007.

Table 3.11 Estimated Unlawful Earnings in The Netherlands, Million EUR (2003)

Types of Crime	Proceeds of Crime, Million €	Proceeds of Crime, Midpoint Estimates in % of Total
(1) Financial, social security, and tax fraud[a]	7735–15,450	73.3
(2) Drugs	1960	12.4
(3) Illegal workers	490	3.1
(4) Prostitution	460	2.9
(5) Theft	345	2.2
(6) Burglary	340	2.1
(7) Fencing	190	1.2
(8) Illegal gambling	130	0.8
(9) Illegal copying	90	0.6
(10) Computer-crime	26	0.2
(11) Violent offenses	6	0.0
(12) Other offenses	187	1.2
Total (1–12) in million EUR	11,959–19,674	
Total (1–12) in million USD	13,500–22,300	
As a percentage of GDP	2.6%–4.3%	

[a] Based on the assumption that between 5% and 10% of the total amounts were discovered and reported.

Unger (2007) estimates the amount of laundered money and its top 20 destination countries; these figures are shown in Table 3.14. In this table, the author presents two estimates, one by Walker (1999, 2007) and one by the IMF. The Walker figure of \$2.85 trillion USD is much larger than the IMF figure with \$1.50 trillion USD (both figures are for the year 2005). Walker's figures have been criticized as much too high which was one reason why the IMF estimates are shown, too. Table 3.14 clearly demonstrates that two-thirds of worldwide money laundering was sent to the top 20 countries listed. One should realize that most of these countries are highly developed and have quite sizeable legal/official economies. What is also amazing is that there are only a few small countries and/or offshore countries (OFCS) and tax havens among them (Cayman Islands, Vatican City, Bermuda, and Liechtenstein).* The majority of countries that attract money laundering flows are economically big players. The United States has the largest worldwide share of money laundering of almost 19.0%, followed by the Cayman Islands (4.9%), Russia (4.2%), Italy (3.7%), but also smaller countries like Switzerland (2.1% of worldwide money laundering), Liechtenstein (1.7%) and Austria (1.7%) are attractive. If one takes the lower IMF value for Austria, Switzerland, and the United Kingdom, roughly 5.5% of the total amount is laundered, which comes close to roughly 10% of the official GDPs of these three countries. However, it needs to be emphasized that it is not clear whether this money is *only laundered* in

* Compare also Masciandaro (2005, 2006), Zdanowicz (2009), Truman and Reuter (2004), and Walker and Unger (2009).

Table 3.12 Estimates of the Income and Profits of Organized Crime in Italy (2009)

Income	In Billion EURO	
(1) Trafficking drugs	60.00	
(2) Trafficking in human beings	0.87	
(3) Arms trafficking	5.80	
(4) Smuggling	1.20	
Subtotal trafficking (1–4)		67.87
(5) Protection racket	9.00	
(6) Loan sharking (usury)	15.00	
Subtotal predatory activities (5 + 6)		24.00
(7) Theft and robbery	1.00	1.00
(8) Procurement	6.50	
(9) Agro-crime	7.50	
(10) Games and gambling	2.50	
(11) Counterfeiting	6.50	
(12) Illegal construction	2.00	
Subtotal—Illegal economic activities (7–12)		25.00
(13) Ecomafia/agromafia	16.00	16.00
(14) Prostitution	0.60	0.60
(15) Financial gains	0.75	0.75
Total income in bn EURO (1–15)	135.22	135.22
Total income in bn USD (1–15)		188.58
Total income in % of GDP		8.9%

Source: SOS Impresa, *XII Rapporto—Le mani della criminalità sulle imprese*, Rome, Italy, January 27, 2010.

these countries or remains in these countries; it may well leave these countries after the laundering process. In general, Table 3.14 demonstrates how substantial the amount of laundered money is and that two-thirds of these funds are concentrated in only 20 countries.

Bagella et al. (2009, p. 881) use a two-sector dynamic general equilibrium model to measure money laundering for the United States and the EU-15 macro areas over the sample 2000:01–2007:01 at a quarterly data basis. Their series are generated through a fully micro-founded dynamic model, which is appropriately calibrated to replicate selected stochastic properties of the two economies. Their model (and the analysis) has a short run perspective. Bagella et al. (2009, p. 881) got the following results: First the simulations show that money laundering accounts for approximately 19.0% of the GDP measured for the EU-15, while it accounts for 13.0% in the U.S. economy, over the sample 2000:01–2007:04. Second, the simulated money laundering appears less volatile than the corresponding GDP. With regard to the EU-15 macro area, the simulated statistics suggests that money laundering volatility is one-third of the GDP volatility; for the U.S. economy, the same statistics produces a figure of two-fifths. Considering these estimates, one can admit that they are pretty high and have some doubts about how plausible these large figures are.

In their latest study, Walker and Unger (2009, p. 821) again undertake an attempt to measure global money laundering and/or the proceeds from transnational crime that are pumped through the financial system worldwide. They criticize methods such as case studies, proxy variables, or models for measuring the crime economy, arguing that they all tend to overestimate money laundering. They present a model that is a gravity model and one that makes it possible to estimate the flows of illicit funds from and to each jurisdiction in the world. This "Walker model" was first developed in 1994, and was recently updated. The authors show that it belongs to the group of gravity models that have recently become popular in international trade theory. The authors demonstrate that the original Walker model estimates are compatible with recent findings on money laundering. Once the scale of money laundering is known, its macroeconomic effects and the impact of crime prevention, regulation, and law enforcement effects on money laundering and transnational crime can also be measured. Walker and Unger (2009, pp. 849–850) conclude that their model still seems to be the most reliable and robust method to estimate global money laundering, and thereby the important effects of transnational crime on economic, social, and political institutions. Rightly they argue that the attractiveness of the distance indicator in the Walker model is a first approximation, but is still not theoretically satisfactory. A better microfoundation for the Walker model will be needed. A microfoundation means that the behavior of money launderers is analyzed, and in particular what makes them send their money to a specific country. Hence, Walker and Unger (2009, p. 850) argue that an economics of crime microfoundation for the Walker model would mean that, similarly to international trade theory, behavioral assumptions about money launderers have to be made. Their gravity model can be seen as a reduced form or outcome of a rational calculus of sending the money to a certain country and potentially making large profits. Using their model in Table 3.14, the amount of laundered money and the top ("most" attractive) 20 destinations of laundered money are shown for 2005. The United States ranks number one, followed by the Cayman Islands and

Table 3.13 Methods of Money Laundering

(1)	Wire transfers or electronic banking	The primary tool of money launderers to move funds around in the banking system. These moves can conceal the illicit origins of the funds or just place the money where the launderers need them. Often the funds go through several banks and even different jurisdictions.
(2)	Cash deposits	Money launderers need to deposit cash advances to bank accounts prior to wire transfers. Due to anti-money-laundering regulations they often "structure" the payments, i.e., break down to smaller amounts. This is also called "smurfing."
(3)	Informal value transfer systems (IVTS)	Money launderers need not rely on the banking sector; other transfer providers, such as the Hawala, are readily available to undertake fund transfers. These systems consist of shops (mainly selling groceries, phone cards, or other similar items), which are also involved in transfer services. IVTSs enable international fund transfers, as these shops are present in several jurisdictions.
(4)	Cash smuggling	Money launderers might mail, Fedex, or simply carry cash with them from one region to another, or even to different jurisdictions.
(5)	Gambling	Casinos, horse races, and lotteries are ways of legalizing funds. The money launderer can buy (for "dirty" cash) winning tickets or casinos chips and redeem the tickets or the chips in a "clean" bank check. Afterward, the check can be easily deposited in the banking sector.
(6)	Insurance policies	Money launderers purchase single premium insurance (with dirty cash), redeem early (and pay some penalty) in order to receive clean checks to deposit. Longer-term premium payments might make laundering even harder to detect.
(7)	Securities	Usually used to facilitate fund transfers, where underlying security deals provide cover (and legitimate looking reason) for transfers.
(8)	Business ownership	Money might be laundered through legitimate businesses, where laundering funds can be added to legitimate revenues. Cash-intensive operations, such as restaurants, are especially well suited for laundering.
(9)	Shell corporations	Money launderers might create companies exclusively to provide cover for fund moves without legitimate business activities.
(10)	Purchases	Real estate or any durable good purchases can be used to launder monies. Typically, the item is bought for cash and resold for clean monies, like bank checks.
(11)	Credit card advance payment	Money launderers pay money in advance with dirty money, and receive clean checks on the balance from the bank.
(12)	ATM operations	Banks might allow other firms to operate their ATMs, i.e., to maintain and fill them with cash. Money launderers fill ATMs with dirty cash and receive clean checks (for the cash withdrawn) from the bank.

Source: Unger, B., *The Scale and Impacts of Money Laundering*, Edward Elgar Publishing Company, Cheltenham, UK, 2007, pp. 195–196.

Russia. With 18.9% of worldwide money laundering, the United States has by far the biggest share, followed by the Cayman Islands with 4.9%.

Cost and Proceeds of Cybercrime: The Latest Development in International Organized Crime

According to Anderson et al. (2012, p. 3), in the last 10–15 years, cybercrime arose from white collar crimes. In the year 2007, the European Commission (EC) (2007) defined cybercrime as follows*:

1. Traditional forms of crime such as fraud or forgery, though committed over electronic communications, networks, and information systems;
2. The publication of illegal content over electronic media; and
3. Crimes unique to electronic networks.

Today, cybercrime takes many forms, like online banking fraud (phishing), fake antivirus, computer programs, fake error scam, and other variants. In a first systematic paper, Anderson et al. (2012) try to give a survey in measuring the cost of cybercrime and/or the criminal proceeds from some types of cybercrime.† Cybercrime is a rather new

* This definition is taken from Anderson et al. (2012, p. 3); compare also Levi and Suddle (1989) as well as Levi (2009a,b).

† Compare also Detica and Office of Cyber Security and Information Assurance (2011), Kanich et al. (2011), Levi (2011), Levi and Burrows (2008), Taylor (2009, 2011), Van Eeten and Bauer (2008).

Table 3.14 Amount of Laundered Money and Top 20 Destinations of Laundered Money, Year 2005

Rank	Destination	% of Worldwide Money Laundering	Walker Estimate $2.85 Trillion USD Amount in Billion USD	IMF Estimate of $1.5 Trillion USD Worldwide Amount in Billion USD
1	United States	18.9	538,145	283,500
2	Cayman Islands	4.9	138,329	73,500
3	Russia	4.2	120,493	63,000
4	Italy	3.7	105,688	55,500
5	China	3.3	94,726	49,500
6	Romania	3.1	89,595	46,500
7	Canada	3.0	85,444	45,000
8	Vatican City	2.8	80,596	42,000
9	Luxembourg	2.8	78,468	42,000
10	France	2.4	68,471	36,000
11	Bahamas	2.3	66,398	34,500
12	Germany	2.2	61,315	33,000
13	Switzerland	2.1	58,993	31,500
14	Bermuda	1.9	52,887	28,500
15	Netherlands	1.7	49,591	25,500
16	Liechtenstein	1.7	48,949	25,500
17	Austria	1.7	48,376	25,500
18	Hong Kong	1.6	44,519	24,000
19	United Kingdom	1.6	44,478	24,000
20	Spain	1.2	35,461	18,000
	SUM	67.1	1,910,922	1,006,500

Source: Unger, B., *The Scale and Impacts of Money Laundering*, Edward Elgar Publishing Company, Cheltenham, UK, 2007, p. 80.

development and is certainly becoming more and more important. What type of cybercrime costs can one observe? Anderson et al. (2012, p. 4) state the following four:

1. Costs in anticipation of cybercrime, such as antivirus software, insurance and compliance
2. Costs as a consequence of cybercrime, such as direct losses and indirect costs, such as weakened competitiveness as a result of intellectual property compromise
3. Costs in response to cybercrime, such as compensation payments to victims and fines paid to regulatory bodies
4. Indirect costs such as reputational damage to firms, loss of confidence in cyber transactions by individuals and businesses, reduced public-sector revenues and the growth of the underground economy

These types of costs are shown in Figure 3.1, where Anderson et al. (2012) try to analyze the costs of cybercrime and also some criminal revenues. From Figure 3.1, one clearly sees that criminal revenues or criminal proceeds, the main topic in this chapter, can be derived from the direct losses of cybercrime, where we have also defense costs and indirect costs. Direct losses (or proceeds of national or transnational criminal activities) include

1. Money withdrawn from victim accounts
2. Stolen software
3. Faked financial transactions

What do we know about the costs (and partly proceeds of criminal activities) in the cybercrime area? Anderson et al. (2012, p. 24) provide an interesting table about a first estimation of the costs (and partly proceeds) of the category of cybercrime.* Considering the four cost components (cost of genuine cybercrime, cost of transitional cybercrime, cost of cybercriminal infrastructure, and cost of traditional crimes becoming "cyber") one clearly realizes, that No. 4 "Cost of crime against public institutions (welfare tax fraud)"

* Table 3.15 is adapted from Anderson et al. (2012, p. 24).

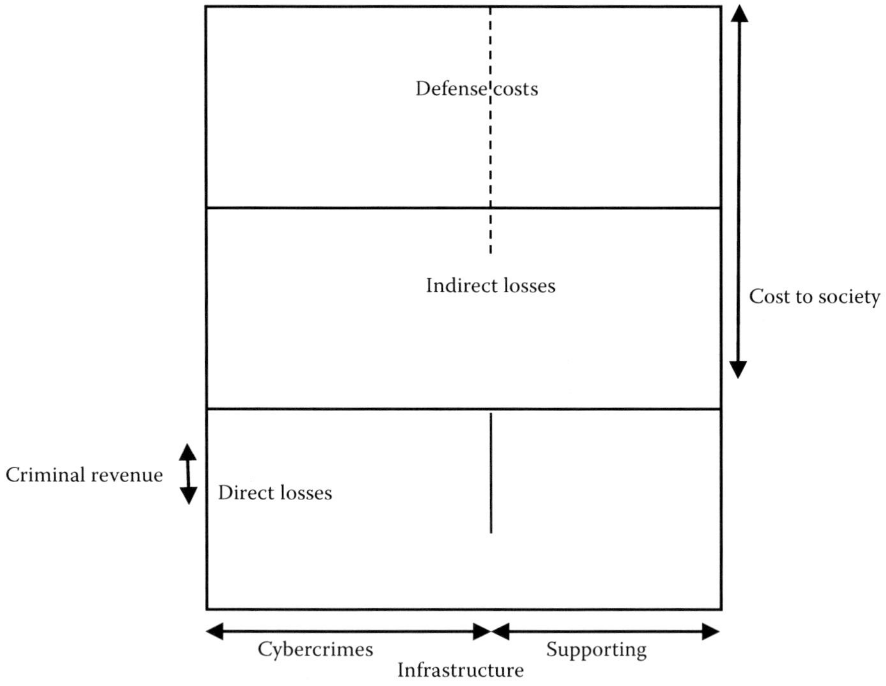

FIGURE 3.1 Framework for analyzing the costs of cybercrime. (From Anderson, R. et al., Measuring the cost of cybercrime, http://weis2012.econinfosec.org/papers/Anderson_WEIS2012.pdf, 2012, p. 5.)

becoming "cyber" is by far the largest part covering 67.5% of all costs of cybercrime, which amount to $150.2 billion USD on a global estimate. If we further turn to the global estimate, we see the cost of "genuine cybercrime" on a worldwide basis is $3.5 billion USD or 1.6% of the total cost of cybercrime. The $3.5 billion USD can also be seen as a large part of the proceeds of genuine cybercrime activities. If we consider no. 2 "Cost of transitional cybercrime," we see that it amounts to $44.2 billion USD or 19.8% of the total cost of cybercrime. With $24.8 billion USD, the cost of a cybercriminal infrastructure is quite sizable; it amounts to 11.9% of the total cost. As already mentioned, the costs of traditional crimes becoming cyber are, with $150.2 billion USD, the largest part of the cost of cybercrime. Again this could at least partly be seen as criminal proceeds of cybercrime activities in these areas, especially tax fraud. In general, Table 3.15 clearly shows that the cost and proceeds of cybercrime activities are sizable. In the future they will certainly rise because the use of electronic networks for crime activities becomes increasingly attractive.

Informal Money Banking (Hawala) System

Obviously, transnational crime organizations prefer to use an informal banking system, in order to make it more difficult for the state authorities to detect it. The most famous and oldest informal banking system is the Hawala banking system, which will be analyzed now.

During the 1990s, international concern grew over the so-called underground banking and its abuse by criminal offenders. Some studies, for example, the ones by Williams (2007), Savona and ISPAC (1997), and El-Quorchi (2003), have explained how informal systems operate, including their risks. The informal value transfer systems (IVTS) change from region to region (Hawala or door-to-door banking). Some scholars (El-Quorchi, 2003; Williams, 2007) argue that Hawala is vulnerable to criminal abuse, and like the other financial institutions, there is evidence that money derived from drug trafficking, illegal arms sales, body parts trade, corruption, tax evasion, and all kinds of fraud have indeed moved through Hawala networks.

Hawala banking still takes place and some authors, like Perkel (2004) or van de Bunt (2007), have analyzed it. These authors point to the need for a regulation of the Hawala banking system, because it can be another way to transfer criminal financial flows. According

Table 3.15 Estimation of the Various Cost Components (Partly Proceeds) of Cybercrime

Types of Cybercrime	UK Estimate (in billion USD)	Global Estimate (in billion USD)	Reference Period	Criminal Revenue	Direct Losses	Indirect Losses	Defense Cost
1. Cost of Genuine Cybercrime							
Online banking fraud							
Phishing	0.016	0.32	2007	x?	x?		
Malware (consumer)	0.004	0.07	2010	x↓	x↓		
Malware (businesses)	0.006	0.20		x↓	x↓		
Bank technology countermeasures	0.050	1.00	2010				x?
Fake antivirus	0.005	0.10	2008–10	x	x		
Copyright infringing software	0.001	0.02	2010	x	x		
Copyright infringing music, etc.	0.007	0.15	2011	x↓			
Patent infringing pharma	0.014	0.29	2010	x			
Stranded traveler scam	0.001	0.01	2011	x↓			
Fake escrow scam	0.010	0.20	2011	x↓			
Advance fee fraud	0.050	1.00	2011	x↓			
Sum of 1	**0.164 (0.9%)**	**3.50 (1.6%)**					
2. Cost of Transitional Cybercrime							
Online payment card fraud	0.21	4.20	2010		(x)		
Offline payment card fraud							
Domestic	0.11	2.10	2010		x↓		
International	0.15	2.94	2010		x↓		
Bank/merchant defense costs	0.12	2.40	2010				x↓
Indirect costs of payment fraud							
Loss of confidence (consumers)	0.70	10.00	2010			x?	
Loss of confidence (merchants)	1.60	20.00	2009			x?	
PABX fraud	0.19	4.96	2011	x	x↓		
Sum of 2	**3.07 (6.7%)**	**44.20 (19.8%)**					
3. Cost of Cybercriminal Infrastructure							
Expenditure on antivirus	**0.17**	**3.40**	**2012**				**x**
Cost to industry of patching	**0.05**	**1.00**	**2010**				**x?**

(*Continued*)

Table 3.15 (*Continued*) Estimation of the Various Cost Components (Partly Proceeds) of Cybercrime

Types of Cybercrime	UK Estimate (in billion USD)	Global Estimate (in billion USD)	Reference Period	Criminal Revenue	Direct Losses	Indirect Losses	Defense Cost
ISP clean-up expenditures	**0.00**	0.04	2010			x?	
Cost to users of clean-up	**0.50**	**10.00**	2012			x?	
Defense costs of firms generally	**0.50**	**10.00**	2010				x?
Expenditure on law enforcement	**0.02**	0.40	2010				x
Sum of 3	1.24	24.84 (11.9%)					
4. Cost of Cybercrime from Fraud against Public Institutions							
Welfare	**1.90**	**20.00**	2011	x	(x)		
Tax fraud	**12.00**	**125.00**	2011	x?	(x)		
Tax filing fraud	—	**5.20**	2010	x	(x)		
Sum of 4	13.90 (75.7%)	150.20 (67.5%)					
Sum of 1–4	18.37 (100%)	222.70 (100%)					

Source: Anderson, R. et al., Measuring the cost of cybercrime, http://weis2012.econinfosec.org/papers/Anderson_WEIS2012.pdf, 2012, p. 24.

Estimating costs and scaling: Figures in boldface are estimates based on data or assumption for the reference area. Unless both figures in a row are bold, the non-boldface figures have been scaled using the UK's share of world GDP unless otherwise stated in the main text. Extrapolations from UK numbers to the global scale should be interpreted with utmost caution. A threshold to enter this table is defined at $10 m for the global estimates.

Legends: x, included; (x), partly converted; with qualifiers x↑ for likely overestimated; x↓ for likely underestimated; and x?, for high uncertainty.

to van de Bunt (2007), Hawala bankers* are financial service providers who carry out financial transactions without a license and therefore without any government control.† They accept cash, checks, or other valuable goods (diamonds, gold) at one location and pay a corresponding sum in cash or other remuneration at another location. Unlike official banks, Hawala bankers disregard the legal obligations concerning the identification of clients, record keeping, and the disclosure of unusual transactions, to which these official financial institutions are subject.

Through this system that forms an integral part of the legal (formal) and informal market economy, Hawala bankers ensure the transfer of money without having to move it physically or electronically. When a payment needs to be made overseas, the underground banker will get in touch with a courier (or more currently using e-mail, fax, or phone) in that country informing him of the details of making the payment. If the recipient of the payment wishes to personally obtain the money, a code referring to the underground banker in the country of payment is given to the recipient. Such a system is almost untraceable since it leaves little if any paper trail. Transaction records are being kept only until the money is delivered, at which time they are destroyed. Even when there is a paper or electronic record of the transaction, it is often in dialects and languages that serve as a *de facto* encryption system.‡

In Table 3.16, some "guesstimates" or estimates of Hawala banking turnover or proceeds are shown. On a global scale, Page and Plaza (2006) estimate $57.53 billion USD as the amount of informal money flows used by Hawala banking in the year 2004. The country sums are much smaller with the exception of the study by Fischer (2002), where he comes up with

* Several traditional terms, like Hundi (India) and Fei-ch'ein (China) remind one of the fact that Hawala banking came up independently in different parts of the world. At present, a range of other terms is used to refer to the same phenomenon, such as "informal banking," "underground banking," "ethnic banking," or "informal value transfer system."

† Compare Schneider (2010a) and van de Bunt (2007).

‡ Mostly these are legal payments and of course can include some illegal payments, but it is unclear whether the Hawala banker knows this.

Table 3.16 Guesstimates or Estimates of the Amount of Informal Money Flow through Hawala Banking

Author/ Source	Country/ Area	Year/ Period	Estimated Amount of Informal Money Flow
Schneider and Caruso (2011)	India	2000–2005	\$5–\$10 billion USD/year
Fischer (2002)	Saudi Arabia	Unknown	\$40 billion USD/year
Fletcher and Baldrin (2002)	Pakistan	2001	\$2.5 billion USD
Viles (2008)	Somalia		\$0.5–\$1 billion USD
Page and Plaza (2006)	Global	2004	\$57.53 billion USD
Omer (2002)	Somalia		
Omer and El Koury (2004)	Somalia	2004	\$0.7–\$1 billion USD/ year
Zaidi (2010)	Pakistan	Unknown	\$2.5–\$3 billion USD/ year
IMF (2001)	Pakistan and Afghanistan	Unknown	\$2–\$5 billion USD/year
Jessee (2006)	Pakistan	Unknown	\$2–\$3 billions USD/year

\$40 billion USD as the estimated amount of informal money flows of Hawala banking for Saudi Arabia per year. Countries like Pakistan or Afghanistan range between \$2.5 and \$3.0 billion USD per year. Table 3.1 should be seen as a first attempt to come up with some ideas of the relative size of the estimated amount of informal money flows via Hawala banking.

According to van de Bunt (2007), there are two different views about Hawala banking. From the first point of view, Hawala banking is regarded as a centuries-old institution, which has not yet outlived its usefulness. Low-income workers and migrant workers, in particular, supposedly put more trust in Hawala bankers than in formal banks. This viewpoint emphasizes the problem associated with subjecting Hawala banking to the same rules as formal banks. Regulation either through registration or licensing is seen as ineffective because it will simply push the system further into the underground, further complicating the already problematic task of controlling Hawala transactions (Perkel, 2004, pp. 210–211; Razavy, 2005, p. 292). Hence, Hawala banking might be the closest thing to a free market banking, without government regulation and it has functioned well for centuries. One should clearly emphasize these advantages of Hawala banking when criticizing it.

From the opposite (second) point of view, van de Bunt (2007) argues that Hawala banking is described as "underground banking," a system that flies under the radar of modern supervision of financial transactions. Underground banking can be considered a threat to the effectiveness of anti-money laundering measures and the fight against terrorist financing. To prevent underground bankers from becoming a safe haven for criminals and terrorists, they should be subject to the standard regulations regarding record keeping, disclosure of unusual transactions, and identification of clients.*

* Compare also Richard (2005) and Rider (2004). This is a general claim in order to be on the safe side. However, to the author's knowledge there is no clear empirical evidence that the Hawala banking system has been infiltrated by the transnational and/or organized crime organizations.

Conclusion

In this chapter an attempt is made to review the literature of the finances of international organized crime organizations with a focus on estimations of the volume of the finances of transnational crime; it comes to the following preliminary findings.

First, the necessity of money laundering is obvious as a great number of illegal (criminal) transactions are done by cash. Hence, this amount of cash from criminal activities must be laundered in order to have some "legal" profit, to do some investment or consumption in the legal world.

Second, to get an estimate of the extent and development of the amount of the financial means of transnational crime over time is very difficult. On a worldwide basis in 2009, \$1.4 trillion USD (or 2.5% of world GDP) is estimated to be laundered coming from all types of crimes (*Source:* IMF, 2010). These figures are very preliminary with a quite large margin of error, but give a clear indication of how important money laundering and the turnover of transnational crime nowadays are.

Third, tax fraud and/or illegal cross-border capital flows are by far the biggest/highest share of all illegal transactions; quite often 66% of all illegal capital flows/proceeds.

From these preliminary results, three conclusions are drawn:

1. The revenues of transnational crime are extremely difficult to estimate. They are defined differently in almost every country, the measures taken against them are different and vary from country to country and it is not at all clear which part of these revenues from transnational crime stays in a country with the consequence of a severe double counting problem.*
2. To fight against transnational crime is very difficult, as there are no efficient and powerful international organizations that can effectively do this job.†
3. Tax fraud and/or other illegal cross-border capital flows should be the prime target for governments to reduce them; for example, a rigorous fight against tax heavens should have high priority.

* The definition of money laundering considerably varies from country to country; also there are no international organized and harmonized efforts to fight money laundering with the result that little has been done thus far; compare D'Souza (2012).

† Some first attempts have been made, like the FATF, or some sub-organizations of the U.N., compare, e.g., UNO DC (2004, 2005), FATF (2004, 2005) and FATF-GAFI (2005, 2006); see also D'Souza (2012).

References

Agarwal, J. D. and Agarwal, A. (2004), Globalization and international capital flows, *Finance India*, 19(1), 65–99.

Agarwal, J. D. and Agarwal, A. (2006), Money laundering: New forms of crime, and victimization, Paper presented at the *National Workshop on New Forms of Crime*, Victimization, Department of Criminology, University of Madras, Chennai, India.

Anderson, R., Chris, B., Rainer, B., Richard, C., Van Eeten Michael, J. G., Michael, L., Tyler, M., and Stefan, S. (2012), Measuring the cost of cybercrime, http://weis2012.econinfosec.org/papers/Anderson_WEIS2012.pdf. (Accessed July 19, 2012.)

Bagella, M., Francesco, B., and Argentiero, A. (2009), Money laundering in a microfounded dynamic model: Simulations for the U.S. and the EU-15 economies, *Review of Law and Economics*, 5(2), 879–902.

Baker, R. W. (2005), *Capitalism's Achilles Heel—Dirty Money and How to Renew the Free-Market System*, Hoboken, NJ: John Wiley & Sons.

Buehn, A. and Schneider, F. (2011, 2013), A preliminary attempt to estimate the financial flows of transnational crime using the mimic method, in Unger, B. (ed.), *Research Handbook on Money Laundering*, Cheltenham, UK: Edward Elgar Publishing Company.

Detica and Office of Cyber Security and Information Assurance. (2011), The cost of cyber-crime, February 2011. http://www.cabinetoffice.gov.uk/resource-library/cost-of-cyber-crime.

D'Souza, J. (2012), *Terrorist Financing, Money Laundering and Tax Evasion: Examining the Performance of Financial Intelligence Units*, Boca Raton, FL: CRC Press.

El Quorchi, M. et al. (2003), *Informal Funds Transfer Systems: An Analysis of the Informal Hawala System*, Washington, DC: International Monetary Fund, pp. 1–53.

European Commission. (2007), Towards a general policy on the fight against cybercrime, May 2007. COM (2007) 267 final, http://eur-lex.europa.eu/LexUriServ/LexUriServ.do?uri=COM: 2007:0267:FIN:EN:PDF.

FATF. (2004), Report on money laundering and terrorist financing, Typologies (2003–2004), Paris, France.

FATF. (2005), Report on money laundering and terrorist financing, Typologies (2004–2005), Paris, France.

FATF. (2007), Financial system abuse, Report, 2007, Paris, France.

FATF-GAFI. (2005), Third mutual evaluation report on anti-money laundering and competing the financing of terrorism, Norway, pp. 1–160, Paris, France.

FATF-GAFI. (2006), Third mutual evaluation report on anti-money laundering and competing the financing of terrorism, Portugal, pp. 1–165, Paris, France.

Fischer, H. S. (2002), *Hawala—What Is It and How to Emasculate It*, Beverly Hills, CA: Study.

Fletcher, N. and Baldwin, J. (2002), Money laundry counter measures with primary focus upon terrorism and the U.S. patriot act 2001, *Journal of Money Laundering Control*, 6(2), 105–136.

Haken, J. (2011), Transnational crime in the developing world. Global Financial Integrity, February 2011, Washington, DC. http://www.gfintegrity.org/wp-content/uploads/2014/05/gfi_transnational_crime_high-res.pdf. (Accessed on January 12, 2012.)

IMF. (2001a), Financial system abuse, financial crime and money laundering, Report Washington, DC: Monetary and Exchange Affairs and Policy Development.

IMF. (2001b), Financial system abuse, financial crime and money laundering-background paper, Washington, DC: Monetary and Exchange Affairs and Policy Development, February 12, 2001.

IMF. (2010), Financial system abuse, financial crime and money laundering—Background paper, Washington, DC: Monetary and Exchange Affairs and Policy Development, February 2010.

Jessee, D. D. (2006), Tactical means, strategic ends: Al Qaeda's use of denial and deception, *Terrorism and Political Violence*, 18(3), 367–388.

Kanich, C., Weaver, N., McCoy, D., Halvorson, T., Kreibich, C., Levchenko, K., Paxson, V., Voelker, G. M., and Stefan, S. (2011), Show me the money: Characterizing spam-advertised revenue, in *Proceedings of the USENIX Security Symposium*, San Francisco, CA, August 2011.

Katkov, N. (2002), Anti-money laundering: A brave new world for financial institutions, *CELENT*, September 2002.

Levi, M. (2009a), Money laundering risks and e-gaming: A European overview and assessment, Final Report, Wales, UK: Cardiff School of Social Sciences, Cardiff University, September 2009.

Levi, M. (2009b), Fear of fraud and fear of crime: A review, in S. Simpson and D. Weisburd (eds.), *The Criminology of White-Collar Crime*, New York: Springer, pp. 84–109.

Levi, M. (2011), Social reactions to white-collar crimes and their relationship to economic crises, in M. Deflem (ed.), *Economic Crisis and Crime*, Bingley, UK: The JAI Press/Emerald, pp. 87–105.

Levi, M. and Burrows, J. (2008),: Measuring the impact of fraud in the UK: A conceptual and empirical journey, *British Journal of Criminology*, 48, 293–318.

Levi, M. and Suddle, M. (1989), White collar crime, shamelessness and disintegration: The control of tax evasion in Pakistan, *Journal of Law and Society*, 16(4), 489–505.

Masciandaro, D. (2004), *Global Financial Crime: Terrorism, Money Laundering and Off Shore Centres*, Aldershot, UK: Ashgate.

Masciandaro, D. (2005), Financial supervisory unification and financial intelligence units, *Journal of Money Laundering Control*, 8(4), 354–371.

Masciandaro, D. (2006), Offshore financial centres and international soft laws: Explaining the regulation gap, *Second Annual Conference*, Società Italiana di Diritto ed Economia, Roma, Italy, pp. 1–49.

Omer, A. (2002), A report on supporting systems and procedures for the effective regulation and monitoring of Somali remittance companies (Hawala), New York: UNDP Report.

Omer, A. and El Koury, G. (2004), Regulation and supervision in a vacuum: The story of the Somali remittance sector, *Small Enterprise Development*, 15(1), 44–52.

Organisation for Economic Co-operation and Development. (1990), Financial action task force on money laundering, Paris, France, in *UNDCP, Economic and Social Consequences of Drug Abuse and Illicit Trafficking*, Vienna, Austria: UNDCP Technical Series No. 6, p. 26.

Organization for Economic Co-operation and Development (OECD). (1999–2010), Observer, Paris, France, various years.

Page, J. and Plaza, S. (2006), Migration remittances and development: A review of global evidence, *Journal of African Economies*, 15(2), 245–336.

Perkel, W. (2004), Money laundering and terrorism: Informal value transfer systems, *American Criminal Law Review*, 41(2), 183–211.

Pickhardt, M. and Prinz, A. (eds.) (2012), *Tax Evasion and the Shadow Economy*, Cheltenham, UK: Edward Elgar Publishing Company.

Razavy, M. (2005), Hawala: An underground haven for terrorist of social phenomenon? *Crime, Law and Social Change*, 44(2), 277–299.

Reuter, P. (2004), Chasing dirty money—The fight against money laundering, Report, Washington, DC.

Richard, A. C. (2005), *Fighting Terrorist Financing: Transatlantic Cooperation and International Institutions*, Baltimore, MD: Center for Transatlantic Relations, Johns Hopkins University.

Rider, B. (2004), The war on terror and crime and the offshore centres, in D. Masciandaro (ed.), *Global Financial Crime: Terrorism, Money Laundering and Offshore Centres*, Aldershot, UK: Ashgate, pp. 61–95.

Savona, E. U. and ISPAC. (Organization) (1997), *Responding to Money Laundering: International Perspectives*, Amsterdam, the Netherlands: Harwood Academic Publishers.

Schneider, F. (2004), The financial flows of Islamic terrorism, in M. Donato (ed.), *Global Financial Crime: Terrorism, Money Laundering and Offshore Centres*, Aldershot, UK: Ashgate, pp. 97–126.

Schneider, F. (2008a), Turnover of organised crime and money laundering: Some preliminary empirical findings, Discussion Paper, Linz, Austria: Department of Economics, University of Linz.

Schneider, F. (2008b), Money laundering from revenues from organised crime: Some preliminary empirical findings, Revised version of a paper which was presented at the *Conference Illicit Trade and Globalization, CES-IFO Venice Summer Workshop*, Venice National University, San Servolo, Italy, July 14–15, 2008.

Schneider, F. (2009), Die Finanzströme von Organisierter Kriminalität und Terrorismus: Was wissen wir (nicht)? *Vierteljahreshefte zur Wirtschaftsforschung, DIW Berlin*, 78(4), 73–87.

Schneider, F. (2010a), The (hidden) financial flows of terrorist and organized crime: A literature review and some preliminary empirical results, Paper prepared for the *EUSECON Conference in Athens*, Athens, Greece, April 12–13, 2010.

Schneider, F. (2010b), Turnover of organized crime and money laundering: some preliminary findings, *Public Choice*, 144, 473–486.

Schneider, F. (2011), The financial flows of transnational crime: Some preliminary empirical results, in A. Georgios et al. (eds.), *Usual and Unusual Organizing Criminals in Europe and Beyond: Profitable Crimes from Underworld to Upperworld, Festschrift for Petrus Van Duyne*, Apeldoorn, the Netherlands: Maklu Publishing Company, pp. 215–232.

Schneider, F. (2013), The financial flows of transnational crime and tax fraud in oecd countries: What do we (not) know? *Public Finance Review/Special Issue: The Shadow Economy, Tax Evasion and Money Laundering*, 41(5), 677–707.

Schneider, F. and Caruso, R. (2011), The (hidden) financial flows of terrorist and transnational crime organizations: A literature review and preliminary empirical results, Paper presented at the *AEA/ASSA Conference 2011*, Denver, CO.

Schneider, F., Dreer, E., and Riegler, W. (2006), *Geldwäsche: Formen, Akteure, Größenordnung—Warum die Politik machtlos ist*, Wiesbaden, Germany: Gabler-Verlag.

Schneider, F. and Ursula, W. (2008), Money laundering: Some facts, *European Journal of Law and Economics*, 26(4), 387–404.

Smith, D. (2011), Black money: The business of money laundering, economy watch, www.economywatch.com, 2011. (Accessed January 12, 2012.)

SOS Impresa. (2010), *XII Rapporto—Le mani della criminalità sulle imprese*, Rome, Italy, January 27, 2010.

Takats, I. (2007), A theory of "Crying Wolf": The economics of money laundering enforcement, Paper presented at the *Conference "Tackling Money Laundering,"* University of Utrecht, Utrecht, the Netherlands, November 2–3, 2007.

Taylor, J. (2011), Overseas cyber-crimewave taking 600£ m a year from the taxman, *The Independent,* December 2011. Retrieved January 12, 2012 from http://www.independent.co.uk/news/uk/crime/overseas-cybercrimewave-taking-600m-a-year-from-the-taxman-6271552.html.

Truman, E. M. and Peter, R. (2004), *Chasing Dirty Money: Progress on Anti-Money Laundering*, Washington, DC: Institute for International Economics, United States, November 2004.

Unger, B. (2007), *The Scale and Impacts of Money Laundering*, Cheltenham, UK: Edward Elgar Publishing Company.

UNO DC. (2004), World Drug Report, United Nations Office for drug and crime prevention (UDCCP), Report, Oxford, UK.

UNO DC. (2005a), World Drug Report, United Nations Office for Drug and Crime Prevention (UDCCP), Report, Oxford, UK.

UNO DC. (2005b), World Drug Report, Vol. 1, Analysis, Vienna, Austria.

UNO DC. (2010), *The Globalization of Crime: A Transnational Organized Crime Threat Assessment*, New York: Documentation.

Van Eeten, M. and Bauer, J. M. (2008), Economics of malware: Security decisions, incentives and externalities. Technical Report OECD STI Working Paper 2008/1, OECD, Paris, France, http://www.oecd.org/dataoecd/53/17/40722462.pdf.

Van de Bunt, H. (2007), *The relation between organized crime and informal markets: The role of Hawala bankers in the transfer of proceeds from organized crime,* CRIMPREV, Gant University, Gant, Belgium, Discussion Paper.

Viles, T. (2008), Hawala, hysteria and hegemony, *Journal of Money Laundering Control*, 11(1), 25–33.

Walker, J. (1999), How big is global money laundering? *Journal of Money Laundering Control*, 3(1), 64–85.

Walker, J. (2000), Money laundering: Quantifying international patterns, *Australian Social Monitor*, 2(6), 139–147.

Walker, J. (2004), *A Very Temptative Exploration of the Relationship between Shadow Economy and the Production and Transit of Illicit Drugs*, New York: UNODC Document.

Walker, J. (2007): Measuring global money laundering, Paper presented at the *Conference "Tackling Money Laundering,"* University of Utrecht, Utrecht, the Netherlands.

Walker, J. and Unger, B. (2009), Measuring global money laundering: The walker gravity model, *Review of Law and Economics*, 5(2), 821–853, doi: 10.2202/1555-5879.1418.

Williams, P. (2007), Warming indicators and terrorist finances, in Jeanne K.G. and Harold A.T. (eds.) *Terrorism Financing and State Responses: A Comparative Perspective*, Stanford, CA: Stanford University Press:

World Bank. Macroeconomic indicators, Washington, DC, various years.

Zaidi, M. A. S. (2010), Understanding the appeal of Taliban in Pakistan, *Journal of Strategic Security*, 3(3), 1–14.

Zdanowicz, J. (2009), Trade-based money laundering and terrorist financing, *Review of Law and Economics*, 5(2), 854–878.

4. Organized Crime and the Mafia between Violence and the Informal Economy

Arije Antinori

«Go to East Berlin»
«And why? »
«The Berlin Wall has fallen»
«And what should I do?»
«You must buy everything, everything, everything,
buy discos, bars, pizzerias,
everything, everything, everything.»

(Wiretapping between two Neapolitan members of Camorra during the "Fall of the Berlin Wall"—November 9, 1989)

First their money arrive,
then they come with their own methods.

(Giovanni Falcone, 1991)

Introduction: Mafia Economic Development and the Enterprise

The development of the economic Mafia system in Italy can be identified mainly through the following four stages characterized by the connection between the social change produced in the macro-scenario and the Italian dynamics of organized crime development at the local, national, and transnational levels:

1. *Paper factory* (*1970s*): The Mafia produced a system of "empty boxes" enterprises. They created false documents and records such as invoices and delivery notes just to set an effective facade to support money management because it was necessary to structure a privileged relationship/network with influential local politicians.
2. *Mafia politicization* (*1980s*): The Mafia strengthened their enterprise by forming strong links between Mafia families and enterprises in order to "grow" public consensus and essential local voters by offering employment and productivity.
3. *Mafia injection* (*1990s*): The Mafia used their assets to infiltrate markets and influence the system of relations at all levels and in many primary sectors of the Italian economy.
4. *Diversion of public resources* (*end of the 1990s*): The consolidation of Mafia systematic economic routine progressively robbed the resources assigned to the virtuous growth of the market, concentrated riches in the hands of a few illegal elites, "cut out" the "clean" enterprises, and discouraged the market entry of new players who gave up doing business in a Mafia-conditioned system.

The criminal economy (Becchi and Rey, 1994) and the "dirty economy" (Ruggiero, 1996) are widely represented by the binary criminal system, which uses formally legal and illegal enterprises. The Mafia enterprise, as an illegal enterprise, must be understood as the systemic and entrepreneurial management of the criminal interest by the Mafia rule of illegal markets such as drug trafficking, usury, extortion, and toxic waste dumping, thanks to the large availability of manpower, skilled workers, professionals, resources, and capitals. The (Mafia) formally legal enterprise represents a strategic threat to the market of free competition. The proliferation of this infiltrative, criminal modus operandi, in the long term, can entirely contaminate and distort the market as a key component of the national democratic development of a country. Indeed, the Mafia can pollute and silently subvert the socioeconomic architecture to reach an informal "Mafia sociality." So the Mafia enterprise represents a strategic tool because it acts in a formally legal way moved by the needs to always promote the Mafia profit through regular psychological and/or physical violence.

For this reason, the Mafia enterprise should consider the following:

1. *Organic tool for achieving profit*: It is the main business/money laundering tool or a tool to reinvest the income from criminal activities, especially drug trafficking.
2. *Influence and power tool*: It is used to generate social relations and to create and strengthen the public consent, especially at the local level.
3. *Penetration tool*: Penetrating the economic system and circuit of legality, it creates intersection areas between "white" economy (legal business) and "black" economy (dirty money).

The development of the Mafia as an "entrepreneur" can be traced back to the early 1980s (Arlacchi, 1983). In order to understand its origins, it is appropriate to abandon a strictly folkloristic vision of the Mafia phenomenon from the late 1990s of the nineteenth century based on the icon of gangster. In this sense, it is important to underline the main role, during the Mafia development, of the Mafia's connection with the Latifundia policy that favored the nationalization and colonization of all Italian regions.

Article 416-bis (Italian Penal Code), introduced in 1982, has been given the opportunity to frame the so-called "foreign Mafias" too; it decrees that the criminally associated must be considered a "Mafia" man and not only as an organized crime man, when the following specific characteristics can be identified:

> Anyone who takes part in a Mafia association formed by three or more persons, shall be punished by the imprisonment from seven to twelve years.
>
> Those who promote, manage or organize the association are punished, just for this reason, by imprisonment from nine to fourteen years.
>
> The association has a mafia character when its members make use of the strength of the associative bond intimidation and the condition of subjection and conspiracy of silence to commit crimes, to acquire directly or indirectly, the management or control of economic activities, concessions, authorizations, contracts and public services or to realize unjust profits or advantages for themselves or others or to prevent or hinder the free exercise of voting rights or procure votes for themselves or others at elections.
>
> If the group is armed, the penalty of imprisonment from nine to fifteen years must be provided in the cases referred to the first paragraph and from twelve to twenty-four years referring to the second paragraph.
>
> The association is considered armed when the participants have access to the achievement of the association purpose, weapons or explosive materials, even if hidden or kept in storage.
>
> If the economic activities the association intends to take or maintain control of are financed in whole or in part with the price, product, or profit from crimes, the punishment set in the preceding paragraphs shall be increased by a third to a half.
>
> Against the convicted is always mandatory the confiscation of the things that were used or were intended to commit the crimes and the things that are the price, the product, the profit or that constitute the act.
>
> The provisions of this Article shall also apply to Camorra 'Ndrangheta and other associations, local derivation, including foreign ones, that apply intimidation force of the association tie follow aims that correspond to those of the mafia associations.

From the beginning, the chapter aims to fight not only the Mafia's illicit profits but also the unjust profits obtained through the constant expansion of Mafia power across many sectors of Italian life and economy, such as tourism, construction, food service, and trade. Therefore, the birth of circularity identity between power and economy should be noted in the Mafia system. In this sense, the new Mafia man, the Mafia enterprise's owner, can be understood within the system in which he operates. Thus, from a socio-criminological perspective, the Mafia man can be known, according to the criminological interpretation of Robert K. Merton's theory of deviance characterized by the relationship between cultural goals and institutionalized means (Marotta, 2007), as the figure of "rebel" because he introduces the use of violence as an alternative tool in the enterprises environment.

Furthermore, the Mafia's capability to pollute the entire socioeconomic fabric is given by the coaction of three elements:

1. *Use of violence*: Direct and/or indirect tools, methods, and behaviors, as well as threats of violence against things and/or individuals
2. *Enterprise functions*: Market integration through the production of useful goods and services to the community by offering employment
3. *Criminal familiarization*: Representation of the core of personality structurization and criminal alphabetization of the Mafia soldier by the family inside the Mafia structure, as one of the primary agents of socialization

Therefore, the use of domination as the founding principle of the entrepreneurial Mafia system identifies the following three "competitive advantages" (Dalla Chiesa, 2012) that favor the Mafia enterprise compared to white enterprises, allowing for the lowering of production costs, both as capitals and workforce:

1. *Violence*: The Mafia use violence as a fundamental tool, especially in the current economic environment, in particular because of its completely external essence.
2. *Intimidation*: The Mafia act against trade union representatives in the enterprise to interrupt the communication link between the outside world and politics to claim in a collective way the workers' main rights.
3. *Availability of autonomous liquidity*: In order to operate in the most articulate manner, corrupting at every level of social, economic, and political environment, the Mafia use their own enormous cash power.

The Mafia approach to economy and finance has origins, since the nineteenth century, in the use of organized violence as a method of management of the land tenures on behalf of the absent noble, as narrated by the historian Renda (Catanzaro, 1988):

> The Mafia in essence makes use of a particular extralegal organization to capitalize in privilege conditions both the advantages of the ordinary original accumulation, obtained by straight violence against the peasants.

All this has given the Mafia a dual role in the systemic dimension of the organized crime phenomenon (Catanzaro, 1987):

- *Social mediator*: It is the subject that helps in collaboration and integration by connecting individuals belonging to different domains.
- *Entrepreneur of violence*: It increases the Mafia's power and riches, thanks to introjection and serialization of aggressive behavior against others. The Mafia man gets the role of the glocal gatekeeper who, by his dual identity of enterprise and person, becomes the entrepreneur of social relations.

Then the assumption of the identity between the figure of Mafia man and entrepreneurial activity (Arlacchi, 1983) marks the turning point of understanding the evolution and the strategic–criminal capacity of the Italian Mafia entities.

Multidimensional Economic Mafia Strategy

The "uncertainty principle of Mafia border" as the virtual absence of a clear and easily distinguishable boundary between licit and illicit systems is promoted, supported, and reinforced by a Mafia pollution strategy of the socioeconomic and cultural assets, which consists of a bidirectional attack on the same target for violent conditioning, controlling, and "expropriating." This could be done by means of two actions-functional interconnections: on one hand through the white enterprises and on the other hand through the black ones.

In this way, the entrepreneur and/or, in the wide sense, the economic player who acts in a specific territory cannot choose a way of doing business external to the polluted economic relationships based on the differential advantages in terms of resources to facilitate illegal supremacy in competitiveness, more expeditious and efficient access to legal services, increasing capacity of differentiation of the exchanges, and, last but not least, availability of considerable capitals that represent a vital resource in times of crisis. As already stated, it is important considering the perfect and "pervert fusion" between some efficient enterprises in Northeast Italy and the Italian Mafia enterprises from Southern Italy to manage the illegal "toxic waste cycle."

The internal "Mafia conditioning" of enterprises can sometimes affect the whole production system, lowering the quality of products to allow greater competitiveness, especially in relation to participation in public tenders, as often proved by criminal investigations on the infiltrative Mafia phenomenon within the so-called "concrete cycle."

The "Mafia model of production" (Santino, 2009) is characterized by a systemic mix of productivity and parasitism given by the interoperability between criminal and legal businesses through the interpenetration of three macrospheres:

1. *Official economy*: The complex of relationships, declared contracts, and related taxes
2. *Underground economy*: The whole of not-declared works and taxes
3. *Illegal economy*: The set of black commercial relationships between criminals

Within official and underground economies, the functional relationships among the participants are ruled through the following ways of competition between agents:

- *Complicity*: Both agents know and share every aspect of the illicit activity.
- *Self-interested coexistence*: The agents share only some aspects of the illicit activity.
- *Forced cohabitation*: Individuals are forced to accept the Mafia supply.
- *Competition*: The common competition in the market.
- *Conflict*: By way of
  - Social exclusion from the market through the relational alienation of competitors and peer groups
  - Legal elimination based on the deceptive use of law against the other agent-victims
  - Physical elimination by killing

In the Mafia economic system, the innovation is given by the transformation of the entrepreneurial identity. So the production of goods and services enables polluted enterprises and/or straight Mafia-managed ones to obtain an exclusive monopoly profit not reachable by the white ones.

The progressive change of the entrepreneurial organization within the Mafia has operated in accordance with a progressive advancement role, in functional terms, across five evolutionary steps:

1. The Mafia support external business.
2. They look for intermediaries in order to invest through satellite activities.
3. They train their affiliates as intermediaries to be included as professionals as well as to directly (without any mediation) participate in business.
4. They transform the enterprise from within, taking control by economic, environmental, and violent conditioning.
5. They turn into a criminal enterprise and train their own young talents in order to structure new enterprises able to project Mafia power outside the national borders.

As mentioned earlier, three economic areas of Mafia infiltration have been identified since the 1990s:

1. The white economy, which is characterized by competition law
2. The gray economy in which the enterprises are a complex Chinese-box system
3. Black illegal markets (customs, weapons, humans, etc.)

Most of the Mafia-polluted enterprises are conditioned because of the payment of "pizzo" (protection money) given by cash and/or as a diversion of some income to the Mafia group that guarantees protection.

Therefore, five categories of entrepreneurs can be recognized (Sciarrone, 2011):

1. *Subordinated entrepreneur*: Subject of extortion by the Mafia to obtain protection for its own business; divided further into two subcategories:
   a. *Oppressed*: Used only to acquire money with no direct interest
   b. *Conditioned*: Represents a functional interest and/or operates in a specific sector of interest for the Mafia organization
2. *Colluding entrepreneur*: Decides to have business with the Mafia through a relationship of mutual benefit, sometimes in order to take advantage of the Mafia networks and interests
3. *Mafia entrepreneur*: Straightly participates in the Mafia enterprise or through a white figurehead

4. *Enterprise participated by the Mafia*: A top, clean enterprise bought by a criminal entity to hide its illicit profile and income, characterized by
   a. Increased capacity of criminal actions and business concealment
   b. Competitive capabilities deep-rooted in the production area
   c. Reputation, reliability, and prestige across the market in which it operates
   d. Capability to express its power through a pseudo-military command-and-control chain
   e. Infiltration tool to penetrate the highest levels of the socioeconomic system
5. *Joint ventures*: Link between Mafia and non-Mafia entities that strengthens a high-profile Mafia class to be used as the engine of colonization of the whole enterprise fabric

A Product Called "Violence"

Although the main Mafia organizations have been transformed, in whole or part, into entities where white collar crime has the key role, they retained their control of the region through the exclusive exercise of violence (threatened or not) and the killing of hostile individuals and/or groups. In this sense, in some areas the Mafia is considered an informal "alter-State" thanks to Mafia enterprises providing work and socializing because of their

1. Monopoly of the use of force
2. Arbitrary use of force
3. Alternative and self-legitimated system code of judgment
4. System of shared subcultural habits
5. Parallel tax system
6. Pseudo-religious system

The Mafia gain power because they replace the concept of ownership with the totalizing concept of Mafia affiliation in terms of sociocultural, economic, and moral aspects. The Mafia enterprise represents a threat because it has the power to promote criminal goals through the establishment of "Mafia welfare" because of the following features:

1. *State enterprise*: A leading player in the system, which can easily multiply, especially in the context of crisis
2. *Social transformation agent*: A socioeconomic actor able to transform society from within through the promotion of (Mafia) values favored by the progressive impoverishment of the cultural and moral dimensions, changing the DNA of the Italian macro-system in the long term

The added value in criminal terms promoted by the Mafia to go into the enterprise system is represented by the provision of private protection through the system of violence, thus renewing the strategy of socioeconomic suffocation by means of capillary (door-to-door) control of the territory and the exercise of violence against opponents. So the Mafia transform, thanks to the threat of force, the mediation by offering protection from itself.

The element of increased exposure to Mafia violence is the proximity of the business to the road. It expresses the vulnerability to be a victim of the dynamics of extortion, racket, and usury. Moreover, the existence of the so-called "turbulent markets" (Gambetta, 1992) must be underlined as where the crystallization of main illicit activities such as drug trafficking takes place. So insecurity needs security, but sadly the providers are always the same, the Mafia men.

According to the findings of police investigations in the last years, especially in relation to the phenomenon of 'Ndrangheta infiltration in Northern Italy, the Mafia have the ability to operate simultaneously in two ways (Block, 1983):

1. *Power syndicate*: Criminal entity that shows its violent control in the territory of interest
2. *Enterprise syndicate*: The business organization dedicated to illicit trafficking

Moreover, in this case there are many "Ianus" enterprises to be addressed as an "enterprise participated in by the Mafia," particularly operating in the "circuit of the Major Projects." Usually, the Major Project protocol helps enterprises have adequate historical and anti-Mafia documentation.

The Mafia modus operandi in relation to the enterprises is based on the injection of illicit capital to reach two main goals:

1. Establishment of a usury system against the entrepreneurs who, already reduced to poor condition, will lose their power such as any sort of right/control of the enterprise

2. Progressive acquisition, in the case of productivity and growth, of the enterprise to have the exclusive power to manage it

So the entrepreneur experiences the function of positive reinforcement given by the money supply, added to the violence and/or its threat. In relation to the interconnection between the external environment and the criminal Mafia environment, the role of the functionally relevant and meaningful conspiracy behaviors emerges. That is the reason why these individuals can be called Mafia supporters who promote and/or participate in external initiatives in order to gain differential advantages.

In the last years, the gradual Mafia spread and monopolization across the entire production areas have reduced the capability to create business committees in bureaucratic politics and business outside the Mafia because its environment of social networking is widely contaminated. In addition, the Mafia interest has been expressed in social practices that, in the medium/long term, crystallize into "Mafia rules," which could often be uncritically introjected.

The pervasiveness of the Mafia method within a given environment involves a substantial change in the social relationships and working conditions of those who want to act as an "informal resistance" against the Mafia colonization. The workers, professionals, and entrepreneurs try to resist, immediately putting their safety at risk. They must be protected and asked to collaborate with the police in order to narrate important infiltrative processes in progress that are not always detectable by external observation.

The violence and fear generated by Mafia pollution cause the so-called "depressing effect" (Grasso and Bellavia, 2011), which makes foreign investors "escape" mainly from Southern Italy. This can be considered one of the causes of the lack of development of the southern enterprises both for single players and interconnected systems. All these negative dynamics determine the "killing of future" for the young generations who decide to leave the country.

Violence is constantly used in any expression of the economic system to increase the power of the Mafia and criminal capital. It has become an integral part of the Mafia enterprise as the main tool of action/economic expansion, according to the circularity loop between profit and power because of the need to control and dominate the territory. In fact, profit without power is nothing, but in a capitalist system, it is not possible to get power without having profit.

The violence characterizes this circularity producing a well-integrated system of

1. Formal enterprises, which aim to get profits through legitimate activities such as pizzerias or construction
2. Informal enterprises, which have a high level of organization to get profits through all illegal activities across both gray and black markets

The profit–power circularity underlies, in strategic terms, the tension of the organizational structure to simultaneously reach multiple interdependent goals. The Mafia hierarchizes them trying to solve the conflict between the ways to reach them. This is the reason why we experience the copresence of the silent infiltrative tactics and very aggressive armed actions. So the Mafia structure stands out for its extreme flexibility and different methods of using violence. In this way, the Mafia can regulate the inner conflicts and preserve the entirety of the "Mafia organism" preventing and/or fighting the rise of micropower systems due to individuals and/or small groups.

Mafia Structurization and Infiltrative Process

The infiltrative Mafia strategy is characterized by segmentation, as evidenced by the fact that among the confiscated enterprises for Mafia crimes, 48.5% constitute limited liability companies, 27.3% individuals, while only 3.3% constitute joint-stock company.*

Mr. Avallone, an entrepreneur, highlighted the 'Ndrangheta ability of adaptive masking in Northern Italy:

> Meanwhile, those who are really only after you find out. They don't come with the gun, but in suit and tie, with clean enterprises, with real operative functions, without a criminal record, and with anti-mafia certification. You understand who is in front of you, when it's too late.†

Judge Paolo Borsellino, victim of Mafia terrorism of the 1990s, said:

* http://www.sosimpresa.it/24:xiii-rapporto-sos-impresa.html.

† Cesare Fiumi, "Io imprenditore lombardo schiavo della 'Ndrangheta, dico: 'basta paura,'" *Sette*, May 26, 2011.

Politics and mafia are two powers that live on control of the same territory, that is why they make war or make agreements.[*] The 13th Research Report released by SOS Impresa, the anti-Mafia association from Confesercenti, points out that the so-called "Mafia S.p.A." (a metaphoric name to identify Mafia to a joint-stock company) can be considered a major Italian economic player that is able to accumulate about 140 billion euros a year. At the same time, it is argued that in Italy, enterprises affected about 1300 crimes per day, about 1 min^{-1}.[†] The report shows how the serialization and organized "colonization" of the territory represent a way to "Mafia mature," as in the case of Camorra, which has progressively become an economic criminal holding.

The interesting research reports a trend of the Mafia to spread to new businesses "to germinate fertile new worlds" with the aim not only to increase their own economic power but also to increase their hegemony as a multiplier of the first. So, four areas of strategic interest can be identified:

1. *Health*: Testing laboratories, private clinics, residential homes, centers for tracking helper, disability-related services for cleaning and administration of food, rehabilitation centers
2. *Sports*: Amateur clubs, above all linked to large businesses such as professional soccer but also the lower categories of professionalism, sports supplies, sports construction, betting services, sports and multipurpose centers/clubs
3. *Trucking*: Local services, tourism, professional transportation
4. *Surveillance*: Nocturnal security guards, security services in nightclubs, construction site security, personal protection services

It is interesting to add the latest infiltrative trends given by the need for real-time money laundering:

- *Gold-for-cash services*: 60% operate as criminal entities to support and favor money laundering and tax evasion, and 20% are linked to organized crime (Razzante, 2012).
- *Gambling*: Casinos, video poker, scratch cards, bingo centers. The gambling business is experiencing a rapid growth throughout the country. Every year, Italians spend an average of 1260 euros, as stated in the interesting report named "Azzardopoli"[‡] by the anti-Mafia association "Libera. Associazioni, nomi e numeri contro le mafie." This phenomenon is extremely important and worrying considering that, according to what is indicated in the aforementioned report, money laundering activities in Italy amount to 10% of the GDP. In this sector the Mafia operate to detect the development of new markets, technologies, and trends, while retaining an interest in the traditional parallel illegal gambling[§] business by directly managing the gambling rooms, the underground betting, the "lottonero" (the black lotto), and fake scratch-offs.

Finally, the Mafia have developed an interest in the Internet and the Deep Web, which are used by several complex criminal phenomena. The cyberworld must be considered the new "playground" where we will very soon experience the rise of de-territorialized cyber-Mafia and other brand new criminal entities. This scenario will find many points of convergence with other kinds of organized cybercrime.

Three specific types of costs, whether direct or indirect, are produced because of the infiltration and/or environmental Mafia conditioning, as noted by Ms. Anna Maria Tarantola, Deputy General Manager, Bank of Italy[¶]:

1. *Costs of anticipation*: This can be defined as preventive costs, including all those costs that entrepreneurs have to manage because they could be victims of the Mafia, according to all the possible methods. Therefore, among these are the costs for the execution of specific assurances as well as video surveillance systems and equipment for safety and security for not only the enterprises but also their families. So, the Mafia must be considered the virus and the antidote at the same time; in fact after threatening, they introduce the entrepreneurs directly or indirectly to agencies working in the private security and close protection services to provide adequate protection.
2. *Costs of consequences*: Theft of goods, robberies, and "pizzo."

[*] Paolo Borsellino, in Lirio Abbate e Peter Gomez, I complici, 2007.
[†] www.sosimpresa.it.
[‡] www.libera.it/flex/cm/pages/ServeBLOB.php/L/IT/IDPagina/5741.
[§] Commissione Parlamentare di Inchiesta sul Fenomeno della Mafia e sulle altre Associazioni Criminali, anche Straniere—Relazione sul fenomeno delle infiltrazioni mafiose nel gioco lecito e illecito—Anno 2010, www.anfp.it/gestionale/upload/cms/elementi_portale/news/documenti/(3)relazione.pdf.
[¶] www.unioncamere.gov.it/download/2970.html.

3. *Costs of reaction*: The entire economic resources, assets, and institutions engaged in fighting the Mafia (Home Office, Police forces, prison systems, judges, etc.).

We must add a fourth category, namely, "costs of amputation." These include losses incurred in all Mafia attacks/aggressions (e.g., arson) that completely or partially destroy some of the assets, properties, and movable items of the enterprises. Thus, the enterprises cannot rise again without injecting large sums of money. Then, the Mafia readily provide money to the entrepreneurs and definitively buy their future.

The infiltration of the Mafia in the socioeconomic fabric may allow, especially in times of crisis and/or economic contraction,

1. Provision of more effective services
2. Provision of services in the most favorable trading conditions
3. Provision of services that could not have been granted because of
   a. Lack of a reliable financial lender
   b. Small or denied banking support

Today, the Italian Mafias are the criminal entities characterized by the perfect fusion between tradition and change, in the order of cultural, economic, media, and military elements.

From the macro-structural level, there is a main difference between the two archetypes of the Mafia entity:

1. The Mafia organization is structured by a well-defined hierarchical architecture through the following:
   a. *Association*: A group of individuals linked together by an honor code based on violence
   b. *Clan*: A familiar group that holds power over a given territory
   c. *Enterprise*: An economic entity infiltrated by the criminal organized interest
2. The Mafia system (Saviano, 2006) is the organizational architecture transformed into sociocultural, economic, and sometimes political colonizing system, which pervades the entire life of citizens.

So the Mafia organization must be studied in its main identity, key concepts, and functions:

1. *Strategic positioning*: To protect and promote the Mafia core business. There is a paradox: the criminal enterprise does not act because of a self-determination that represents the spirit of capitalism, but the strategic decisions, positioning, and projection of it are dictated from an external actor, the Mafia leadership of the organization.
2. *Intended/proposed purposes*: To commit crimes with the aim
   a. To manage/control economic activities through intimidation and arbitrary use of violence
   b. To get illicit profits and/or benefits
3. *Means and/or assets*: Violence, subjection, conspiracy of silence used to guarantee the aforementioned purposes.
4. *Authority of status*: Powers and criminal functions given by the structure in relation to the role of the affiliate.
5. Division of activities in roles that correspond to precise responsibilities and duties.
6. *Ideology*: For the Mafia entrepreneur, the business risk is characterized by two opposite principles:
   a. *Spread*: The ability to have much higher economic resources (than the competitors) because of illicit activities.
   b. *Contraction*: Thanks to illegal alteration of the principles of fair competition, the Mafia entrepreneur projects his business strategically but not in a long period, because he knows that he can suddenly lose everything as a consequence of confiscation of property. So he has a specific and not ordinary approach to
      i. His own business
      ii. His wealth
      iii. His power of influence
      iv. His personal freedom
      v. His life, particularly in the case of competition with players from other criminal organizations and/or inner conflicts inside the same structure

The Mafia express a totalizing function to colonize the socioeconomic and political culture through a multidimensional strategy implemented by means of specific expertise and structured roles to rule the following main strategic functions:

- *External functions*: Outsourcing of individuals colluding with the Mafia.
  - *Recon-informative*: Analysis and identification of key issues and key players to achieve.
  - *Relational*: Establishment of links between the Mafia and the non-Mafia worlds, such as the justice system, police forces, and other institutions.

- *Health*: Care system to illegally support the affiliates involved in criminal actions, especially fugitives.
- *Professional*: People such as surveyors, engineers, architects, etc., who provide services to support the Mafia interest.

- *Inner functions*: The "cultivation," alphabetization, and socialization through the construction of a complex "Mafia environment."
  - *Family/education*: The primary socialization agents that favor criminal learning, in terms of values and practices.
  - *Logistics*: Designed to provide all the support for moving affiliates across territories and favoring the settlements of Mafia individuals and groups.
  - *Business*: Criminal economic markets.
  - *Military*: Supply of weapons, explosives, and guerilla commandos.
  - *Technology*: Acquisition and management of digital devices and intelligence.
  - *Accounting*: Managing/tracking fees and distribution of money to affiliates.
  - *Media*: Managing Mafia interests through the web and Deep Web.

An element of particular interest regarding the strategic positioning of the Mafia enterprises is that the Mafia organizations "spread" their own interests in diversifying business, especially across small entities and areas of infiltration, including drug trafficking, construction, (toxic or nontoxic) waste cycle, legal gambling, food retail, and catering service. During the last 10 years, one of the most relevant sectors for Mafia business infiltration is the so-called "great works"—major projects such as architecture, engineering, communications, roads, railways, bridges, harbors, and airports—usually realized because of globalized public events, such as the next world EXPO, which will take place in 2015 in the city of Milan. To prevent the Mafia infiltration in public procurements related to this important event, the Italian Government has established G.I.C.EX., Central Interagency Group for Expo, a special police task force consisting of detectives from the Polizia di Stato, Carabinieri and Guardia di Finanza under the command of D.C.P.C., the Italian Central Directorate of the Criminal Police at the Ministry of the Interior.

It focuses on the main role of enterprises through the Mafia environment where they acquire a triple role as expressions of the following:

1. *Mafia circularity*: They are perfectly set to interconnect power and money in the criminal loop.
2. *Affiliation tie*: They must collect individuals' inspirations, convoy and interconnect them to the expansionist and accumulative project of the Mafia as a criminal collective and complex identity.
3. *Mafia identification*: They facilitate the social recognition and the Mafia autoidentification as subcultural identity opposite to the State.

It is necessary to the identity of the Mafia/criminal enterprise because it highlights the power of the Mafia strategy directly given by the fusion of economic, political, and social spheres as represented through the three-step modus operandi of Mafia collusion:

1. *Step 1*: The Mafia set a package of votes to support a politician, as the direct expression of occult governance of a given territory. There is, therefore, another actor, the covert enterprise close to and/or directly controlled by the Mafia, which gives the money to finance the electoral support.
2. *Step 2*: The Mafia-supported politician is elected, who then favors and gives, directly or indirectly, contracts to the first polluted enterprise, which uses part of the income to develop Mafia businesses and spread their power in the territory through other new Mafia enterprises.
3. *Step 3*: The Mafia loop process between business and power starts across the aforementioned three spheres, excluding everything that does not pertain to the Mafia fabric.

Therefore, as reported in many judicial findings and records, we can identify three main strategic and operational models that the Mafia use to infiltrate and colonize the socioeconomic and political environment:

1. *Convergent*: Direct connection between high-rank subjects in politics, the Mafia, and enterprises.
2. *Coincident*: As an evolution of the previous model, the Mafia subject and politician are the same person.
3. *Divergent*: Used in particular local areas where there is a threat to the criminal power, for example, due to the direct control of the local administration by the Ministry of Interior because of the Mafia infiltration. Thus, the Mafia representative of the territory decides to manage/control their interest from an external "safety distance."

Analyzing the large 'Ndrangheta infiltration in Lombardy Region, we experience the set and act of very complex and hidden operative strategies structured and supported by the socioeconomic, subcultural, and political Mafia assets, as follows:

1. *Threshold subject*: The Mafia represent the entity that is able to allow the privileged access of the enterprise to public contracts, thanks to a large and long-established system of corruption, collusion, and connivance.
2. *Business accelerator*: The Mafia provide a large amount of capitals to be managed by the controlled enterprise, which becomes competitive in a short term compared to other competitors. So in the short term it can sign contracts and can acquire a very good reputation from all the suppliers and commercial partners and institutions involved in the business.
3. *Anabolic steroid*: The Mafia instantaneously inject large capitals in the enterprise. These assets are immediately used to purchase machinery, equipment, tracks, etc. All that causes an "explosive growth" of the enterprise, which has the power to "pollinate" the entire field of action by the establishment of a monopoly based on Mafia violence and money. An interesting example of this strategy can be found in the so-called "concrete cycle" criminally interconnecting excavation, soil moving, and waste dumping across the following steps:
   a. Creation, infiltration, or control of an enterprise
   b. Signature of relevant contracts especially in the public sector
   c. Recruitment of Mafia-trusted subjects with no assignments
   d. "Oppression" of trade union delegates
   e. Identification of transport routes, loading and unloading of toxic waste through covert activity, as in the contract
   f. Consolidation and increasing capacity of routes, thanks to the introduction of additional tracks "cannibalized" (obtained by the Mafia) to other smaller enterprises and individuals
   g. Hyper-exploitation and depletion of each strategic investment for the future development of the enterprise, which goes bankrupt in a few days/months

   All the aforementioned individuals taking part voluntary, involuntary, or under threat in the explained steps represent the "Mafia social capital."
4. *Politics agent*: The Mafia create transversal strong and close ties with corrupt politicians, men from both Left and Right parties, as key players in local government, thanks to bribes.

The Mafia enterprise is a totally twisted entity because it does not give resources to the community in which it operates, but it takes them away through the creation and support of economic, organizational, and social processes. That is why, nowadays, about 1 million entrepreneurs are victims of crimes related to the Mafia, as reported by C.E.N.S.I.S.*

Mafia-polluted people are the multipliers of criminal wealth. In a criminal entity such as the Mafia, which is known for its ability to penetrate the socioeconomic fabric, the crisis is an inexhaustible propellant in terms of increase in consent, power, and authority. Indeed the depletion of the overall system and the widespread need for cash and credit create and reinforce a sort of popular "legitimacy" and enrichment of people. But this is not real because the citizens day by day become victims of the Mafia's own interest, as individuals, families, and communities.

* www.interno.gov.it/mininterno/export/sites/default/it/assets/files/15/0110_Censis-Sintesi_completa.pdf.

Mafia Entrepreneur Profile

"At the local level, the head of a family was and still is the king of his territory."† So it is important to explore the behavioral profile of the Mafia entrepreneur. He is characterized by the will, aspiration, and continuous intent to act in the direction of criminal business familiarization through the fusion of family and enterprise. It renews and reinforces the attestation of its role within the organized crime structure while infusing energy

† Vittorio Zincone, "Sette"—*Corriere della Sera Magazine*, November 6, 2009.

and expanding strategic resources in the hands of the Mafia man.

From a behavioral point of view, the Mafia-affiliate entrepreneur represents an interesting typicalness because on one side, he is the expression of power, prestige, open-mindedness, and "innovation" and, on the other side, a dominated soldier who must comply only with the Mafia leaders' orders. He lives his life as a subject in constant conflict, a man at war to war. He must protect the Mafia business and his "homeland Mafia" in which he is completely integrated and which he recognizes and is recognized in subcultural terms. He is moved from exercising its supremacy in the environment in which it is undertaking, to be "accepted" as deviant and then fully recognized within the criminal entity membership of the subculture of which he is also constantly the ambassador.

He has a double identity in the Mafia subculture:

- Deviant in relation to the state and its institutions, moral and constitutional principles, rules
- Compliant to the Mafia subculture, its own social-relational environment that he can bring with him and/or replay in transnational and transcontinental scenarios

The Mafia entrepreneur operates in a production environment as an innovator and as a supplier of products. In this sense, it has been stated that the only element of effective innovation is the introduction of violence in entrepreneurial acting (Arlacchi, 1983), thanks to his enhanced ability to compete and win. This violence, as a means of doing business, can itself become a business product to be placed on the market, together with the measures and devices for the prevention of and defense against violence.

There is also an additional element of identity reinforcement inherent in the progressive geographization of Mafia enterprises. It is based on the occurrence of the following elements among the individuals who take part in the same context:

1. The same area of origin/geographical operations identified in Southern Italy, in the territories of birth and historically rooted Mafias
2. The same sector of employment
3. Belonging to the same environment as closely related to the sector of employment
4. Same corporate structure (small/medium enterprise)
5. Same functional interdependencies
6. Adherence to the same Mafia subculture, in particular, related to violent strategies and tools to make business

The systematic presence of these elements explains how the Mafia strategy is relevant in terms of

1. Productive specialization
2. Selection operating on the trust in the conspiracy of silence
3. Territorialization as (1) self-preservation to fight the State authority and (2) united projection/export territories that are considered criminally "fertile"
4. Subcultural promotion as (1) self-identity promotion and (2) group-identity promotion
5. System reliability
6. Substitution function of the agents operating in the legal market and State institutions

All these can be only because of the routine use of violence as the real "Mafia know-how" essential to get the following targets:

1. Opening of new markets
2. Expansion of existing markets
3. Centralization of markets and peripheral interests
4. Massification of small criminal business
5. Instantaneous repositioning of the economic interest
6. Create connections through new sources of economic supply
7. Establishment of monopoly in relation to sale and/or purchase
8. Conversion and/or dual use of existing markets
9. Enterprise inner governance
10. Finding and creating new money laundering opportunities
11. Taking part in the planning activities of large commercial projects to money laundering

In the end, the violent behavior is an element that can short-circuit the circular economy, development, and innovation of modern capitalism at least theoretically, since the absence of development, in favor of accumulation and concentration of illicit capital, prevents innovation that is itself acquisition, as well as more extensive and widespread sharing, not pursuing particular interests and in this case criminals.

Change as a Factor of Strengthening Mafia Business: "Cosa Nuova"

Antonio Maria Costa, Executive Director of the United Nations Office on Drugs and Crime until 2010, said:

> With the outbreak of the financial crisis—and in the middle of a cash crisis—too many banks are open to the money laundering coming from illegal and criminal activities.*

The persistence of the conditions of economic crisis favors the fragmentation of the system of rules on which the main productive and commercial sectors of the Italian economy are based, such as trade, crafts, and more generally the small and medium enterprises.

It points out the occurrence of a particular Mafia infiltrative strategy, which can be named "Deal with the Devil," a mechanism where the supply of capital represents a very attractive power "pushing" the shopkeeper, the artisan, and the entrepreneur into the "mouth" of the Mafia. Nowadays, this criminal organization has been considered the "first bank in Italy"† in terms of cash availability and access to credit. In this sense, it is very important to investigate the dynamics of the so-called "fatal attraction" (Dalla Chiesa, 2011, 2012). In fact, as stated by the author, in terms of the satisfaction of needs through the interconnection between legal and illegal business, the importance of four key principles causally related to it can be identified:

1. *Calculation*. The white entrepreneur assesses the benefits of "Mafia doping Mafia" for his business. Its conditions of impoverishment do not allow him to carry out a strategic evaluation in terms of cost and benefit... . The prospect of being able to access undisturbed, thanks to money injection from the Mafia, the procurement market determines a strong behavioral conditioning for the entrepreneur, because of the following:
    a. It twists the moral value system, which should be based on fair competition.
    b. It encourages the belief founded on the illusion that, thanks to the signed contracts, he can really emancipate himself in the medium term. He cannot perceive and/or rationalize the fact of being a living Mafia tool.
2. *Fear*: The exercise of the power of intimidation, which is a foundational element of the Mafia essence, is revealed through the central use of terror in terms of conditioning
    a. *Sociocultural aspects*: Diffusion, consolidation, and passive acceptance of the Mafia values, including the deliberate use of violence, abuse of power, and submission to criminal authority, are the bases of the social system.
    b. *Business*: The more or less silent infiltration determines the spread and becomes a structured appeal to fear as an "ordinary" mechanism in use within the dynamics of employment and production. In this sense, fear can also be determined top down and bottom up through every professional in the production cycle, from the entrepreneur to the worker, the counselor, the accountant, the lawyer, and the carrier.
    c. *Family*: The potential risk of opposing the Mafia is a primary element of conditioning not only for individuals but also for the entire families. The Mafia do not condemn just the family but each member, directly or indirectly, to the dependence on the Mafia interests, but they can inevitably condemn the future of their young members, not only from the point of view of material resources but above all by the possible transmission of cultural values of the Mafia, thus helping to reduce the prospects of choosing their own life.
    d. *Subjective*: Fear for safety is favored by the knowledge of lethal and violent "exemplary" practices against others. The so-called "demonstrative action" consists of the damage done to the property of the subject and/or ultimately directly injuring individuals to threaten them.

Mafia violence produces the complete subversion of the conceptual condemnation perspective of the entrepreneur's life by joining the Mafia. His notion that joining the Mafia is a means to economic salvation is not only influenced by the pervasive violence of the Mafia, but also by the difficulty, if not impossibility, of gaining access to banking credit, as well as the stagnation of the market. Moreover, the choice of the Mafia interlocutor does not take place through a cost–benefit system of calculation. Because criminals are the only subjects in the business environment, the map of enterprises operating in a given area becomes the map of families, groups, and criminal interests since everything

* Speech at the "Royal Institute of International Affairs," 2012.

† Antonio Ingroia, Anti-Mafia prosecutor, Interview in Nadia Francalacci, "La prima banca in Italia? Oggi è la mafia," *Panorama*, January 11, 2012.

is Mafia-polluted. The Mafia today are both the first enterprise, with a yearly income of approximately 140 billion euros,* and, as already mentioned, the "first bank of Italy" for cash availability.

Temporary work, especially in big Italian cities, became the "recruitment constituency" where the Mafia act to promote the systemic spread of self-interest by encouraging the black market and evasion. This allows, among other things, "popularization" in this case without any violent and armed actions of its affiliates. The recruited workers are far from the direct participation, violent behaviors, and Mafia interests. These people are laid off and unemployed workers or are college students who do not have the resources to support their studies. Their recruitment is based on the lack of awareness to participate in organized criminal interests, as evidenced by these statements:

> I do without asking too many questions what they ask… I need money to live, I do and I'm only able to be a metalworker. If they call me for a task, they give me the opportunity to survive. As soon as I finish my work I go back home, just thinking to myself. I just did some welding.—Blaise (2013)

The Mafia are able to intercept trends and social changes to identify the socioeconomic and cultural enrichment and consensus of the territory. Just 3 years after the "Fall of the Berlin Wall", during a prosecution for money laundering, prominent criminal interconnections were recorded between the small Calabrian town of Locri, a stronghold of 'Ndrangheta power, and some banks in Moscow that manage the dirty money acquired through drug trafficking. This is a typical case of link between illicit proceeds and legal business, as evidenced by statements made in 2012 by Piero Luigi Vigna, a former National Anti-Mafia Prosecutor, who said:

> Our mafias collect 190 billion Euros a year, and a large part of this money is not intended for illicit markets but to businesses that, in this period of credit crunch, put in danger the legal enterprises. This is a magic moment for the mafia and for the usury, too†

Indeed, the so-called "credit crunch" determined a progressive reduction in the ability to access credit by white entrepreneurs, compressing significantly their ability to invest in the future, then actually interrupting the natural drive toward the future as the engine of economic development of a country. This condition is exacerbated by the chronic delay in the public administration's remittance for the services provided by many enterprises. For example, 59-year-old entrepreneur of "Eurostrade 90" (Peraga of Vigo, Padua) John Schiavon, who killed himself by shooting and left a note *"I'm sorry, I cannot do more"* in reference to the debts he had been obliged to pay following the continuing failure, with a credit from the State of 200,000 euros.‡

Considering that in the Italian economic system where the small and medium enterprises sector is formed by 95% less than 10 employees, 98% less than 20 employees, 99.5% less than 50 employees, and 0.5% more than 250 employees—according to the last national census§—the report from "Fondazione Impresa" in 2012 points out that 43.3% of small enterprises have experienced critical difficulties in accessing credit.¶ Furthermore, the Krls Network of Business Ethics report in 2012 shows that Italy is the first country in terms of tax evasion, which gives rise to an underground economy of around 340 billion euros a year, equivalent to 21% of the national GDP.** This scenario allows the Mafia to infiltrate enterprises at every level of production, where the presence of usury and extortion must be always considered "early-warning crimes" of Mafia infiltration. In this sense, it is necessary to explain that the traditional, as not organized in a Mafia strategy/modus operandi, usurer and extorter behavior is different from that of the Mafia where the criminal structure wants to obtain a double advantage:

1. To avoid the creation of a united front of merchants, entrepreneurs, and workers committed to "resist" the spread of Mafia
2. To revive competition among enterprises in a polluted way by increasing the conspiracy of silence and by penetrating the social fabric of the economic system in a less shocking and more pervasive way and generating public consensus

The Mafia create covert financial enterprises to give cash to the "walking-dead" enterprises, requiring a commitment to return the debt with interest

* www.sosimpresa.it/10_documentazione.html.

† Agenzia Nazionale Stampa Associata (ANSA)—May 15, 2012.

‡ Francesca Sironi, "Suicidi, un massacre silenzioso," *L'espresso* April 12, 2013.

§ www3.istat.it/salastampa/comunicati/non_calendario/20101209_00/testointegrale20101209.pdf.

¶ www.fondazioneimpresa.it.

** hargomenti.ilsole24ore.com/krls-network-of-business-ethics.html.

rates up to 180%–200% and through the recovery actions that "strangle" the entrepreneurs, described as follows:

1. Land knowledge and monitoring
2. Identification of strategic areas
3. Focusing on the entrepreneurs in a critical economic and financial situation
4. Proposal for funding through intermediaries, often complacent indigenous entrepreneurs who work in the same socioeconomic context and/or through covert enterprises
5. Informal and violent action of mafiosa affiliates as delegates of credit recovery companies and/or covert ones too
6. Mafia recovery of credit through the direct management of enterprises, through the cannibalization of their assets
7. Assimilation of territory, plus the Mafia cultural infiltration . . . [leading to] the spread of the "Mafia idiom" to favor ... the relation through individuals and the building of the Mafia identity
8. Spread of the polluted system, thanks to the link with the representatives of local administrations and politics

The bankruptcy and the final closing of some enterprises are the expressions of Mafia power. So the intermediary role of the entrepreneur is very important because he can share the same critical conditions, language, and dialect.

The last two annual anti-Mafia reports to Parliament,* realized by the national intelligence agencies, show that Mafias are implementing the criminal economic diversification, from public procurements to the creation of consensus and jobs. The diversification key is represented by the capability to promote criminality, thanks to the organizational and subcultural reticular system.

Mafia penetration has spread like wildfire in the national economic system, and it has an interconnected supply and demand generating a sort of "Mafia tax" (Dalla Chiesa, 2012) applied across every enterprise and production process, either directly or as a result of further fiscal pressure that affects the legal actors in terms of tax evasion. So, according to the same author, the "Mafia tax" becomes a sort of tax on tangible goods, but it must be identified as a polysemic operative concept, described as follows:

1. Force subtraction of private resources
2. Subtraction of public resources
3. Additional disbursement for the community, in terms of cost for justice and security
4. Additional disbursement for the community, in terms of costs for environmental destruction
5. Distortion as inefficiency of the system of allocation of resources
6. Decreasing the number of subjects creating wealth and discouraging businesses
7. Raising the threshold for market access

The informal application of the "Mafia tax" can affect such intangibles as relationships, individual achievements, the harmony of the community in regard to the fulfillment of the natural integration of human beings with the environment, as well as with nature. In short, it can affect everything relative to the concepts of freedom. Environment, beauty and happiness...

The most powerful Italian Mafia, the ʻNdrangheta, currently referred to by its members as "Cosa Nuova" (New Thing), is primarily a socio-criminal organization. It has the ability to handle criminal interests as differentiated financial transactions, particularly in its primary role as manager of transatlantic drug trafficking, local enterprises and public procurements. ʻNdrangheta obtained a dominant role through enterprises not only in the so-called "concrete cycle" and "the "waste cycle" and also in the so-called "economy of catastrophe" (Dalla Chiesa, 2012). The development of new businesses for the criminal organization emerged with the activities of reconstruction following catastrophic events, such as the earthquakes in Irpinia, L'Aquila, and Emilia. It is important to understand that in order to successfully combat the twenty-first century criminal complex phenomenon such as "Cosa Nuova", we need new tools to be used in monitoring/knowledge, analysis and counter-intelligence able to make focus on the sociocultural dimension of the Mafia as a key factor of its criminal complexity.

* www.interno.gov.it/mininterno/export/sites/default/it/sezioni/sala_stampa/dossier/.

References

Antinori, A. (2009). *L'"activité des force de police dans la lutte contre le criminalité organisée de type mafieux en Italie in Cahiers de la Sécurité" janvier-mars*, vol. 7. Institut National des Hautes Etudes de Securite, Paris, France.

Arlacchi, P. (1983). *La Mafia imprenditrice*. L'etica mafiosa e lo spirito del capitalismo, Il Mulino, Bologna, Italy.

Becchi A. and Rey G. M. (1994). The Criminal Economy. L'economia criminale. Laterza, Bari-Roma, Italy.

Biagio, S. (2013). *I padroni della crisi*. Il Saggiatore, Milano, Italy.

Block, A. (1983). *East Side-West Side: Organizing Crime in New York*, University College of Cardiff Press, Cardiff, UK.

Catanzaro, R. (1987). *Imprenditori della violenza e mediatori sociali. Un'ipotesi di interpretazione della mafia, in Polis*. Ricerche e studi su società e politica in Italia, vol. I, no. 2, Istituto Carlo Cattaneo, Il Mulino, Bologna, Italy.

Catanzaro, R. (1988). *Il delitto come impresa. Storia sociale della mafia*. Liviana, Padova, Italy.

Dalla Chiesa, N. (2012). *The mafia enterprise. Between violent capitalism and social control.* Cavallotti University Press, Milano, Italy.

Gambetta, D. (1992). *La mafia siciliana*. Un'industria della protezione privata, Einaudi, Torino, Italy.

Grasso, P. and Bellavia, E. (2011). *Soldi sporchi. Come le mafie riciclano miliardi e inquinano l'economia mondiale*. Baldini Castoldi Dalai editore, Milano, Italy.

Marotta, G. (2007). *Teorie criminologiche*. Da Beccaria al postmoderno. LED Edizioni Universitarie, Milano, Italy.

Razzante, R. (2012). Evasione fiscale e riciclaggio, un intreccio perverso, in *GNOSIS*, no. 1/2012, Agenzia Informazioni e Sicurezza Interna, Roma, Italy.

Ruggiero V. (1996). Dirty economies. The criminal enterprise in Europe. Bollati Boringhieri, Torino, Italy.

Santino, U. (2009). *Storia del movimento antimafia*. Dalla lotta di classe all'impegno civile, Editori Riuniti, Roma, Italy.

Saviano R. (2006). Gomorrah: A Personal Journey into the Violent International Empire of Naples' Organized Crime System. Mondadori, Milano, Italy.

Sciarrone, R. (2011). *Il Patto con la zona grigia, in "Narcomafie,"* Giugno 2011, Libera, Associazione Gruppo Abele Onlus, Torino, Italy.

5. The Informal Economy

The Connection to Organized Crime, White Collar Crime, and Corruption

Peter C. Kratcoski

Introduction: Illustrations of the Informal Economy

Case 1: Rosa Guerraras, a single mother of three children, is employed as a clerk in a government agency. In order to make ends meet, she also works as a babysitter during evenings and weekends. In a good week she often makes $200 USD or so for which she is always paid in cash. These cash payments for her services are not listed on her tax records.

Case 2: Tommy, age 15, started his own lawn mowing/yard cleanup business. He established regular customers, predominantly the house owners in the neighborhood. During the summer months of June, July, and August, he averaged more than $250 USD per month. His customers paid by cash or check. Tommy does not file an income tax return.

Case 3: Terrance Luskey, a retired electrician, generates his income from social security retirement and from a pension provided by the company he was employed with when he retired. He also completes a number of electrical service jobs for which he receives remuneration. The referrals for these assignments come from contractors, clients he worked for before he retired, and by word of mouth. The amount of income earned from these jobs varies a great deal month by month. However, regardless of the amount earned, the money earned is never reported, nor is it included in his tax statements.

Case 4: Al Serafin is a waiter in a restaurant noted for expensive dinners. Al never reports the total gratuities he receives. Al has worked out a formula by which he reports a substantial portion of the gratuities he receives on a good night, perhaps as much as 50%. On slow nights, he reports a much lower proportion, perhaps as low as 25%.

Case 5: In 1927, the U.S. Supreme Court ruled that illegally earned income had to be declared for income taxation. Al Capone was convicted for income tax evasion in 1931 and was sentenced to a federal prison for 11 years and required to pay several hundred thousand dollars in back taxes, with interest.

Case 6: Theresa and William Vanderpool are co-owners of a large home-building company. During a year, they have a number of full-time regular employees, but they also employ a number of workers on a part-time basis and subcontract with various technicians such as plumbers, electricians, and carpenters. When filing income tax returns, the Vanderpools report the salaries and wages of part-time, temporary employees and subcontract workers at a higher figure than the actual payment for increasing the costs of operating the company. This results in the payment of a lower amount of taxes.

No doubt almost every adult in the United States either contributes to the informal economy in some way or at least knows someone who has contributed. An adolescent girl or boy contributes to the informal economy when a home owner hires her or him to watch their children, mow lawns, walk dogs, or feed pets, or for some other services, and pays in cash without any record of the transaction. As adults, our experiences with the informal economy may be related to having an electrician, plumber, or carpenter complete a job "under the table," that is, no record of the work in terms of the amount earned is filed with the tax collection authorities. Other examples include waitresses and waiters who only report a portion of the amount of gratuities they receive and, of course, anyone who deliberately distorts the amount of money earned. When we consider all the contributors to the informal economy, often referred to as the "underground" economy, the loss of revenue in tax collection amounts to billions of dollars each year. Of course, some of those in the examples mentioned earlier are exempt from filing income tax reports because of their small income. In the other examples given, as well as in other more large-scale schemes, the behavior constitutes fraud.

Definitions of Formal and Informal Economies

The formal economy of a nation is defined in several ways, but in general it is the totality of individual and corporate incomes. The sources of the economy include the amount of employment, production, and revenue generated. The formal economy is difficult to measure, but an estimation can be made by knowing the tax bases for various levels of income generated and having some notion of the extent of the informal economy, that is, income generated but not recorded for taxation.

The funds for nongovernmental organizations (NGOs) (2009, pp. 1–2) describes the difference between formal and informal economies from the perspective of an employee. In a formal economy, the worker has a contract with the employer in which job responsibilities and work conditions are predefined.

In addition, the employee has a fixed income, is employed for a specific duration of time, and is a member of an organized group of people who are covered by some form of social security and who are aware, socially and legally, of their rights. In an informal economy, the worker does not have a formal contract with the employer, does not have specified work conditions and fixed hours of work, gets paid irregularly and unevenly, has no formal avenues to express grievances, and does not benefit from a social security system. The perception of the informal economy presented earlier is especially appropriate for developing countries in Africa and Asia as well as other countries around the world that are in a stage of economic development. It implies that when a country is predominately based on an informal economy, the workers are likely to be exploited, particularly when there is a surplus of workers available to fill a limited number of jobs. In addition, the opportunities for the employers to engage in various types of criminal acts, such as bribery, corruption, and tax evasion, are plentiful.

The California Department of Insurance (2014, p. 1) notes that the "Underground Economy is a term that refers to those individuals and businesses that deal with cash and/or use other schemes to conceal their activities and their true tax liability from government licensing, regulatory, and taxing agencies. Underground economy is also referred to as tax evasion, tax fraud, cash pay, tax gap, payments under the table, and off the books." This conception of the informal economy concentrates on the type of questionable business transactions and crimes that in their totality make up the informal economy.

Feige (2003) notes that a variety of terms are used to designate the informal economy, including the gray market unreported economy, clandestine economy, unrecorded market, second market, and the shadow economy. Other more narrow concepts of the informal economy equate it to the "black market," which is a system for the purchase and sale of totally illegal goods and services. However, this concept is too narrow, since not all activities related to the informal economy are illegal and the person who engages in an informal economy transaction may or may not be committing a crime, depending on the circumstances, context, and even the laws of the country in which the transaction takes place.

According to Feige (2003), there are several specific underground economies that can be identified:

- The illegal economy consists of income obtained through economic activities that violate the legal statutes for legitimate forms of commerce, for example, trafficking of illegal drugs, weapons, humans, and others.
- The unreported economy consists of economic activities that are legal but evade the provisions of the codified tax codes. In short, the activity or transaction should have been recorded, but it was not. Perhaps this is the most common way how millions of individuals in the United States engage in the informal economy, thus causing a loss of hundreds of billions of dollars in tax revenue each year (Feige, 2009).
- The informal economy consists of that portion of the economy that is not taxed, nor regulated in any way by any government agency. The informal sector of the economy is characterized by unreported employment in which the income from the employment is hidden from the government agencies responsible for recording the income of workers for the purpose of taxes, social security, and labor laws.
- In a broad sense, the informal economy also includes the substantial amount of money and property owned or generated by corporations or businesses that is not subjected to taxation due to subsidies granted to these corporations, special tax breaks, and other benefits not provided to the common citizen. Kristof (2014) mentions welfare subsidies for private planes, private yachts, hedge funds and private equity, America's biggest banks, as well as large welfare subsidies for U.S. corporations from cities, counties, and states that are trying to attract a corporation to their location or trying to convince a corporation not to move out of their location in which the corporation or business has been in operation.

The so-called "black market" is a portion of the informal economy, and it specifically refers to contraband (goods illegally purchased, stolen, or traded) sold above or below the market price. The transaction may or may not be recorded for tax purposes.

Organized and "White Collar" Crimes Related to the Informal Economy

Any illegal act involving financial gain in which there is no official record of the money received is an act related to the informal economy. The term "official record" should be emphasized, since most organized crime syndicates, including drug-trafficking cartels, keep records of financial transactions. Of course, these records are not open to scrutiny by government agencies and thus the money received from illegal transactions is not taxed. Antinori (2012, p. 151), writing on the relationship of organized crime, the Mafia, and white collar crime in Italy, notes that

> The Mafia economic and financial ecosystem is characterized by a "money-for-money" cycle consisting of (1) accumulating money from illegal activities; (2) using money to pay bribes; (3) creating businesses in new economic sectors; (4) laundering money to produce capital. These steps consolidate crime, politics, and the economy into a system that approaches the systematic planning of public policies.

Although the four-step process described earlier is in reference to the relationship between organized criminal groups, legitimate financial organizations, and government officials in Italy, the process can be applied to most other countries of the world. Thus, more explanation of each step in the process is needed. In the first step, accumulating money from illegal activities, any type of criminal activity that involves making money, would apply. The second step, paying bribes, typically requires some type of corruption between the criminal element and legitimate businesses or government officials. For example, Hetzer (2012, p. 217) states that "... more and more cases show that corruption has become a functional principle even in business conglomerates with traditional and worldwide operations. Some companies are high efficiency centers in which practices of organized crime have become routine in the conduct of business." *Corruption* is generally defined in the context of abuse of power for trying to achieve an unlawful advantage. Hetzer (2012) states that "In principle corruption is a situation in which a person who is responsible for performing certain duties pursues improper or unfair advantages for actions or omissions in the performance of those duties" (p. 218). Not all corrupt activities are motivated by the desire for making financial gain.

Thus, some forms of corruption do not directly pertain to the informal economy. Obviously, if a political figure takes money as a bribe in return for supporting a specific piece of legislation that would benefit the person or organization providing the bribe, that official is not likely to report the income. Thus, it becomes part of the informal economy, unless the money is "laundered" into the formal economy. However, some person may engage in corrupt activities for enhancing their prestige or to illustrate to others how much power they have, or as a favor to someone. For example, a political figure might try to "fix" a traffic ticket for a friend even though there is no apparent payback. In some instances, the motivation for the person engaging in corruption is not apparent. Take, for example, the case of Ben Suarez (*Akron Beacon Journal*, July 6–7, 2004). He was tried for illegally contributing to the political campaigns of two political figures who were running for state offices. The scheme was as follows:

Suarez, owner of Suarez Corporation Industries, was accused of "conspiring to use his top-paid executives as 'straw donors' in order to raise about $200,000 USD in 2011 for the GOP re-election campaign of U.S. Representative Jim Renacci and the failed U.S. Senate bid of Ohio Treasurer Josh Mandel." He was charged with violating federal campaign laws, lying to federal agents, obstruction of justice, and witness tampering (*Akron Beacon Journal*, July 7, 2014, p. A7). Suarez was acquitted of seven of the eight charges, but "he was found guilty of attempting to influence the pending grand jury testimony of his longtime friend, SCI controller Barb Housos, in the summer of 2011 during the FBI probe of the case" (*Akron Beacon Journal*, July 9, 2014, p. A1).

The third step in the money-for-money cycle described by Antinori (2012, p. 151) requires investing money obtained through illegal means into businesses in new economic sectors. This step in the process can be achieved in several ways. For example, money gained illegally (dirty money) can be joined with money obtained legally and invested in a legitimate business. Once the money that is obtained by legal means and the money that is obtained by illegal means are integrated into the flow of money, it is difficult to trace the source of the illegal money.

The fourth step, laundering money to produce capital, requires transforming the illegally obtained money into legitimate money or other assets such as property. Layton (2014, p. 1) describes the practice of money laundering in terms of criminals who disguise the origins of the money obtained through illegal means and try to make it appear as if the money was obtained through legal activities. The three-step money laundering process described by Reuter (2004) includes (1) introducing the illegally obtained money into the financial system, (2) completing complex financial transactions to hide the source of the "dirty" money, and (3) acquiring "clean" money from the investments made with the "dirty" money now integrated into the formal financial system. There are several methods that can be used to hide the source of the illegal money and transform it into legal money. These include depositing smaller amounts of money into several different banks, smuggling the money to another country by creating shell companies and trusts, and layering the money deposits by which legitimate money and money obtained illegally are integrated.

Factors Facilitating the Development and Maintenance of a National Economy

Today, many countries continue to maintain an economy based on the customs and traditions developed many years ago. In addition, there are numerous countries that are in a state of development and are in the process of changing their economy from an informal economy based on custom, informal laws, and traditions to a formal economy based on contracts and regulatory laws. Edelbacher and Theil (2012) indicate that numerous factors, many of them beyond the control of the government, influence the development of the national economy. These include exogenous and endogenous factors. Exogenous factors include the following:

- *Population size*: Countries with huge populations have traditionally been based on the informal economy.
- *Amount and types of natural resources*: Are there natural resources such as coal, oil, and wooded areas that can be developed.
- *Susceptibility to natural disasters*: Such as earthquakes, floods, hurricanes, and droughts.

- *Territorial location*: If the country is isolated and not located on waterways to transport goods to other countries, it is difficult to develop a formal economy.
- *Movement of populations*: As people emigrate from poor countries to the wealthier ones that have a formal economy, often a clash between the traditions, cultures, and religions of different people can be observed.

Endogenous factors affecting the economy include the following:

- *Changes in moral and ethical values*: As the needs of the family and the community are considered less important than serving the wants and needs of the individual, the economy tends to develop around producing more material goods that are not essential for the welfare of the group or the community.
- *Changing values on the rule of law*: If the leaders of a country's industry, corporation executives, bankers, and financial investigators are predominately concerned with making profits for their companies rather than with the welfare of the customers who purchase their products, there will likely be an increase in various forms of financial crimes, including fraud, price-fixing, and corruption, which will ultimately have a negative effect on the economy.

The Informal Economy, Financial Crime, Corruption, and Terrorism

The definition of *white collar crime* has not changed significantly since Sutherland first introduced the concept in 1939. However, the scope and the types of crimes that are included under the concept have expanded significantly. Sutherland (1949) used the term to refer to crimes committed by persons of respectability and high social status in the course of their occupations. White collar crime overlaps with corporate crime as well as financial crime, which can be defined as an act or failure to act relating to the business or financial sector of society that is in violation of the country's laws against criminal activity. The recent developments in electronic communications, transportation, and technology have led to a need for numerous new laws related to financial activities, as well as more specific regulations and involvement by law enforcement agencies.

Research on white collar and financial crime has found that some past practices of leaders of large, illegal industrial corporations, investment firms, and banks were not even considered to be criminal and thus were either ignored or treated as civil law violations. The typical U.S. citizen trusted the financial institutions, and there was a belief that the banks and security institutions were sound and that regulations and mechanisms were in place to avoid the economic disasters that occurred in the 1930s.

However, when such criminal activities as price-fixing, corruption of officials, Ponzi schemes, insider trading, money laundering, and racketeering were shown to be connected to the financing of terrorist activities and posed a threat to national security, the government began a concerted effort to prevent and control financial criminal activity (The 9/11 Commission Report, 2014). The 9/11 Commission Report revealed the fallacies of many of the assumptions the government had about the effectiveness of the laws, regulatory agencies, and security agencies meant for curtailing financial crime and providing financial security for the nation. These deficiencies were most apparent in international matters.

According to Heyman and Ackleson (2010, p. 49), the strategies and responses by government security agencies to terrorist threats were disjointed and often confusing. Recognition of the deficiencies in the policies and resources to respond to terrorist attacks eventually led to the consolidation, reorganization, and expansion of the existing agencies and the creation of new agencies dedicated to protecting homeland security. The National Commission on Terrorist Attacks Upon the United States was created for the specific purpose of determining what went wrong and what could be done to prevent future attacks. Specifically, "The report emphasized the connections of criminal activities of terrorist organizations and other forms of crime, including trafficking of drugs, money and weapons, illegal immigration, human trafficking, forgery of documents and currency, money laundering, and other crimes" (Kratcoski, 2011, p. 375).

The importance of the informal economy in the financing of the operations of terrorist organizations throughout the world cannot be overstated. Edelbacher and Kratcoski (2010) noted that "Many times the same trafficking routes that are used to traffic drugs and humans from Asia to Europe and North American are used for trafficking arms, other military equipment, and money from the United States to Europe and Asia. These goods and money are then used to support terrorist operations" (p. 90).

Recognizing the importance of money laundering in the financing of terrorist operations, a key recommendation of the 9/11 Commission Report was to "Target terrorist money. Identify terrorist financiers and freeze their assets" (The 9/11 Commission Report, 2002, pp. 361–398).

Title III of the USA PATRIOT Act, referred to as the International Money Laundering Abatement and Anti-Terrorism Act of 2001, provided means for the United States to detect and prosecute those involved in money laundering and financing of terrorist groups. In addition to increasing the capacity of investigative and law enforcement agencies to enforce the provisions of the law, it also strengthened and expanded the provisions of the Money Laundering Control Act of 1986 (18 USC: 981), developed procedures for the forfeiture of assets of those suspected of money laundering/and or financing of terrorist activities, and included provisions that would prevent U.S. financial institutions from receiving personal gain through the actions of corrupt foreign officials or sale of stolen assets (Kratcoski, 2012, pp. 376–377).

Relationship of Globalization to the Informal Economy, Fraud, and Corruption

Aas (2007, p. 11) noted that one of the major effects of globalization had been a change in the role of the nation state. The changes apply to control of the borders, migration, global agreements and methods to control transnational crime, new ideologies developing on state control, and many other changes that are directly or indirectly related to the globalization movement. He notes that "The challenges to state sovereignty come, significantly, not only from the increasingly interconnected and autonomous global economy, but also from the global illicit economy."

Onwudiwe (2002, pp. 1–27) developed a world systems theory to demonstrate how a global economy is related to international crime. Based on the notion that all nations are in some way dependent on all other nations in some way, he developed three categories of nations: controlling, semi-controlling, and exploited.

Controlling nations have large amounts of wealth and resources and are in a position to determine the direction of the global economy as well as to exploit the governments and resources of poorer nations. Semi-controlling nations are in the middle; they have some power to exploit poorer nations but are themselves in a position to be exploited by the richer, more powerful nations. The exploited nations are generally poor in terms of natural and economic resources, although some of these countries may have either human resources (cheap labor) or a key natural resource (oil, timber, minerals) that other nations desire. Often their governments and economies are in a state of transition, and thus they are very vulnerable to exploitation by both legitimate and illegitimate enterprises. Often the poorer nations are the most reluctant to give up any of their sovereignty for engaging in cooperative agreements with other nations to control and prevent international crime, since they fear that they might eventually be "swallowed up" by the more powerful countries. The lack of technological and human resources in some of the poorer nations can be an important factor in their attempts to combat crime, both domestic and international.

Edelbacher and Kratcoski (2010, p. 133) point out that after 9/11, organized criminal groups and terrorist organizations have become more efficient and effective by decentralizing their operations, thus making it more difficult for law enforcement officials to destroy them.

Effects of Private and Government Corruption on the Economy

Globalization has led many poverty-stricken countries to develop economically as a result of agreements with foreign nations and the leaders of private corporations establishing trade agreements, locating factories, exporting natural resources, and other ventures. However, in many countries, the long tradition of corruption among the leaders has seriously inhibited economic development. Millard (2003) notes that the strong link between organized crime, terrorist organizations, and corrupt political and corporation leaders has inhibited economic progress. Once the criminal elements have established a foothold in the country and have successfully corrupted government and private enterprise leaders, very little can be done to stop them. Using Mexico as an example, he reports that Mexican citizens automatically assume that the police, government officials, and military leaders are corrupt, and the facts, as established from various reports, confirm the suspicions of the public (Edelbacher and Kratcoski, 2010, p. 112).

Legislation Pertaining to Crimes Related to the Informal Economy

If one uses the definition of *informal economy* as income that has not been recorded for taxation and is not exempt from taxation, and thus it should have been recorded as income, almost all crimes committed by persons or organizations engaged in illegal acts under the state and federal criminal codes would be subject to enforcement by local and state law enforcement agencies.

The first major legislation designed to combat organized crime was the Racketeer Influenced and Corrupt Organizations Act, commonly referred to as RICO, passed by the U.S. Congress in 1970. Champion (2005) defines RICO as "A federal statute permitting law enforcement officers to charge or sue criminal enterprises or organizations, passed by Congress in 1970 to attack and prosecute organized crime. The Act also authorizes both civil and criminal assets forfeiture" (p. 212) This law has been modified and expanded several times during the latter part of the twentieth century. While it was originally passed to combat racketeering, that is, organized crime groups using legitimate organizations as a front for illegal activities, revisions of the original legislation led to the inclusion of many other state and federal crimes, including gambling, murder, kidnapping, extortion, arson, robbery, drug trafficking, bribery, counterfeiting, theft, embezzlement, fraud, money laundering, and slavery (Free Public Record Search, Racketeering/RICO, 2014, p. 1).

A new and far-reaching legislation was passed by the U.S. Congress after the 9/11 terrorist attack on U.S. soil. While this legislation was geared toward preventing terrorism and establishing the mechanisms to improve and maintain the security of the United States, some of the major provisions applied directly to organized crime and financial crime.

The USA PATRIOT Act

The Uniting and Strengthening America by Providing Appropriate Tools Required to Intercept and Obstruct Terrorism (USA PATRIOT) Act of 2001 has 10 titles. Nine of the 10 titles or sections of the act "pertain to domestic security, the collection of electronic evidence, regulation of and restriction on banking activities suspected of financing terrorist activities, increased security of U.S. borders, detention of suspected terrorist, sharing of intelligence by federal law enforcement agencies, adding new laws for curtailing terrorist activities, criminalization of cyberterrorism and authorization of searches of suspected terrorist mail" (Kratcoski, 2012, p. 376). The 10th title clarifies various definitions of terms and provides for grants for training and program implementation for state and local law enforcement agencies. Of particular significance is Title III of the USA PATRIOT Act, since it directly applies to organized crime and financial crime. Title III, among other important provisions, includes measures to "provide the means for the U.S. to prevent, detect, and prosecute those involved in international money laundering and the financing of terrorism" and "prevents U.S. financial institutions from receiving personal gain through the actions of corrupt foreign officials or sales of stolen assets" (Kratcoski, 2012, pp. 376–377). Another important section of Title III is to create the Financial Crimes Enforcement Network, which set up the mechanisms for federal, state, and local law enforcement agencies to share and exchange intelligence pertaining to the identification of possible criminal activity (Kratcoski, 2012, p. 379). The U.S. Congress authorized the creation of the Department of Homeland Security in 2013. Kratcoski (2012) states that "The overall mission of the department is to have federal, state, and local law enforcement and investigative agencies coordinate their activities by cooperating in investigations of all matter pertaining to U.S. security" (p. 385).

Legislation Pertaining to Financial Crime

The worldwide financial crisis that began in 2007 brought about new legislations and revisions of existing laws pertaining to commercial and investment banking and the protection of consumer rights in the United States. Many of the regulations of the U.S. Securities & Exchange Commission (SEC) pertaining to investments were strengthened, and others that were not being enforced were now strictly enforced by the SEC. The Dodd–Frank Wall Street Reform and Consumer Protection Act was passed by the U.S. Congress in 2010. Its main purpose was to "promote the financial stability of the United States by improving accountability and transparency in the financial system, to end 'too big to fail' institutions, to protect the U.S. taxpayer by ending bailouts, to protect consumers from abusive financial services practices, and for other purposes" (H.R. 4073-8//: www.sec.gov/).

Law Enforcement Efforts Directed toward the Prevention of Organized and Financial Crimes

Sedgwick (2008) stated that all five of the U.S. Government Departments—Justice, Defense, Homeland Security, Treasury, and State—were involved in various cooperative programs that were directed toward preventing and curtailing organized crime in 90 countries located in various parts of the world. In addition, the federal investigating and policing agencies cooperate with 18,000 local and state policing agencies by assisting in task forces directed toward the investigations and prosecutions of members of organized crime and terrorist organizations.

Almost all the federal law enforcement agencies as well as the state and local agencies are involved in some way in the investigation of crimes related to the informal economy. In this section, several of the federal agencies that investigate and arrest those who violate federal laws most closely related to the informal economy will be highlighted.

The Federal Bureau of Investigation (FBI, 2014) has the responsibility for investigating federal crimes that fall within its jurisdiction. In addition to its 56 field offices and 400 satellite offices located throughout the United States, there are legal attaché offices attached to the U.S. embassies in more than 50 countries. The FBI Units of Criminal Priorities Division focus on public corruption, civil rights violations, organized crime, white collar crime, violent crime, and major theft.* The Organized Crime Unit, recognizing the danger international organized crime presents to the U.S. society, has expanded its mission in recent years to focus more on working with law enforcement officials from other countries to prevent international criminal organizations from establishing a foothold in the United States.

The White Collar Crime Unit of the FBI investigates all forms of fraud and other illegal activities relating to businesses, securities, and government organizations, including bankruptcy, money laundering, illegal corporate activities, health care fraud, hedge-fund fraud, insurance fraud, mortgages fraud, and securities fraud. In addition, this unit is responsible for investigating identity theft, price-fixing, public corruption, antitrust violations, Internet and computer fraud, and many other crimes related to business and government activities.†

The U.S. Drug Enforcement Administration (DEA) has the responsibility for enforcing all federal laws pertaining to controlled substance laws and regulations. This agency, along with the FBI, is directly involved with the suppression of organized crime. Several of the primary tasks of the DEA are as follows:

- Investigation and preparation for the prosecution of major violators of controlled substance laws operating at interstate and international levels
- Investigation and preparation for the prosecution of criminals and drug gangs who perpetrate violence in our communities and terrorize citizens through fear and intimidation
- Management of a national drug intelligence program in cooperation with federal, state, local, and foreign officials to collect, analyze, and disseminate strategic and operational drug intelligence information
- Seizure and forfeiture of assets derived from, traceable to, or intended to be used for illicit drug trafficking
- Enforcement of the provisions of the Controlled Substance Act as they pertain to the manufacture, distribution, and dispensing of legally produced controlled substances
- Coordination and cooperation with federal, state, and local law enforcement officials on mutual drug enforcement efforts and the enhancement of such efforts through the exploitation of potential interstate and international investigations beyond local or limited federal jurisdictions and resources
- Coordination and cooperation with federal, state, and local agencies, as well as with foreign

* FBI (2014:1), White Collar Crime Unit, http://www.fbi/gov/about-us/investigate. Retrieved August 10, 2014.

† http:www.fbi./gov/about-us/investigate/corruption. Retrieved 8/10/2014.

governments, in programs designed to reduce the availability of illicit abuse-type drugs on the U.S. market through reinforcement methods such as crop eradication, crop substitution, and training of foreign officials
- Responsibility, under the policy guidance of the Secretary of State and the U.S. ambassadors, for all programs associated with drug law enforcement counterparts in foreign countries
- Liaison with the United Nations, Interpol, and other organizations on matters relating to international drug control programs.

The U.S. Secret Service has several missions, including safeguarding the U.S. financial infrastructure and preserving the integrity of the economy and protecting the nation's leaders. The strategic plan of the Secret Service is multifaceted and is focused on engaging in the cooperative planning and programming with other federal and local law enforcement agencies in preventing, detecting, investigating, and mitigating the effects of financial crime; improving and expanding its ability to combat criminal operations related to the counterfeiting of currency, personal identification documents (pass boards), and other documents (securities); and using the most advanced technology, research, and intelligence to develop the most advanced plans to reduce the risk in safeguarding protected persons, sites, and events in which these protected persons participate.

The Financial Crime Division of the Secret Service is responsible for investigating fraud committed against financial institutions, access device fraud, fraudulent use of credit cards, personal identification numbers, computer password fraud, and fraud related to computer systems that are of "federal interest" (Taylor et al., 2006, p. 265).

In order to achieve the goals of the several dimensions of the mission, considerable cooperation with other investigative agencies, both at home and abroad, is needed. When the U.S. Secret Service was included under the structure of the Department of Homeland Security, it was given the responsibility of "organizing task forces of federal, state, and local law enforcement personnel to address international and domestic computer fraud." This task is completed by "providing educational briefings and seminars on financial and electronic crimes to state, federal, local, and foreign law enforcement partners to expand investigative skills and capabilities" (U.S. Secret Service, 2011, p. 9).

The Postal Inspection Service, a component of the U.S. Postal Service, was created to "exercise investigative jurisdiction over more than 200 postal related statutes pertaining to 'assaults' against the service or its employees and the misuse of the national postal system." (Ackerman, 1999, p. 45.) In addition to investigating those crimes that directly affect the Postal Service, such as mail theft, possession of stolen mail, mailed bombs and narcotics, and the counterfeiting of stamps, the agency also shares responsibility with other federal agencies in the investigation of embezzlement, child pornography, money laundering, various types of fraud, identity theft, violation of laws pertaining to hazardous materials, and child pornography.

Effects of Legislation and Law Enforcement on Crimes Pertaining to the Informal Economy

The expanded efforts to prevent and control criminal activities related to the informal economy through legislation and enhanced law enforcement have been rather successful when the increase in prosecutions and convictions for such crimes as fraud, tax evasion, and corruption is considered. Between 2000 and 2010, more than three-quarters of a million offenders were sentenced for federal crimes in the United States (Radnoisky et al., 2014, p. 16). In addition to the prosecutions and convictions of offenders by the Departments of Justice, Treasury, and Homeland Security, thousands of offenders were investigated by various government regulatory agencies. Radnoisky et al. remark: "Government agencies of all stripes have become the front-line enforcers for many of the laws Congress has written for the past four decades. Not only do the agencies enforce these laws, they also write voluminous regulations needed to put the laws into effect and govern federal programs" (Radnofsky et al., 2014, p. 14).

Regardless of the enhanced efforts to combat financial crimes and other crimes related to the informal or shadow economy, there is still a lack of commitment because of the large number of people who either engage in criminal activities, know someone who engages in criminal activities relating to the informal economy, or benefit from such criminal acts. For example, it is difficult to even estimate the number of people who have purchased "black market" merchandise at one time or another for a lower price than the price would have been if purchased in a retail store, or who have paid a person "under the table" for a service, knowing full well that the person providing the service will not report the income to the tax authorities.

In regard to large-scale financial crimes committed by corporations and business leaders and powerful political leaders, many think of such practices as price-fixing, bribing government officials from foreign countries, violations of labor laws, insider trading on the stock exchange, accepting "kickbacks," making illegal contributions to political candidates, and other questionable activities as sound business practices, not criminal acts. Furthermore, the power of lobbyists to influence federal, state, and local politicians through one means or another and to convince these politicians to support questionable legislation favorable to their clients is well known.

In addition to the aforementioned factors, the laws and rules pertaining to the types of financial transactions made by banks and investment firms are often not clear and difficult to interpret. For example, Crovitz (2011) noted "Federal prosecutors tried and failed to bring criminal cases relating to mortgage-backed securities against AIG, Countrywide Financial, Washington Mutual and Goldman Sachs" (p. A17). In an interview with a former FBI investigator for financial crimes, David Cardona said that "the reasons prosecutors can't prove criminal intent is that in many cases bankers were simply trading in compliance with the regulations governing them." He recommended a more deliberate targeting on banks and other security agencies that are clearly fraudulent in operations.

Another factor that hinders the investigations and prosecutions of those involved in large-scale financial criminal activity is that the resources available to leaders of financial and corporate institutions generally far exceed the resources available to federal and local law enforcement agencies to take on the "big people."

Law Enforcement Agencies Responsible for Investigating Crimes Related to the Informal Economy

A number of U.S. federal, state, and local law enforcement and investigative agencies have had considerable success in the investigation, prosecution, and conviction of individuals and organizations involved in organized and financial crimes. There have been headline stories of leaders of powerful corporations and financial magnates being convicted for crimes and sentenced to prison.

The following are examples of various corporations, criminal gang leaders, and individuals that have been either criminally or civilly prosecuted or both:

> Bridgestone Corp. has agreed to plead guilty in a price-fixing conspiracy and pay a $425 million criminal fine in a Justice Department probe that has swept the automotive parts industry. (Yost, 2014, p. A9)

> For years, John Junker enjoyed the prestige of running the Fiesta Bowl organization, pulling in a six-figure salary, mingling with powerful people and taking advantage of the perks of the job such as spending $33,000 USD in bowl money on his birthday bash. (Billeaud, *Akron Beacon Journal*, July 10, 2014, p. D1)

> On being fired as Fiesta Bowl Chief executive for running an illegal campaign contribution scheme, "His troubles were punctuated Thursday when he was sentenced to eight months in federal prison for participating in a scheme in which bowl employees made illegal campaign contributions to politicians and were reimbursed by the nonprofit bowl." (Billeaud, 2014, p. D1)

> **Nashville, Tennessee**: The truck stop company owned by Cleveland Browns owner Jimmy Haslam and Tennessee Gov. Bill Haslam has agreed to pay a $92 million penalty for cheating customers out of promised rebates and discounts, authorities announced Monday. In an agreement with the U.S. Attorney's Office for the Eastern District of Tennessee, Pilot Flying J has accepted responsibility for the criminal conduct of its employees, 10 of whom have pleaded guilty to participating in the scheme. (Loller, 2014, p. A10)

> **Washington**: An Army program meant to increase the number of recruits during the Iraq and Afghanistan wars developed into an illegal free-for-all that could cost taxpayers close to $100 million, military

investigators say, describing new details of what they called a long-running scheme among National Guard recruiters that went undetected for years. (Cooper, 2014, p. A5)

New York: J.P. Morgan Chase & Co., already beset by costly legal woes, will pay more than $2.5 billion for ignoring obvious warning signs of Bernard Madoff's massive Ponzi scheme, authorities said Tuesday. The nation's largest bank will forfeit a record $1.7 billion to settle criminal charges, plus pay an additional $543 million to settle civil claims for victims. It also will pay a $350 million civil penalty for what the Treasury Department called "critical and widespread deficiencies" in its programs to prevent money laundering and other suspicious activity. It took until after the arrest of Madoff, one of the worst crooks this office has ever seen, for J.P. Morgan to alert authorities to what the world already knew. (Hays, 2014, p. A7)

Cleveland: John A. Miller, 53, was charged with one count of conspiracy to commit mail fraud, nine counts of mail fraud, three counts of money laundering in connection with a scheme to defraud his company, according to the U.S. Attorney's Office. (Farkas, 2014, p. A5)

Cleveland: A man convicted of masterminding a $100 million, cross-country Navy veterans fraud was sentenced to 28 years in prison on Monday. The Ohio attorney general's office which handled his trial, asked the judge in a filing last week to sentence him to 41 years in prison. (Sheeran, 2014, p. B10)

Bloomberg News: U.S. authorities have dismantled one of the most sophisticated and prolific counterfeiting rings in U.S. history, the Justice Department said. The organization was responsible for more than $77 million in fake $100 bills that were distributed up and down the U.S. East Coast since at least 1999, according to court papers. "This case is a perfect example of the Secret Service combining traditional investigative methods with the cutting-edge technology to resolve a long-term and complex counterfeiting currency investigation," Secret Service Director Julia Pierson said in a news release. (*Bloomberg News*, 2014, p. B10)

Conclusion

An exact definition of the "informal economy" is difficult to develop. The concept, along with several other concepts such as the "hidden economy," "gray market," "shadow economy," "second market," and "underground economy," has been used to designate that part of the total economy of a nation that is concealed for tax liability from government agencies responsible for recording and collecting taxable income.

Determining the full extent of the "informal economy," in terms of who participates and the amount of money involved, with any degree of accuracy is also difficult. As shown in this chapter, it is certain that when using a very broad definition, millions of Americans participate in the informal economy in some way and the amount of money involved is billions of dollars.

While some transactions related to the informal economy are legal, the vast majority are illegal. Any form of property crime in which the proceeds gained from the crime were not recorded would constitute a crime related to the informal economy. Even violent crimes, for example, being paid for committing a murder or armed robbery, are part of the informal economy since the proceeds from the crime are hidden.

The primary focus of this chapter was on the effect organized crime and financial crime has on the national economy and the security of the United States. Although some of the methods used to commit the crimes may vary, the overall effects of the criminal activities, in terms of weakening the national economy and creating mistrust of public officials, corporate, and financial leaders are the same when the public becomes aware that some of these officials and leaders have become corrupted by accepting bribes or engaging in other illegal practices.

The final section of this chapter is devoted to an explanation and discussion of the various legislations that have been passed by the U.S. Congress to combat organized crime and financial crime, as well as the activities of domestic and foreign terrorist organizations, which have been linked directly or indirectly to organized criminal groups and financial institutions.

In addition, the functions of several key federal agencies, including the FBI, DEA, Secret Service, Postal Inspection Service, and the Department of Homeland Security, are considered, as well as the results of several successful investigations undertaken by these agencies.

References

Aas, K. (2007). *Globalization and Crime*, Los Angeles, CA: Sage Publications.

Ackerman, T. (1999). *Guide to Careers in Federal Law Enforcement*, Traverse City, MI: Sage.

Antinori, A. (2012). Organized crime, the mafia, white collar crime, and corruption. *Financial Crimes: A Threat to Global Security*, eds. M. Edelbacher, P. Kratcoski, and M. Theil, Boca Raton, FL: CRC Press, pp. 147–162.

Bloomberg News. (July 9, 2014) U.S. indicts 13 people in counterfeiting ring, *Akron Beacon Journal*, D3.

California State Department of Insurance. (2014). Bureau of Investigation. https//oag.cagov/bi. (Accessed on July 15, 2014.)

Champion, D. (2005). *The American Dictionary of Criminal Justice*, 3rd ed., Los Angeles, CA: Roxbury Publishing Company.

Cooper, H. (February 2014). Fraud in Army could cost U.S. $100 million, *Akron Beacon Journal*, A5.

Crovitz, G. (2011). Federal prosecutors tried and failed to bring criminal cases against AIG, Countrywide, Washington Mutual and Goldman Sachs, *Wall Street Journal*, A17.

Farkas, K., (July 2014). U.S. charges Solon man with $1.5 million fraud, *Akron Beacon Journal*, A5.

FBI. (2014). Legal attache' offices. http:// www.fbi.gov/contact/ Legat/legat.htm. Retrieved August 11, 2014.

FBI. (2014:1). White Collar Crime Unit. http://www.fbi/gov/about-us/investigate. Retrieved August 10, 2014.

Feige, E. (2003). Defining and estimating underground and informal economies: The new institutional economics approach. *World Development*, Elsevier 18:7.

Feige, E. (2009). The underground economy and the currency enigma. *Public Finance (Finances Publiques)* 49 (Suppl): 119–136.

Feige, E. (2011). New estimates of U.S. currency abroad, the domestic money supply and the unreported economy. MPRA Paper 34778, Munich, University of Munich Library.

Free Public Record Search. (2014, 1). Racketeering/RICO. http:// criminal-charges/racketeering-rico.html?DCMP=GOO-CRIM_Racketeering-RiCODefine&HBX_PK=rico+law+d. Retreived August 10, 2014.

Funds for NGO. (2009, 1–3). What is the difference between formal and informal economy? Retrieved August 6, 2014.

Edelbacher, M. and Kratcoski, P. (2010). Protecting the borders in a global society: An Austrian and American Perspective. *Border Security in the Al Qaeda Era*, eds. J. Winterdyk and K. Sunberg, Boca Raton, FL: CRC Press, pp. 77–119.

Edelbacher, M. and Theil, M. (2012). White collar crime. *Financial Crime: A Threat to Global Security,* M. Edelbacher, P. Kratcoski, and M. Theil. (eds.), Boca Raton, FL: CRC Press, pp. 83–117.

Hays, T. (January 8, 2014). Madoff scheme will cost JP Morgan, *Akron Beacon Journal*, A5.

Hetzer, W. (2012). Financial crisis or financial crime? *Financial Crimes: A Threat to Global Security,* eds. M. Edelbacher, P. Kratcoski, and M. Theil, Boca Raton, FL: CRC Press, pp. 217–264.

Heyman, J. and Ackleson, J. (2010). United States border security after 9/11. *Border Security in the Al Qaeda Era*, eds. J. Winterdyk and K. Sundberg, Boca Raton, FL: CRC Press, pp. 77–120.

H.R.4173-6, http://www.sec.gov/.

H.R. 4173-8, http:// www.sec.gov/.

Kratcoski, P and Kratcoski, L. (2010). Police without borders: An overview. *Police without Borders: The Fading Distinction between Local and Global*, eds. C. Roberson, D. Das, and J. Singer, Boca Raton, FL: CRC Press, pp. 1–26.

Kratcoski, P. (2011). Legislative and programming initiatives to prevent and control financial crimes in the United States. *Financial Crimes: A Threat to Global Security*, eds. M. Edelbacher, P. Kratcoski, and M. Theil, Boca Raton, FL: CRC Press, pp. 373–389.

Kristof, N. (2014). Welfare that makes for wealthy takers, *Akron Beacon Journal*, A1.

Layton, J. (2014). How money laundering works. How stuff works, http:// money.howstuffworks.com/money-laundering.htm. Retrieved August 6, 2014.

Loller, T. (July 15, 2014). Pilot to pay $92 million, *Akron Beacon Journal*, A1.

McCarthy, J. (2014). Company controller testifies against Suarez, *Akron Beacon Journal*, July 1:A1

Millard, G. (2003). The forgotten victims of narco-terrorism in Latin America. *Meeting the Challenges of Global Terrorism*, eds. D. Das and P. Kratcoski, Lanham, MD: Lexington Books, pp. 159–170.

Onwudiwe, L. (2002). *The Globalization of Terrorism*. Hampshire, UK: Ashgate.

Radnofsky, L., Fields, G., and Emshwilller, J. (2014). Federal police swell to enforce a widening array of criminal laws. *Wall Street Journal*, CCLVIII(143), 1, 2.

Reuter, P. (2004). Chasing dirty money. http:// bookstore.piie.com/ book-store//381.html. Peterson. Retrieved August 6, 2014.

Sedgwick, J. (2008). International challenges to law enforcement: Policing in the global age. Key Note Address at the *15th Annual International Police Executive Symposium*, Cincinnati, OH, May 12–16, 2008.

Sheeran, T. (June 2014). Man is given 28 years in Navy charity scam, *Akron Beacon Journal*, B10.

Sutherland, E.H. (1949). *White Collar Crime*. New York: Dryden Press.

Taylor, R., Caeti, T., Loper, D., and Tritsch, E. (2006). *Digital Crime and Digital Terrorism*. Upper Saddle River, NJ: Prentice Hall.

The 9/11 Commission, 2002. *The 9/11 Commission Report*. New York: W.W. Norton and Company.

U.S. 107th Congress, USA Patriot Act of 2001. Title III: Sections 301–377. Washington, DC: U.S. Government Printing Office.

U.S. 107th Congress, Dodd-Frank Wall Street Reform & Consumer Protection Act. H.R. 4173-6, 4173-8. Washington, DC: U.S. Government Printing Office.

U.S. Secret Service. (2011). *Strategic Plan*. Washington, DC: Department of Homeland Security. www.secretservice.gov.

6. The Insurance Industry and the Informal Economy

Michael Theil

Introduction

Economic activities that are not recorded by authorities are known under a plethora of designations, such as shadow, informal, hidden, black, underground, gray, clandestine, illegal, and parallel (Fleming et al., 2000, p. 387). Most of these designations imply, to various degrees, that such activities are negative. This, however, does not necessarily mean that they are also illegal. As has been discussed thoroughly elsewhere, it is not clear without ambiguity where to draw the line between *official* and *unofficial* activities (Fleming et al., 2000, p. 388 ff).

Since the following is devoted to an analysis of insurance business economics, we will leave this definition to others: in the end, the question is a legal one, often a matter of court judgments and therefore not in the scope of an economist. Rather, we will point out situations where potentially illegal activities in the area of insurance business may occur, or describe cases that already have occurred. In doing so, we prepare the ground for an approach to capture the interaction between insurance and informal economic activities.

To this end, we start discussing circumstances where an insurer himself or herself is the main actor. Next, we will go into situations, where service providers in the insurance business other than the insurer himself or herself carry out illegal activities. Finally, we refer to interconnections to insurance fraud—all that can be seen as some sort of shadow economy within the core insurance business. However, there is also an area, where illegal activities are undertaken in some other part of the economy, but have implications to insurance business. We will discuss this in a later section. Finally, we provide conclusions of what we can learn from an analysis of insurance in a shadow economy context.

Insurers Carrying Out Illegal Activities

In the first scenario we consider an insurance company that is carrying out informal activities. We will first analyze primary insurers as a prototypical form of an insurance company and discuss other forms subsequently.

Primary insurers are such that have a direct contractual relationship to policyholders. As for all insurance companies, their core business is accepting risks that are in such a way transferred from the insured to the insurer and organizing risk portfolios in a manner that those portfolios become balanced. Another area is capital investment. Since insurance premiums are most usually paid in advance, and potential compensations for loss are paid in, sometimes near, sometimes remote, future, insurance companies have very high amounts of capital to invest. Naturally, those amounts vary by type of insurance. For instance, most life insurance contracts are long-term businesses, possibly lasting for decades and involving considerable sums of money. Contrary to this, and as an opposite example, travel insurance is usually taken out for days or weeks of a journey, involving much smaller amounts of money. As we can see, capital investment is in such sense secondary that it requires insurance transfer and payment of premium in advance. Simply put, balancing of portfolios means that most insurance contracts do not result in any claims at all. A balancing effect can also be achieved in that you have a very large fraction of insurance contracts with very small claims and very few contracts with relatively high claims. Typical loss ratios (claims in relationship to total premiums earned) are 65%–75%, underlining the importance of this part of insurance business (Versicherungsverband Österreich, 2012, p. 127 ff).

Since primary insurance companies are economic entities involving very large amounts of money, and since it has proven necessary to protect customers against insurance companies, because the former have a considerable weaker level of information and much less market power, primary insurers are subject to extensive supervision (Farny, 2011, p. 108 ff; Theil, 2012, p. 269 ff; for example, §4 Versicherungsaufsichtsgesetz). In order to establish an insurance company, considerable amounts of your own capital are required together with a business plan that makes the evolvement of a sustainable healthy insurance business believable. That makes it unattractive to set up an insurance company for purposes other than a long-term business, and it becomes very unlikely that an insurance company as a whole is determined to serve illegal purposes.

Nevertheless, primary insurers may still serve illegal purposes as part of their business. Turning again to transfer of risk as their core business, insurers may, for instance, accept overrated risks. A quite simple example in property and casualty insurance would be to promise cover for an item (or building, liability, or any other) in the amount of, say, 150,000 euros, while it is only worth 100,000 euros. In case of loss, the insured would then receive an excessively high compensation. Analogous cases in health insurance were to accept coverage for diseases that are commonly excluded (for instance, lung cancer for smokers).

Given the previously described nature of the insurance business, such activities must be on a (very) small scale relative to total business, since portfolios would become unbalanced very soon. But even on a small scale, with accepting very many, but only slightly overrated risks, they may be attractive for criminals, because by and by, they may involve high sums of money. An opposite approach, to accept a few, highly overrated risks, does not appear promising: claims above particular sizes are usually subject to additional internal revision, thus bringing additional risk of detection. Having said this, it becomes clear that insurance lines in retail business are more suitable for such activities rather than situations in which the insurance taker is a company.

A second way for primary insurers for illegal activities in risk transfer may be to charge inappropriate risk premiums. Generally, the starting point in calculating any insurance premium is the so-called risk-adequate or fair premium. That is the amount of money that reflects expected individual (as opposed to collective) loss. Furthermore, security loading, loading for non-risk-related costs, and profit margin are added. The insurance company is very much interested to implement this calculation procedure, since it results in what we call portfolio neutrality. That means that adding or removing risks to and from a portfolio, respectively, does not have an effect upon this particular portfolio's balance.

However, price discrimination is nevertheless part of an insurance company's set of marketing tools. In the given context, this implies that in some cases premiums will differ from those previously described in size. This is nothing else as every other enterprise does, for instance, to attract new groups of customers, and certainly not illegal. But it becomes problematic, if this deviation becomes excessive. Charging exorbitantly low premiums is in effect largely equivalent to accepting overrated risks, as we have already discussed. So we will turn to a case, where excessively high premiums are charged, now.

The following (potential) case has been in discussion for several years: The marginal tax burden of an economic entity may be higher than that of a given insurance company, especially if the latter is situated in a low-tax country. In order to transfer money from one (high-tax) country to another (low-tax), insurance with excessively high premiums may be an appropriate vehicle. In particular, enterprises in the construction and in the glass industry were suspects in these cases. The insurance companies involved were to a large part or even as a whole owned by the respective enterprises. It seems that these discussions remained speculative; at least there has not been any further report on that. To give an impression concerning mere numbers, there were between 28.9 and 30.9 m risks insured in property/casualty insurance lines in the past years—in the small country of Austria (Versicherungsverband Österreich, 2012, p. 103).

The second most important area of insurance business is capital investment, a multibillion € amount (Versicherungsverband Österreich, 2012, p. 110, for Austria). A significant share of investments (more than 6%)

is in real estate, and quite often, related transactions have been a matter of suspect, in particular that objects have been sold at too low, or bought at too high, prices (Hodoschek, 2014). Nothing specific has been reported over the past years, but since the mere amount of money is that high, there is certainly some appeal to enrich oneself.

Unlike primary insurers that conduct business directly with policyholders, reinsurance companies offer insurance for other insurers. Until recently, reinsurers have been supervised only to a very small extent. By now, supervision is similar to that of primary insurance companies, with some facilitation concerning the business plan (Farny, 2011, p. 128 ff).

In principle, this field of business offers the same possibilities for criminal conduct as discussed before. A problem area of some importance has been reinsurers owned in part or wholly by a single other enterprise. Such constructs have been suspects to tax evasion, when the reinsurer was located in low-tax countries, like the Bahamas or the Channel Islands. The problem appears to remain unsolved (Pine and Wright, 1986, p. 14; Kenealy, 2013, p. 37).

From what has been stated above, it is obvious that at least some collusion with people outside of a particular insurance company is necessary. For instance, concerning overrated risks, it needs an insurance buyer to participate and some flow back of money to people within the insurance company. For the tax-savings scenario, at least two companies will be involved. Their collusion is in most cases easier to implement, when they have the same ownership. For fraud when buying or selling investments, there will also be outsiders involved.

Illegal Activities by Other Participants in the Insurance Process

In this section we consider economic entities that are not insurers themselves, but play a role in the insurance process. As we have described previously, the core business of an insurer is to get risks transferred from the policyholders and to balance them within its portfolio, which we call the risk process.

Other elements of the insurance business, ranging from marketing, business acquisition, and loss assessment to claims settlement may be carried out by the insurance company itself, but also be sourced out to other companies. These are the cases we will discuss in the following.

A wide range of various forms of intermediaries engages itself in insurance sales. Their function is not only to acquire business, but in many cases also to risk assessment. Generally, the same problems with overrated risks may arise in such situations, similar to the case, when the insurer does risk assessment on his or her own. However, since portfolios are continually monitored by the insurer, who has a good statistical knowledge base, such activities cannot be concealed without collusion on the part of the insurer.

Intermediaries sometimes also collect premiums. In a recent case, intermediaries promised policyholders to pay all follow-up premiums (i.e., the insured pays only the first premium), a model that totaled in a 5.6-million euro loss within a single year. The matter is currently on trial (http://wien.orf.at/news/stories/2626452/, accessed on January 2, 2014).

Another function that is regularly sourced out is that of loss assessment. The intermediary often has conflicting interests, since policyholders are disappointed when loss is not at all or not entirely covered and blame the intermediary for that. He then might be tempted to settle the matter in favor of the policyholder. Again, any unusual behavior carried out more often than just a single time, will leave its traces in the insurer's statistics. Sometimes, for instance, for specific losses, loss settlement is completely carried out by specialized companies. That makes it very difficult for the insurer to detect anomalies on a statistical basis and makes him quite vulnerable.

The Insurer as the Damaged Party: Insurance Fraud

Insurance fraud is a presumably widespread phenomenon, presumably, because the actual dimensions are unknown: estimates are in a wide range from 10% to 40% of claimed losses (Edelbacher and Theil, 2008, p. 19, for a synopsis).

Insurance fraud appears in the following most important forms (Fechtenhauer, 1999, p. 205; Nell/Schiller, 2002, p. 2 f; Tennyson, 2002, p. 35; Viane and Dedene, 2004, p. 314 f):

- Damage is caused deliberately.
- Damage is faked.
- An actual damage is utilized, either by exaggerating the size of the loss or by redefining the type of loss that would remain uninsured otherwise.
- The insurance contract is concluded illegally.

Examples for situations where damage is caused intentionally are manifold: one of the most prominent examples is that of the sinking of the ship Lucona (http://en.wikipedia.org/wiki/Lucona; Edelbacher and Theil, 2008, p. 112 f). The ship has been sunken deliberately by use of a time bomb; furthermore, scrap metal was on board, instead of valuable machinery. Therefore, the sinking of Lucona is also an example for other forms of insurance fraud. Most notably, it took quite a long time to uncover this crime, not only because proofs were difficult to supply, but also because highly influential politicians were involved and the case was very complex.

More day-to-day examples often involve motor vehicles. For instance, taxi drivers staged several hundred accidents. In reaction to that, insurers set up an information system in order to detect such kind of crime more efficiently (Edelbacher and Theil, 2008, p. 115). Ethnic groups, sometimes people from neighboring villages on the Balkans, cooperated in producing car accidents, sometimes during illegal car races (Edelbacher and Theil, 2008, p. 120). International criminal gangs were charged to have staged several hundred accidents with some complexity, for instance, with a car registered in Italy, a German driver, and the accident happening on a Hungarian motorway (Edelbacher and Theil, 2008, p. 125; http://www.oe24.at /oesterreich/ chronik/wien/Versicherungsbetrueger-fingierten-300-Unfaelle/109183074).

In a very prominent case of faked events of damage, the CEO of an insurance company in person produced wrong damage reports. A large network of people participated in these activities (Edelbacher and Theil, 2008, p. 114). More commonplace are cases where people organize groups to produce incorrect damage reports, for instance, motorcyclists (Edelbacher and Theil, 2008, p. 114 f) or workers in a garage (Edelbacher and Theil, 2008, p. 117 f). Cases committed only by a single person appear rare and nonrecurring (Edelbacher and Theil, 2008, p. 123 f). Some cases involve nonexistent vehicles or life insurance claims with counterfeit death certificates (Edelbacher and Theil, 2008, p. 116 ff).

Since insurance companies work in a similar manner everywhere in the world, fraud against private insurers does also happen in a similar way. Concerning social insurance, the case is quite different: social security systems vary considerably and so does fraud in social insurance.

Unemployment insurance may be defrauded when the offender is formally unemployed, but derives his income from other sources (Edelbacher and Theil, 2008, p. 118 f). This is often the case, when someone is actually working in the shadow economy, but remains unemployed officially.

The construction industry is especially notorious for practices, where large numbers of workers are not employed officially; the company does not pay social security contributions and goes bankrupt soon after having received payment from the principal. Often, large and complex networks of companies are established to shadow those practices (http://wirtschaftsblatt.at/home/nachrichten/europa/1545884/Grossrazzia-wegen-Betrug-am-Bau; http://de.wikipedia.org/wiki/Kettenbetrug; http://diepresse.com/home/wirtschaft/economist/1466444/Betrugsnetz-von-Baufirmen-aufgeflogen).

In statutory health insurance, people often receive benefits for pretended sicknesses: examples range from aid for the blind (http://www.spiegel.de/wirtschaft/soziales/sozialbetrug-in-griechenland-die-insel-der-scheinblinden-a-912222.html) and retirement pensions for deceased people (http://www.fr-nline.de/schuldenkrise/rentenbetrug-griechenlandzahlte-acht-milliarden-euro-an-tote,1471908,11083270.html) to fraud by using others' or counterfeit social security cards (http://kurier.at/chronik/oesterreich/betrug-aerzte-verursachten-millionenschaden/3.711.340).

How the Shadow Economy Affects the Insurance Business

The previously described fraudulent activities with respect to social insurance have already shown that the shadow economy affects insurance. Specifically, when illegally working, no contributions are paid and no benefits, be it for unemployment, sickness, or accidents, can be drawn from this activity.

When people still try to receive benefits, they usually pretend a suitable situation, which makes it fraud. So fraud follows activities in the shadow economy, or shadow economy makes fraud necessary, since accidents, sickness, and others do also happen in the shadow economy, if not more often than in the official sector, for instance, because of missing industrial safety.

While this is clear for social insurance, what is the situation like in private insurance? For most forms of insurance, the matter is not different to that of social insurance: Since it would be illegal to take out insurance for illegal activities, the real situation is masked either for the purpose of concluding an insurance contract for it or for the purpose to receive compensation for an activity other than the actual one.

A special case is that of liability insurance. There, the contract is concluded between the insurer and the insured, but the beneficiary is a third party. We can easily assume that the probability for damage against a third party is not lower for illegal than for legal activities; as a consequence, there must be numerous cases, where the damaged third party will not receive compensation.

Conclusion

What can we derive from what has been said? First, the possibilities for individuals to carry out illegal activities are somewhat limited. They can of course, be active in all the areas of insurance. However, control and supervision mechanisms in the field of insurance are manifold and it is generally expected that they will be able to uncover misdoings. Statistical analysis is quite powerful in detecting exceptional losses, in particular if they can be attributed to individuals from inside and outside an insurance company alike. In case of single attempts, statistical methods are much weaker for multiple ones, so there is some potential that illegal activities stay undetected as long as they remain onetime events.

Detection and supervision methods can be outmaneuvered when they are known in detail to perpetrators and when they are able to scatter their activities. This, in turn, requires some level of organization: as we have seen, in past cases with high amounts of damage, offenders took shared roles, thus undermining control mechanisms. Taking these facts into account, insurance appears to be a suitable field for organized crime.

A second point is that the insurance industry aggregates enormous sums of money, which attracts criminals. Although we lack a complete picture, we can assume from the past that even single event can reach high levels of damage.

Third, figures concerning the magnitude of illegal activities are uncertain and incomplete, and moreover, there is even dissent on how uncertain and incomplete they are. Higher estimates concerning the share of fraudulent insurance claims go up to slightly less than half of all claims. In a worst-case scenario, a similar percentage rate for all shadow activities may be true.

Finally, indirect effects, where shadow activities in other parts of the economy affect the insurance business may also be of considerable importance. In part, they will result in several forms of insurance fraud, while under other circumstances, the risk related to shadow undertakings remains untreated, with the usual consequences of uninsured losses.

References

Edelbacher, M. and Theil, M. (2008): *Kriminalität gegen Versicherungen*; Wien, Vienna, Austria.

Fetchenhauer, D. (1999): Zur psychologie des versicherungsbetrugs; in Fischer, L., Kutsch, T. and S., Ekkehard (eds.): *Finanzpsychologie*; Oldenbourg, München, Germany, pp. 188–213.

Fleming, M., Roman, J., and Farrell, G. (2000): The shadow economy; *Journal of International Affairs* 53(2): 387–409.

Hodoschek, A. (2014): Anklage gegen Ex-ÖBB-Chef Huber ausgeweitet; http://kurier.at/wirtschaft/wirtschaftspolitik/anklage-gegen-ex-oebb-chef-huber-ausgeweitet/46.314.529 KURIER online, January 16, 2014.

Kenealy, B. (2013): Controversy over foreign reinsurance taxes continues; *Business Insurance* 47(21): 37.

Kettenbetrug, http://de.wikipedia.org/wiki/Kettenbetrug. diepresse.com.

Nell, M. and Schiller, J. (2002): Erklärungsansätze für vertragswidriges *Verhalten von Versicherungsnehmern aus der Sicht der ökonomischen Theorie*, Working Papers of Risk and Insurance; Hamburg University No. 7, Hamburg.

Pine, S. and Wright, B. (1986): Barbados, Bermuda, and the U.S. Excise Tax; *Risk Management* 33(1): 14.

Tennyson, S. (2002): Insurance experience and consumers' attitudes towards insurance fraud; *Journal of Insurance Regulation* 21(2): 35–55.

Theil, M. (2012): Dealing with insurance: What can be learned; in: Edelbacher, M., Kratcoski, P., and M. Theil (eds.): *Financial Crimes. A Threat to Global Security*; CRC Press, Boca Raton, FL, pp. 269–287.

Versicherungsverband O. (2012), p. 127 ff.

Viane, S. and Dedene, G. (2004). Insurance fraud: Issues and challenges; *Geneva Papers on Risk and Insurance* 29(2): 313–333.

wien.orf.at.

www.fr-online.de.

www.kurier.at.

www.oe24.at.

www.spiegel.de.

www.wirtschaftsblatt.at.

7. The Role of Lawyers as Defenders of White Collar Criminals

Petter Gottschalk

Introduction

Lawyers are competent in general legal principles and procedures and in the substantive and procedural aspects of the law; thus they have the ability to analyze and provide solutions to legal problems (Dibbern et al., 2008). Lawyers, as knowledge workers, apply a variety of knowledge categories such as declarative and procedural knowledge. Most lawyers spend several hours a day answering queries, generally the types of queries you cannot really capture or look up in a how-to database. As part of the execution of knowledge processes, knowledge lawyers can decide for themselves and are free to decide whether and what knowledge they need and what knowledge they want to evaluate, develop, implement, and communicate. When several lawyers work on a case, there is often an independence of professionals working together, which might be characterized as collective individualism or individualistic collectivism that makes the sharing of knowledge both dynamic and random. Lawyers, as knowledge professionals with a great deal of autonomy, are free to choose an individual approach to knowledge processes, including the need, storage, access, sharing, application, creation, and evaluation of knowledge. Autonomy of the performance is an important structural feature that can promote knowledge processes, since such autonomy encourages individuals to develop new knowledge. At the same time, several people using their natural powers (brains) who look at the same problem can come up with different, novel approaches to solving the problem.

Characteristics of White Collar Crime Lawyers

A lawyer is a person who does legal knowledge work for clients. A lawyer is a typical knowledge worker, who combines legal insights with client problems to find a good or even optimal solution to problems. A white collar crime (WCC) lawyer is a defense attorney for *white collar* individuals prosecuted in court, when a white collar suspect is accused of financial crime (Kopon and Sungaila, 2012). The white collar suspect is on trial to be convicted or dismissed from the case. It is decided in court whether the person is guilty of financial crime committed in the course of occupational activities. The trial in court is concerned with a privileged person who has a competent and knowledgeable lawyer to carry out the defense (Sutherland, 1940, 1949, 1983).

The privileged person, a white collar suspect, has committed financial crime as part of the profession. The competent lawyer may be well paid by the client, and thereby improves the access to positive justice and to advantages in the court process and in the potential imprisonment. These advantages are quite abundant if compared to other suspects such as street criminals (Attanasio, 2008).

A white collar crime (WCC) lawyer is a defense attorney in criminal court cases, which are concerned with financial crime. Both knowledge and behavior of WCC lawyers distinguish them from other defense roles. Lawyer knowledge is about business insights, understanding of economics, experience in reading accounting statements, and knowledge of tax regulations and other laws and regulations related to the justice system as well as to financial crime. Lawyer behavior in WCC cases is different from other cases, for example, in terms of resources and in terms of ambiguity whether the action was not just unethical, but also illegal. Breaking rules is different from violating laws, and there is often significant uncertainty whether a white collar suspect has done something that may lead the person to imprisonment. Furthermore, there are challenging tasks related to facts. In a murder case, the facts are usually quite clear: A person is found killed and dead. In a financial crime case, the facts are not that obvious, as financial transactions can have different purposes and justifications.

While the judge typically is a generalist, the lawyer is a specialist. Simply stated, a generalist is a person who knows little about a lot, while a specialist is a person who knows a lot about a little. When the WCC lawyer defends an executive or shareholder in court, the lawyer is on his or her home turf, while the judge is often unfamiliar with factual as well as the legal issues in the case. On the day before, the judge may have passed a verdict in a child abuse case, a murder case, or a traffic violation case. The lawyer, however, may have helped another WCC client in a similar financial case the day before.

Gillers (2012) argues that specialization in legal fields is a complement to the movement toward conformity of law. Specialization will make each lawyer better able to get up to speed on (be competent in) the law in the area of specialization. Specialists know what variations to look for. Specialization is increasingly defined by expertise in areas of law. Specialized knowledge will often define the borders of a lawyer's competence with greater assurance than will the geographical borders of his or her clients.

A concept might be defined in its own right, or in terms of difference from other terms. For example, a man could be defined as such, or as different from a woman. Thus, a white collar lawyer is characterized by the clients, who are white collar criminals. Similar terminology is used for celebrity lawyers and divorce lawyers, who have clients of fame and clients of marriage breakdown. It is the client who defines the lawyer. When lawyers have different clients, then they are different kinds of lawyers.

Normally, lawyers are defined in terms of their area of expertise. Some are tax lawyers, while others are merger-and-acquisition lawyers or maritime lawyers. When lawyers have different areas of expertise, then they are different kinds of lawyers. A WCC lawyer can work in several legal areas, as long as the client is a white collar suspect. For example, WCC cases may range from tax fraud via accounting fraud to corruption.

Attanasio (2008) argues that there are a number of issues where a knowledgeable defense lawyer can help the WCC client early on in the process:

> One of the most pressing challenges facing white collar crime defense counsel early in an investigation is to persuade an intelligent, successful and proactive client to engage in what he or she will likely think is counter-intuitive behavior. Many executives, however, wind up in federal prisons not because of the conduct that was initially being investigated – but because of statements they made afterwards to government agents or even to co-workers and friends (all of whom are potential witnesses once an investigation is underway). One of the most common mistakes that a white collar target can make is to think that "all of this will end if I can just tell everybody what really happened." (p. 58)

Similarly, there are a number of issues where the knowledgeable defense lawyer can help the WCC client late in the process. If the client is convicted to a prison sentence, then the lawyer may help ease conditions during imprisonment. The lawyer may argue by the special sensitivity hypothesis, which claims that white collar offenders are ill-equipped to adjust to the rigors of prison life (Stadler et al., 2013, p. 2):

> Termed the "special sensitivity hypothesis," the claim is made that white collar offenders experience the pains of imprisonment to a greater degree than traditional street offenders. Upon incarceration, they enter a world that is foreign to them. In the society of captives, status hierarchies found in the larger community are upended, as those with more physical prowess and criminal connections "rule the joint". White collar offenders discover that they are no

> longer in the majority in a domain populated largely by poor and minority group members – in fact, prison is a place that a researcher suggests is the functional equivalent of an urban ghetto.

Furthermore, Stadler et al. (2013) found that research investigating the sentencing of white collar offenders has revealed that federal judges often based their decisions not to impose a prison sentence for white collar offending on a belief that prison is both unnecessary for and unduly harsh on white collar offenders.

Even when WCC lawyers argue the case of special sensitivity for their clients, Stadler et al. (2013) found that the historical pattern of lenient treatment of white collar offenders appears to be waning. Following widespread public outrage and condemnation of white collar criminals in regions such as Northern Europe and North America, for the lavish lifestyles, unscrupulous deeds, and fraudulent actions of corporate executives and stock market acrobats, the prosecution of WCC has become increasingly common.

Furthermore, the special sensitivity hypothesis for white collar criminals sometimes argued by their personal lawyers is not necessarily true. In research conducted by Stadler et al. (2013), they found that white collar inmates were in fact better at prison adjustment, experienced fewer difficulties in prison, had less trouble sleeping, had less need of safety in prison, experienced fewer problems with current and former cellmates, and made easier friends in prison, than other inmates in the prison.

A challenge for WCC lawyers is sometimes the lack of guilt perceived by their clients (Stadler and Benson, 2012):

> Indeed, a distinguishing feature of the psychological makeup of white collar offenders is thought to be their ability to neutralize the moral bind of the law and rationalize their criminal behavior. (p. 294)

In the United States, it is argued that white collar sentencing has been strengthened after the devastating collapse of Enron and other major American corporations such as WorldCom, Tyco, and Xerox. Congress enacted the Sarbanes-Oxley Act, which was passed hastily by a seemingly shaken legislature. The act included a multitude of reforms aimed at preventing another meltdown (*Harvard Law Review*, 2009, p. 1728):

> One particular area of reform was white collar criminal sentencing: included in the Act was the White Collar Crime Penalty Enhancement Act of 2002 (WCCPA), which sharply increased penalties for various forms of fraud.

Lawyers as Knowledge Workers

Basic knowledge is required for a lawyer as a professional to understand and interpret information, and basic knowledge is required for a law firm as a knowledge organization to receive inputs and produce outputs (Galanter and Palay, 1991). Advanced knowledge is knowledge necessary to get acceptable work done (Zack, 1999). Advanced knowledge is required for a lawyer as a knowledge worker to achieve satisfactory work performance, and advanced knowledge is required for a law firm as a knowledge organization to produce legal advice and legal documents that are acceptable to clients. When advanced knowledge is combined with basic knowledge, then we find professional knowledge workers and professional knowledge organizations in the legal industry (Mountain, 2001; Nottage, 1998; Phillips, 2005). Innovative knowledge is knowledge that makes a real difference. When lawyers apply innovative knowledge in analysis and reasoning based on incoming and available information, then new insights and possible novel solutions are generated in terms of situation patterns, actor profiles, and client strategies. Knowledge levels were here defined as basic knowledge, advanced knowledge, and innovative knowledge (Parsons, 2004).

An alternative approach is to define knowledge levels in terms of knowledge depth: know-what, know-how, and know-why, respectively. These knowledge depth levels represent the extent of insight and understanding about a phenomenon. While know-what is the simple perception of what is going on, know-why is a complicated insight into cause and effect relationships about why things are going on:

1. *Know-what* is knowledge about what is happening and what is going on. A lawyer perceives that something is going on, that might need his or her attention. The lawyer's insight is limited to the perception of something happening. The lawyer understands neither how it is happening nor why it is happening.
2. *Know-how* is a lawyer's knowledge about how a legal case develops, how a criminal behaves, how

investigations can be carried out, or how a criminal business enterprise is organized. The lawyer's insight is not limited to the perception that something is happening; he or she also understands how it is happening or how "it is." Similarly, know-how is present when the lawyer understands how legal work is to be carried out and how the client will react to advice put forward in the process.

3. *Know-why* is the knowledge representing the deepest form of understanding and insights into a phenomenon. The lawyer does not only know that it has occurred and how it has occurred, but he or she also has developed an understanding of why it has occurred or why it is like this. It is a matter of causal understanding, where cause and effect relationships are understood.

A law firm is a business entity formed by one or more lawyers to engage in the practice of law. Most law firms use a partnership form of organization. In such a framework, lawyers who are highly effective in using and applying knowledge for fee earning are eventually rewarded with partner status, and thus own a stake in the firm, resulting in an income often 10 times as much as initially earned.

In many countries, lawyers and law firms enjoy privileges that make them attractive to white collar criminals and crime. For example, money placed in a client account at a Norwegian law firm is strictly confidential. The law firm does not have to tell tax or other authorities about names or amounts. Knowing that some of this money flows freely to and from tax havens like the Cayman Islands and knowing that some of the money originates from WCC makes the job of the prosecution extremely difficult (Vanvik, 2011).

Another example is Danish law firms where there is an "in kassu" system. Many in kassus are run by law firms, and they buy debts and chase "debtors" for many companies in Denmark. The reason is that unlike nonlaw firms, they are authorized and not subject to regulation. The only way a complaint can be filed is through the law firm's own organization Board of Lawyers (Trustpilot, 2013).

Iossa and Jullien (2012) distinguish between higher-quality and lower-quality lawyers. The first category comprises lawyers who graduated from elite institutions, serve business clients, and charge high fees. Here, we typically find knowledgeable WCC lawyers. The second category serves more individual clients and comprises lawyers who graduated from lower-tier schools, charge lower fees, and provide largely routine, noncontested legal services. Depending on their category, lawyers are then employed in different law firms, with the most reputable firms employing the most talented and well-trained lawyers.

Knowledge Competition in Court

From a legal perspective, a court situation is characterized by efforts to conclude whether the charged persons and company are guilty or not guilty. From a knowledge perspective, this situation is characterized by a competition as illustrated in Figure 7.1. Depending on the relative knowledge levels of prosecution and defense, a knowledge rivalry with three alternative situations might exist as illustrated in Figure 7.1:

1. Defense lawyers are experts, while prosecutors are not experts in areas such as international tax regulations, tax havens, global company operations, and management of international operations. Defense lawyers have innovative knowledge (know-why), while prosecutors have core knowledge (know-what).
2. Prosecutors are experts, while defense lawyers are not experts in Norwegian laws and regulations. Defense lawyers have core knowledge (know-what), while prosecutors have innovative knowledge (know-why).
3. Both parties are at about the same knowledge level, leading to a real knowledge competition in court between the defense lawyers and prosecutors.

While in Norway, street criminals such as burglars and rapists seldom can afford several top defense lawyers for weeks and months in court, white collar criminals often can afford it. This discrepancy emphasizes the importance of Sutherland's (1949) seminal work on WCC. The most economically disadvantaged members of society are not the only ones committing crime. Members of the privileged socioeconomic class are also engaged in criminal behavior (Brightman, 2009; Croall, 2007) and the types of crime may differ from those of the lower classes. Some examples of the former are business executives bribing public officials to obtain contracts, chief accountants manipulating balance sheets to avoid taxes, procurement, and managers

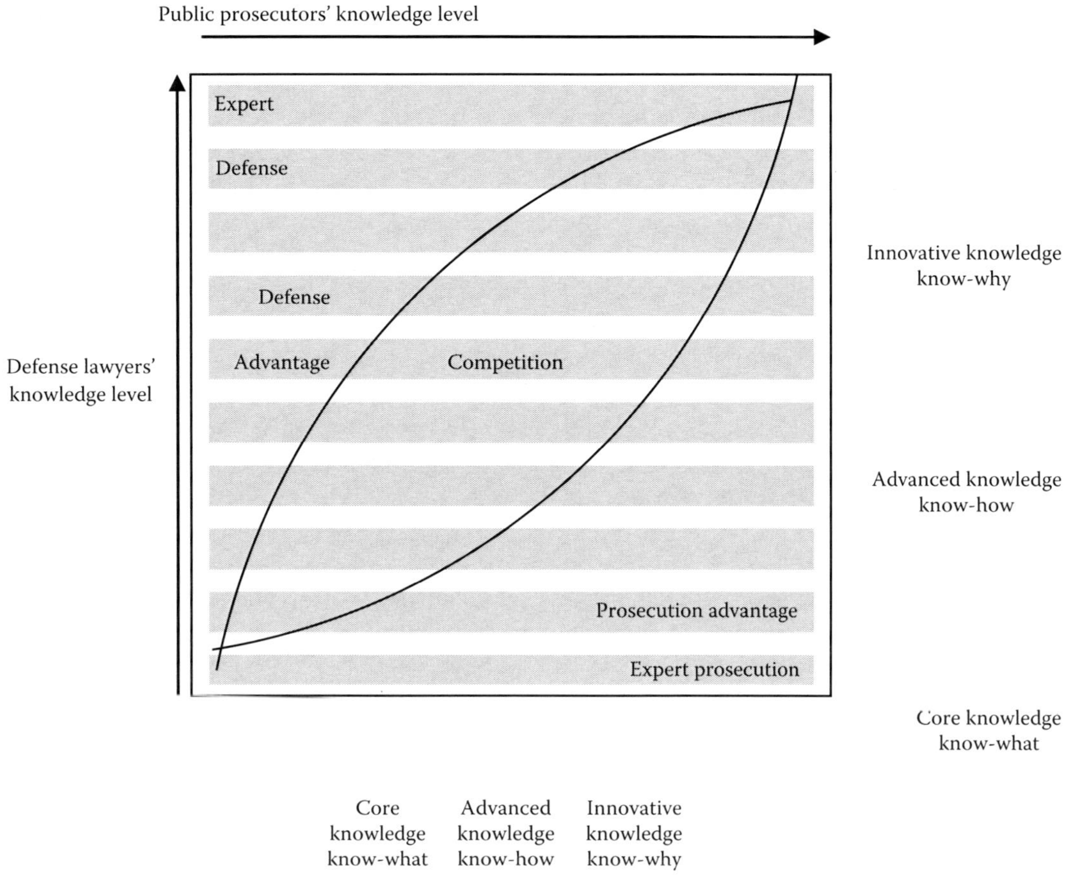

FIGURE 7.1 Knowledge rivalry between the prosecution and defense in court.

approving fake invoices for personal gain (Simpson and Weisburd, 2009). The elements of competition and rivalry make practicing law an entrepreneurial endeavor, but ultimately a defense lawyer has an advantage in that he or she knows the full extent of the client's guilt. The lawyer has insider knowledge.

Criminal behavior by members of the privileged socioeconomic class is routinely labeled WCC when a financial crime occurs (Benson and Simpson, 2009; Simpson, 2011). As mentioned earlier, Sutherland (1949), in his or her seminal work, defined WCC as crime committed by a person of respectability and high social status in the course of his or her occupation. According to Brightman (2009), Sutherland's theory of WCC from 1939 was controversial, particularly since many of the academics in the audience perceived themselves to be members of the upper echelon of American society, where white collar criminals can be found. Despite his or her critics, Sutherland's theory of white collar criminality served as the catalyst for an area of research that continues today. In particular, differential association theory proposes that a person associating with individuals who have deviant or unlawful mores, values, and norms learns criminal behavior. Certain characteristics play a key role in placing individuals in a position to act illegally. These include the proposition that criminal behavior is learned through interaction with other criminal persons in the upper echelon and the interaction that occurs in small intimate groups who might be involved in corruption, money laundering, or embezzlement (Hansen, 2009).

Sutherland argued that criminal acts are illegalities that are contingently differentiated from other illegalities by virtue of the specific administrative procedures to which they are subject. Some individual white collar offenders avoid criminal prosecution because of the class bias of the courts (Tombs and Whyte, 2007). As a consequence, WCC is sometimes considered creative crime (Brisman, 2010) and something to be grudgingly admired. Brightman (2009) differs slightly from Sutherland regarding the definition of WCC. While societal status may still determine access to wealth and property, he argues that the term white collar crime should be broader in scope and include virtually any nonviolent act committed for financial gain, regardless of one's social status. For example, access to technology, such as personal computers and the Internet, now allows individuals from all social classes to buy and sell stocks or engage in similar activities that were once the bastion of the financial elite. In Sutherland's definition of WCC, a white collar criminal is a person of respectability and high social status who commits crime in the course of his or her occupation. This excludes many kinds of crime of the higher class, for example, most of their cases of murder, adultery, and intoxication, since these are not customarily a part of their white collar business activities (Benson and Simpson, 2009). It also excludes lower-class criminals committing financial crime, as pointed out by Brightman (2009). What Sutherland meant by respectable and high social status individuals, is not quite clear, but in today's business world we can assume he is referring to business managers and executives. They are, for the most part, individuals with power and influence that are associated with respectability, trust, and high social status. Part of the standard view of white collar offenders is that they are mainstream, law-abiding individuals. They are assumed to be irregular offenders, not people who engage in crime on a regular basis (Benson and Simpson, 2009, p. 39).

Unlike the run-of-the-mill common street criminal who usually has had repeated contact with the criminal justice system, white collar offenders are thought not to have prior criminal records.

However, it might be that they have not been caught previously. As part of the white collar criminal definition, the role of class has been highly contested, because the status of an offender may matter less than the harm done by someone in a trusted occupational position. Croall (2007) argues that the term crime is also contentious, since many of the harmful activities of businesses or occupational groups are not subject to criminal law and punishment but administrative or regulatory law and penalties and sanctions. Therefore, some have suggested a definition of WCC as an abuse of a legitimate occupational role that is regulated by law, typically representing a violation of trust. It is also apparent that white collar defense lawyers are predominantly drawn from the elite too. Indeed, Osiel (1990) referred to a class of lawyers as being monopolists, aristocrats, and entrepreneurs.

White Collar Crime Law Firms

Lawyers or attorneys who defend white collar criminals are sometimes labeled WCC lawyers, white collar defense attorneys, or simply white collar lawyers. Lawyers work in law firms, and some law firms have specialized on WCC cases. Here is an example of a firm named White & Case presenting itself on the Internet (http://www.whitecase.com/whitecollar/):

> The White Collar Practice offers clients around the world first-rate skills in dealing with government investigations and enforcement matters. Our lawyers have substantial experience defending clients through all phases of investigations as well as criminal and civil enforcement proceedings. These capabilities are enhanced by the resources of a preeminent international law firm, including local law proficiency and familiarity with local enforcement authorities in major business centers around the world. Clients include large corporations, banks, and other institutions, as well as individuals prominent in business and political affairs.
>
> The White Collar group serves clients around the world in civil and criminal matters. The common element is the involvement of a government agency engaged in fact-gathering or enforcement proceedings. The group is prepared to defend the interests of domestic and international clients, offering them immediate access to high-caliber legal counsel with substantial experience in complex as well as controversial matters. These include financial fraud, public and private corruption, money-laundering, securities fraud, environmental, tax and antitrust cases.

One of the white collar cases handled by White & Case LLP was referenced in *Harvard Law Review* (volume 124, 2011). The case was concerned with courts that were authorized to issue protective orders limiting the disclosure of evidence produced in civil the discovery.

Another example of a white collar law firm is Covington & Burling, which applies the term "white collar lawyers" about themselves and who present their defense competence in WCC cases on the Internet (http://www.cov.com/practice/white_collar_and_investigations/):

> Our white collar lawyers successfully represent both corporations and individuals in criminal and regulatory investigations by the U.S. Department of Justice, federal regulatory agencies, and state and local prosecutors and regulators throughout the nation. Covington's White Collar Defense & Investigations Practice is widely recognized not only for litigating

and winning high-profile criminal cases, but also for devising creative legal strategies to resolve cases long before they draw public scrutiny. Covington's longstanding record of excellence in defending clients in complex criminal and regulatory enforcement cases has earned the firm a deep and invaluable reservoir of credibility with courts, prosecutors and regulatory agencies nationwide.

Our white collar practice includes 30 partners, most of whom are former prosecutors and SEC enforcement attorneys who have held senior positions in United States Attorney's Offices, the U.S. Department of Justice, the White House, the Securities and Exchange Commission, and other government agencies involved in white collar criminal and regulatory enforcement.

Transocean Court Case

Transocean was accused of having underpaid taxes by up to 10 billion Norwegian crowns ($1.8 billion USD) in 2000–2002, according to the police unit that investigates economic crime, Økokrim, in Norway. The Norwegian National Authority for Investigation and Prosecution of Economic and Environmental Crime—Økokrim—is similar to the Serious Fraud Office in the United Kingdom. Police say the alleged underpayments stem from several transactions in connection with the sale of 12 oil rigs from Transocean's Norwegian subsidiary to other company units in the Cayman Islands. Taxes are a key part of Transocean's strategy since its rigs move between jurisdictions, as "it is common in the oil rig business," says Stephen L. Hayes, executive vice president of tax matters at Transocean. The company, after growing to become the world's largest drilling contractor via three acquisitions of rivals worth $27 billion USD in the decade to 2009, rebased to Switzerland from the Caymans for tax reasons. The company, which had operational headquarters in Houston before the Swiss move, has also shifted assets between subsidiaries over the years, which are at the heart of the Norwegian case (Klesty and Reddall, 2011).

Norwegian authorities indicted two companies owned by offshore drilling rig contractor Transocean Ltd. and three tax advisers over suspicions of tax fraud.

> "From 1996/97, the Transocean Group's master plan was to concentrate the ownership of the Group's Norwegian rigs in companies registered in the Cayman Islands," Økokrim said in the 24-page indictment issued this week. The final decision in the Norway tax case was to be made by a Norwegian court, said Morten Eriksen, a lawyer for Økokrim. Transocean denied the allegations and said it intended to clear its name in court. "The indictment is based on an inadequate comprehension of the facts," defense counsel Erling O. Lyngtveit said in the statement. "Moreover in our opinion Økokrim base their conclusions on peculiar and original interpretation of Norwegian and international tax legislation."
>
> **Klesty and Reddall (2011).**

The largest tax evasion case in Norwegian history started in December 2012, with prosecutors claiming that tax advisors for the rig firm Transocean must have known they were misleading tax authorities. Raids on Transocean's offices in Stavanger in Norway and years of investigation by Økokrim led to the firm, its advisers, and affiliates being charged with evading taxes. Prosecutors claimed that Transocean's tax planning was managed in detail from its Houston headquarters, with Norwegian tax advisers at Ernst & Young as central players. A tax attorney at the Oslo law firm Thommessen is also involved in the case, but local Transocean management in Norway is not believed to have been involved. Prosecutors claim the alleged tax evasion was conducted from Houston headquarters (News, 2012).

Oslo District Court started its proceedings in the Transocean case on December 5, 2012. It was scheduled to last for 8 months. A total of 29 persons were presented in court, including

- Public prosecutor Morten Eriksen with four associates (5 persons)
- Accused six Transocean executives from the United States with six defense lawyers (12 persons), prosecuted because of tax fraud
- Accused lawyer Sverre E. Koch with three defense lawyers (4 persons), prosecuted for tax fraud advice
- Accused lawyer Klaus Klausen with three defense lawyers (4 persons), prosecuted for tax fraud advice
- Accused lawyer Einar Brask with three defense lawyers (4 persons), prosecuted for tax fraud advice

It was estimated that the accused persons and Transocean would pay about $10 million USD for their defense lawyers, even though defense can be obtained for free in Norwegian courts. It is interesting to note that the prosecution had only 17% of the engaged personnel in the court room. In addition to the prosecution and defense, there were 3 judges in the district court on this case, making a total of 32 persons for 8 months in court.

While street criminals such as burglars and rapists can seldom afford several top defense lawyers for weeks and months in court, white collar criminals often can afford it. This discrepancy emphasizes the importance of Sutherland's (1949) seminal work on WCC. The most economically disadvantaged members of society are not the only ones committing crime. Members of the privileged socioeconomic class are also engaged in criminal behavior (Brightman, 2009) and the types of crime may differ from those of the lower classes. Some examples of the former are business executives bribing public officials to obtain contracts, chief accountants manipulating balance sheets to avoid taxes, procurement managers approving fake invoices for personal gain (Simpson and Weisburd, 2009), or tax evasion as in the Transocean case. The Oslo District Court acquitted Transocean and some of its advisors of tax fraud in July 2014. However, Norway is appealing the decision. (Skonnord and Fouche, 2014). It is expected that the case will move on into a court of appeals, and possibly the Supreme Court may consider a final judgment in the Transocean case in 2016 or 2017.

This research is not concerned with whether or not the persons and the company are guilty as charged. Rather, this chapter has presented the knowledge management view on WCC cases, where white collar criminals can afford a much better defense than street-level criminals. This discrepancy emphasizes the importance of the WCC concept as defined by Sutherland (1940, 1949, 1983). The agency theory further emphasized role importance of principal (criminal) and agent (lawyer) for privileged white collar criminals.

Attorney–Client Privilege

The attorney–client privilege is one of the oldest privileges known to the common law in the United States. The privilege ensures that a client may provide information to his or her attorney, in confidence, with the knowledge that such information is protected, and neither the client nor the attorney may be forced to disclose the information that has been shared with their judicial adversaries (Kopon and Sungaila, 2012). Similar privilege exists between clients and attorneys in most other democratic societies. The privilege may extend to information concerning money, where a client has placed an amount in a law firm account. If the police suspect the money to originate from crime, or it is suspected that the money is moved illegally to tax havens, the attorney–client privilege allows the attorney to deny the police insight into accounts. The attorney–client privilege shields from discovery any information communicated to an attorney to enable the attorney to render legal advice (Oh, 2004).

An attorney's ability to advise a client is directly dependent upon that client's willingness to engage in such full and truth-oriented communication. According to Kopon and Sungaila (2012), the privilege serves both the immediate needs of the individual client and public ends by ensuring sound and fully informed legal advice and advocacy.

An attorney has both the ethical duty of confidentiality as well as the attorney–client privilege. The former is a rule of professional responsibility. The latter is an evidentiary privilege. Both principles seek to permit the client to control confidences shared with his or her lawyer. Professional responsibility generally prohibits a lawyer from knowingly revealing a confidence or secret to the client's disadvantage, without the client's consent (Bryans, 2009).

Attorney–Client Asymmetry

There is an asymmetry in knowledge between the lawyer and the client. The lawyer is an expert on laws, verdicts, and legal procedures. The client is an expert on business transactions, management, and leadership. Knowledge asymmetry can benefit and hinder defense work. It can benefit defense work by combining knowledge and creating knowledge synergies. It can hinder defense work because of misunderstandings where there is a lack of minimum knowledge overlap between attorney and client.

Susskind (2010) emphasized another kind of asymmetry between the commercial interest of law firms and those of their clients. In the ordinary course of events when a client needs help from a lawyer it will generally be the hope of the client that the involvement of the lawyer and the resultant fee can be kept to a bare minimum. Most clients would prefer to minimize legal expenses.

References

Attanasio, M. (2008). Handling criminal investigations, *Financial Executive*, December, 56–58.

Benson, M. and Simpson, S. (2009). *White Collar Crime: An Opportunity Perspective, Criminology and Justice Series*, Routledge, New York.

Brightman, H. (2009). *Today's White Collar Crime: Legal, Investigative, and Theoretical Perspectives*, Routledge, Taylor & Francis Group, New York.

Brisman, A. (2010). "Creative crime" and the phytological analogy, *Crime Media Culture*, 6(2), 205–225.

Bryans, H. (2009). Business successors and the transpositional attorney-client relationship, *The Business Lawyer*, 64, 1039–1086.

Croall, H. (2007). *Victims, Crime and Society*, Sage, Los Angeles, CA.

Dibbern, J., Winkler, J., and Heinzl, A. (2008). Explaining variations in client extra costs between software projects offshored to India, *MIS Quarterly*, 32(3), 333–366.

Galanter, M. and Palay, T. (1991). *Tournament of Lawyers. The Transformation of the Big Law Firm*, The University of Chicago Press, Chicago, IL.

Gillers, S. (2012). A profession, if you can keep it: How information technology and fading borders are reshaping the law marketplace and what we should do about it, *Hastings Law Journal*, 63, 953–1022.

Hansen, L. (2009). Corporate financial crime: Social diagnosis and treatment, *Journal of Financial Crime*, 16(1), 28–40.

Harvard Law Review (2009). Go directly to jail: White collar sentencing after the Sarbanes-Oxley Act, *Harvard Law Review*, 122, 1728–1749.

Iossa, E. and Jullien, B. (2012). The market for lawyers and quality layers in legal services, *RAND Journal of Economics*, 43(4), 677–704.

Klesty, V. and Reddall, B. (2011). Norway indicts transocean over alleged tax fraud, *Thompson Reuters News & Insights*, http://newsandinsight.thomsonreuters.com/Legal/News/2011/06_-_June/Norway_indicts_Transocean_over_alleged_tax_fraud/. (Accessed January 2, 2012.)

Kopon, A. and Sungaila, M. (2012). The perils of oversharing: Can the attorney-client privilege be broadly waived by partially disclosing attorney communications during negotiations? *Defense Counsel Journal*, July, 265–277.

Mountain, D. (2001). Could new technologies cause great law firms to fall? *Journal of Information, Law and Technology*, 1, 1-6. http://www2.Warwick.ac.UK/fac/Soc/law/eli/jilt/2001_1/mountain/. (Accessed July 26, 2015.)

News (2011). Convicted executive faces two years in prison, *Norway International Network*, www.newsinenglish.no, published October 5, 2011.

News (2012). Rig evasion case underway, views and news from Norway, http://www.newsinenglish.no/2012/12/09/rig-tax-evasion-case-underway/. (Accessed January 2, 2012.)

Nottage, L. (1998). Cyberspace and the future of law, legale education and practice in Japan, *Journal of Current Legal Issues*, 5, 1–20, http://www.gailiii.org?UK/other?Journals/Web.JCLi/1998/Isue 5/nottage 5.5/JML. (Accessed July 27, 2015.)

Oh, J. (2004). How (Un)ethical are you? Letters to the editor, *Harvard Business Review*, March, 122.

Osiel, M. (1990). Lawyers as monopolists, aristocrats and entrepreneurs, *Harvard Law Review*, 103(8), 2009–2066.

Parsons, M. (2004). *Effective Knowledge Management for Law Firms*, Oxford University Press, Oxford, UK.

Phillips, D.J. (2005). Organizational genealogies and the persistence of gender inequality: The case of Silicon Valley law firms, *Administrative Science Quarterly*, 50, 440–472.

Simpson, S. (2011). Making sense of white collar crime: Theory and research, *The Ohio State Journal of Criminal Law*, 8(2), 481–502.

Simpson, S. and Weisburd, D. (eds.)(2009). *The Criminology of White Collar Crime*, Springer, New York.

Skonnord, P. and Fouche, G. (2014). Norway appeals acquittal of Transocean in tax fraud case in Reuters News, U.S. edition, July 16, 2014.

Stadler, W. and Benson, M. (2012). Revisiting the guilty mind: The neutralization of white collar crime, *Criminal Justice Review*, 37(4), 494–511.

Stadler, W., Benson, M., and Cullen, F. (2013). Revisiting the special sensitivity hypothesis: The prison experience of white collar inmates, *Justice Quarterly*, I First, 1–25.

Susskind, R. (2010). *The End of Lawyers? Rethinking the Nature of Legal Services*, Oxford University Press, Oxford, UK.

Sutherland, E. (1940). White collar criminality, *American Sociological Review*, 5, 1–12.

Sutherland, E. (1949). *White Collar Crime*, Holt Rinehart and Winston, New York.

Sutherland, E. (1983). *White Collar Crime: The Uncut Version*, Yale University Press, New Haven, CT.

Tombs, S. and Whyte, D. (2007). *Safety Crimes*, Willan Publishing, Cullompton, UK.

Trustpilot (2013). Egeparken anmeldelser (Egeparken complaints), Trustpilot, http://www.trustpilot.dk/review/www.egeparken.dk. (Accessed January 3, 2013.)

Vanvik, H. (2011). Diamantring fra skatteparadis (Diamond Ring from Tax Haven), *Dagens Næringsliv* (*Daily Norwegian Business Newspaper*), Thursday, February 3, pp. 4–5.

Zack M.H. (1999). Developing a knowledge strategy, *California Management Review*, 41 (3), 125–145.

8. Falsified Prospect Theory in the Context of Corruption and Foreign Direct Investment*

Benjamin Potz, Dominik Sporer, Christian Zirgoi, and Briget Burbeck

* This chapter is a short version of a seminar paper written by the following team members: Gonzalez Daniela, Pötz Benjamin, Sporer Dominik, Reiter Fabienne, and Zirgoi Christian, supervised by Dr. Brigit Burbeck (formerly Gusenbauer). The seminar paper was written throughout the course "Marketing Research Methods" in the master program "Business in Emerging Markets." The results were presented and discussed in June 2013 at the United Nations Office. The students were challenged by the research process and the fruitful discussion with many experts. We owe special thanks to Mr. Maximilian Edelbacher, who gave us valuable insights into the diverse topic of crime and corruption at the beginning of this course and also organized the final presentation at the UNO in Vienna.

Introduction

Due to globalization and technological innovations, new investment opportunities attract the attention of companies, especially in emerging markets. As corruption is widespread, particularly in these markets, controversial discussions about the influence of corruption on foreign direct investment (FDI) exist. This chapter is using falsification in order to test the usefulness of the prospect theory (PT) and to explain the impact of corruption on FDI in China and Russia. The results show that the widely used PT cannot serve as a theoretical model in this context.

Globalization and technological innovations have created opportunities for companies all over the world to expand their business by investing in international markets. One such opportunity is called *foreign direct investment* (FDI) (Harrison, 2011). Transition and emerging economies are becoming more open to international business, which attracts foreign investors and increases FDI (Primorac and Smoljic, 2011).

Heated discussions about FDI are ongoing, and expert opinions diverge enormously. The key factors for the discussions are the dramatic increase in the annual global flow as well as the consequences of the rise in its relative relevance as a source of investment funds for numerous nations. Additionally, FDI is regarded as a key driver of the continuing integration of the world economy, which is commonly known as globalization. FDI can serve as a factor that leads to an increase of efficiency regarding usage of the world's limited resources and can act as a stimulator for innovation and competition, as well as for savings and capital formation that positively contribute to job creation and economic growth (World Trade Organization, 2013).

Chapter 8

Emerging markets are very attractive targets for FD, since these countries show high economic growth as well as enormous population growth. Due to that fact, these emerging economies will turn to a high aggregation of wealth, which helps them to get an attractive position in the world market (Lynn et al., 2011). In fact, China is the world's largest country with a population of 1.3 billion people and a GDP of $5.89 trillion USD in the year 2010, yet it is still seen as a transition country (Lynn et al., 2011). Russia was badly hit by the world's financial crisis that led to a shrinking of the economic growth rates. After this incident, several figures show that the Russian economy is recovering again, especially if the population, which increased to nearly 143 million people in 2012, is taken into consideration; it has to be pointed out that the Russian market offers enormous opportunities for foreign investors (The World Bank, 2013a). Also the GDP (official exchange rate) of Russia in 2012 with an observed amount of $2.022 trillion USD serves as evidence of a promising market (Central Intelligence Agency, 2013). The effects of the financial crisis caused a drop in the extent of FDI, but the latest values show an increase (The World Bank, 2013).

Figure 8.1 shows the development of FDI and the Corruption Perceptions Index (CPI) in China. The FDI increased steadily over the years. In the year 2009, the FDI inflows declined and recovered again in 2010. The development of corruption shows a declining but volatile trend. Starting with a score of 7.6, the general trend was downward, which shows a score of 6.4 in the year 2011.

Figure 8.2 shows the same variables for Russia. The FDI inflows reached its peak in the year 2008, with approximately $75.000 million USD, but declined in 2009. In contrast to China, the FDI inflows in Russia have not yet recovered totally since 2009 but the development is rising. The corruption scores show a higher volatility in Russia, which reached its highest scores of nearly 7.9 in the years 2000 and 2010, but declined in the year 2011 to 7.6.

Due to the fact that Russia and China are still in an ongoing process of change from a communistic structure to a more free and open market economy, these two countries serve as ideal bases for our research purpose. Another reason for focusing on China and Russia is that these countries possess considerable amounts of FDI inflows, although they show high levels of corruption.

A significant increase in FDI flows during the 1990s has led to several studies dealing with the impact of corruption on FDI (Lynn et al., 2011). The costs of corruption are viewed as additional costs of doing business or sometimes called tax on profits. In other words, corruption may decrease a company's expected profitability of an investment project in a country. The level of corruption in a host country is of particular interest when entering a new market. Moreover, the level of corruption may influence the decision on whether to invest abroad or not. However, the empirical literature dealing with the effects of the host country's corruption level on FDI inflows has not found these theoretical expected effects (Al-Sadig, 2009).

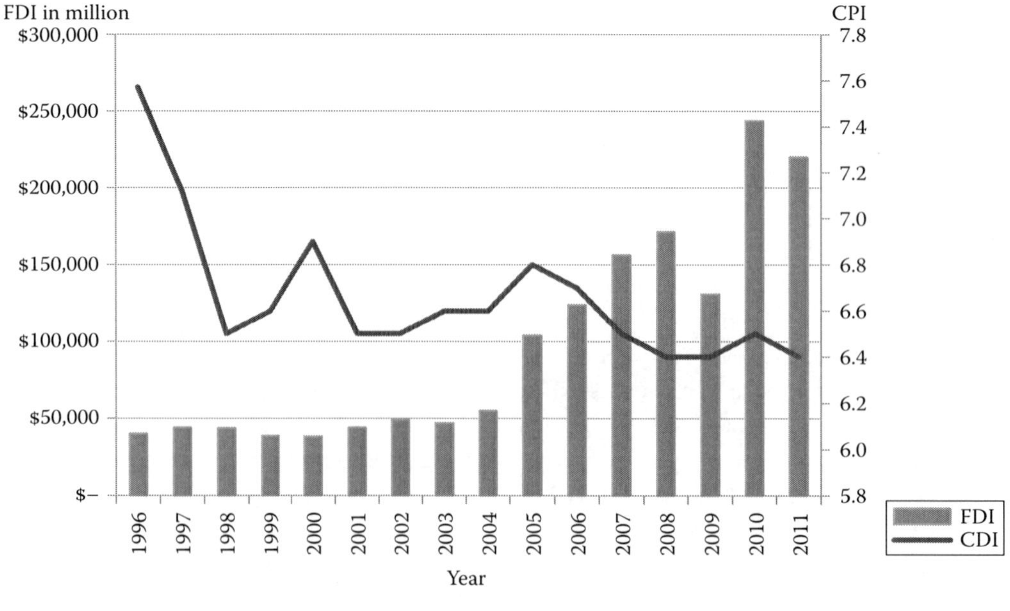

FIGURE 8.1 Development of FDI and corruption in China from 1996 until 2011.

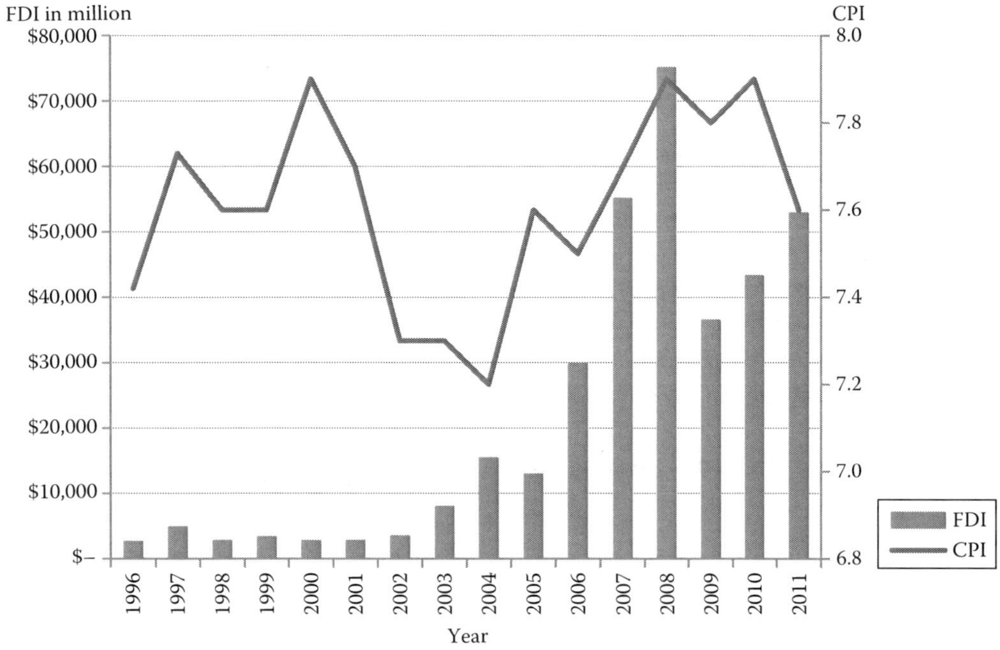

FIGURE 8.2 Development of FDI and corruption in Russia from 1996 until 2011.

Cuervo-Cazurra (2008) points out not only the negative but also the positive sides of corruption. He mentions that corruption can be seen as both the *grabbing hand* and the *helping hand*. The theory of the grabbing hand is also supported by Habib and Zurawiciki (2002), because corruption fosters precariousness in business outcomes and also creates bottlenecks, which is considered as morally wrong. In contrast, Lui (1985) points out that the theory of the helping hand appears most of the time concerning economic efficiency and notes that corruption is able to grease the wheel of ineffective bureaucracy, mostly in transition economies.

Up to the present time, no consensus has been found about whether corruption has a positive or a negative impact on FDI inflows. For example, Mauro (1995) provides evidence of a negative link between corruption and FDI inflows, Al-Sadig (2009) can't find any significant relationship, and according to Bardhan (1997) corruption can also have positive effects on FDI, because fixed regulations and ineffective bureaucracy can be duped by side payments.

Hakkala et al. (2005) conclude that corruption decreases the probability of investment. However, these authors also find that the effects of corruption are asymmetric. Their model showed that the impact of corruption may be asymmetric in two different dimensions. First, corruption may affect the probability that a firm chooses to invest, but not the size of affiliate activities once the firm has decided to invest. Second, corruption may have a differential effect on the type of investment, as measured by different types of affiliate activities.

Qian et al. (2012) examine the asymmetric effect of corruption distance on FDI. In their study, they found that positive and negative corruption distance impacts bilateral FDI behavior asymmetrically. An asymmetry in this context means a different impact of corruption on FDI.

In order to explain asymmetric effects, the prospect theory (Kahnemann and Tversky, 1979) in Figure 8.3 can be used. The characteristics of the hypothetical value function of the prospect theory are the

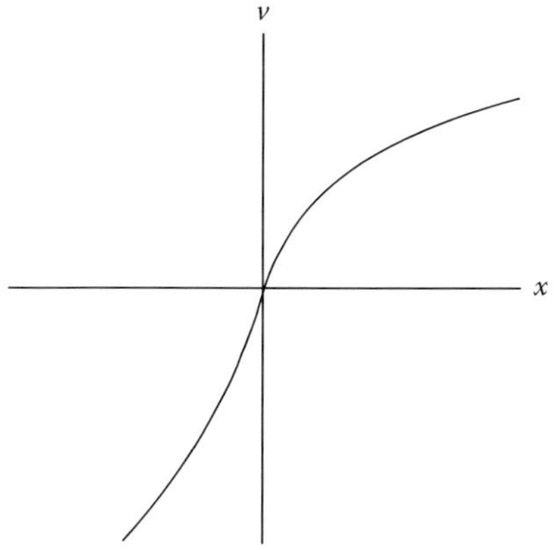

FIGURE 8.3 Prospect theory. (From Eisenführ, F. and Weber, M., *Rationales Entscheiden*, Vol. 4, Auflage, Berlin-Heidelberg, Germany, New York, 2003, p. 378.)

(1) reference point dependence, (2) concave for gains and convex for losses (diminishing sensitivity), and (3) steeper for losses than for gains (loss aversion).

Although several researchers have used the prospect theory in various fields (Gusenbauer, 2012; Levy and Wiener, 2013; Mittal et al., 1998), the research has failed to test the usefulness of the PT in the context of corruption and FDI. Of course a question arises concerning how the rigor of a theory test can be judged. Theory testing must be approached broadly and must include empirical representation of the explanatory constructs specified by the theory. This can be achieved by measuring the independent variables. The acceptability of the theory depends on the influence of the independent on the dependent variables representing some specified criterion of the construct (Sternthal et al., 1987). Calder et al. (1981) distinguish between effect application and theory application research. Effect application should be used for relationships in a particular real-world situation, whereas theory application is based on a desire for scientific knowledge about relationships that occur in a variety of real-world situations.

The aim of this study is to identify whether the prospect theory can be used to provide a general understanding of the relationship between corruption and FDI. Theory research calls for falsification of testing procedures. These procedures are used to test the theory within different contexts and measuring effects within the context in order to confirm or refute the theory. Theories that continually survive rigorous falsification attempts are accepted as scientific explanation and are useful for application (Calder et al., 1981; Popper, 2002). Therefore, our research question is: "Can the relationship of corruption and FDI in Russia/China be explained by the characteristics of the PT?" Figure 8.4 shows the relationship of our framework. The dashed line implies relationship with the testing procedure, while the continuous line shows the relationship of the independent on the dependent variable.

In order to test the prospect theory, three hypotheses for each country are tested. The hypotheses $H1_0/H1_1$ and $H2_0/H2_1$ for China and Russia, respectively, are developed to measure the loss aversion that is described by the prospect theory, which suggests that losses loom larger than gains (Einhorn and Hogarth, 1981). In other words, the value function is steeper in the negative area than in the positive. More precisely in the case of this investigation, negative outcomes on the independent variable corruption should have a greater impact than equal amounts of positive outcomes on the dependent variable FDI in China and Russia. Therefore, the following applies:

$H1_0$: Negative performance on corruption will have no greater impact on FDI than positive performance on corruption in China.

$H1_1$: Negative performance on corruption will have a greater impact on FDI than positive performance on corruption in China.

$H2_0$: Negative performance on corruption will have no greater impact on FDI than positive performance on corruption in Russia.

$H2_1$: Negative performance on corruption will have a greater impact on FDI than positive performance on corruption in Russia.

The hypotheses $H3_0/H3_1$ and $H4_0/H4_1$ for China and Russia, respectively, are developed to investigate the diminishing sensitivity. Diminishing sensitivity indicates that at high levels of corruption, the FDI inflows should not be affected as dramatically as it does at intermediate levels of corruption. Therefore, we arrive at the following conclusions:

$H3_0$: At high levels of corruption, FDI in China will be more affected than at intermediate levels of corruption.

$H3_1$: At high levels of corruption, FDI in China will be less affected than at intermediate levels of corruption.

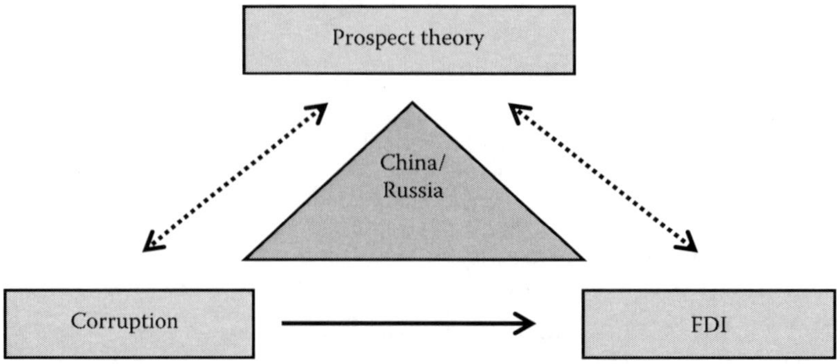

FIGURE 8.4 Overview of the framework.

$H4_0$: At high levels of corruption, FDI in Russia will be more affected than at intermediate levels of corruption.

$H4_1$: At high levels of corruption, FDI in Russia will be less affected than at intermediate levels of corruption.

Data

Data used to measure the perceived level of corruption are derived from Transparency International. This nongovernmental organization offers data on corruption for 183 countries around the world. Furthermore, it investigates how corruption is perceived in different sectors such as international relations, education, poverty and development, as well as health (Transparency International, 2013). The second source is the World Bank database. This international organization provides data for a wide range of countries and years. In addition, the database offers information for many topics related to economics. Most relevant for this study are the indicators for economic policy and external debt (World Bank, 2003).

The level of corruption is defined as the independent variable. Transparency International defines corruption as *the abuse of entrusted power for private gain*, which can be applied to both the public and private sectors. Corruption comprises illegal activities, which can be revealed through scandals, investigations, or prosecutions. The CPI, published annually by Transparency International, has been used as an indicator to measure the overall level of corruption by many researchers, including Cuervo-Cazurra (2008) and Hossain et al. (2012). This index combines the interpretations of many reliable institutions and experts living and working in the country. The focus of the CPI is on the public sector, observing the behavior of public official, servants, and politicians. Based on a survey, which contained questions relating to bribery of officials, graft in public procurement, and the effectiveness of anticorruption initiatives, a single score for each country was developed. The index ranges from 0 to 10. A score of 10 reflects a very clean country, where almost no corruption is present. In contrast, the lowest score 0 denotes a highly corrupt country (Transparency International, 2013).

Our research aims to be as comprehensible as possible. The analysis includes the data for all available years for both China and Russia, starting from 1996 to 2011. In addition, the index was rescaled, a score of 10 indicating a high level of corruption and 0 a low level, to enable a better comparison later on.

The dependent variable is FDI, net inflow, which is measured in U.S. dollar derived from the World Bank. The database uses the following definition to collect the relevant values: FDI is defined as the investment to attain a lasting management interest (at least 10% of voting stock) in a company, operating in a different economy than that of the investor. The values are the sum of equity capital, reinvestment of earnings, and other long-term and short-term capital as displayed in the balance of payments. The World Bank compromises the data from the International Monetary Fund, Balance of Payments database, the United Nations Conference on Trade and Development, and official national sources (World Bank, 2013).

Since data for corruption were available only from 1996 onward, the same time period was used for the independent as well as the dependent variables for both countries. The CPI was rescaled so that a score of 10 indicated a high level of corruption and 0 a low level, to enable a better comparison. The data on FDI inflows were divided by 1 million to reduce the complexity and enable a better overview of the FDI data.

Analysis

The analysis follows the procedure of Mittal et al. (1998) and Ting and Chen (2002). Descriptive statistics are used to define the point of reference in the analysis of the asymmetry. The mean, or average value, is given by the sum of all scores within a data set divided by the total number of scores. Following Field (2013) and Brosius (2013), the reference point of each variable consists of each mean.

As the goal of this research is rather to measure the impact of corruption in both countries separately than the overall impact, two equations need to be set up. Hence, the asymmetric and nonlinear impact of corruption on the FDI inflows in China is modeled as follows:

$$FDI_{ch} = Intercept + LN\_CO_{CH} + LP\_CO_{CH}$$

Adapting the model for the analysis of the impact in Russia results in the following equation:

$$FDI_{RU} = Intercept + LN\_CO_{RU} + LP\_CO_{RU}$$

In both equations the corruption variable is divided into *LN_CO* and *LP_CO*. Furthermore, *L* stands for the natural logarithm of each measure *L_CO* and *P_CO*. *N* and *P* indicate the negative and positive deviations or performances, respectively, from the mean level of corruption. The decomposition into negative and positive deviations is conducted this way: If the deviation from the first value is negative, the measurement variable for negative performance, *LN_CO*, equals ln(*CO*) and *LP_CO* equals to zero. As natural logarithms do not exist for negative numbers, the minus for *CO* for negative deviations is essential to make the final outcome positive. This means that a negative score of −4 yields to +4 by setting the variable to −(−4), enabling to take the natural logarithm. On the contrary, if the deviation is positive, the *LP_CO* equals to ln(*CO*) and *LN_CO* is zero. The following example targets to demonstrate the transformation process: If the first value has a negative deviation of −4, $LN\_CO_{CH} = \ln[-(-4)]$ and consequently $LP\_CO_{CH} = 0$. Inversely, if a score is 3, $LP\_CO_{CH} = \ln(3)$ and $LN\_CO_{CH} = 0$ (Brosius, 2013; Mittal et al., 1998; Ting and Chen, 2002).

This method results in two coefficients for each country (β_1 and β_2). As suggested by Mittal et al. (1998) and Ting and Chen (2002), a linear regression is conducted, which applies FDI as the dependent variable and *LP_CO* and *LN_CO* as the independent variables.

This measurement method supports the achievement of three relevant goals of this research. First, this procedure eases the comparison of the coefficients in order to test the hypothesized asymmetry, since it enables the researchers to compare the absolute value of the coefficients. For example, if one country has a larger coefficient in absolute values for negative performance than its coefficient for the positive performance, the negative asymmetry, characterizing the prospect theory, can be supported. In addition to that, the absolute value of the coefficients allows the researchers to analysis the magnitude of the effect, meaning the greater the absolute value of the coefficient, the greater the impact of corruption on FDI. Second, the relationship between corruption and FDI can be ascertained, due to the positive and negative algebraic signs. Third, the application of the natural logarithm reveals in case of a significant coefficient, the diminishing sensitivity (Mittal et al., 1998; Ting and Chen, 2002). Thus, a significant coefficient for negative performance on corruption in China would support the proposed hypothesis.

Results

Table 8.1 displays the results of the regression analysis for China and Russia. The unstandardized coefficient for LN_CO_{CH} is 3708.315 with a significance of 0.885. The unstandardized coefficient for LP_CO_{CH} is 4796.838 with a significance of 0.864. The coefficient for LN_CO_{RU} is 206.680 with a significance of 0.965. The coefficient for LP_CO_{RU} is −6148.682 with a significance of 0.518.

Interpretation

As can be seen, the goal is to investigate and explain the impact of corruption on FDI in China and Russia with the characteristics of the PT. Apart from the reference dependence, asymmetry, the diminishing sensitivity is also considered. Therefore, the first part of this chapter interprets and discusses the asymmetric impact between corruption and FDI in China and Russia. The second part interprets and discusses whether or not diminishing sensitivity is supported.

Table 8.1 Regression Analysis for China and Russia

		LN_CO		LP_CO	
	Intercept	Regression Coefficient for Negative Deviation (β1)	Significance	Regression Coefficient for Positive Deviation (β2)	Significance
China	104,227.71	3708.315	0.885	4796.838	0.864
Russia	17,561.49	206.680	0.965	−6148.682	0.518

Negative Asymmetry

Following Mittal et al. (1998) and Ting and Chen (2002), the unstandardized coefficients are used in order to determine a negative asymmetric relationship between corruption and FDI in China and Russia. A negative asymmetry requires *LN_CO* (β_{C1}) > *LP_CO* (β_{C2}) for each country. According to the results in Table 8.1, (β_{C1}) > (β_{C2}) can't be held, either for China or for Russia. This means that negative performance of corruption won't have a greater impact on FDI than a positive performance. In other words, instead of identifying a negative asymmetry, we found a positive asymmetry. Therefore, $H1_0$ and $H2_0$ have to be rejected and $H1_1$ and $H2_1$ have to be accepted for the time being.

However, the higher the absolute value of a coefficient, the higher the impact on the dependent variable (Ting and Chen, 2002). The absolute value of the coefficient in Russia is higher than the coefficient of China; therefore, corruption has a higher influence on FDI in Russia than in China. The negative β_{C2} of Russia indicates that a higher level of corruption might decrease the FDI inflows into the country. On the contrary, the positive coefficient of China implies that the impact of corruption on FDI in China is positive.

Diminishing Sensitivity

To prove the diminishing sensitivity in China and Russia, it is necessary to observe significant values for β_{C1} and β_{C2}. A significant beta coefficient, which is based on a natural logarithm, indicates diminishing sensitivity. Therefore, the beta coefficients of the negative (*LN_CO_CH*) and positive (*LP_CO_CH*) deviations need to be significant to reject $H3_0$.

As indicated in Table 8.1, β_{C1} and β_{C2} for China are not significant, displaying a significance levels of 0.885 and 0.864, respectively, which exceed the critical level of 0.05. Similarly, here is the result for the Russia: β_{R1} has a significance level of 0.965 and β_{R2} a value of 0.518, indicating also nonsignificant values.

This means that for China as well as for Russia, the results do not give evidence for a diminishing sensitivity and we have to accept $H3_0$ and $H4_0$. In other words, at high levels of corruption, FDI in China and Russia will be more affected than at intermediate levels of corruption.

Discussion

Comparing our results with other conducted studies reveals that research findings on the influence of corruption on FDI are very controversial. Dahlström and Johnson (2007) conclude that host country corruption has a negative effect on the size of FDI inflows, since side payments to corrupt bureaucrats decrease the expected profitability of multinational enterprises (MNEs). Moreover Shleifer and Vishny (1993) and Wei (1997) observe that corruption deters FDI, since it may act as a tax on investment or increase risk about costs.

Wu (2006) and Qian et al. (2012) also find evidence that the corruption impact on FDI might be negative or positive, depending on the corruption distance to the home country. This means companies tend to invest into host countries that have a similar or lower level of corruption to their home country rather than into host countries with a higher level.

Interestingly, Barassi and Zhou (2012) state that without control of the location of the selection process for FDI, corruption has a negative effect on FDI and can be seen as a *grabbing hand*. In contrast to that, they point out that with a control of the selection process, the impact of corruption on the level of FDI stock can be seen as positive. In other words, when MNEs once have chosen a country in which they want to invest, a higher corruption level may increase FDI stock and can be seen as a *helping hand*. This result can be compared with the conclusion reached by Wei (2000a,b), who points out that MNEs that invest in foreign markets are less corruption averse than those companies that do not undertake FDI.

In contrast to many other studies who find evidence for an asymmetric relationship between FDI and corruption, the results of the analysis from Al-Sadig (2009) show a negative linear relationship between those two variables. In more detail, it was found out that a 1-point increase in the corruption level leads to a reduction in per capita FDI inflows by about 11%. But it has to be noted that after controlling the *quality of institutions*, the negative effects of corruption disappear. In fact, it is pointed out that the quality of an institution is more crucial in attracting FDI than the level of corruption in a country (Al-Sadig, 2009).

Pupović (2012) states that corruption is a highly complex phenomenon and that this fact is ignored in several investigations. There are relationships between numerous other characteristics of the host country, including the quality of institutions, the lack of competition, and cultural values. In addition, it is also possible that there are time-invariant unobserved effects that vary from country to country and are associated with corruption. Corruption is not only an independent variable. The level of corruption might also be influenced by other variables in the host country, including the level of economic development, the quality of institutions, and cultural characteristics.

Conclusion

In China as well as in Russia, investors are confronted with rather high levels of corruption when entering the market. Nevertheless, these markets attract continuously increasing amounts of FDI. The economic literature discusses the relationship between corruption and FDI quite differently. A wide range of literature has been reviewed, but no valid generalizations about the impact of corruption on FDI can be made thus far. The research presented here sought to analyze how the characteristics of the prospect theory can contribute to explaining this controversially discussed economic issue.

The comparison of the results for both countries shows that the impact of corruption on FDI is indeed asymmetric. Interestingly, the prominent factor in Russia and China is the positive coefficient. The fact that China and Russia have a larger β_2 than β_1 (or $\beta_1 < \beta_2$) indicates that the asymmetry in both countries is positive. Thus, the negative asymmetric characteristic suggested by the PT is not applicable to describe the relationship between FDI and corruption in China and Russia. This means that in both countries, a higher level of corruption may influence the impact of corruption on FDI stronger than a low level of corruption.

A comparison of the absolute value of both coefficients for a positive deviation points out that the magnitude of the impact in Russia and China differs. The investigation shows that the influence of corruption on FDI in Russia is relatively higher than in China. Furthermore, the results suggest that the level of corruption can influence the FDI inflows positively as well as negatively. In the case of China, the analysis indicates that a higher level of corruption might also lead to more FDI inflows. In contrast, in the case of Russia, the results imply that a higher level of corruption may decrease the amount of FDI inflows.

Since the coefficients of both countries are not significant, the results of the research have to be interpreted with caution. Moreover, the low level of significance reveals that there is no evidence for the diminishing sensitivity at high as well as low levels of corruption in Russia and China. One reason why the results might not be significant is that the available values are not sufficient, meaning the period of time from 1996 to 2011 is too narrow. Another possible explanation can be found in the study of Abdellaoui et al. (2007), which suggests that the size of the outcome might influence the concavity and convexity of the value function. Small outcomes can result in less convexity for losses than larger outcomes (Abdellaoui et al., 2007).

In conclusion, due to the positive asymmetry as well as the unproven diminishing sensitivity, the characteristics of the prospect theory do not explain the impact of corruption on FDI either in China or in Russia.

Limitations

Several limitations reduce the generalizability of the findings, which can be taken as starting points for future researches.

The major limitation of the research is due to the low level of significance of the results for Russia and China. Therefore, researchers could further elaborate if the characteristics of the prospect theory can explain the relationship between corruption and FDI in other countries. In addition, studies in the future could use different variables for measuring the impact of corruption on FDI. Although the CPI of Transparency International is widely accepted as an appropriate measure of the level of corruption, other indexes, including those discussed by Thompson and Shah (2005), could lead to different results.

In addition, researchers could question the level of corruption as a measurement of corruption per se. For example, an interesting approach could be to investigate if the characteristics of the prospect theory can explain the impact of corruption distance on FDI.

References

Abdellaoui, M., Bleichrodt, H., and Paraschiv, C. (October 2007). Loss aversion under prospect theory: A parameter-free measurement. *Management Science*, 53(10), 1659–1674.

Al-Sadig, A. (2009). The effects of corruption on FDI inflows. *Cato Journal*, 29, 267–294.

Barassi, M. R. and Zhou, Y. (January 11, 2012). The effect of corruption on FDI: A parametric and non-parametric analysis. *European Journal of Political Economy*, 28(3), 302–312.

Bardhan, P. (1997). Corruption and development. A review of issues. *Journal of Economic Literature*, 35(3), 1320–1346.

Brosius, F. (2013). *SPSS 21.* Heidelberg, Germany.

Calder, B., Phillips, L., Tybout, A. (1981): Designing research for application. *Journal of Consumer Research*, 8, 197–207.

Central Intelligence Agency. (June 10, 2013). Central Intelligence Agency. Retrieved June 17, 2013, from https://www.cia.gov/library/publications/the-world-factbook/geos/rs.html.

Cuervo-Cazurra, A. (2008). Better the devil you don't know: Types of corruption and FDI in transition economies. *Journal of International Management*, 14(1), 12–27.

Dahlström, T. and Johnson, A. (2007). Bureaucratic corruption, MNEs and FDI. CESIS—Electronic Working Paper Series, Paper No. 82, 1–39.

Einhorn, H. J. and Hogarth, R. M. (1981). Behavioral decision theory: Processes of judgement and choice. *Annual Review of Psychology*, 32, 53–88.

Eisenführ, F. and Weber, M. (2003). *Rationales Entscheiden*, Vol. 4. Auflage, Berlin-Heidelberg, Germany.

Field, A. (2013). In *Discovering Statistics Using IBM SPSS Statistics*, Vol. 4. (M. Carmichael, Ed.) Sage Publications Ltd., Los Angeles, CA.

Gusenbauer, B. (2012). Der beitrag der prospect theory zur Beschreibung und Erklärung von Servicequalitätsurteilen und Kundenzufriedenheit im Kontext von *Versicherungsentscheidungen*, Peter Lang, Vienna, Germany.

Habib, M. and Zurawicki, L. (2002). Corruption and foreign direct investment. *Journal of International Business Studies*, 33(2), 291–307.

Hakkala, K., Norbäck, P.-J., and Svaleryd, H. (2005). Asymmetric effects of corruption on FDI: Evidence from Swedish multinational firms. The Research Institute of Industrial Economics, IUI Working Paper No. 641, 1–54.

Harrison, M. (2011). Can corrupt countries attract foreign direct investments? A comparison of FDI inflows between corrupt and non corrupt countries. *International Business and Economics Research Journal*, 2(9), 93–100.

Hossain, T., Keep, W., and Peters, S. (2012). Corruption and foreign direct investment: The moderating effect of bilateral tax treaties. *International Journal of Business Insights and Transformation*, 4, 40–48.

Kahneman, D. and Tversky, A. (March 1979). Prospect theory: An analysis of decision under risk. *Econometrica*, 47(2), 263–291.

Levy, H. and Wiener, Z. (2013). Prospect theory and utility theory: Temporary versus permanent attitude toward risk. *Journal of Economic and Business*, 68, 1–23.

Lui, F. (1985). An equilibrium queuing model of bribery. *Journal of Political Economy*, 93, 760–781.

Lynn, D., Wang, T., and Mehlum, C. (2011). Investing in emerging markets: China, India and Brazil. *Real Estate Issues*, 36(2), 21–28.

Mauro, P. (August 1995). Corruption and growth. *The Quarterly Journal of Economics*, 110(3), 681–712.

Mittal, V., Ross, W. T., and Baldasare, P. (1998). The asymmetric impact of negative and positive attribute level performance on overall satisfaction and repurchase intentions. *Journal of Marketing*, 62, 33–47.

Popper, K. (2002). *The Logic of Scientific Discovery*, Taylor & Francis Group: London.

Primorac, D. and Smoljic, M. (2011). Impact of corruption of foreign direct investment. *Megatrend Review*, 8(2), 169–190.

Pupovic, A. (2012). Corruption effects on foreign direct investments—The case of Montenegro. *Economic Review—Journal of Economics and Business*, 10(2), 13–28.

Qian, X., Sandoval-Hernandez, J., and Garrett, J. (2012). *Corruption Distance and Foreign Direct Investment.* SUNY Buffalo State College, Buffalo, NY.

Shleifer, A. and Vishny, R. (1993). Corruption. *Quarterly Journal of Economics*, 108(3), 599–617.

Sternthal, B., Tybout, A., and Calder, B. (1987). Confirmatory versus comparative approaches to judging theory tests. *Journal of Consumer Research*, 14, 114–125.

Thompson, T. and Shah, A. (2005). Transparency International's Corruption Perceptions Index: Whose perceptions are they anyway? World Bank. http://citeseerx.ist.psu.edu/viewdoc/download?doi=10.1.1.370.4882&rep=rep1&type=pdf.

Ting, S. and Chen, C. (2002). The asymmetrical and non-linear effects of store quality attributes on customer satisfaction. *Total Quality Management*, 13, 547–569.

Transparency International. (2012a). Transparency International. Retrieved May 30, 2013, from http://www.transparency.org/whoweare/organisation/faqs_on_corruption.

Transparency International. (2012b). Transparency International. Retrieved June 02, 2013, from Politics and Government: http://www.transparency.org/topic/detail/politics_and_government.

Transparency International. (2012c). Transparency International. Retrieved June 16, 2013, from http://www.transparency.org/research/cpi/overview.

Transparency International. (2012d). Transparency International. Retrieved June 16, 2013, from http://cpi.transparency.org/cpi2012/results/.

Transparency International. (2013). Transparency International. Retrieved June 07, 2013, from http://www.transparency.org/.

Wei, S. (1997). Why is corruption so much taxing than tax? Arbitrariness Kills. NBER Working Paper No. 6255, 1–27.

Wei, S. (2000a). How taxing is corruption on international investors? *The Review of Economics and Statistics*, 82, 1–11.

Wei, S. (2000b). Local corruption and global capital flows. *Brookings Papers on Economic Activity*, 2, 303–354.

World Bank. (2013). World Bank FDI database. Retrieved June 3, 2013, from http://data.worldbank.org/indicator/BN.KLT.DINV.CD?order=wbapi_data_value_2005%20wbapi_data_value%20wbapi_data_value-first&sort=desc.

World Bank. (2013a). The World Bank. Retrieved June 17, 2013, from http://data.worldbank.org/indicator/SP.POP.TOTL.

World Bank. (2013b). The World Bank. Retrieved June 17, 2013, from http://data.worldbank.org/indicator/BX.KLT.DINV.CD.WD.

World Bank Group. (2013c). The World Bank. Retrieved May 31, 2013, from http://web.worldbank.org/WBSITE/EXTERNAL/EXTABOUTUS/0,contentMDK:2 3272490~pagePK:5112364 4~piPK:329829~theSitePK:29708,00.html.

World Trade Organization. (2013). World Trade Organization. Retrieved June 17, 2013, from http://www.wto.org/english/news_e/pres96_e/pr057_e.htm.

Wu, S. (2006). Corruption and cross-border investment by multinational firms. *Journal of Comparative Economics*, 34(4), 839–856.

9. "Construction Mafia?" Social Fraud and Organized Crime—The Austrian Perspective

Martin Meissnitzer

Introduction

More than 10 years ago, the notion of the "construction mafia" (*Baumafia*) evolved in Austria as part of catchy headlines: "Tax authorities seize 40 Mn Euros construction mafia finds new loopholes"* or "Construction mafia: public servant exposes social fraud"† and, more recently, "€140 Mn damages: construction mafia network exposed."‡ Consequently, there is a widespread perception of the Austrian construction sector being infested by the "mafia" that is responsible for "organized social fraud" amounting to alleged damages of 800 million euros to 1 billion euros per year.§ In the following, this chapter tries to go beyond the headlines in order to explain what type of criminal phenomenon is covered by the highly ambiguous terms "construction mafia" and "organized social fraud" in order to establish the ties between a particular evasion scheme regarding social security contributions as well as wage taxes and structures of organized crime.

In order to approach this topic, a few terminological clarifications will be essential: the term "mafia" is commonly used for different groups and phenomena. In the following context, mafia shall be synonymous with the term "organized criminal group," that is, "a structured group of three or more persons, existing for a period of time and acting in concert with the aim of committing one or more serious crimes or offences [...] in order to obtain, directly or indirectly, a financial or other material benefit."¶ For the term "social fraud," however, there is no common understanding. Usually it tends to be associated with defrauding the social security or welfare system by claiming different types of benefits without being legally entitled to them. In the Austrian context, however, it is often used synonymously with what is usually referred to as "undeclared work," relating to paid activities that are not illegal in themselves, but not sufficiently declared to the authorities.** In this sense, it was already used by the Austrian government to coin one of the first legal initiatives, the "Social Fraud Act," trying to tackle the construction mafia in 2005.†† The steps taken

* *Die Presse*, February 13, 2013, http://diepresse.com/home/wirtschaft/economist/209320/Fiskus-pfaendete-40-Millionen-Euro_Baumafia-hat-neue-Schlupflocher?from=suche.intern.portal (accessed on July 10, 2014).

† *Die Presse*, July 17, 2004, http://diepresse.com/home/wirtschaft/economist/167922/Baumafia_Beamter-deckt-Sozialbetrug-auf?from=suche.intern.portal (accessed on July 10, 2014).

‡ *Die Presse*, July 8, 2014, http://diepresse.com/home/wirtschaft/economist/3834939/140-Mio-Euro-Schaden_BaumafiaNetz-aufgeflogen?from=suche.intern.portal (accessed on July 10, 2014).

§ Estimation for 2004, EBRV 698 BlgNR XXIV.GP 5.

¶ Art 2 lit a United Nations Convention against Transnational Organized Crime.

** Cf. the respective definitions of the EU in European Commission (2007) and the OECD (2004, p. 232).

†† "Social Fraud Act," BGBl I 152/2004.

in this initiative focused exclusively on the evasion of social security contributions by employers and did not include any fraudulent benefit claims in their understanding of "social fraud." Taking into account that the evasion of social security contributions and wrongful benefit claims frequently occur hand in hand, this perception might be insufficient. Thus, this chapter follows the more global approach of the European Union defining "social security fraud" as "any act or omission to act, in order to obtain or receive social security benefits or to avoid obligations to pay social security contributions, contrary to the law of a Member State."*

* Art A 2 b Resolution of the Council and the Representatives of the Governments of the Member States, meeting within the Council of April 22, 1999 on a Code of Conduct for improved cooperation between authorities of the Member States concerning the combating of transnational social security benefit and contribution fraud and undeclared work, and concerning the transnational hiring-out of workers, OJEU C 125/1, June 5, 1999.

Organized Social Fraud in Austria

Austria is a country with comparatively high labor costs,† mostly due to a significant level of social security contributions and wage-related taxes. In general, the employer is legally required to immediately register a new employee at the competent social security institution, deliver the necessary contribution data, and eventually pay social security contributions and wage taxes. Bearing in mind the increasing competition and a continuing race to the bottom in order to reduce prices and win tender offers, there has always been a high incentive for employers to reduce labor costs. Traditionally, this could be achieved by simply not declaring the employment of workers and paying them "cash in hand." This scenario, however, always had two shortcomings: On the one hand, the increasing number of on-site inspections by different authorities led to a high risk of being exposed and having to pay severe administrative fines. On the other hand, many full-time workers insisted on a declared employment so that they (and their families) would be covered by social insurance. As a result, a new evasion scheme evolved: instead of hiding the employment altogether, it consisted in concealing the identity of the actual employer by outsourcing employees to letterbox companies. This phenomenon gave and still gives thousands of workers access to social insurance without paying the related social security contributions and wage taxes into the system.

Modus Operandi

How does it work exactly? In Austria, there are numerous transient limited liability companies who do not have any (formal) economic activity and only serve as vehicles for declaring employees as well as various billing purposes. Officially, such letterbox companies are run by a single person, who acts as registered shareholder and managing director at the same time and who is either a front man from abroad or using a false identity. In one case, the Austrian police identified a suspect who acted as a front man for at least 15 letterbox companies using 12 different identities within a period of 5 years (Meissnitzer, 2013b, p. 11). The real wire-pullers of those companies typically act behind the scenes and do not occupy any formal position within the company. In order to minimize labor costs, employers can turn to the people controlling such a company and have them register their workers with the Austrian social security system as employees of the letterbox company. In return for this "outsourcing service," the actual employer pays a fee that usually varies between 150 euros and 350 euros per month per worker, which is still cheaper than paying the social security contributions and wage taxes. Once the workers have been registered as active employees, they are covered by all branches of the Austrian social security system, including sickness, pension, accident, and unemployment insurance (Meissnitzer, 2013a). Whenever an on-site inspection takes place, the encountered workers are all registered in the social security database, thus avoiding fines for nondeclaration of employment. As mentioned before, neither contributions nor wage taxes are paid. Providing that the registered person actually works, they are legally entitled to claim social security benefits, despite the fact that their respective employer never paid into the system.

Although this phenomenon has been known for many years, it still takes up to 1 year until the authorities discover an active letterbox company and initiate bankruptcy proceedings in order to take it "off the market." At this moment in time, the workers are deregistered from the social security system. The perpetrators, however, already have the next company lined up, ready to start again from scratch. During its lifetime, the people running one of those companies try to offer their *outsourcing services* to as many employers

† Cf. Eurostat figures on labor costs, retrieved at http://epp.eurostat.ec.europa.eu/statistics_explained/index.php/Wages_and_labour_costs (July 10, 2014).

as possible. Consequently, a single letterbox company usually registers hundreds, in some extreme cases even more than 1000 employees with the Austrian social security system. In one recent case, four main suspects allegedly registered up to 7500 persons as employees of 20 letterbox companies over a period of about 5 years leading to damages of 140 million euros; their mere profits from "registration" fees are estimated at about 3 million euros.*

Subcontracting Pyramids

Mostly, an active letterbox company is discovered during on-site inspections or audits by different inspection services. Especially on big construction sites, they are confronted with highly elaborated subcontracting chains. On top, you would find a general contractor subcontracting parts of his or her contract to other companies, who themselves work with subcontractors. As a result, there are up to five or more levels of subcontractors. The majority of the required workforce is usually registered with letterbox companies on the lowest level, thus creating the impression that they are, in fact, legitimate construction companies or temporary work agencies. In reality, the workers are usually directly employed by a company on a higher level in the subcontracting chain and outsourced as described earlier. The people controlling the letterbox company are usually not involved in the construction project; they only provide their company as a billing vehicle for the required workforce including a bogus subcontract for the actual employer in order to conceal his employer status (Reindl-Krauskopf et al., 2012, p. 47).

Kickback Payments, Black Funds, and Corruption

The second major source of profit, besides the registration fees, lies within issuing pro forma—or fake—invoices in the name of a letterbox company that serve a wide array of purposes. By certifying fictitious expenditures, they can be "bought" by entrepreneurs in order to reduce their taxable profits and, henceforth, their tax load. More commonly, employers intending to outsource their workers also require an invoice to cover the *cash in hand*—salaries as well as the registration fees they are paying off the books. Finally, it is an effective way to launder money as well as to create black funds financing bribes to win tender offers (Reindl-Krauskopf et al., 2012, p. 50).

Police investigations have shown that the entrepreneur usually transfers the invoice sum to one of the letterbox company's bank accounts, where the money is withdrawn in cash on the same day. The people behind the letterbox company deduct a commission of about 5%–10% of the invoice sum before handing the money back over to the entrepreneur. In the aforementioned case, the group allegedly issued 2600 of these fictitious invoices covering invoice sums of 25 million euros over a period of 5 years.†

Ties to Other Types of Criminality

The vast availability of letterbox companies also enables different types of criminality due to the widespread "trade" with social security registrations. Besides giving access to all different kinds of social security benefits, those registrations also serve as proof of an employment, a steady income, or, more general, sufficient resources and therefore play a crucial role in the Austrian society. As a result, registrations with the Austrian social security system are not only sold to employers trying to minimize labor costs for their workers but to merely anyone who manages to pay the registration fees, irrespective of whether the person is legally entitled to social insurance. This led to the emergence of a virtual black market for bogus social security registrations. In those cases, the registered persons as well as their next of kin enjoy full coverage without meeting the legal requirements for social security. Moreover, they can declare any amount of salary, thus fraudulently increasing the amount of income-related cash benefits (e.g., sickness, maternity, unemployment, or pension benefits). In practice, it is merely impossible to establish whether the persons registered by a letterbox company actually work and are therefore entitled to claim benefits or not. Recently, the Austrian Financial Police estimated the average number of bogus registration, that is, registrations of inactive persons, at around

* "Wie das aufgedeckt Baumafia-Netzwerk operierte," *Der Standard*, July 9, 2014, http://derstandard.at/2000002866815/Wie-das-aufgedeckte-Baumafia-Netz-operierte (accessed July 10, 2014); "140 Mio. Euro Schaden: Baumafia-Netz aufgeflogen," *Die Presse*, http://diepresse.com/home/wirtschaft/economist/3834939/140-Mio-Euro-Schaden_BaumafiaNetz-aufgeflogen?from=suche.intern.portal (accessed July 10, 2014).

† "Wie das aufgedeckt Baumafia-Netzwerk operierte," *Der Standard* 09.07.2014. http://derstandard.at/2000002866815/Wie-das-aufgedeckte-Baumafia-Netz-operierte (accessed July 10, 2014).

25% of all registrations by letterbox companies.* Besides fraudulently obtaining social security benefits, those registrations are also used to obtain visa and residency permits, bank loans, etc.

Furthermore, there is also anecdotal evidence of informal agents offering pregnant women abroad the opportunity to give birth in Austrian hospitals as well as access to maternity benefits (in hand as well as cash). After being registered as employees of a letterbox company, those women take their maternity leave after 2 or 3 weeks and return to their home countries shortly after the delivery (Reindl-Krauskopf and Meissnitzer, 2013, p. 14). Apart from the latter, bankruptcy allowances are particularly affected as well. Whenever a letterbox company goes bankrupt, many of the registered employees claim bankruptcy allowances by stating that they were not paid their last salaries. In reality, most of them either were not working at all or received their full salary *cash in hand* (Reindl-Krauskopf et al., 2012, p. 51).

Networks and Structures

As far as we know, it can be argued that especially the people controlling those letterbox companies belong to organized criminal groups, often affiliated with particular ethnic groups. Apart from enabling employers to evade social security contributions and taxes or other persons to commit individual forms of benefit fraud, they are often involved in other forms of white collar crime as well as "traditional" fields of organized crime, that is, money laundering, drugs, and extortion. Police investigations showed that they are applying highly elaborate shielding measures to avoid being identified. From their perspective offering, their service is just another highly effective way to make enormous profits with a very low risk of detection and prosecution. However, the term "construction mafia" might be misleading, insofar as it limits the scope to the construction sector. Although the phenomenon is particularly common in construction, it appears in many other economic sectors having a high demand especially for low-skilled workforce. Thus, the persons registered as employees of a letterbox company work not only in construction but also in the transport sector, agriculture and forestry, gastronomy, security business, meat industry, etc. Moreover, by selling bogus employment registrations and wrongfully giving access to social insurance to people who are not entitled to it, their activities raise questions far beyond compliance issues in the construction sector.

In a nutshell, the organized groups managed to create a system in the best economic interest of all involved actors: the construction mafia itself makes enormous profits with a comparatively low risk of being exposed. On the demand side, there are employers and individuals who are usually not affiliated with the organizations behind the companies. The employers simply seize the opportunity to reduce labor costs and tax loads. They decide to collude with an organized group in order to gain a competitive advantage on the market, leading to significant distortion of competition. In some sectors, this practice became widespread, thus gradually forcing law-abiding entrepreneurs to either engage in social security fraud or leave the sector altogether.

The individuals who are registered as employees of a letterbox company form a rather heterogeneous group. If they are inactive, that is, not working at all, they have to be considered as fraudsters themselves, requiring the bogus registration for benefit scams, unemployment insurance, medical health benefits and other assistance programs. If they are actively working, they are entitled to social security benefits. Mostly, those workers further benefit from the system by earning relatively high cash-in-hand salaries, due to the evasion of contributions and taxes. In other cases, however, those workers might be exploited themselves, being subject to severe working conditions and gaining only a fraction of the relevant minimum wage.

* "Baumafia: Paradefall für organisiert Abgabenkriminalität," *Die Presse* June 9, 2014, http://diepresse.com/home/wirtschaft/economist/3835360/Baumafia_Paradefall-fur-organisierte-Abgabenkriminalitaet?from=suche.intern.portal (accessed July 10, 2014).

Tackling the Construction Mafia in Austria

During the past several years, numerous steps were taken on regulatory as well as organizational level in order to eradicate the "construction mafia," including repressive as well as preventative measures. In the following, I will focus on the two most visible ones, relating to each side of the spectrum.

In 2005, the Austrian government tried a repressive approach by introducing new criminal sanctions in the "Social Fraud Act."† Shortly afterward, the Austrian police reacted by establishing a joint

† Sozialbetrugsgesetz, BGBl I 152/2004.

investigations team with members of the police, the tax fraud investigation unit of the financial administration, and representatives of the social security institutions (Reindl-Krauskopf et al., 2013, p. 134). They succeeded in exposing eight major groups controlling more than 200 letterbox companies over a period of approximately 5 years. Due to meticulous investigations, key figures of those groups could be tried in court and eventually convicted thus dismantling the functioning of those particular groups. However, the void they left behind on the black market for social security registrations was quickly filled by other groups. So despite the initial success, the exclusively repressive approach focusing on the organized groups was not enough to effectively tackle the construction mafia.

In 2010, the Austrian government tried a different approach by introducing a system of joint and several liabilities for social security contributions and wage taxes in the construction sector.* The law provides that a contractor can be held liable for a certain amount of his subcontractor's overdue social security contributions and wage taxes. The concerned contractor may avoid liability by either choosing a subcontractor from a "green list" of companies that are deemed to be in compliance with the law or by deducting a certain amount of the subcontractor's remuneration and transferring it directly to a clearing office of the social security system. At this clearing office, those funds may then be used directly to cover unpaid debts or forwarded to the subcontractor if he appears to be compliant. Since 2010, there have been almost no cases where the actual liability had to be enforced, because contractors tend to choose one of the preventative tools to avoid liability. As a result, damages could be significantly reduced by increasing the number of subcontracts with companies from the "green list" or by directly receiving funds from the contractors. Furthermore, this preventative approach helped to reduce profits for organized groups and gave law-abiding companies a possibility to effectively check the reliability of their subcontractors.

This approach was not enough to tackle the problem and still has a number of shortcomings. Due to the fact that the law does not provide for an actual chain liability,† the liability only applies at one level of the contracting relationship; thus it might be circumvented by simply interposing more companies in a subcontracting chain, especially foreign subsidiaries or subcontractors. Furthermore, the liability only applies in the construction sector and has no impact for subcontracting schemes in other sectors and does not provide any solution for selling social security registrations to inactive individuals who do not exercise any professional activity. Contrary to the repressive approach focusing only on the organized groups, the system helped nonetheless to drain profits of those organized groups, thus making it less attractive or at least more expensive to engage in this type of fraudulent behavior.

* Cf. §67a ASVG and §82a EStG.

† Regarding the distinction between chain liability and joint and several liability cf. Houwerzil and Peters (2008, p. 2).

Conclusion

In conclusion, the Austrian cases of letterbox companies controlled by organized criminal groups serve as a perfect example for the interaction of organized crime and the vast field of undeclared work and social security fraud.

Nevertheless, the notion of the construction mafia might be misleading by indicating that the phenomenon is limited to the construction sector and a particular organized group, separated from the formal economy. In reality, the organized structures can be found in virtually any sector with a high demand for rather low-skilled, manual labor. By offering companies as tools for various aspects of social security fraud, those groups respond to an existing demand for ways to reduce labor costs or to fraudulently obtain social security coverage. This phenomenon mutually benefits the members of the "mafia," the employers, and in most cases also the workers, although there have been cases where the workers were exploited as well.

Different efforts to tackle the problem may not have eradicated the problem, but succeeded in draining profits and increasing the risk of being prosecuted. Due to the newly raised awareness, the organized groups started shifting their business model to foreign letterbox companies, who offer a whole new range of evasion of social security contributions, wage taxes, and minimum wage standards. Those transnational phenomena require a high level of international cooperation and cross-border data exchange between the authorities and are going to be the next defining challenge in the fight against social security fraud.

References

European Commission. (2007). Stepping up the fight against undeclared work, Communication from the Commission to the Council, the European Parliament, the European Economic and Social Committee and the Committee of Regions, COM (2007) 628 final.

Houwerzijl, M., Peters, S. (2008). Liability in subcontracting processes in the European construction sector. http://www.ft.dk/samling/20121/almdel/beu/spm/69/svar/931966/1199657.pdf. Accessed July 10, 2014.

Meissnitzer, M. (2013a). *Sozialbetrug, Schwarzarbeit, Schattenwirtschaft*. Verlag für Polizeiwissenschaft, Frankfurt, Germany.

Meissnitzer, M. (2013b). Scheinfirmen und Massenanmeldungen, kripo.at 11/2013, pp. 11–13. http://www.kripo.at/ZEITUNG/2013/05%20Oktober%2013/11-scheinfirmen.pdf. Accessed July 10, 2014.

OECD. (2004). Employment outlook 2004. http://www.oecd.org/employment/emp/oecdemploymentoutlook2004.htm. Accessed July 10, 2014.

Reindl-Krauskopf, S., Kirchmayr-Schliesselberger, S., Windisch-Graetz, M., Meissnitzer, M. (2012). Endbericht zum Forschungsprojekt "Sozialbetrug, auch im Zusammenhang mit Lohn und Sozialdumping," Vienna, Austria. https://www.bmask.gv.at/site/Startseite/News/Endbericht_zum_Forschungsprojekt_Sozialbetrug_liegt_vor. Accessed July 10, 2014.

Reindl-Krauskopf, S., Meissnitzer, M. (2013). Types of social security fraud—A legal analysis. *Bulletin luxembourgeois des questions sociales* 30: 7–20.

10. Organized Crime and the Informal Economy

The Austrian Perspective

Maximilian Edelbacher

Introduction

For decades, daily police work has been confronted with the phenomenon of organized crime, white collar crime, and corruption. The informal economy, also termed the shadow economy, was not a primary target of policing. Tax authorities, of course, are steadily confronted with the phenomenon of the informal economy. It is well known that nearly every citizen tries to avoid taxes and looks for possibilities to do so.

What happened in 1989 can be seen as a paradox. We in Europe were confronted with the "Fall of the Iron Curtain." This was like a miracle, because it seemed unbelievable that the Soviet Union would ever collapse. On the one side, enormous hopes came through that a new era of freedom had begun, but on the other hand, the breakdown of the Soviet Union was the starting point of exporting crime all over the world, because Russian organized crime gangs established themselves in America and especially in Europe. By this dramatic challenge, we were immediately confronted, not only with a geographically unified Europe, an area of freedom, but also with a dramatic increase of crime, especially organized crime and corruption, coupled with an increase in the informal economy. Many people from the former Eastern Bloc countries offered themselves as cheap workers and offered cheap products from the East. At the same time, cars were stolen all over Western Europe, the number of burglaries increased, and all kinds of expensive goods, which were not available in the former Eastern Bloc countries, were delivered illegally to the East. These challenges changed the economic balance between the East and the West. These new resources entered the economy and expanded the informal economy dramatically. For example, a very dramatic development was illegal immigration. Thousands of women came to Western Europe as sex workers, and millions of young men and women left their home countries to find better working possibilities in Western Europe or America.

After 2008, in different meetings and talks, experts discussed the question of how much organized crime influenced the financial crisis, how much it caused it, and if it can be proved that organized crime played an important role. If the financial crisis was started mainly because of financial crimes as an outcome of organized crime activities, it seems to be logical that a link between them exists. In this chapter I elaborate on these topics, and the first thesis is that the financial crisis and organized crime showed up as the so-called twin brothers.* The second thesis deals with the assumed link between financial crimes, organized crime, and informal crime. There exists an impression that white collar crime and financial crimes concentrate in the actual development of informal crime.

* Bojan Dobovšek presented the idea to link organized crime and the informal economy first time at the meeting of the European Society of Criminology in Ljubljana in 2011.

Frame Conditions of Crime

Watching the developments of the last century and trying to predict future trends, it seems that the goals of the new millennium are

- Growing of population
- Growing migration
- Global warming
- Problem of waste
- Global economy
- Tendency to growing cities
- Multicultural and multiethnic societies
- Growing gap between rich and poor
- People becoming older
- Unemployment rate of young people

From the standpoint of a sociologist and criminologist, a lot of problems are involved with such megatrends. In Europe, we were confronted with illegal immigration, an increase of crime, and economic problems, especially increases in the unemployment rate, an economic breakdown after 2008, and a very slow recovery of that situation. There are two sides of the coin: On the one side, we have a decreasing birth rate. The average European family has only one child. If we did not have immigration, the population in Europe would shrink. But, on the other hand, we do not select who is coming to Europe as is done in Canada, the United States, or Australia. The consequence is that a lot of uneducated and very simple people are migrating to Europe. Their standard of education and knowledge is so poor that they need to be supported. Even if they are young, they cannot be used in our economic system.

Densely connected with illegal and legal migration is the criminal exploitation of women and children.* Organized criminals are bringing women and children of poorer classes to Western Europe or America. They tell women living in small villages that they have organized excellent working possibilities for them in Western Europe. On the way to the countries of destination, they force them into prostitution by violence. It is very difficult for police in Western Europe to convince such victims of crime to provide information about their pimps, because very often it is difficult for the victims to trust the police. Police in their home countries are very often corrupt.

* Criminal exploitation of women and children was discussed at the *IPES Conference in Vancouver* in 2004.

"Fall of the Iron Curtain"

The "Fall of the Iron Curtain" was the sensation of the last millennium. After the end of World War II, the "Cold War" started, and in this economically prosperous period in Europe and America, it was nearly hopeless to think about a "One Europe." Europe was divided into two spheres of influence, the Western sphere and the Eastern sphere. The "Iron Curtain" was a dramatic border where many refugees were killed. People who tried to cross this "Iron Curtain" were shot by the guards of the Eastern Bloc countries, and it was very rare that somebody was lucky enough to come through. From 1945 to 1989, we had virtually no idea how people lived in East Germany, the Czech Republic, or Hungary.

I remember very well the experiences of the Hungarian Revolution in 1956 and the Czech Revolution in 1968. Austria became free in 1955 after 10 years of occupation. One year later, the Hungarian Revolution started. We in Austria suffered with the Hungarian people and wanted them to have the freedom back that we had already received. We supported them by sending goods and food and welcoming their refugees crossing the Austrian borders. The year 1966 was the first time that I visited Budapest, 10 years after the revolution was over.

In 1968, the Czechs revolted against the Russian occupation. They started the so-called Czech Spring by a new government that tried to overcome the communists. The idea of freedom lasted very shortly. As in Hungary, the Russians again sent their tank army and stopped these movements of freedom. When Austria became a free country in 1955, it declared "neutrality," but we supported the Czech people and refugees as we did the Hungarians. We in Austria were afraid that the Russians would cross the borders of Austria to follow the Czech refugees on their way to Austria. Our military, which was watching the Austrian borders near Czechoslovakia, would have been much too weak to stop the Russian military.

The Hungarians and the Czechslovakian people wanted to become free like the people in Western Europe, but were stopped very brutally by the Russian tanks and forced to stay part of the communist system. The dream of freedom seemed to be impossible. When in 1989 the "Berlin Wall" and the "Iron Curtain" fell, there was the fear that the Russians would send their army again, but Gorbaschev, the president of Russia at this time, was a completely different personality, and history did not repeat.

Global Challenges

There are so many aspects that change our life. All people are confronted with the global challenges of population growth, climate change, and global warming. As was mentioned earlier, these conditions are influencing all our lives. If millions of people have to leave their home countries because there will not be enough water and food to survive, the inhabitants of all continents will be confronted with this fact.

The international world organizations, like the United Nations (UN),* try to deal with these challenges, but the outcome seems to be very poor. The powerful groups, the lobbyists of the economical branches, like the oil branch or the atomic lobby, are able to stop activities protecting human beings. Economic conditions are so important that aspects of surviving are neglected. Even in Austria we were confronted with several catastrophes that did not change this attitude. That is a tragedy seen in the quest for global understanding.

Challenges of Global Crime Development

In reviewing the last 50 years of history, lots of challenges can be seen. As was already mentioned, the "Fall of the Iron Curtain" and the "Fall of the Berlin Wall" in 1989 were dramatic challenges to all of us in Europe and throughout the world.

In 2001, the terrorist attack against the World Trade Center in New York was a shock. Nobody would have expected such an aggression against the number one world power. A consequence of this attack was that the level of security at borders, airports, harbors, and even homes was increased dramatically, and the issues of personal freedom and integrity were limited.

* UNODCP: At the yearly meetings in Vienna in April or May each year—in Vienna special trends in crime, terrorism, organized crime, drugs, and prevention of crime are discussed—the Academic Council on the United Nations System (ACUNS) Vienna Liaison Office arranges the so-called side events at these meetings.

Spying on Everything and Everybody

Since 9/11, resources in spying activities by the United States were increased. All kinds of communication by telephones and computers were and are intercepted, checked by intelligent software, and analyzed to determine if there is any relevance to terrorist activities. Many individuals suffer by this reduction and control of personal freedom. Millions of people are frustrated and helpless against these powerful attacks in the name of security and safety. Very often it is discussed whether our system of democracy is still checked and balanced in the right way. The "critics" about NSA activities in 2014 are typical. Many people around the world believe that the "fear of terrorism" is misused by state authorities or world powers to spy against other countries and their people.

Financial Crisis

The financial crisis started with the crash of the Lehman brothers in 2008 in the United States. In Europe, the crisis continued, especially in Spain, because of speculations similar to those that happened in the United States. Because financial institutions all over the world speculated with immobilization and false estimations of their worth, the crisis continued. As a consequence, all continents and economies were dramatically damaged. Since then, the crisis has not ended. Europe still experiences a euro crisis, an economic crisis, and a loan crisis.

Did Organized Crime Cause the Financial Crisis?

As a former criminal investigator in Austria, especially after 1989, it was usual for me to be confronted with organized criminal activities. Criminal groups from the South, Italy, and East, Russia, chose to use Austria for their meetings and sometimes to commit crimes (Edelbacher, 1989). Criminals working together planned their activities, structured their organization, and split their fields of activities, based on their professionalism. We could analyze patterns of behavior performed by their experts.

Analyzing actions of the so-called international financial experts, it has to be recognized that a lot of criminal energy seems to be involved in their activity. Otherwise, it is not understandable that without any responsibility, speculations over such a long period of time are pushed in a permanent greed-driven way. An example is the Cyprus case. Financial institution in Cyprus offered a much higher interest rate than other institutions in Europe. Many Russians and other customers opened bank accounts in Cyprus banks, and for many years, more than 8 years, they gathered over 30% interest. Now, the Cyprus financial system has enormous problems and has asked the European Union Central Bank to cover their expenses and support them; otherwise, they would crash.

Meeting of Experts in Europe (Edelbacher et al., 2012)

It was interesting to experience a meeting of international experts in the year 2010 in Germany. About 80 experts came together, invited by Alexander Siedschlag, a German professor, who moved his activities from Munich to Vienna at the Sigmund Freud private University to push research in the fields of security and safety. One of the initiatives was to organize this international conference on security issues in February 2010 (Edelbacher et al., 2012). The goal of the conference was to elaborate on early warning mechanisms to protect people against all kinds of threats, like avalanches, floods, and earthquakes. Two years after the financial crises occurred, nobody wanted to speak about the financial crises and what we could do to protect people from losing their money by wrong and fraudulent promises.

Because we missed such a discussion about the financial crisis and what could be done to prevent another crisis, two experts, including myself, started to cooperate on that issue and set up different round tables, one at the yearly meeting of the European Society of Criminology in September 2011 in Ljubljana, one at the meeting of the Crime Commission in Vienna at the UN in May 2012, and one at the House of the European Union in Vienna in autumn 2012. CRC Press/Taylor & Francis Group accepted our book proposal to report the findings of these meetings, and in September 2012, the book *Financial Crimes: A Threat to Global Security*, by Max Edelbacher, Peter C. Kratcoski, and Michael Theil, was published.

When the book was ready to be presented, I asked representatives of the Austrian federal bank if they were interested in the topic and if the book could be launched in their institution. The answer was very clear: "No interest!" For the financial sector, it is impossible to look in the mirror, and even the idea of discussing if criminal energy was involved in the financial crisis was "unthinkable." Today, everybody on the street knows that a lot of criminal energy was and still is involved in the financial sector. Greed and cheating the simple customer are driving powers, but nobody wants to speak about that issue.

Organized Crime and the Informal Economy

The idea to research and discuss the relationship of organized crime and the informal economy was started by University Professor Bojan Dobovšek from the University of Maribor in Ljubljana, Slovenia. The first time we discussed this was at the yearly conference of the European Academy of Criminology in 2011 in our small group of researchers and practitioners with University Professors Branislav Simonovic from the University of Kragujevac, Serbia; Arije Antinori from Sapientia University, Rome, Italy; and, director and specialist on fraud management Ronald Wörner, Zürich Kosmos Insurance Company, Switzerland. We enlarged the discussion by including links of organized crime (OC), the shadow economy, corruption, and fraud. This book will deepen this idea of linking research about the relationship of organized crime and the informal economy and integrating the relevance of fraud and corruption, because all these fields seem to be connected densely. If you study law and work in the field of crime fighting and crime prevention, first, you are confronted with traditional forms of crime. Murder, robbery, extortion, theft, fraud, drug trafficking, and drug consuming are standard fields. Therefore, it seems important to discuss the various kinds of crimes.

Traditional Crime Development

Police organizations react to such experiences with an organizational answer. Because murder, robbery, high jacking, and extortion are dramatic threats to the average society, police organizations try to concentrate primarily on solving such crime cases. For example, in the Austrian Police Organization, Vienna always is confronted, as the capital of Austria, with about 40% of all crimes that happen in Austria. As the former chief of the Major Crimes Bureau (Edelbacher, 2008), it was my main duty to solve murder cases, cases of robbery, and other major crime cases each year. At the end of each year, it was always the burning question of how our crime statistics looked and what percentage of major crimes had been solved.

This importance was reflected by the structure of the Major Crimes Bureau. About 200 investigators were employed, and they were split into groups dealing with clarifying murder, robbery, burglary, trafficking of human beings and criminal exploitation of women, thefts, fraud, and drugs. For example, in the 1980s, we were confronted with about 40–50 murder crime cases in Vienna, about one-third of all murder crimes in Austria. If we could clarify more than 90% of these murder crimes, we would show a rather good performance rate. At the end of the year and in the beginning of each year, a statistical overview was prepared, and the public was informed by a press conference. There was a lot of pressure by the media, the public, and the Ministry of the Interior to present an efficient picture of police investigative work. Nothing has changed since I retired. There are similar circumstances and pressure for the police leadership. The inhabitants of Vienna and Austria want to feel safe, and the yearly published police crime statistics is enormously important to the parliament, the public, and the media.

If a spectacular crime case occurs, there is always a discussion about the difference of objective and subjective feelings of being safe. A spectacular crime case, like the murder of a child, can influence such feelings very dramatically. I remember in the late 1980s when we were confronted with the murder of two children in Vienna, and it took some time to solve these crimes. Immediately, inhabitants of the area—the tenth district of Vienna, called Favoriten, where more than 180,000 inhabitants live—felt insecure and wanted to protect themselves using their own civil guards, because they did not trust police anymore. It was hard work to convince people to trust the police and to reduce their feelings of being insecure. We had to do a lot of public work, information, and discussion with the citizens. The best prevention is solving such crimes.

Violence is the number one issue in policing. People fear very much the rate of murders and robberies. For example, as people become older, an important problem is violence against the elderly. Two groups of victims are very vulnerable, the elderly and the young ones. If a lot of violence is reported in the media, it influences the feeling of security and safety enormously.

In 2013, the German Organization of Criminal Investigators invited representatives of the media and the international society to a symposium on the topic of "Elderly Victims of Crimes." This topic produced a lot of reactions in the public society and in the media. Elderly as victims of crime is a burning issue in the European and American societies because as people become elderly, they are much more vulnerable. In a symposium at the Vienna Police Headquarters in 2013, we compared measures to prevent crime against the elderly in the countries of Germany, Switzerland, and Austria. In May 2014, this topic was represented at the Crime Commission meeting at the UN in Vienna.

People in the richer countries suffer very much by burglary and thefts. Seventy percent of all crimes are property crimes. Thefts and burglaries are on a high level. In Austria, we experience more than 20,000 burglaries every year. Burglaries into houses and flats are on a very high level. Another issue is thefts in public areas like public transportation facilities, markets, streets, and shops. Breaking into cars and stealing of cars are on a high level, too. Another side of property crimes is the development of fraud cases. More and more people become victims of fraud. The Internet as a communication platform is an ideal opportunity for criminals to cheat people who are interested in buying and selling via the eBay system. Internet crime has increased in Austria more than 150%–200%. Millions of the so-called advanced-fee-fraud letters are sent to customers all around the world by the Internet. All kinds of promises are made to create interest in starting a correspondence with the offenders. More than 20 years ago, criminal investigators of the FBI reported at a conference of the International Association of Financial Crimes Investigators that such letters were sent from Nigeria and the offenders lived in rather poor accommodations just running computers and the Internet. The modus operandi of the fraudsters was very simple: They informed the customer that he or she has won money or that he or she was selected as a successor of a "last will." In the e-mail, it is told that some payments have to be invested to get the benefits. This starting of a correspondence offers the hope to become rich in a short time, and even clever, critical persons are convinced by such letters to pay advanced fees.

Modern Crime Development

Criminals are very innovative and learn faster than the police. Therefore, law enforcement agencies are confronted with a whole punch of new crime activities and new modus operandi. After the "Fall of the Iron Curtain," Central Europe was confronted by organized crime, just as the United States was in the time of prohibition of alcohol in the 1930s.

Quantity of Crime

Between 1989 and 1994, but the *quality of crime* and the *quantity of crime* created problems. Under *quality of crime* has to be understood the groups of organized criminals coming especially from the East, the so-called Russian Mafia. In the middle of the 1990s, they began arrangements with the Italian "Mafia organizations" and met very often together in Vienna. This was geographically the best area to meet, and it became an enormous problem for the Austrian police to watch these meetings but not be able to investigate what was going on. At this time period, the Austrian penal and procedural law did not allow surveillance of these meetings. It was a fact that Austrian criminal investigators watched the meetings in the special hotels but could only register a profile of mobility of the representatives of these organized crime groups. They could not intercept what they were speaking and dealing with.

Quality of Crime

In 1996, the boss of the Georgian Mafia was killed during his summer vacation in Vienna. He was out for dinner with his fiancée and walked alone without bodyguards. The criminals were informed and used this opportunity to shoot him and wound his girlfriend. It was a prepared action and revenge for a lot of his criminal activities. Although police work was of high quality and the international police cooperation was effective, the problem was the justice system. Police prepared a summary paper about the background of the organizations behind that murder crime case, but the highest court of Austria did not accept that it was an organized crime and just ended that case as a *simple murder case.* This was a great step backward for the high-quality investigation team. This case was symptomatic for the justice system in Austria, and even for Europe, because of the fact that the topic of organized crime slowly taking over business and crime in Europe was neglected.

Anti-Mafia Fight

At this time, Italy was much better off. Italian judges, like Falcone and Borsalino, had knowledge about the Mafia organization. Anti-Mafia laws were passed by the Italian Parliament, and the so-called Pentiti regulations allowed deals with core members of Mafia clans. In the 1990s, the Italian justice and anti-Mafia law enforcement agency had some tremendous successes in the fight against organized crime. The Italians followed the American way of fighting organized crime by the so-called Racketeer Influenced and Corrupt Organizations (RICO) laws. The anti-Mafia laws of Italy were structured the same way. Core members of organized crime groups were allowed to keep half of their illegal incomes if they were informing the anti-Mafia justice and law enforcement agencies about the organization.

Italy in the 1990s was an excellent model in efficiently fighting organized crime. There was hope that the long-lasting tradition of a partnership between corrupt politicians and capos of the Mafia could be broken. Meanwhile, the current situation in Europe is not so hopeful. After experiencing the political scandals and the economic crisis, we have to understand that the *war against organized crime* was not won. In Italy, we experienced the periods of election of Berlusconi as prime minister. It seems that his time is over, but who knows? In Russia, Putin is in power again. There is information of insiders that Putin has dense connection with Russian organized crime groups from the St. Petersburg area. It seems to be clear that both leaders are not figures where you can trust in an organized-crime-free system.

Europeen de luffe Anti-Fraude (European Bureau Against Fraud and Corruption)*

Each year in February, a conference at the Academy of European Law in Trier, Germany, takes place. The European Bureau Against Fraud and Corruption, the highest anticorruption and antifraud institution in the European Union, reports about the situation in Europe. The report shows that corruption and fraud are increasing problems of the European Union. Europe sponsors the most projects internationally, but nearly one-third are asked by fraudulent actions. OLAF can identify a lot of the fraudulent requests, but cannot act. Even a newly implemented whistle-blower system could not stop this development. Another handicap of OLAF was and is that, although the mostly clever investigators are active in the organization, there can be produced only reports, but no sanctions. Two years ago, a very prominent participant said: "OLAF is a tiger without hands and legs."

United Nations†

The United Nations Office on Drugs and Crime (UNODC) is based in Vienna. United Nations Office on Drugs and Crime is the center in fighting terrorism and organized crime. The UN are very active in fighting terrorism, organized crime, and corruption. Three conventions were passed to address the issue of

- Organized crime, by the Palermo Convention in 2000
- Terrorism, by the Convention against Terrorism in 2001
- Corruption, by the Convention against Corruption in 2004

Each year, the Crime Commission organizes meetings in Vienna and other countries to discuss the status quo of organized crime, terrorism, and corruption. In Vienna and New York, nongovernmental organizations

* Max Edelbacher, several unpublished reports about the yearly meetings of OLAF at the European Law Academy in Trier—these reports were drafted for AVUS Group International based in Graz, Austria, whom I am advising.

† Since 2008 Max Edelbacher is a member of ACUNS, Vienna Liaison Office. ACUNS organizes several side events each year at the meetings of the Crime Commission.

(NGOs) are very strongly involved in supporting these activities. For example, the Academic Council on the United Nations System (ACUNS) Vienna Liaison Office organizes each year in January, April, May, and sometimes September side events on special topics. Since 2008, ACUNS has organized several round tables on the issues about organized crime, white collar crime, financial crimes, and corruption. For example, in May 2014, two round tables took place on the topic of

1. Relationship of organized crime, the informal economy fraud, and corruption
2. Elderly victims of corruption

International Anti-Corruption Academy (IACA)

A very promising institution was implemented by the cooperation of the Republic of Austria and the UN in Vienna. In 2011, the International Anti-Corruption Academy was founded and established in Laxenburg, based near Vienna. Representatives of NGOs are trained to draft reports about the corruption situation in their countries. That can be very dangerous for them, because in some countries, more people are killed reporting about the dimensions of corruption than journalists reporting about wars. These training courses are based on the Convention against Corruption.

The Relationship between Organized Crime, the Informal Economy, White Collar Crime, Fraud, and Corruption

In this book, we want to elaborate on the relationship of organized crime, the informal economy, white collar crime, fraud, and corruption. As a law enforcement agent, it is very clear to me, based on practical experiences, that there are strong links between these special fields of crime. There are definitions of organized crime that are not accepted completely, but they do provide a picture about the topic. The following excerpt from the UN Convention shows one of many approach possibilities.

The UN Convention against Transnational Organized Crime, adopted by the General Assembly Resolution 55/25 of November 15, 2000, defines *organized crime* in Article 2: Use of Terms as follows:

For the purpose of this Convention:

(a) "organized criminal groups" shall mean a structured group of three or more persons, existing for a period of time and acting in concert with the aim of committing one or more serious crimes or offenses established in accordance with the Convention, in order to obtain, directly or indirectly, a financial or other material benefit;
(b) "Serious crime" shall mean conduct constituting an offense punishable by maximum deprivation of liberty of at least 4 years or a more serious penalty;
(c) "Structured group" shall mean a group that is not randomly formed for the immediate commission of an offense and that does not need to have formally defined roles for its members, continuity of its membership or a developed structure;
(d) "Property" shall mean assets of every kind, whether corporeal or incorporeal, moveable or immovable, tangible or intangible, and legal documents or instruments evidencing title to, or interest in, such assets;
(e) "Proceeds of crime"! shall mean any property derived from or obtained, directly or indirectly, through the commission of an offense;
(f) "Freezing" or "seizure" shall mean temporarily prohibiting the transfer, conversion, disposition or movement of property or temporarily assuming custody or control of property on the basis of an order issued by a court or other competent authority;
(g) "Confiscation", which includes forfeiture where applicable, shall mean the permanent deprivation of property by order of a court or other competent authority;
(h) "predicate offense" shall mean any offense as a result of which proceeds have been generated that may become the subject of an offense as defined in article 6 of the convention;
(i) "Controlled delivery" shall mean the technique of allowing illicit or suspect consignments to pass out of, through or into the territory of one or more States, with the knowledge and under the supervision of their competent authorities, with a view to the investigation of an offense and the identification of persons involved in the commission of the offense;
(j) "Regional economic integration organization" shall mean an organization constituted by sovereign States of a given region, to which its member States have transferred competence in respect of matters governed by this Convention and which has been duly authorized, in accordance with its internal procedures, to sign, ratify, accept, approve or accede to it; references to "States Parties" under this Convention shall apply to such organizations within the limits of their competence.

Organized Crime

In the literature and in practical experience, it is very well known what can be done against organized crime. The leadership of the Italians and Americans in the fight against organized crime allowed us to gather experiences. In the United States, the "RICO regulations" and, in Italy, the so-called anti-Mafia laws, the Pentiti regulations are sharp instruments to fight this phenomenon. Of course, the success still is limited because there are relationships between politicians and organized crime bosses. Both in Italy and in the United States that is difficult to stop, because corruption is the oil that makes the "machine running." Methods of supporting and sponsoring elections and parties and the influence of lobbyists of all kinds are so strong that criminals find their way into the centers of governments and parliaments. The goal of organized criminals is to gather influence and political power. They use media, personal contacts, society events, and charity events, and they cannot be stopped.

The Informal Economy

The informal economy shows two sides, a so-called bad side, even sometimes a criminal side, because the state loses money and taxes by the activity that is performed by not regularly registered companies, firms, or individuals, while the good side is the production itself. The brutto national product (BNP) is increasing, and goods and houses that are produced stay in the country. The wealth of a country is growing and people become richer, but the state authorities are losing income. The country itself becomes richer, much wealthier, but the state power does not see effects or participate in this profit. The public power, the state, the regional governor, and the village authorities are all cheated by the individual unlawful activities that are taking place. The informal or shadow economy is a deviant behavior of everybody. In Austria, for example, it happens all the time that houses are built where friends, parents, and family, who are specialists in various trades, work together to construct them. Even if they have other jobs, they work on the weekends or in the evenings, do the work on the houses, and use their knowledge and expertise and get a salary that is tax-free. These specialists work for hours, days, or weeks and get a relatively high income that cannot be registered by the tax authorities. Therefore, the BNP is growing, but the state stays weak. Many studies show that the so-called shadow economy is much stronger in a country, if the taxes are rather high. It is well known that high taxes produce a high level of informal economy.

Who Profits and Who Loses?

Who profits and who loses if dramatic historical changes happen? Such changes were regularly the starting point for new winners and losers, especially the so-called newcomers, the winners of a war, or the winners of the breakdown of societies. A shortage of products and services opens new opportunities to provide members of the society with the missing things that are desired. When I was a child in the time period after the end of World War II, I remember very well that my parents were looking for food and other goods to stay alive, to heat the flat, and to care for us children. It was a terrible time, and if families had no opportunities to be supported by their relatives living in the countryside, who provided the family members in the cities with necessary materials, they suffered very much. We as children sometimes were lucky, because as a child you would find someone who would offer you a piece of bread or sweet. Walking around, showing the impression of being poor sometimes opens the hearts of the richer ones. When I was walking around with my sister, even American soldiers liked us and gave us some chocolate. But this was only a single experience. The important deals were made by the "Winners of the War," who had excellent contacts to new powers and used their contacts to launch big businesses.

Illegal Markets

All over the world, dealers provide legal and illegal markets with goods and services that are needed when there is a shortage. As a police chief of the Major Crimes Bureau, the daily fight was the fight against the drug traffickers. For example, there is a market of about 30,000 drug addicts in Vienna, and everyday they need heroin, cocaine, synthetic drugs, and soft drugs. This fact opens excellent opportunities for dealers. In the 1980s and 1990s, Kosovo Albanians, drug families, settled down in Bratislava and Vienna to provide the market with illegal drugs delivered through the "Balkan route." When the Balkan War started in the 1990s, these families moved back to their home countries, because they had much better opportunities to deal with all kinds of goods at home. They started smuggling petrol, cigarettes, and prostitutes from Moldavia because thousands of young men, soldiers of the UN peacekeeping missions, made good money and had no opportunity for sex.

The Internet

The largest growing rates of crime offer the opportunity to sell and buy via the Internet. The anonymity of this platform is an ideal opportunity for fraud crime by cheating. Identity can be covered or wrong identities are used and are the basics for criminal activities. It is a tragedy that the Internet offers a world of freedom and communication, but in reality, it is used by criminals too much.

Hacking

The Internet market is so powerful because it is used not only for communication and for legal business but also for illegal business. Hackers can gather practically all information, and the protection against them is nearly impossible. The main problem is the theft of data. Legal transfers of financial institutions are an excellent opportunity to be hacked. Personal financial transactions are used illegally to plunder accounts and information. As soon as criminals hack such data, they abuse them for their transfers and steal the money amounts they can get. As early as the mid-1970s, thefts of data by members of the so-called Chinese Mafia in Hong Kong allowed them to hack into the credit card numbers of customers. In Europe, we were confronted by international credit card fraudsters, who used the billings for purchases in restaurants and shops to scan the credit card data and to abuse these data for the so-called white plastic cards. Today, this modus operandi is much more sophisticated and done only through the Internet and computers.

Example 1

Even when I was a retired police officer, several individuals asked for help and support because they became victims of Internet business. International police cooperation is so weak that criminals can act internationally without any danger. For example, an Austrian was interested in buying an English car, an "old-timer," and got an offer by "eBay platform." He paid the costs for transportation and insurance in advance, but never got the car. Although he suffered more than 4000 British pounds damage, Interpol London does not start an investigation if the damage is lower than 5000 British pounds. It is so easy for criminals to cheat because the authorities are inflexible, not efficient, and overburdened by the daily business. Even if evidence to start an investigation exists, in reality, nobody cares to do something against criminals.

Example 2

Another example shows the same result: A couple, both merchants, were selected by an e-mail correspondence to get in touch with a lawyer in South Africa, because they inherited funds from a rich man. The advanced fee fraud, which is very well known to police, started, and they received an offer to come to Madrid to see part of the money they would inherit. They had to pay fees for the lawyer, for opening an account in South Africa, and they traveled to Madrid to see their money. The meeting happened, they could see the money—more than $1 million USD—but the money was not given to them. Again they had to pay for costs of transfer. Of course they never got any money and never inherited anything. They just became victims of fraud. There existed a lot of evidences, identities, a paper trace through the correspondence, and names and addresses. The Interpol correspondence was started, but with no success—the South African authorities did not start any investigation.

What Are the Costs of Deviant Behavior?

In 1991,* shortly after the "Fall of the Iron Curtain," the former police president of Vienna and I were invited by the most important top leaders of the Austrian insurance companies—there are four big players in Austria, like Generali International Ltd., Veisz Alliance Ltd., Uniqa (at that time they were called Bundesländer Versicherung), and the Vienna Insurance Group—to speak about problems the insurance industry was confronted with after the dramatic increase of crime. The costs for insurance increased, because criminals came as the so-called crime tourists from the poorer part of Eastern Europe to the richer part of Western Europe and were stealing cars, shoplifting, and breaking into houses and flats and generally became a terrible

* Max Edelbacher, contribution in the yearly report of Kuratorium Öffentliche Sicherheit, published in 1992, by the Ministry of the Interior, Vienna, Austria.

burden for insurance companies. This meeting was an "outcry" of the insurance industry that they were not willing any longer to suffer by these developments and initiated an open discussion about what could be done against that burning issue of losses. The ambience of the symposium was very nice because the meeting took place in a wonderful area in Salzburg, at the Lake Fuschl. The president of police in Vienna spoke about a more philosophical approach on the topic of "policing and security." I prepared a paper about estimated damage to the insurance industry caused by crime. In this chapter, I have tried to elaborate on the dimension of damage that was caused by the increase of crime after the "Fall of the Iron Curtain." In 1989, the "Iron Curtain" fell, and immediately, Austria was confronted with a dramatic increase of burglary into house flats and shops, theft of cars, and shoplifting. Crime increased from 370,000 offenses in 1988 to more than 500,000 offenses in 1992. This development influenced the business of the insurance industry heavily, because they had to cover the costs of crime. Confronted with this topic, many questions arose. Where does deviant criminal behavior originate, who are the offenders, and how much damage is caused by this deviant behavior in Austria. The paper and presentation "What Are the Costs for Insurance Industry by Crime Development?" was based on the police criminal statistics of the Ministry of the Interior and the average payment statistics of the Austrian insurance industry. All deviant behavior was considered, and we tried to enumerate the costs. The multiplication of the numbers of crimes (e.g., 22,000 burglaries into houses and flats multiplied by the average damage costs of a single burglary) with the costs showed the extent of the expenses for the insurance industry. These costs could be estimated for the different fields of damages. It was rather easy to estimate the costs of thefts of cars, burglary into homes, and average costs of violence, but it was difficult to estimate the costs of a person being killed. The question was as follows: "Is the life of a university professor worth more than the life of a poor man?" The whole process was a starting point for discussion. Later on, the chief of the Austrian Statistical Center, Hofrat Mag. Franz, tried to find better and useful basics to get more exact data. The problem was to find mathematical-based methods to give exact data about the dimension of damage. This was rather complicated, because it was impossible to enumerate exactly these dimensions, but generally, this idea led to a new approach in evaluating the problem to compare costs of security with the costs of damage.

Outcome of the 1991 Discussion

The very first step of this very simple comparative approach showed that the costs of crime and damages, even in a small country like Austria, were enormous. The conclusion was that it could be estimated that the yearly losses were about one-third of the budget. Because of the fact that it is difficult to find efficient exact parameters, the Austrian Center for Statistical Research could only partly prove the dimensions of damage. A discussion was started, and one of the conclusions was that investments into security make sense. One of the changes, for example, was that the private security industry started booming. Law enforcement agencies could no longer handle all security issues. One of the reactions was that the monopoly of security was split in the 1990s, the duties of police were reduced, and private security services took over parts of the security market. The situation in Austria still is not comparable to that of the United States. Today, in Austria, about 30,000 employees work for the police and about 12,000 work in the private security industry. In the United States, about 1.5 million work in the different police organizations and about 3 million work in the private security business.

Does Organized Crime Influence the Economy?

The costs of fighting organized crime have exploded, and the damage caused by organized crime has increased. Each year, UNODC in Vienna launches a report on the dimensions of the costs of organized crime. It is estimated that about $2 billion USD are the dimensions of organized crime. Trafficking of human beings, trafficking of drugs, and trafficking of weapons are the main income sources of organized criminals. As the gap between poor and rich people is growing each day, millions of young people living in the poorer parts of the world try to change their living conditions and look for a better life in a country that is not their home country. Each day, thousands of refugees from Africa try to cross the Mediterranean Sea by simple boats that are not safe for transporting them. Coast guards in Italy, Spain, Greece, and other European countries have to save these refugees. You can watch such reports on television every hour. The refugee industry is one of the largest illegal industries. In addition, the informal economy is more and more in the hands of organized crime groups. Counterfeits of all kinds of products, including clothing, technical products like watches, and computers are produced illegally and sold into the legal markets.

Are Organized Crime and the Informal Economy Linked?

As the practical analysis of the different fields of economy shows, there seems to be a definite link between organized crime and the informal economy. University Professor Bojan Dobovšek, who works as an expert on organized crime, white collar crime, and corruption, made us aware that we needed to concentrate on the topic of the relationship between organized crime and the informal economy. He argued there are a lot of proofs of this existing relationship that can be elaborated in a scientific way. His understanding of the relationship between organized crime and the shadow economy is supported by Professor Friedrich Schneider, who uses mathematical instruments to prove the connection. This book and several round table discussions are the outcomes of dealing with the issues of organized crime, white collar crime, and financial crimes, especially the financial crisis of the year 2008, and our recognition of its relationship to the informal economy and corruption. The difficulties are that this phenomenon is difficult to fight, because in daily life, a melting process between the formal and the informal economy occurs, and it is nearly impossible to determine which quantity and quality of the economy are based on illegal or legal business. Of course, illegal incomes are invested as fast as possible into legal business; therefore, it is difficult to analyze and prove the way money has moved. The relationships between politicians, criminals, and entrepreneurs usually are not transparent, deals cannot be openly reconstructed, and the process of decisions is hidden. Nobody knows why and how they are made and what the real background was. If the state authorities or the authorities of a city decide on investments to build hospitals, schools, roads, public buildings, or undergrounds, sometimes many years later, it may be discovered by journalists or members of NGOs that illegal contacts and businesses were connected with such decisions. Very often it is covered up that kickbacks and corruption money are involved. A new information mechanism tries to motivate persons to reveal what they know about these practices. The so-called whistle-blower regulations of OLAF or anticorruption agencies in different countries offer protection to informants so that they are not vulnerable against the institutions that covered up illegal activities. Whistle-blowing goes back to the RICO laws and anti-Mafia laws. By legal processes, informants are offered special treatment by the police and justice system.

The Informal Economy and Corruption

Corruption has many dimensions. To law enforcement experts, it is well known that corruption figures as the backbone of all kinds of criminal activities. Terrorism, organized crime, and white collar crime cannot happen without corruption. The first step of organized criminals is to gain financial influence. The first step of terrorists is to threaten thousands by killing one. Often a very prominent victim is selected. The second step is to gather political influence. The use of corruption is a popular method to gain this influence. The narcissi of politicians can be used as the entrance door. Many stories can be reported of how politicians are caught by different methods. Criminals and terrorists are very eager to learn about the weak link of a person or a system. Criminals and terrorists learn very fast, sometimes much faster than the official authorities. It can be money, since most deviant behavior is based on greed. It can be any addiction; it can be women, drugs, or just friendship that motivates individuals to support deviant behavior. Sometimes it is not even clear what was really going on. If the network is established, it is rather difficult to stop the bad influence and to end it. If you try to analyze corruption, each one of us can be corrupted. Each of us is vulnerable and has a weak point or weak side. It is a question of personal stability and personal development to be strong enough to just say *no* to any attempt. If the offer is hidden, it may not be recognized immediately.

Dangers of the Relationship of Organized Crime: The Informal Economy, Fraud, and Corruption

The main dangers are based on the relationship between organized crimes, all other crimes like fraud and corruption and the informal economy. The informal economy can be understood as the "crime of everybody." People in high-tax countries try to avoid the payments of these high taxes, and this approach opens a relationship to organized crime. Organized criminals use cheap workers, import them by trafficking human beings, extort them, and generate a market for their services. Organized criminals do not care about human rights standards. They use the market of pull and push factors in the liberalized atmosphere of the European Union. The so-called freedom of movement is misused because there is less control.

Who Pays for These Crimes?

In 2013, Professor Friedrich Schneider presented actual numbers regarding the informal economy in his paper, *Schattenwirtschaft* (*The Shadow Economy*); he provided the following figures:

- Informal economy: 21 billion euros
- Tax fraud: 5 billion euros
- Tax evasion: 4 billion euro
- Costs of corruption: 17 billion euros
- Costs of robbery, burglary, and theft: 2 billion euros
- Costs of violent crimes: 3 billion euros
- Insurance fraud: 1 billion euros
- Social fraud: 3.5 billion euros

In Austria, we have an authority in the field of informal economy. We prefer to call it the shadow economy. It is University Professor Dr. Friedrich Schneider at the Johann Kepler-University in Linz, Upper-Austria. For more than 20 years, he has presented a report each year about the shadow economy in Austria. His evaluation of the shadow economy presented in this book influenced comparative international studies very much.

Prevention and Repression Measures

The phenomena of organized crime, terrorism, white collar crime, and corruption are enormous dangers for democratic societies. Public and private institutions that have to protect people against these dangers have to be proactive to reduce the risks. What are answers to the challenges?

Awareness, Transparency, and Information of the Public

Working as an international expert for the UN, the Council of Europe, and the European Union, it was important for me to learn and to understand that there are similar principles that can be useful for solving the challenges of organized crime, terrorism, white collar crime, drug trafficking, and corruption. The exchange of knowledge and experience of practitioners and academics shows that awareness building, transparency, and an open communication with the public build confidence and trust and make people aware of the risks.

Preventing Organized Crime, White Collar Crime, and Corruption

Many meetings, talks, discussions, literature reviews, and exchanges of knowledge confirm the fact that, as a German chief prosecutor once mentioned, "The criminals sit in the jet, the police sit in a Porsche and justice sit on a horse." This saying hits exactly the problem of modern investigations. Criminals are not restricted by any limitation of sovereignty, competence, or legal conditions. They are able to communicate and cooperate as much seems to be necessary for them. In 1923, the former president of police in Vienna, Dr. Johann Schober, founded Interpol that was based in Vienna until 1938. The concept of Interpol was a modern one at that time. Today, in the age of Internet communication and modern technology, new ways of policing have to be achieved. Two years ago, we discussed in a symposium: "What shall a police officer look like in 2020—what are the main challenges?" The profile of modern police officers needs

1. Understanding of culture and languages in a multicultural society
2. Technical knowledge to use and understand these developments
3. Human and sociopsychological expertise to interrogate offenders and victims

On the one hand, national and international cooperation becomes more and more important, but on the other hand, this special profile of individual capacity has to be built by education and training. Policing is a very challenging work. It will be difficult to find enough young men and women who are willing and able to fulfill these expectations.

Bibliography

Albrecht, J. and. Das, D. (2010). *Effective Crime Reductions Strategies*. Boca Raton, FL: CRC Press.

Das, D. and Otwin Marenin, O. (eds.) (2000). *Challenges of Policing Democracies*. Amsterdam, the Netherlands: Gordon & Breach.

Edelbacher, M. (1989). *OrganisierteKriminalität in Europa* (*Organized Crime in Europe*). Vienna, Austria: Linde Publisher.

Edelbacher, M. (2008). *Polizei Inside*. Vienna, Austria: Amalthea Publisher.

Edelbacher, M., Kratcosk, P., and Theil, M. (eds.) (2012). *Financial Crimes: A Threat to Global Security*. Boca Raton, FL: CRC Press.

Einstein, S. and Amir, M. (1999). *Organized Crime: Uncertainties and Dilemmas*. Chicago, IL: University of Chicago Press.

König, D. and. Das, D. (2001). *International Police Cooperation*. New York: Lexington Books.

Marenin, O. and. Das, D. (2009). *Trends in Policing*, London, UK: CRC Press/Taylor & Francis Group.

United Nations Office on Drugs and Crime, Vienna, Austria. www.unodc.org. (Accessed June 19, 2014.)

Winterdyk, D. and Sundberg, K. (2010). *Border Security in the Al-Qaeda Era*. Boca Raton, FL: CRC Press.

11. Symbiosis of Politics, the Shadow Economy, Corruption, and Organized Crime in the Territory of the Western Balkans

The Case of the Republic of Serbia

Branislav Simonović and Goran Bošković

Introduction

This chapter emphasizes that the shadow economy is the *Achilles' heel of a state* (for instance, see Andjelković 2002, p. 407). A high level of the shadow economy represents a symptom of deeper disturbances in the economic structure, weak enforcement of laws, and bad functioning of institutions. The shadow economy is a response to weak functioning of authority (government) and state in the sense of their incapability to enforce laws and regulations (Vujović et al., 2013, p. 6).

The problem of the shadow economy in Serbia is to a certain extent more pronounced than in other East European countries that have also undergone the transition in government and economy considering the wide range of causes and the specificity of the situation in Serbia. Serbia has been in transition for a very long time (extended transition characterized by stagnations in privatization processes and the changes of principles in its implementation). In addition, the economic growth rates in Serbia are low, the rule of law is at a low level, the government institutions are caved in, the law enforcement is weak, and there is a high level of corruption,* among other factors. In addition to the problems mentioned, Serbia is characterized by a high unemployment rate, low quality of public services, low tax-related moral and tolerant attitudes of the citizens

* The Corruption Perception Index (CPI) supports this fact. Serbia is at 72nd position out of 177 in 2013, with index 42, compared to the countries in the neighborhood that have taken much better positions. Slovenia is at 43rd place, and at better ranked are also Croatia at place 57 and Montenegro and Macedonia, both at place 67. The website in which this can be found is the Corruption Perceptions Index 2013, Transparency International, Brochure, http://cpi.transparency.org/cpi2013/results. Accessed July 20, 2014.

toward the shadow economy, and its high participation in GDP (compare Vujović et al., 2013, p. 13). Also in the most recent history, Serbia has been pressurized by the sanctions of the international community, wars, political conflicts, and various other social tensions, which all influenced in one short period its economic development and its government stability. Thus, Serbia became a classic country for the development of a shadow economy. Expressed tolerance and conscious helping to the development of a shadow economy by (a part of) the state apparatus, interconnectedness of certain important factors in the government structure and carriers of a shadow economy, and the fusion of *bad parts* of government structure and a shadow economy (Kostić, 2004, p. 10) have left consequences that are still felt during the present time. All the aforementioned factors represent only some of the important factors of the shadow economy in Serbia.

The shadow economy in Serbia is a multidimensional, multilayered phenomenon and its dimensions are rather diversified, starting from relatively benign smuggling to particularly economically destructive phenomena (Čudan et al., 2014). According to the *Economic Dictionary*, shadow economy is a set of economic activities that are carried out outside the institutionalized economic environment. It includes criminal business management, fictitious economy, the informal economy, and other covert and unlawful business transactions (*Economic Dictionary*, 2010, p. 175). Bearing in mind the said entries, and for the purpose of this chapter, it can be said that the shadow economy in a wider sense means performance of economic activity outside relevant legal regulations (the informal economy) or against the regulations (illicit economy, black economy) (Morić et al., 2004, p. 13). The important determinants of the shadow economy in Serbia are first of all primary and destructive influences of the authority, that is, political factors and corruption on its formation and persistence, These factors will be accentuated in this chapter.

Influence of the Disintegration of Yugoslavia and the Sanctions of the International Community on the Shadow Economy in Serbia

During the last decade of the twentieth century, the expansion of the shadow economy in Serbia was considerably influenced by several unfavorable processes that simultaneously unwound, and therefore their effects were united and multiplied. In particular, the negative influence of the disintegration of the former Yugoslavia, the war in the neighboring countries, which started due to the disintegration of the country, the beginning of transition, and economic sanctions and economic blockade imposed to Serbia by the United Nations should be mentioned.

The disintegration of the former Yugoslavia also caused the collapse of a unique economic and monetary system of the country; the disappearance of a huge market (of 22 million consumers), which further influenced the breaking of economic ties between economic subjects of the disintegrated country; new problems in manufacturing, distribution, and selling of products; and the powerful economic crisis. Over 650,000 refugees from the former Yugoslav republics fled into Serbia due to the war in the neighborhood, which caused great social crisis and unemployment (Report, 2006, p. 6; Hovy, 2011, p. 33).

At the same time, along with the disintegration of the former Yugoslavia, the transition started, as well as the transfer from socialist principles of economy to liberal and *market* mechanisms. The experiences of the countries in which the privatization process is completed or near its end show clearly that this sphere is burdened to a large extent by criminal actions, the goal of which was first to make the capital worthless (to lower the value by wrongful trading) and then to make its inaccurate estimation so that the social wealth will be redirected into private hands (Simonović, 2004, p. 620). The change of ownership in countries in transition by itself is not sufficient to obtain successful economic results; this can be expected only when there are legal and regulatory institutions that support private ownership and when they function in such a way that the owners can exercise their rights and improve productivity and profitability (Zinnes et al., 2001, p. 148). Therefore, liberalization in the sphere of economy and low quality of legal regulations connected to it, as well as the laws not adapted to new economic conditions, created the conditions for transition and the privatization processes of large and medium enterprises that were based on social injustice, corruption, political influences, manipulations, and economic machinations, for instance, frauds related to company value estimations, causing false bankruptcies. In the privatization transition, those who were a part of management structure in the privatized companies or were close to political power centers appeared as the new owners of capital. It is emphasized in the research literature that sudden market liberalization pushed inexperienced companies toward a rather severe competition, and the decline of companies that were previously owned by the state resulted in large-scale layoffs of workers, proclaiming redundancies, with constantly high level of unemployment.* The restructuring of a social protection system was left to be dealt with later, which forced the employees of all profiles as well as small entrepreneurs to seek the alternative survival strategies (Šćepanović, 2011, pp. 154–155). This led to the sudden rise of the shadow economy.

The development of the shadow economy was to a large extent influenced by the sanctions and embargoes on business operations with the world, which the international community and the UN imposed on Serbia. This led to total economic and financial blockade and isolation of the country. Considering that nothing could be imported by legal channels, the entire foreign trade and international connections went into the *gray zone* (Paunović and Kosanović, 2009, p. 10). This was particularly expressed in the sphere of the import of oil, cigarettes, weapons, and other strategic products. The entire foreign trade of strategic products went into the smuggling zone organized by the state, that is, some of its structures that had the greatest power and possibility of control were involved in the smuggling. The possibility of illegal imports of larger quantities of products was given to *the chosen ones* who were close to the political authority or represented some of its parts. Illegal import of strategic products also implied illegal export of foreign currency from the country considering that legal banking transactions with the world were blocked. The control of money that was illegally brought out of the country was inexistent, and the financial aspects of the business moves that were made in the name of the country were unknown. In this way, large amounts of money were kept and appropriated by the individuals who concluded business deals for Serbia in the illegal world market.

The sanctions of the international community brought about the widespread corruption of foreign partners in the foreign trade of the country with the world in purchases of goods, forgery of documents, and smuggling, that is, illegal import of goods. In this way, the sanctions of the international community had influence on the increase of the shadow economy, corruption, and smuggling at both national and international levels. Since many foreign partners were politically against the imposing of sanctions on Serbia, or because of the profit to be made, they entered into corruption schemes, forgery of documents, and money laundering. In the short period of time of international sanctions on Serbia, a stratum of extremely wealthy individuals who gained their wealth on the bases of the shadow economy, smuggling, and corruption; who managed to keep their wealth, political power, and influence; and who had excellent international ties in foreign trade was formed. Their wealth and power have their roots in the shadow economy, money laundering, and corruption. The greatest lesson these *successful businessmen* learned was that money and corruption can do anything and that they open the doors to power and big *business enterprises* at both national and international levels.

International sanctions and a total embargo on business operations of Serbia with the world (in the fields of the economy, science, and the entire international communication and exchange of ideas, and suspended cooperation of the Interpol with the Serbian police) led to not only great economic, political, social, and security consequences in the country, but also a backlash influence outside the country. Due to the economic collapse and growth of unemployment, even the ordinary citizens who are not close to those in power got involved in the shadow economy, by way of small-scale smuggling inside the country or illegal shifting of deficient products from abroad into the country in order to survive. The sanctions of the international community imposed on Serbia contributed to hyperinflation and the collapse of the domestic currency.† What was left of the economy also went from legal business operations

* In the report of Social and Economic Council of the Republic of Serbia, "The Effects of Privatization in Serbia," there is a conclusion that the results of privatization are rather defeating, despite the fact that the income earned is about 2.6 billion euros. That is, in Serbia in the last decade, more than three thousand companies were privatized, but 65% stopped working or were on the verge of bankruptcy. The price for the economy is huge, that is, around 83,000 jobs; in other words, two-thirds of jobs that existed before the privatization are lost. The privatization agency annulled 636 privatization contracts, mainly because the new owners failed to pay installments, did not manage to keep continuous business operations, and did not hold on to the agreed social programs (Report, 2011, p. 14).

† The years 1992 and 1993 will be remembered as the years of the devastating hyperinflation that caused the growth of prices beyond any proportion. The busiest factory in Serbia in 1993 was the mint. In 1993 only, 20 new bills were printed with nominal value of the last bill of record-braking 500,000,000,000 dinars, after the denomination that removed six zeros. Otherwise, the bill would have had eighteen zeros. The biggest denomination was done in 1994 by removing 23 zeros. The hyperinflation brought about the destruction of monetary and fiscal systems of the country, created many difficulties in supply of the population, contributed to drastic impoverishing of people, and created even better conditions for shadow economy to spread (Djuric, 2003, p. 53).

into the sphere of the shadow economy, which led to shortages of goods in the legal market, and the only possibility to buy these goods was in the gray market. The "Shadow economy as a deviation from the official economy in the time of crisis, i.e. in the period of sanctions, turned into the main flow of purchase of energy generating products and some consumer goods" (Pilić-Rakić, 1997, p. 12).

During the period of hyperinflation and the sanctions of the international community, the banks could not serve the direct interests of the economy. They became the centers of estranged economic and financial power. Huge assets were placed to the privileged groups and individuals without the knowledge and influence of the economy that created these assets, in the background of which were often the aspirations of individuals or groups to get rich in an easy manner by corruption and other forms of crime (Morić et al., 2004, p. 66).

For example, it is necessary to mention only some data from that period, although they can be accepted only conditionally since the exact and precise research, measuring, and estimations were not carried out. The direct consequence of war and sanctions resulted in a decrease of industrial production in 1992 of 40%. At the same time, the loss of market was 50%. In Serbia, the shadow economy in 1992 achieved the level of 40.5%, and in 1993 even as much as 53.2% of the registered domestic product (Sokić, 2000, p. 20; Milošević, 2005a, pp. 584–585).

The Shadow Economy in Serbia in the Period Following the Democratic Changes and the Return of the Country into International Economic Systems

The previously ruling socialist structure at the level of state administration and at the level of the economy restructured quickly in the transition process and adapted to new conditions in which the interest (primarily personal or of a narrow group) and money (for the purpose of personal enrichment) became the main measure of value and success. Within the context of transition processes in the Republic of Serbia, the continuous changes of legislative environment, often inconsistent and selective application of law, and unstable economic and political environment generated a symbiosis of the shadow economy, corruption, and organized crime. Marinković points out that the system of domination of politics over economy represents a death penalty for market economy or equal market match. In such a social environment, it is neither technology, work organization, nor knowledge that is the most important for the success of a company, but closeness or affiliation to the political elite in power (Marinković, 2004, pp. 462–463). In other words, the calculations related to all business operations should include the amount of bribery that should be given to government exponents as an item that enables uninterrupted business operations. In such circumstances, the norms (laws) are valid and binding for some and are not valid and binding for the others. Therefore, the entrepreneurship exists, but all those who have entered into that process without connecting to political structures cannot survive. Thus, all the principles of market economy, competition, rivalry, improvement of services, and similar traits do not apply in Serbia. These principles of market economy are not important to many businesses, since the reason that these businesses are successful is not because of their superior product or operations but because no one is allowed to jeopardize them, because they are ensured by rather perfidious and sophisticated methods with criminal sign.

In the process of destroying the old system and building the new transitional one, forming of interest groups plays a decisive role (starting from political parties and on), which results in the symbiosis of those who possess real power at the level of state administration (politics), economy, and organized crime. The influence of interest groups on the appearance of the shadow economy is best described by Kostić: "They impose to society the adoption of norms (measures of economic policy) which are in their interest, and not in the interest of the entire society by creation of imbalance in the market and privileged position of some participants in it" (Kostić, 2004, pp. 19, 33). On the other hand, imposing to the society the measures that get a part of economic factors into privileged position brings about the appearance of response by those economic factors that are harmed, and this can find a field of manifestation within the shadow economy. Even more drastic situation appears when the creation and implementation of economic policy is influenced by the interest groups whose interests are directly or indirectly linked to the gray market (Kostić, 2004, p. 71). The interest groups make wide space for possible influence of political corruption and organized crime on economic flows in the country.

Such a state of affairs makes a favorable ground for *flourishing* of criminal activities and illegal capital accumulation, through the activities in the sphere of the gray economy, corruption, and organized crime, by which social and state resources are illegally transferred into the hands of criminal structures. This is also emphasized by the European Parliament in Article 17 of the *Resolution on the European integration process of Serbia* no. B7-0000/2012, which calls on the Serbian authorities to review immediately the controversial privatization and sale of 24 companies for which the European Commission found serious doubts concerning their legality. This is just a tip of an *iceberg* of misuses in all spheres of economic life whose parts *rise to the surface* every day filling the newspaper columns, but this is all left without an adequate response by the structures in power.

The existence of interest groups and economic policy, which is predominantly in their interest and not in the interest of the citizens, may explain the fact that even after the hyperinflation was restrained and with the democratic change of power, the shadow economy in Serbia still remained strong and ranges (depending on the measuring method and the field of economic business operations) somewhere around one-third of GDP: (Djurić, 2003, p. 53; Stojanović, 2003, p. 623), although the great difficulties in making these estimations should be noted (Report 2013, p. 4; Vujović et al., 2013, p. 12).* The shadow economy is the most expressed in trading, catering industry, tourism, and the construction industry.

* In the report by the Foundation for Development of Economic Science titled "Shadow economy in Serbia—New findings and recommendations for reforms," the scope of shadow economy in Serbia was estimated by using three methods: MIMIC (Multiple Indicators Multiple Causes), household tax compliance (HTC), and the survey on the conditions of company business activities. Therefore, based on the MIMIC method (multiple indicators, multiple causes), the shadow economy in all sectors in 2010 was 30% of GDP. Based on the data for the same year, the shadow economy that can be identified based on income and expenditures of the population (HTC method) was 23.6% of GDP. According to the survey on the conditions of business activities, the shadow economy in the sector of companies for two of the most important forms of evasion (illegal turnover of goods and unregistered labor) was around 21% of GDP. Based on these results, it can be concluded that the entire shadow economy in Serbia is 30% of GDP, which is considerably higher than European average that is around 20% of GDP. That is, in European territories, only Bulgaria has a shadow economy rate higher than Serbia, which is around 32% of GDP (Report, 2013, p. 47).

The Causes for the Development of a Shadow Economy in Serbia

In order to define a successful strategy to suppress the shadow economy, it is necessary to determine its causes and at the same time separate the main causes from the unessential ones, in order to determine the causes leading to this phenomenon from its consequences. As pointed out by Marinković: "The sources of shadow economy in Serbia are connected to another issue, how to recognize and define key footholds of shadow economy. This is even more important because the key footholds of shadow economy are at the same time the key footholds of similar phenomena, including black market and organized crime" (Marinković, 2004, p. 460).

As discovered by Serbian experts and the scientific research literature pertaining to the Serbian shadow economy, there are many causes for the development of the shadow economy. These causes, which are more or less of intensity, individually but primarily together, influence its maintenance and/or important continuance even though the authoritarian government has changed and the country is no longer isolated. Despite the many attempts to suppress it, as a rule, these attempts have had no great effect.

The results of one recent research study (consisting of a representative sample of 1251 registered companies and entrepreneurs) reveal that the respondents' opinions on the causes of the shadow economy in Serbia include the following:

- Inappropriate tax policy, especially in work-related taxing
- Inefficient and selective law enforcement
- High administration burden on business operations
- Low quality of regulations and legal insecurity
- High level of corruption and low level of tax moral
- Economic crisis and decreased possibilities of employment
- Lost confidence in the state and public institutions
- High taxes
- The fact that there is a considerable portion of cash transactions within overall payment transactions (Report, 2013, p. 18)

In another recent research study (2011), in which unreported (illegal) employment was researched, 838 people from the territory of Serbia participated. Out of the entire number of respondents, 20% were engaged in the shadow economy and 11% were engaged in the shadow economy in addition to their work in the formal sector.

Also, 55% of the total number of respondents who were unemployed found some source of existence in the shadow economy. The question "What enables the maintaining of shadow economy?" was answered by the respondents with the following: the state, the government, the ministries, not enough jobs, inadequate law enforcement, inspections, state bodies not doing their jobs, badly arranged economic system, high unemployment rate, politicization and corruption, privatization, bad control, mentality of people. (Manual, 2011, p. 56)

A group of authors from the Institute of Economic Sciences state that according to a rather spread opinion, the causes of the shadow economy in Serbia are considered to be an unbalanced tax system and excessive economic regulations, which appears to have the economic consequences of suffocating regular business operations and redirecting commerce into the so-called informal zone (Jović et al., 2003, p. 286). Some authors state that the most important causes of the shadow economy include the domination of politics over the economy, the shortcomings of the tax system, insufficiently restrictive laws, restrictive politics toward private sector, and low salaries (for instance, see Stanojević, 2003), while others point to the following causes: the lack of expertise and trust in the official institutions (for instance, in the legislator, judicial authorities, and public administration), often inefficient and corruption-prone administration, the development of informal and unofficial institutions with negative performance resulting in the creation of organized crime, inappropriate enforcement of laws and regulations, heavy burden of taxes that together with inappropriate rendering of public services bring about a lack of acceptance of formal rules and laws, and the low probability that persons without work permit and tax evaders will be detected and punished. In addition, the participation in the shadow economy is sometimes important for survival or for starting up of new business activity (Petrović and Vesić, 2008, p. 850).

The most comprehensive classification of the causes of the shadow economy in Serbia classifies the causes into several main groups. The starting basis of this classification is the attitude that there is a high degree of interdependence between the shadow economy and the nature of political and economic systems. According to this view, numerous and diverse sources of the shadow economy may be classified into the following basic groups:

1. Sources stemming from economic and political system
2. Sources stemming from local and regional specificities
3. Sources stemming from tradition, culture, way of life, or historical heritage as a whole (the lack of social judgment, the appearance of widespread cheating of the state)
4. Sources related to personal characteristics of people and their individual systems of values (for instance, inclination toward risk) (Marinković, 2004, p. 461)

In this chapter, we shall dwell only upon the elaboration of the first cause, that is, political and economic factors contributing to the development and persistence of the shadow economy in Serbia, since the authors believe the interplay of the political and economic factors is crucial for the appearance of this phenomenon. Thus, according to this view, the shadow economy in Serbia is just a consequence of a far more serious problem that is reflected in the lack of political will of the ruling elites to put the shadow economy under control. For instance, Kostić points out that the shadow economy is usually observed as a phenomenon opposed to the state and its legal institutions. However, observing the manifesting forms of the shadow economy in contemporary societies, it is possible to observe trends that speak about a different relationship between a shadow economy and state bodies. There appears a higher form of a shadow economy that not only coexists peacefully with the state but also grows together with the elements of economic and political apparatuses. It is possible to talk about such a higher form of a shadow economy in the full sense in a situation where symbiosis is present, even fusion of a shadow economy not only with the parts of economic–political structures and the state apparatus but also with the financial apparatus in a certain country (Kostić, 2004, p. 15).

Marinković states the same thesis even more directly:

> Among the sources of shadow economy it should analyze particularly the following groups: legal system; political system; economic system; measures of economic policy. This is undoubtedly the most powerful group of sources of shadow economy on which all other groups of sources lean. It is undoubted that the concept of arranging all three stated sub-systems depends on the interests and commitment of those political authorities which are currently in power, or said in the words of the modern politics on the political will of the ruling elite. In other words, understated and underdeveloped system, which in our society represents a ground for shadow economy, is the result of not only ignorance, inexperience, or objective

> limitations, but of the lack of political will of the ruling elite to make the system more qualitative and economically more efficient, i.e. to create the appropriate macro-economic environment for equal market game. This open form of conflict of interest of the ruling elite and the entire society is powerfully expressed from the beginning of transition and represents one of the biggest obstacles to successful economic and social reforms. (Marinković, 2004, p. 462)

The declarative attitude that the state creates equal opportunities for everyone is not confirmed in practice. For instance, Morić et al., in their research, point out the following:

> Every non-commercial credit does not automatically mean that politics is involved. However, if a favourable credit is granted to "a person from power" or the favourable credit is obtained based on the recommendation by the "party in power," then we can talk about the politicization of the banking system. The affairs related to business operations of some banks, the manners of credit granting, the involvement of individuals in power in the functioning and work of certain banks became everyday business. (Morić et al., 2004, pp. 104–105)

It is a rather frequent occurrence in Serbia or, better to say, practice both before and after the democratic changes and until today that tax and other laws are not enforced on all people in the same manner and in the same scope. There are legal persons and economic subjects (enterprises, companies, public enterprises) in which financial police and external controls do not enter, which do not pay taxes, utilities, and other contributions and duties to the state regardless of their millions of debts.* The public explanation for this includes political and social reasons (for instance, saving large enterprises from bankruptcy or keeping jobs). However, in the background of this phenomenon, there are financing of political parties, corruption, and enrichment of those who manage these enterprises. The consequences of such practices are a market game unequal for all economic subjects, the favorable position of some at the expense of the others, chronic deficiency in the state budget, and distrust of citizens in the tax system and the state, which further contributes to the evasion of tax payments and the shadow economy.

* The Tax Administration of the Republic of Serbia published the list of the biggest tax debtors on March 26, 2014, according to which one of the biggest tax debtors (not only for this year but also for the previous years) was the company Simpo AD with tax debt amounting to 4,263,365,763 dinars (around 37 million euros) (http://www.poreskauprava.gov.rs/biro-za-informisanje/novosti/1018/spiskovi-najvecih-duznika-na-dan2603201http://www.poreskauprava.gov.rs/biro-za-informisanje/novosti/1018/spiskovi-najvecih-duznika-na-dan2603201 4-godine.html, accessed May 8, 2014). The president of the board of directors of this company is a prominent member of a political party that participates in power for a number of years.

The Relationship between the Shadow Economy, Corruption, Organized Crime, and Money Laundering

The Shadow Economy and Corruption

All the studies, as well as expert and scientific papers dealing with the shadow economy in Serbia, suggest the close relationship between this phenomenon and corruption. The corruption of civil servants most often appears as a method to cover up the shadow economy or the means that facilitates its implementation. Regardless of whether the corruption results from or precedes the shadow economy, the relationship between these two phenomena is directly correlated. The more the shadow or black economy in a society, the higher the degree of corruption, and *vice versa*. The institutions eroded by corruption are weak obstacles to the interests of widespread criminal structures. The corrupt exponents of power do not have sufficient authority or ethics to counter the shadow economy and criminal structures efficiently, which the latter use to generate criminal profit. The relationship between the shadow economy and corruption is particularly expressed in the societies where there is a dominant influence of politics on economic flows, as is the case in Serbia. It is worth mentioning the opinion that Morić et al. present, that is, the politicization of economic processes that results from the connections between political and economic circles undoubtedly leads to corruption and represents its main source. In the countries where corruption takes a dominant place, the connection between the politics and informal sector is very powerful (Morić et al., 2004, p. 106).

The connection between the shadow economy and corruption can be direct or indirect. The direct connection exists when civil servants are involved in racketeering or demand bribes using blackmail and making conditions to economic subjects in various ways.

The evolution and existence of the shadow economy is enabled by corrupt power, since the shadow economy represents a resource for them, which is used for personal enrichment or for financing political parties. On the other hand, a corrupt environment stimulates transformation and the creation of new segments of criminal markets that exist on the margins of both legal and illegal spheres, while criminal structures are imposed as the *managers* of these processes and exponents of the interests of criminal organizations. The practice shows that corruption is the most profitable business of quasi-democratic powers; the shadow economy is their strongest social program, and *racketeering* is the most favored method of *taxation* (Tomaš, 2010, p. 53). This is reflected through the phenomena that stimulate the creation of a shadow economy, the activities of tax evasion, through either avoiding to register the income or declaring a lower amount than actually earned, which makes up a considerable part of the totality of the shadow economy. Therefore, the tax payers must use a considerable part of evaded taxes for the corruption of exponents of power as specific forms of racketeering, which essentially means that in order to survive in a shadow economy, they must pay gray taxes. The mechanism is rather simple: in order to do business and survive in a shadow zone, you must pay corrupt representatives of power so that they will not *make interruptions* in your business. The existence of a positive correlation between the shadow economy and corruption is confirmed by the research in this field, but the influence of a shadow economy on the appearance of corruption is considered to be more intensive than *vice versa* (Buehn and Schneider, 2009, p. 27). It is important at this point to note that the shadow economy functions as a model to gain illegal profit, not a manner of maintaining the existence of those who are most endangered.

The connection between corruptive demands of the exponents of state power and the participants in the sphere of a shadow economy is manifested in various manners. Kostić rather subtly notices that the state in all its activities, including those within the economic sphere of social life, is personalized in the face of public officials and civil servants and must leave space for new occurrences to develop such as bribery and corruption and even the activities of asking the rent. If we start from an undoubted fact that people at the aforementioned positions are guided by personal interests, we must come to the conclusion that they will protect state interests only to the extent that helps in achieving their personal interests. Considering all that has been said, it is realistic to expect that in a situation when a personal interest and state interest get in conflict, when a public official or a civil servant is making his or her decisions, the personal interest will prevail (Kostić, 2004, p. 47). Negative consequences of such a state of affairs are numerous: various forms of lobbying, the bribery of civil servants who can help obtain important licenses, and the fight among these servants to get to and remain in the positions that will be beneficial for them. The said process can lead to imbalance in the market; it can increase to such proportions that it can almost entirely destroy the legal economy in some economic sectors and instead impose the shadow economy as a functioning framework (Kostić, 2004, p. 51).

In practice, these relations are most often manifested in corruption schemes related to obtaining of import–export licenses, or granting licenses, granting quantities for import/export of certain goods, attaining approval of exclusive rights to import certain kind of goods, taking a percentage from concluded agreements, and acquiring participation in the work of a company's board of directors, when a public official can provide benefits in the company's business operations, in illegal financing of political parties in power (compare Marinković, 2005, p. 12), tax evasion, and so on.

One research study conducted in Serbia suggests that a certain behavior of the official administration that expects to be given bribe can also lead to evasion of legal flows and entering into the shadow zone of business operations. In these cases, entering into the shadow zone results from the effort to avoid the pressure of criminal groups and gangs and payment of racketeering (Morić and Tošić, 2002, p. 161).

The relationship between the shadow economy and corruption of civil servants has also indirect consequences that reflect in moral erosion of a society and erosion of tax moral. One more recent research study in Serbia showed that a high level of corruption is destimulating for the readiness of tax payers to pay taxes, considering that it creates an impression that the taxes they pay will not be used in an appropriate manner to finance public sector but to become private gain of certain categories of people. In addition to this, according to the results of the poll that was a part of the said research, corruption was identified among the respondents as the fourth most important cause of the shadow economy in Serbia (Report, 2013, p. 41).

Marinković suggests that indirect losses are even far greater, which cannot often be seen at first sight and which in the long run leaves very difficult consequences. Corruption destroys systematically and permanently the healthy tissue of a society, all organizations and institutions, permanent moral and social values, and lives and destinies of individuals and their families; it devalues the basic goals to which a society is striving. Destruction of basic system of values, in other words moral destruction of a society, is by all means the most severe consequence of corruption considering that it attacks the basic foundations of the society. Under the conditions of corruption, the risk of market game and all efforts and investments (material and human) that are necessary to make in order to survive in the market are very gladly replaced for the benefits offered by closeness to political authorities or those who perform legislative and executive power. The owners of capital, instead of improving technologies and work organizations with new production programs or new entrepreneurship initiatives, are directed at establishing and strengthening ties with carriers of political functions and public authorizations (Marinković, 2005, pp. 13, 15).

The Shadow Economy, Organized Crime, and Money Laundering

The roots of the new *economic elite* in Serbia reach back to the past, from the 1990s to the period of absolute dominance of a totalitarian regime that started the process of *criminalization* of the society. Under the conditions of international sanctions, alternative mechanisms were developed for procuring deficient goods to the market under the control of security services and under the influence of the politicians and active participation of criminal structures. These alternative models of market supply were followed by alternative payment mechanisms, which were developed through the establishment of banks or participation in the management of banks or economic subjects in Cyprus and other offshore centers, which enabled the misuses to be covered up. The goods and money, which flowed through shadow economy channels, were controlled by criminal structures that infiltrated all pores of economic relations. Therefore, organized crime based the largest part of their power on the money gained through illicit activities, and this money represented an economic *lever* of power of criminal organizations that enabled their inclusion into legal economic activities and the corruption of government bodies (Bošković, 2005, p. 595). This trend continued after the democratic changes of 2000; only now these criminal structures started to use the same mechanisms and ties together with corrupt exponents of the new *democratic* power.* The ties between organized crime and the authority primarily reflected in the process of privatization of companies in Serbia. On the one hand, criminally gained money was invested in the purchase of the companies; in other words, the money is of doubtful or unverified provenance. The buyer of the company did not have to prove the origin of money; in other words, the true buyer could hide his or her identity. On the other hand, the companies that were worth a lot of money were bought for a mere trifle and then destroyed while tens and hundreds of thousands of workers were left jobless, and then they were not given any other (real) possibility but to enter the sphere of the shadow economy or to invest their work (the only thing they had) at the black labor market.

Morić indicates that in the periods of big crises and spreading of shadow economy, the boundaries between gray and black zones (economies) become blurred, and the shadow economy often transfers into the black zone (Morić et al., 2004, p. 10). Bearing in mind the period that Serbia had to pass in the most recent history, it is not odd that many cases are recorded of cooperation between civil servants at various levels of hierarchy and the business deals with hardened criminals from the sphere of organized crime. There was not a single big affair when a drug lord, a drug clan, or a big organized crime group was discovered that there were not police officers who directly cooperated with them as direct members of these groups, offering them protection, information, or logistics. Organized crime in the sphere of traditional crime or organized crime in the sphere of economic crime have both influence on the levers of the power both in the domain of high-level politics and economy and in the domain of judiciary. The problem is that there are too many headlines in the yellow press that deal with these problems; too much leads in the everyday functioning of the state, its economy, and justice system; but too little court procedures with meritorious court decisions.

Marinković says that the shadow economy and its inevitable companion, the black market, show exceptional resilience and capability to adapt and survive under the various social circumstances. In order to

* According to the data for 2004, the National Bank of Serbia recorded payment declarations to Cyprus to the amount of $760,540,000 USD for the goods, the customs bodies recorded that the goods that entered the country amounted to $40,000,000 USD, and according to the data from Cyprus on the export of goods into our country the reported goods amounted to $1,400,000 million USD. By simple comparison of the stated data it can be observed that there is a considerable discrepancy of $720,500,000 USD between the data of the National Bank of Serbia and customs bodies and the discrepancy of $759,100,000 USD between the data of the NBS and the data from Cyprus. There are also similar data for 2003, where the discrepancy is $776,100,000 USD (OECD, 2006, p. 29). These could be the cases of the so-called *fictitious import*, which is paid by the amounts considerably higher than the real prices or the goods is paid that will never enter the country. These types of abuses are carried out with the following purpose: to decrease the profit of the company in the country and to evade paying taxes; to bring the money out of the country which then begins its journey through world financial system in order to *be laundered*; to harm the company (most often public enterprises) by the responsible persons when the *discrepancy taken out* is used for illicit property gain and similar.

define shadow economy and its relationship with other similar phenomena, it is a considerably important fact that shadow economy never appears alone. To be more precise, it cannot appear and exist on its own. Its inevitable companions are even worse. They are the black market, including the black labor market and various forms of crime, whereas the central position is taken by organized crime. If observed outside this context, the shadow economy looks like a forced source of existence of marginal social groups. On the contrary, only within the aforementioned context are the true dimensions and consequences of this problem recognized (Marinković, 2004, p. 458).

That there is a relationship between organized crime and legislative bodies in Serbia is best pointed out by the adoption of the Law on Prevention of Money Laundering. The Assembly of Serbia in the mid-2001 adopted the law on prevention of money laundering defining that the law will start to be applied on July 1, 2002. Therefore, the law was adopted exactly a year before it started to be implemented. This both factually and legally left a 1-year period for *all interested parties* to launder the dirty money!

The most recent example of laundering of drug-related money is the case of the drug lord, Darko Šarić, who was importing cocaine from Latin America to Europe. The money earned from selling cocaine in Europe was predominantly invested into real estate in the economy in Serbia. In this way he laundered 22 million euros (Politika of March 29, 2014). There are many pieces of evidence suggesting that the state authority could not have known about the origin of the money; however, it has still enabled him to place the money into the economy of Serbia. The contacts of the closest associates of the drug lord went as far as the prime minister and the Ministry of Internal Affairs in the previous term of office and the current minister in the government of Serbia and the president of one of the biggest political parties in Serbia. The aforementioned politician denied these contacts, although the nature and content of these ties and relations has never been investigated.

Problems in Implementing the Measures to Suppress the Shadow Economy

As a rule, the crime perpetrators in the field of the shadow economy are very skillful, capable, and ready to use their position. They apply the multiple sources of knowledge they have in order to cover their tracks, use to the maximum all the benefits that the existing legislation provides, and take advantage of the weaknesses of the preventive and repressive system whose task is to prevent, detect, and process their criminal behavior. For instance, in one research study conducted immediately following the democratic changes in Serbia, the profiles of perpetrators in the field of the shadow economy whom the police brought charges were investigated. The results of the research showed that in the structure of reported individuals, at the top of the pyramid, there were perpetrators from the most important structures of the former political power that created and misused the most influential para-state centers of power and decision making. According to their importance, right behind them were the perpetrators from among the managers and responsible individuals in public enterprises; big economic systems and state-owned enterprises, banks, and other financial organizations; then the owners and responsible individuals in private companies and the owners of shops; and finally large- and small-scale smugglers, regraters, forgers, tax evaders, foreign currency dealers, loan sharks, and others (Morić et al., 2004, p. 110).

The great challenges in detecting and processing these activities are that the educational profile of these perpetrators and their positions on the social ladder are far higher than in the average population of criminals. In addition to this, they can employ the entire teams of experts who help them cover up their illegal activities. They have ties and contacts with the powerful people since as a rule, they are also powerful and use their strongest weapon, that is, corruption. Sokić suggests that in this kind of crime, there is an expressed misuse of expert knowledge for the purpose of gaining large profits and great wealth of the perpetrators in the area of the shadow economy. He continues: "Almost an 'entire army' of strategists in the sphere of shadow economy is seeking the ways and forms of 'jumping over hurdles' of all kinds and minimizing the consequences of legal and normative acts and activities of the state in suppressing the existence and effects of shadow economy" (Sokić, 2000, p. 4).

The practice shows without any doubt, as Sokić also correctly observes, that opposing the shadow economy is not satisfactory in almost all of the countries of the postsocialist transition. The causes are related primarily to inconsistent legislation, weak functioning of state bodies, unsuccessful measures of economic policy, failures in tax reforms, and stagnation in reforms. The causes of the shadow economy also result from the integrations with the environment, as well as from an almost frantic maintenance of old relations (Sokić, 2000, p. 17).

All the mentioned weaknesses of preventive and repressive systems are expressed in Serbia. In Serbia, there are many state bodies whose tasks and legal authorizations are to prevent offenses and detect and gather evidence of crimes in the field of the shadow economy such as the financial police, tax administration, customs administration, market inspectorate, organizations of social security, foreign currency inspectorate, budget inspectorate, labor inspectorate, crime-investigation police, attorney's office, and the courts. Despite the number and variety of agencies, in practice these bodies appear incompetent and rather inefficient, since a large number of crimes in the field of shadow economy remain undetected and unpunished (for instance, see Milošević, 2005a, p. 592). One of the biggest problems in the work of state organs dealing with control and suppression of the shadow economy in Serbia is the insufficient or bad cooperation and coordination among these agencies. There are problems of overlapping competencies, bad conduct of the control procedure, or interpretation of legal regulations. In some cases, there are even conflicts that make direct cooperation impossible. Also, there is no dissemination and exchange of data among the state organs (Morić et al., 2004, pp. 156–157).

The problem of all state bodies in Serbia is the political factor, since all managers are appointed based on political deals and influences of the ruling parties. When managers in state bodies are elected, it is political eligibility that is primarily considered, while expertise, integrity, or experience is completely neglected. In this way, the ruling political parties have direct influence on the work of state bodies, which is the cause of many misuses and inefficiency of the legal system in Serbia. Among other things, such practice has negative influence on the work of state bodies that are authorized by the law to suppress the shadow economy.

For instance, it is possible to observe numerous weaknesses in the work of inspectorates whose task is to control economic subjects. The work of some inspectorates is not sufficiently regulated by the law. There are certain legal regulations that make it difficult, or even disable the performance of inspection supervision in certain areas (for instance, the impossibility to perform inspection supervision of unregistered companies). It is notable that state bodies are insufficiently involved in suppression of informal work and the shadow economy. The inspection supervision is insufficiently regulated. Punishing policy of inspections is unequal. There is not a qualitative coordination of several inspections regarding the issues where joint jurisdiction and action is prescribed. Inspectorates are insufficiently technically equipped to carry out inspections as far as staff and their qualifications are concerned. It has been noted that inspectors are not sufficiently competent and that they are not familiar with the changes in regulations that are in force and that inspections are not connected with each other into one information system. This is shown by the fact that the supervisions in some companies are carried out several times without having an appropriate time lapse between the inspections, while the inspections of other companies have not been carried out for several years (Vujović et al., 2013, pp. 27, 29, 32). Corruption and political influence often make it conditional for the inspection supervision in certain economic subjects to be carried out very frequently, while in some others it is not performed at all (selective control). In one recent research, which included the sample of 838 respondents from the territory of Serbia, one of the questions was to review the work of inspections. The results revealed that 38% of employers reviewed it as nonexistent, while 56% reviewed it with a failure mark. Thus, 86% of the employees who responded reviewed the work of the inspection bodies as either *fail* or *inexistent* (Manual, 2011, p. 56).

Financial police have similar legal, staff-related, and technical problems as inspection bodies. Its work is also made difficult by bad regulations, insufficient technical and staff support, political influences, and corruption. This is why tax collection and observation of irregularities in this area are rather inefficient. For instance, frequently certain cases are not processed (they are kept for years inside the drawers of financial police managers) since powerful people are interested in these cases or there are political pressures or corruption and other misuses are in their background.

The courts in Serbia are very inefficient and slow institutions, so that the procedures last for years and there is often a statute of limitation in criminal cases. The same destiny is with cases in the field of economic crime and shadow economy. For instance, Morić points out that the activities conducted by the police on the detection and proving crimes in the field of the shadow economy and their perpetrators in the largest number of cases are not adequately pursued by the judiciary, which considerably diminishes the effects of police work. On the other hand, inadequate punishing policy contributes to the lacking in the effects of general crime prevention measures and also leads to the increase of multiple recidivist of the perpetrators within the structure of the detected criminals who have committed crimes related to the shadow economy (Morić et al., 2004, p. 97). This fact is confirmed by the results of a recent poll, in which over two-thirds of the respondents consider that the probability of adequate punishment for those detected for tax evasion is low, that is, at the level of a random guess (50%) and even less. The research suggests that the judicial bodies are not ready and capable to process cases of tax evasion efficiently and effectively, particularly in those cases regarding the more complex forms of tax evasion (Report, 2006, p. 57; Report, 2013, p. 30).

Conclusion

A long history of *nurturing* the values that affirm the models of illegal business operations, or possession of property, has integrated in Serbia's everyday life. It is a fundamental activity of the state in this area to bring into connection the sources of income with their spending, investment, or possession of property through defining a clear legal framework to examine the origin of property.

The measures aimed at *tearing apart* the symbiosis of the shadow economy, corruption, and organized crime represent a challenge for every serious and responsible government who wishes to free the society from criminal *restraints*. This also applies to the Serbian government and society.

The first group of measures should be more general in character and should refer to establishing rule of law through the mechanisms that will not only stimulate higher responsibility of the government and higher risk of losing power and then a decisive fight against corruption and organized crime and consistent law enforcement but also insist on suppressing monopoly and stimulating free market, more efficient tax policy, and high-quality public sector services.

The second group of measures should focus on certain *vulnerable* areas in order to enable implementation of strategic and operative projects of control of the shadow economy. For instance, it is necessary to take stimulating measures for the transfer of the shadow economy into legal economic flows; to insist in the application of methods of financial investigation in all cases of property-motivated criminal activities, particularly in the domain of economic relations; to introduce into the criminal code a crime of *illicit enrichment* (defined by Article 20 of the UN Convention against Corruption); to create a unique methodology for gathering data on crime; and to integrate databases of various state bodies into a unique electronic system, among other provisions.

In addition to the aforementioned, many other measures should be incorporated into the existing strategic documents and future strategic commitments and also implemented in practice. It is necessary to form a comprehensive and efficient system for the fight against organized crime, corruption, and the shadow economy together with timely implementation and efficient enforcement of the measures aimed at reduction of profitability of criminal activities. In this way, the strategic measures would destroy the economic levers of power of criminal structures. The best chance for these aims to be realized lies in the accession of Serbia to the European Union, which would hopefully impose the depoliticization of the economy, putting the state and its finances in order and introducing a more efficient fight against corruption.

References

Andjelković, M. (2002). Siva ekonomija kao globalni društveno-ekonomski fenomen, fiskalna dimenzija. *Pravni život*, No. 10, Beograd, Serbia: Kopaonička škola prirodnog prava, pp. 407–415. [Andjelkovic, M. (2002). Shadow economy as global social-economic phenomenon, fiscal dimension. Legal life, No. 10, Belgrade, Serbia: Kopaonik School of Natural Law, pp. 407–415.]

Bošković, G. (2005). Organizovani kriminalitet i legalno poslovanje, *Organizovani kriminalitet-stanje i mere zaštite*. Beograd, Serbia: Policijska akademija, pp. 593–602. [Boskovic, G. (2005). Organized crime and legal business activities, Organized crime—Status and measures of protection. Belgrade, Serbia: Police Academy, pp. 593–602.]

Buehn, A., Schneider, F. (2009). Corruption and the shadow economy: A structural equation model approach. IZA Discussion Papers, No. 4182. http://nbn-resolving.de/urn:nbn:de:101:1-2009061268. (Accessed April 22, 2014.)

Čudan, A., Lajić, O., Petković, A. (2014). Siva ekonomija na pragu trećeg milenijuma, stanje i perspektive. *Dani Arčibalda Rajsa—Tematski zbornik sa konferencije međunarodnog značaja*, 1. Beograd, Serbia: Kriminalističko-policijska akademija, pp. 375–385. [Cudan, A., Lajic, O., Petkovic, A. (2014). Shadow economy at the threshold of third millennium, status and perspectives. Archibald Reiss Days—Thematic Collection of Conference Papers, Paper No. 1. Belgrade, Serbia: Academy of Criminalistic and Police Studies, pp. 375–385.]

Djurić, Z. (2003). Siva ekonomija i korupcija. Zubin Potok, Kosovo: Ekonomski fakultet. [Djuric, Z. (2003). Shadow economy and corruption. Zubin Potok, Kosovo: Faculty of Economics.]

Ekonomski rečnik. (2010). Beograd: Ekonomski fakultet. [*Economic Dictionary*. (2010). Belgrade: Faculty of Economics.]

Hovy, B. (2011). Koliko ih je napustilo zemlju. Raseljavanje građana bivše Jugoslavije. *Migracije, krize i ratni sukobi na Balkanu sa kraja XX veka*. Beograd, Serbia: Društvo demografa Srbije, pp. 27–49. [Hovy, B. (2011). How much people have fled the country. The Displacement of citizens of former Yugoslavia. Migrations, crises and war conflicts in the Balkans at the end of XX century. Belgrade, Serbia: Association of Demographers of Serbia, pp. 27–49.]

Izveštaj. (2013). *Siva ekonomija u Srbiji, novi nalazi i preporuke za reforme*. Beograd, Serbia: Fond za razvoj ekonomske nauke, USAID Srbija. [Report. (2013). Shadow economy in Serbia, new findings and recommendations for reforms. Belgrade, Serbia: Foundation for Advancement of Economics, USAID Serbia.]

Jović, M., Spariosu, T., Jovanović, M. (2003). *Institucije i mere za legalizaciju sive ekonomije*. Beograd, Serbia: Institut ekonomskih nauka. [Jovic, M., Spariosu, T., Jovanovic, M. (2003). Institutions and measures of legalization of shadow economy. Belgrade, Serbia: Institute of Economic Sciences.]

Kostić, L. (2004). *Zašto je siva ekonomija tako žilava*? Beograd, Serbia: Zadužbina Andrejević. [Kostic, L. (2004). Why shadow economy is so resilient? Belgrade, Serbia: Andrejevic Foundation.]

Manual, (2011). *Manual For Decent Work Against Informal Economy*, European conference on Decent Work and Informal Economy, Belgrade, 19–20.

Marinković, D. (2004). Siva ekonomija i crno tržište u Srbiji. Paralelni svet oko nas. *Ekonomski vidici*, 9(3): 455–467. Beograd, Serbia: Društvo ekonomista Beograda. [Marinkovic, D. (2004). Shadow economy and black market in Serbia. Parallel world around us. *Economic Perspectives*, 9(3): 455–467. Belgrade, Serbia: Belgrade Society of Economists.1]

Marinkovic, D. (2005). Corruption in history and today, have we choice. *Economic Perspectives*, 10(1): 5–20. Belgrade, Serbia: Belgrade Society of Economists.

Milošević, G. (2005a). Uzroci i pojavni oblici sive ekonomije u Srbiji. *Organizovani kriminalitet stanje i mere zaštite*. Beograd, Serbia: Policijska akademija, pp. 569–593. [Milosevic, G. (2005a). Causes and manifesting forms of shadow economy in Serbia. Organized crime—Status and measures of protection. Belgrade, Serbia: Police Academy, pp. 569–593.]

Milošević, G. (2005b). *Porez i izbegavanje poreza*. Beograd, Serbia: Službeni list. [Milosevic, G. (2005b). Tax and tax evasion. Belgrade, Serbia: Official Gazette.]

Morić, L., Tošić, M. (2002). Suzbijanje sive ekonomije kao deo reformi u privredi i društvu. *Zbornik radova nastavnika VŠUP-a*, N 4. Beograd, Serbia: Viša škola unutrašnjih poslova, pp. 155–164. [Moric, L., Tosic, M. (2002). Suppressing shadow economy as a pert of reforms in economy and society. Collection of papers of Police College Teaching Staff, No. 4. Belgrade, Serbia: Police College, 155–164.]

Morić, L. et al. (2004). *Javna bezbednost i problemi sive ekonomije*. Istraživački projekat, Beograd: Viša škola unutrašnjih poslova. [Moric, L. et al. (2004). Public security and problems of shadow economy. Research project. Belgrade, Serbia: Police College.]

Paunović, S., Kosanović, R. (2009). *Siva ekonomija, Hidden Economy*. Beograd, Serbia: International Trade Union Confederation (ITUC). [Paunovic, S., Kosanovic, R. (2009). Shadow economy, hidden economy. Belgrade, Serbia: International Trade Union Confederation (ITUC).]

Petrović, P., Vesić D. (2008). Siva ekonomija i institucionalne promene u tranzicionim zemljama. *Pravni život*, 11. Beograd, Serbia: Kopaonička škola prirodnog prava, pp. 845–854. [Petrovic, P., Vesic, D. (2008). Shadow economy and institutional changes in transitioning countries. Legal life, No. 11. Belgrade, Serbia: Kopaonik School of Natural Law, pp. 845–854.]

Pilić-Rakić, V. (1997). *Siva ekonomija*. Beograd, Serbia: UNDS. [Pilic-Rakic, V. (1997). Shadow economy. Belgrade, Serbia: UNDS.]

Priručnik za dostojanstven rad protiv neformalne ekonomije. (2011). *Evropska konferencija na temu dostojanstvenog rada i neformalne ekonomije*, Beograd, Serbia, Maj 19–20, 2011. Beograd: Fondacija Centar za demokratiju. [Manual for decent work against informal economy. (2011). *European Conference on Decent Work and Informal Economy*, Belgrade, Serbia, May 19–20, 2011. Belgrade: Foundation Center for Democracy.]

Report. (2006). Report on Money Laundering and Predicate Crime in Serbia 2000–2005. (2006). Belgrade, Serbia: OECD Mission to Serbia http://polis.osce.org/library/f/2641/378/OSCE-SRB-RPT-2641-EN-378.pdf. (Accessed March 21, 2014.)

Report. (2011). *Efekti privatizacije u Srbiji*. Beograd, Serbia: Socioekonomski savet Republike Srbije. [Report. (2011). The effects of privatization in Serbia. Belgrade, Serbia: Social and Economic Council of the Republic of Serbia.]

Šćepanović, R. (2011). Dinamika ekonomskih reformi: uloga sive ekonomije u zemljama u tranziciji. *Pravo, teorija i praksa*, 28(10–12): 150–181. Novi Sad: Univerzitet Privredna akademija, Pravni fakultet za privredu i pravosuđe. [Scepanovic, R. (2011). Dynamics of economic reforms: The role of shadow economy in countries in transition. *Law, Theory and Practice*, 28(10–12): 150–181. Novi Sad: University Economic Academy, Legal Faculty of Economics and Judicature.]

Simonović, B. (2004). *Kriminalistika*. Kragujevac, Serbia: Pravni fakultet. [Simonovic, B. (2004). Criminalistics. Kragujevac, Serbia: Faculty of Law.]

Sokić, S. (2000). Ekstradohodak i ekstra profit kao deo sive ekonomije. *Srpska slobodarska misao: časopis za filozofiju, društvene nauke i političku kritiku*, 1(1): 3–31. Beograd, Serbia: SRS. [Sokic, S. (2000). Extra-income and extra profit as parts of shadow economy. *Serbian Libertarian Thought: Journal of Philosophy, Social Sciences and Political Critique*, 1(1): 3–31. Belgrade, Serbia: SRS.]

Stojanović, M. (2003). Razmere sive ekonomije i mere za njeno suzbijanje. *Bezbednost*, 4. Beograd, Serbia: Ministrstvo unutrašnjih poslova Republike Srbije, pp. 621–627. [Stojanovic, M. (2003). Proportions of shadow economy and measures for its suppression. Security, 4. Belgrade, Serbia: Ministry of Internal Affairs of the Republic of Serbia, pp. 621–627.]

Tomaš, R. (2010). *Kriza i siva ekonomija u Bosni i Hercegovini*. Sarajevo, Bosnia: Friedrich-Ebert-Stiftung BIH. [Tomas, R. (2010). Crisis and shadow economy in Bosnia and Herzegovina. Sarajevo, Bosnia: Friedrich-Ebert-Stiftung BIH.]

Vujovic M., Nikolić, N., Ružić, B. (2013). *Dostojanstven rad i siva ekonomija*. Beograd, Serbia: Fondacija Centar za demokratiju. [Vujovic M., Nikolic N., Ruzic, B. (2013). Decent work and shadow economy. Belgrade, Serbia: Foundation Center for Democracy.]

Zinnes, C., Eilat, Y., Sachs, J. (2001). The gains from privatization in transition economies: Is "change of ownership" enough? IMF Staff Papers, No. 48 (special issue 4), pp. 146–170.

12. The Relationship of the Shadow Economy and Corruption in China

Li Xiangxia

Introduction

This chapter focuses on the relationship between corruption and the shadow economy in China. The general trend of the shadow economy and how it relates to corruption; the relationship between power of seeking rent, corruption, and the shadow economy; and the proposals that have been offered to combat serious corruption in China are explored.

The data and information used in the analysis were taken from the annual working reports of the Supreme People's Procuratorate of the People's Republic of China using the data from 2004 to 2013, the 5-year working reports from the Supreme People's Procuratorate of the People's Republic of China from 2004 to 2013, and the annual working report for 2013 of the People's Procuratorate at the provincial level.

Since 2013, the Chinese government has made great efforts to combat corruption. China is one of the largest countries in the world, and in 2013, its GDP was approximately $9.3 trillion USD.* China has become the second largest economic giant in the world. However, the shadow economy was not counted in the statistics, and corruption is one of the major manifestations of the shadow economy (Weiting, 1996). How much does the shadow economy or the black economy relate to corruption in China? What is the real situation of the relationship between the black economy and corruption in China? After checking some Chinese databases, it was found that there are few available research reports or statistics that directly analyze the relationship between the black economy and corruption in China. This article tries to find some clues on the basis of the annual working report of the Supreme People's Procuratorate of the People's Republic of China from 2004 to 2013, the 5-year working reports of the Supreme People's Procuratorate of People's Republic of China from 1993

* Online news, retrieved on May 16, 2014 from http://www.guancha.cn/economy/2014_01_20_200873_s.shtml.

to 2012, and the annual working report of the People's Procuratorate at the provincial level in 2013.

One of the goals of this chapter on the informal economy in China is to let the readers form a broad understanding of the crime of corruption, as defined in the Chinese Criminal Code. In the first part of this chapter, I have briefly introduced what is the exact definition of corruption in the Chinese Criminal Code. The second part focuses on analyzing the annual working report of the Supreme People's Procuratorate of People's Republic of China from 2003 to 2013, the annual working report of the People's Procuratorate at the provincial level in 2013, and some statistics related to pecuniary losses, which were the result of corruption. In the third part, the chapter takes a number of typical cases concerning corruption, by means of analyzing the case facts in detail. It is evident that the black economy is behind these corruptions. Based on the work of the second part and third part, the fourth part of this chapter reveals the relationship of the black economy and corruption in China. Furthermore, this chapter proposes some countermeasures to combat the serious crime of corruption. Finally, in the conclusion, we will examine the relationship between the shadow economy and corruption in China at the international level.

Definition of Corruption in the Chinese Criminal Code and by the United Nations

The definition of corruption under the context of the Chinese Criminal Code is slightly different from most European countries, so it is necessary to make a brief introduction about corruption in the context of the United Nations (UN) Convention against Corruption and the Chinese Criminal Code.

According to Articles 15, 16, 17, 18, 19, 20, 21, and 22 of the UN Convention against Corruption, the definition of corruption is a general term for a series of offenses, which include bribery, embezzlement, misappropriation, trading in influence, abuse of functions, illicit enrichment, bribery in the private sector, and embezzlement of property in the private sector, and other offenses.* So, generally speaking, corruption is used as a broad term under relevant contextual information. However, Antinori (2012) identified some behaviors, which are considered to be corrupt as follows:

- *Corruption*—A crime against general interests. It can be defined as an illegal contract by a public officer who represents a state and its citizens. The public officer receives on his or her own behalf or for a third-party remuneration for acting outside his duties. Corruption ensues even if no money or goods are received.
- *Extortion*—This crime is a type of reverse corruption. A public officer abuses his or her power function and forces a subject to give or to promise money or other goods to the officer or a third party in exchange for actions against the officer's duties. Extortion constitutes a type of blackmail by a public officer against citizens who have the right to seek services granted by law.
- *Peculation*—A public officer takes possession of other people's property and money in the custody of a public office. This is a type of embezzlement against the officer's employer.

Obviously, Antinori's concept of corruption is different from the UN Convention against Corruption.

Under the Chinese Criminal Law, the provisions, which are used to punish corruption,† are more compatible with the UN Convention against Corruption. According to the different identities of criminals, there are two categories of corruption that are regulated in different chapters in the Chinese Criminal Code: One category is that the offenders work as the staff of the private sector, and the corruption that is committed by this type of offenders is laid down by Articles 163, 164, and the first clause of Articles 183, 184, and 185. Accordingly, these provisions are in Chapter 3 of the special provisions of the Chinese Criminal Law, and Chapter 3 is laid down to penalize the crime of disordering the order of socialist market economy; another category of the Chinese Criminal Code pertains to the corrupt activities that were committed by civil servants or state personnel who work in the state organs. In the special provisions of the Chinese Criminal Law, there is an individual chapter used to regulate corruptions, which were committed by civil servants or state personnel, all of the articles in Chapter 8 are set to punish this type of offenders, and Chapter 8 is named corruption and bribery, starting with Article 382 through 396.

* See UN Convention against Corruption. Online resources, from http://www.unodc.org/unodc/en/treaties/CAC/index.html#UNCACfulltext. (Retrieved on May 21, 2014.)

† Here, corruption is used as a broad term that refers to a series of criminal behaviors, such as embezzlement, bribery, and misappropriation.

Dates and Statistics Concerning Corruption in China

In order to understand the real situation of corruption in China and get some useful clues to further analyze the relationship between corruption and the black economy in China, this part of the chapter is based on the statistics of the annual working report of the Supreme People's Procuratorate of the People's Republic of China from 2004 to 2013 and the annual working report of the People's Procuratorate at the provincial level in 2013.

Table 12.1 reveals the general situation of corruption in China from 1993 to 2012. Table 12.2* shows the quantity, number of involved persons, sum of illicit money, and number of corruptors concerning corruption per year between 2004 and 2013. These corruption cases were filed to investigate by the People's Procuratorate across China, and they had been reported in the annual working report of the Supreme People's Procuratorate of People's Republic of China from 2004 to 2013.

Table 12.1 Corruption in China from 2004–2013

	Caseload	Number of Involved Persons	Sum of Illicit Money (Hundred Million RMB)
1993–1997	387,352	181,873	229.2
1998–2002	207,103	More than 102,894	220
2003–2007	179,696	209,487	244.8
2008–2012	165,787	218,639	553

Table12.2 General Situation of Corruption in China from 1993 to 2012

	Caseload	Number of Involved Persons	Sum of Illicit Money (Hundred Million RMB)	Number of Corruptors
2004	No available data[a]	43,757	45.6	—
2005	—	41,447	74	—
2006	33,668	40,041	No available data	—
2007	—	—	—	—
2008	33,546	41,179	—	—
2009	32,439	41,531	71.2	3194
2010	32,909	44,085	74	3969
2011	32,567	44,506	77.9	4217
2012	34,326	47,338	—	—
2013	37,551	51,306	101.4	5515

In the table, when the corresponding data is missing, I replace *no available data* with "—."

Based on the information provided in Tables 12.1 and 12.2, Figures 12.1 through 12.4 can be made. Figure 12.1 depicts the general declining trend of corruption caseloads from 1993 to 2002. The peak appeared in

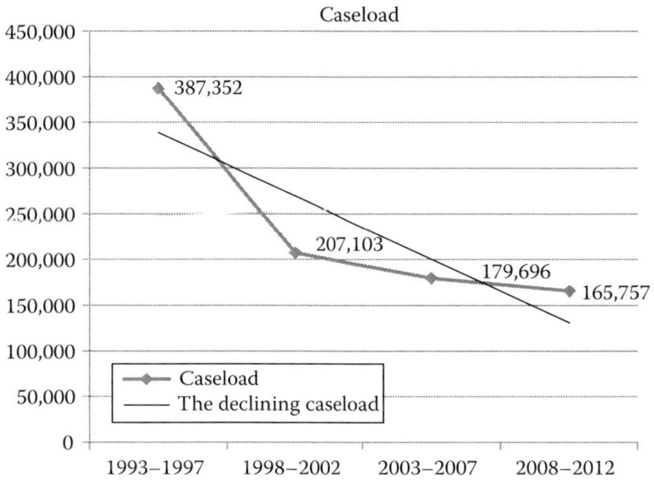

FIGURE 12.1 General trend of the caseload concerning corruption from 1993 to 2012.

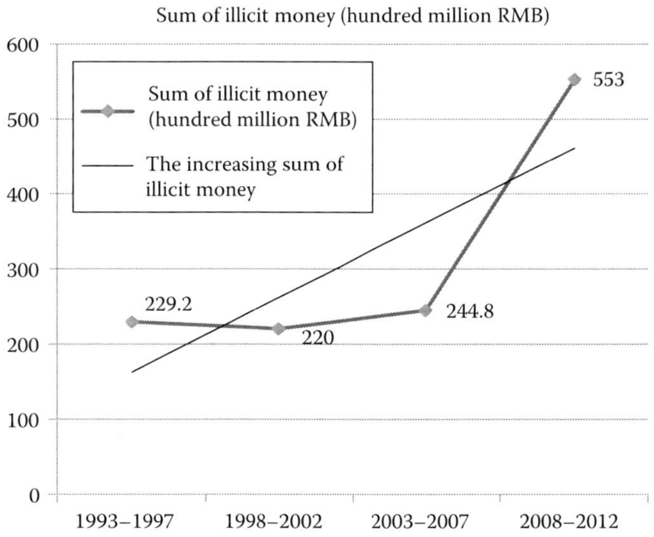

FIGURE 12.2 General trend of the sum of illicit money that was generated through corruption from 1993 to 2012.

* Both Tables 12.1 and 12.2 and the figures that follow were developed by the author of this article.

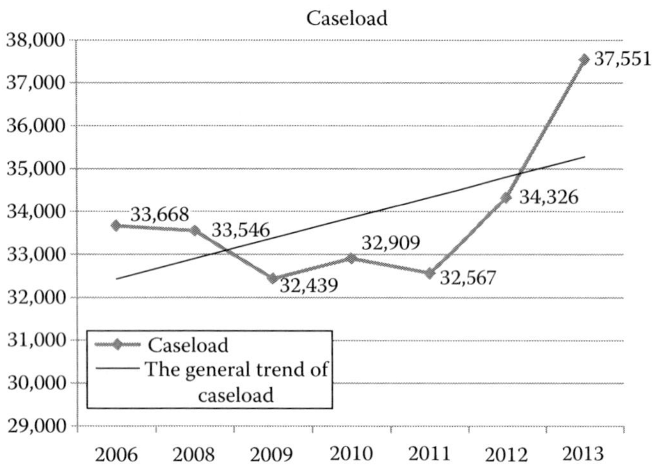

FIGURE 12.3 General trend of the caseload concerning corruption from 2006 to 2013. (No data for 2007 could be found.)

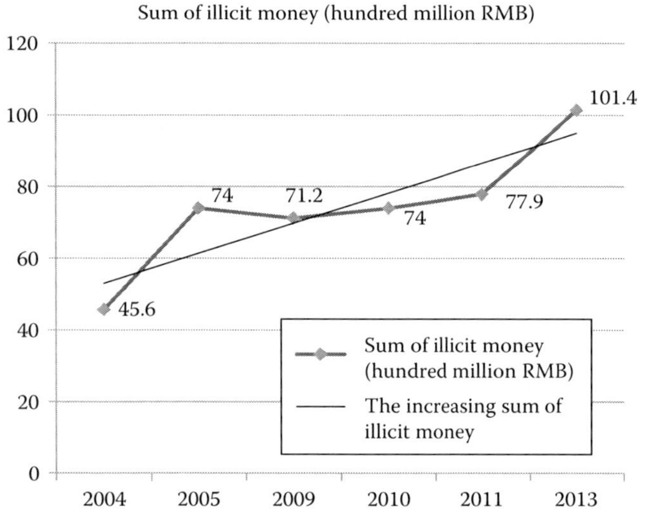

FIGURE 12.4 General trend of the sum of illicit money that was generated through corruption from 2004 to 2013. (There were no available data for the years 2006, 2007, 2008, and 2012.)

the years 1993–1997, which reached 387,352 corruption cases. Compared with the maximum years of corruption, the minimum years emerged in the period of 2008–2012. There were 165,757 cases reported during those years.

Even though the corruption caseload revealed a decreasing trend, the amount of illicit money that was generated by corruption from 1993 to 2002 increased year by year. Compared with the trend of caseloads during this period, the latter was a totally converse tendency. According to Figure 12.2, the bottom was 229.2 (hundred million RMB) during the period of 1993–1997. The amount increases year by year and reached the maximum of 553 (hundred million RMB) in the years of 2008–2012.

Figure 12.3 shows the increasing trend of corruption caseload between 2006 and 2013.The data for 2007 are not available, but it appears to have little effect in the analysis of the general trend of corruption caseloads during these years. The minimum number of corruption cases was 32,439 in 2009, and the number rose to 37,551 during the peak year 2013. The reason why the maximum number appeared in 2013 is that there is a close correlation between the strengthened measures against corruption that were taken in 2013, after the new Chinese government took office, and the number of corruption cases that were discovered and prosecuted as a result of the strengthening of the laws and law enforcement.

Figure 12.4 depicts the sum of illicit money that was caused by corruption from 2004 to 2013. However, in these years, the data are only available for 2004, 2005, 2009, 2010, 2011, and 2013. These data can be found in the official website of the Supreme People's Procuratorate of People's Republic of China. In viewing Figure 12.4, it is obvious that the lowest sum of money was 45.6 (hundred million RMB), which appeared in 2004. In contrast, the maximum sum emerged in 2013, the amount being 101.4 (hundred million RMB).

In order to gain insight on the relationship between corruption and the black economy in China, the author further examined the annual working report of the People's Procuratorate at the provincial level in 2013. Based on these annual working reports, Table 12.3 was constructed. It shows the caseload, number of involved persons, and sum of illicit money (hundred million RMB) in different provinces of China.

Based on the information provided in Table 12.3 and Figure 12.5, the reader can gain an intuitive understanding about the caseload and number of involved persons concerning corruption in 23 provinces of China. As shown in Figure 12.5, the maximum of both the caseload and number of involved persons appeared in the eastern and central region of China. In accordance with the geographic division, Beijing, Shanghai, Tianjin, Zhejiang, Hebei, Jiangsu, Fujian, Shandong, and Guangdong are located in the eastern region and Shānxi, Inner Mongolia, Jilin, Anhui, Hubei, and Hunan lie in the central region. Accordingly, Chongqing, Shǎnxi, Guangxi, Guizhou, Yunnan, Sichuan, Tibet, and Gansu belong to the western region.

Figure 12.6, also constructed on the basis of Table 12.3, reveals the sum of illicit money concerning corruption in Tianjin, Zhejiang, Hebei, Guangdong, Shānxi, Inner Mongolia, Shǎnxi, Guizhou, Yunnan,

Table 12.3 General Situation of Corruption in Different Provinces in 2013a

	Caseload	Number of Involved Persons	Sum of Illicit Money (Hundred Million RMB)
Beijing	299	357	No available data
Shanghai	325	405	—
Tianjin	272	397	4.7
Chongqing	634	771	—
Zhejiang	1046	1341	3.47
Hebei	1351	1932	3.23
Shănxi	491	1421	1.2
Shānxi	1248	1538	1.6
Inner Mongolia	857	1375	9.24
Guangxi	1002	1399	—
Jilin	1693	2438	—
Jiangsu	1393	1646	—
Anhui	1278	1575	—
Fujian	895	1197	—
Hubei	—	1826	—
Hunan	—	1235	—
Shandong	2105	3260	—
Guangdong	—	2347	6.07
Guizhou	922	1158	1.99
Yunnan	1236	1496	4.51
Sichuan	1443	1933	3.5
Tibet		39	0.14
Gansu	603	999	1.44

There were no available data for Henan, Jiangxi, Ningxia, Xinjiang, Heilongjiang, Liaoning, Hainan, and Jiangxi.

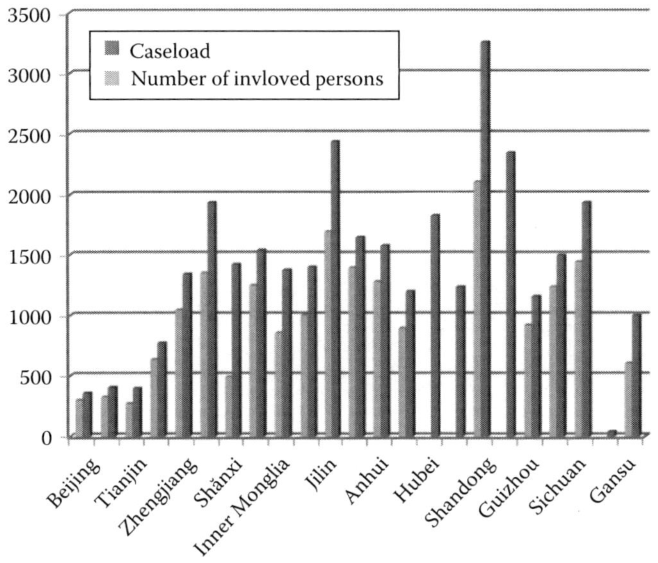

FIGURE 12.5 Caseload and number of involved persons of corruption at the provincial level in 2013. (The data for 23 provinces are shown.)

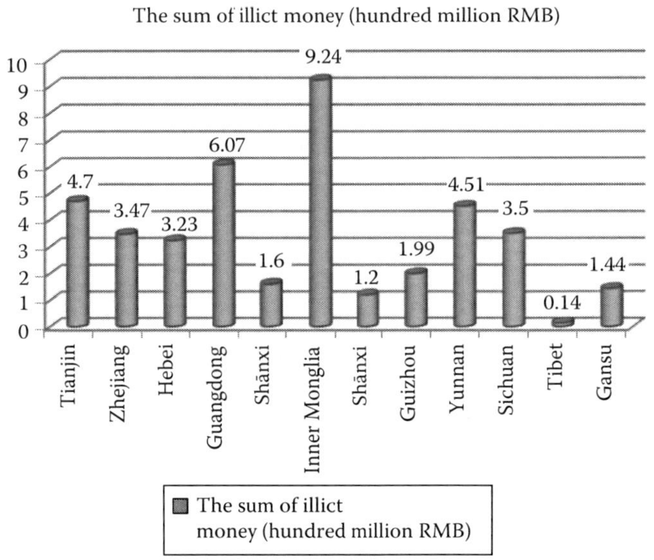

FIGURE 12.6 Sum of illicit money concerning corruption in different provinces in 2013.

Sichuan, Tibet, and Gansu in 2013. Inner Mongolia had a maximum of 9.24 (hundred million RMB) and the lowest number appeared in Tibet, which is the province with the lowest economic development level.

This graph shows three regions of China according to their geographical location, namely, the eastern region of China, the central region of China, and the western region of China. The eastern region includes Tianjin, Zhejiang, Hebei, and Guangdong; the central region includes Shānxi and Inner Mongolia; the western region includes Shănxi, Guizhou, Yunnan, Sichuan, Tibet, and Gansu. Figure 12.7 in the succeeding text was constructed on the basis of the information provided in Figure 12.6.

Based on Figures 12.6 and 12.7, where Figure 12.8 is made out, it reveals the different percentage of illicit money concerning corruption in the eastern region, central region, and western region of China. According to Figure 12.6, the total sum of illicit money was 41.09 (hundred million RMB), which includes 17.47 (hundred million RMB) in the western region, 10.84 (hundred million RMB) in the central region, and 12.78 (hundred million RMB) in the eastern region. Since the author was only able to examine the annual working report of the People's

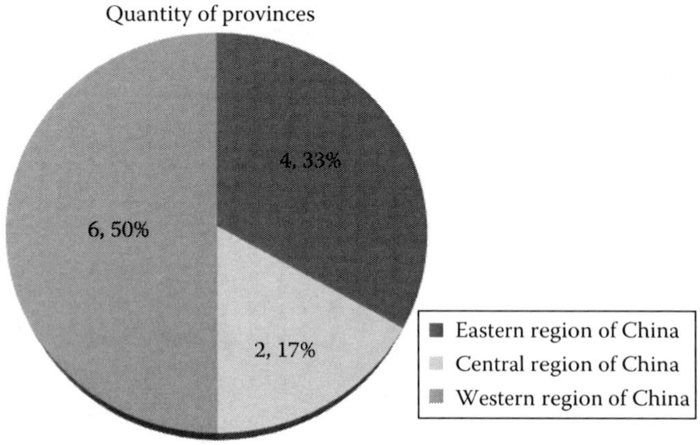

FIGURE 12.7 Quantity of provinces in different geographical locations as depicted in Figure 12.6.

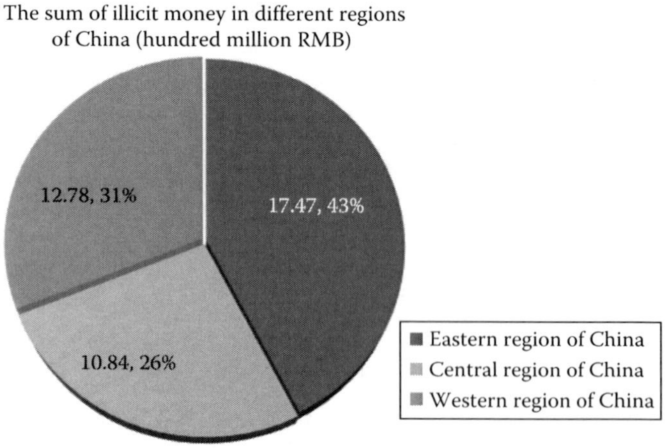

FIGURE 12.8 Sum of illicit money in different regions of China.

Procuratorate at the provincial level for the year 2013, only the data concerning the sum of illicit money of the aforementioned 12 provinces (Tianjin, Zhejiang, Hebei, Guangdong, Shānxi, Inner Mongolia, Shǎnxi, Guizhou, Yunnan, Sichuan, Tibet, and Gansu) are available. As it has been revealed in Figure 12.7, only four provinces are located in the eastern region, two provinces lie in central region, and six provinces are in the western region. It should be noted that the eastern region is the region with the highest economic development level in China, followed by the central region, with the western region located at the bottom. Looking at three figures in Figure 12.8, the sum of illicit money of four provinces in the eastern region accounts for 43% of the total. The two provinces of the central region account for 26% of the total, and the sum of illicit money of the six provinces in the western region accounts for 31% of the total. So it can be concluded that the black economy concerning corruption in China has a close correlation with the local economic development level; in other words, the higher the economic development level of the region, the more likely the serious and rampant effects of the black economy will be felt.

Origins of the Shadow Economy Related to Corruption

The second part of this chapter focuses on the processing of the data of corruption in China. According to these graphs, the conclusion can be made that the caseload and the sum of illicit money increased year by year, and both of them are most active in the areas with a well-developed economy. It is also evident that the ties to the shadow economy and corruption are the most pronounced in the most developed regions. In other words, one can make an assumption that the informal economy is the origin of much corruption. The basis for this assumption can be researched by means of an examination of the provincial and ministerial officers involved in corruption from December of 2012 to December of 2013. There were 18 former significant officers who had been investigated for corruption and bribery during that period of time. These officers are Li Chuncheng, Yi Junqing, Liu Tienan, Guo Yongxiang, Ni Fake, Wang Suyi, Jiang Jiemin, Li Daqiu, Liao Shaohua, Ji Jianye, GuoYouming, Chen Bohuai, Tong Mingqian, Chen Anzhong, Li Dongsheng, Xu Jie, Li Congxi, and Fu Xiaoguang.* Of course, if the past years are included, the officers who were involved in corruption or bribery would not be limited to the 18 officers mentioned earlier. These 18 significant officers are just the cases with serious criminal influences in China. After the examination of corruption and bribery concerning these 18 officers, the truth is revealed that all of these significant officer cases were closely correlated with the officers having the power of seeking rent.

Seeking rent is a term of economics; it refers to the activities that manufacturers are engaged in to get monopoly profits. These activities are unproductive and profit oriented, and they are the performance of the market economy losing self-adjustment.†

* Online news, received on May 25, 2014, from http://www.jcrb.com/xztpd/2013zt/201312/ffnzch1/index.html.

† Online news, received on May 25, 2014, from http://baike.baidu.com/view/477.htm?fr=aladdin.

Furthermore, seeking rent is also used in politics. It means that the public officers use the public's power to seek their own economic profits without contributing to productive activities. As a matter of fact, the power of seeking rent uses the same type of power as the capital to participate in the commodity exchange and market competition and to seek all sorts of material benefits (Xiaoli, n.d.). So the power, which is held by the public officers, brings all sorts of benefits, and thus it becomes the motivation for engaging in corruption. In the following section, some major origins of corruption are discussed.

Commercial Bribery

Commercial bribery refers to situations in which the business dealers aim to eliminate fair market competition and its competitors. In order to win trading opportunities, they give money or other benefits to the trading counterparts or other persons who can influence the trade.* Commercial bribery can be carried out by the following ways:

- Paying or accepting cash bribes
- Paying or accepting all sorts of costs, such as sponsorships, remuneration, red paper containing money as a gift, and other precious gifts
- Paying or accepting valuable material objects, such as upmarket household items, luxuries, collections, real estate and cars, and other material goods
- Paying or accepting marketable security, such as debenture certificate and stocks
- Paying or accepting kickbacks
- Paying or accepting brokerage expenses without entering the ledgers
- Other paying or accepting, such as abating a debt or providing a guaranty and free charge of entertainment or tourism

* Online news, retrieved on June 1, 2014 from http://baike.baidu.com/view/60211.htm?fr=aladdin.

Power of Seeking Rent during the Process of Administrative License and Approval

Since China is an economically transition country, there are a large number of administrative licenses and approvals that are involved in trade and commerce that must be obtained in the administrative system before the owners and corporation leaders can pursue their trades. When trying to obtain these permits, there are obstacles for the citizens and other legal entities who want to get the administrative licenses and approvals, and these obstacles provide opportunities for the public official who grants the licenses and approvals to use his or her power for seeking rent (Xiaoli, n.d.).

Becoming Shareholders of Corporations or Other Commercial Entities

If the public officers accepted shareholdings that were provided by the corruptors and as the counterpayment for the favors granted by the public officers, these public officers violated their duties by providing illegal benefits and also acted criminally by accepting the bribes from the corruptors (Supreme People's Court and the Supreme People's Procuratorate of China).

The Financial Industry and Monopoly State-Owned Enterprises

Among the corruption cases discussed earlier, the financial industry and monopoly state-owned enterprises are the hardest hit by corruption, especially in the area of those persons involved, who ran off to other countries with the illegal money. The staff of the financial industry and monopoly state-owned enterprises accounted for 87.5% of all of the corruptors who ran off to other countries.†

† Online news, retrieved on June 1, 2014, from http://finance.sina.com.cn/china/20120605/011112220954.shtml.

Transportation, the Administration of Land, and Building Industry

It is well known that the transportation, administration of land, and building industry are booming in China. However, all industries need land, and the fact is that the government is the owner of the land. Land in China is state owned. Consequently, transportation, administration of land, and the building industry became another hard hit area of corruption.*

Tax Revenue Collection, Trading, and Other Investing Departments

In the Chinese Naked Officials* Report, it was reported that the corruptors who ran off and went abroad were involved in the departments of tax revenue collection, trading, telecommunication, tobacco industry, oil industry, tourism, and other investing departments.†

* *Naked officials* means that the Chinese official's spouse and children settle abroad or obtain foreign nationality without the sake of working, or they have obtained the right to permanent residency abroad.

† See Chinese Naked Officials Report, online news, retrieved on June 1, 2014, from http://www.360doc.com/content/13/1015/00/2457585_321507892.shtml.

Countermeasures to Contain the Shadow Economy Related to Corruption

The shadow economy related to corruption in China has brought great harm to the Chinese society. First, it erodes the trust of citizens in the government and the other national organizations. Second, in the economic life, it jeopardizes the fair competition between different economic entities. Finally, in order to change the nature of illicit money to clean money, it causes money laundering. Even though it has been recognized that corruption is a chronic problem in China and various measures have been taken to address the problem, there is still a need to take further countermeasures to cut off the correlation between the shadow economy and corruption.

Upgrading the Salaries of Public Officers

Compared with the western countries, the salaries of public officers in China are relatively lower. According to a report in October of 2013, there are four levels of public officers' salaries, categorized by the economic development level of the region where the officers are employed. The highest level is more than 3000 RMB per month in some well-developed cities and areas, such as Beijing, Shanghai, Guangdong, and Zhejiang. Next is 1800 RMB per month, and the next lower level is 1200 RMB per month. Finally, the lowest level is 1000 RMB every month in the underdevelopment areas.‡ It is obvious that the lower salaries of public officers in China are an incentive factor toward corruption. Also, the public officer's workload in China is much heavier than in other countries. As one of the countermeasures to corruption, upgrading the salaries of public officers to satisfy their basic material requirements is needed. Other recommendations include

- Adjusting the penalty of corruption in the Criminal Code.
- Corruption is an economic crime. Even though the majority of provisions concerning corruption in the Chinese Criminal Code are fixed with pecuniary penalties, some are not fixed, and it is still a question why some provisions are fixed with the death penalty. Since corruption is a crime of lusting for benefits, all of the provisions concerning the punishment should be set with pecuniary penalties. In order to make the penalty for corruption more reasonable than before, it is necessary to adjust the penalty for corruption in the Criminal Code.
- Establishing and improving the prevention mechanism against corruption.
- There are no particular regulations or laws that set the family property declaration system and the financial real-name registration system concerning the public officer and his or her family's property. This is a loophole in regard to combating and preventing corruption. It is urgent and necessary to establish and improve both of these two systems to prevent increasingly serious corruption.
- Strengthening the surveillance mechanism. Every power needs to be circumscribed, or it may be followed by corruption. Strengthening the surveillance mechanisms can control serious corruption to some extent.
- Strengthening the role and functions of the People's Procuratorate.
- In China, the People's Procuratorate is the agency that takes charge of investigating and prosecuting corruption, but in practice, there are a great number of cases concerning corruption that are investigated by the Commission for Discipline Inspection. This means that the functions of the People's Procuratorate were executed by the latter. This practice violates laws concerning corruption. In fact, the Commission for Discipline Inspection's functions should be executed according to the surveillance mechanism.

‡ Online news, retrieved on June 6, 2014, from http://www.chgwy.cn/24337.htm.

- Strengthening the data statistics concerning corruption and the shadow economy. There is a scarcity of data statistics concerning corruption and the shadow economy in Chinese official reports. Even though some can be found, significant information and points are often lost. In order to provide convenience for further research on the problems of corruption and the shadow economy, the amount and quality of data statistics need to be strengthened and reported to the public.
- Establishing and strengthening international cooperation. Corruption beyond the national border is becoming an international problem. In view of the fact that many Chinese officers ran off to other countries with a great amount of illicit money, it is necessary to establishing and strengthening multiple or bilateral agreements with other countries concerning corruption. An agreement for investigating corruption and criminal cooperation is needed that requires banks and other financial agencies of each party state to take the responsibility of providing bank and other financial information on their clients to their counterparts who needs this kind of information for the sake of investigating corruption. This would be an effective countermeasure against international corruption. It would also provide help for researching the relationship between corruption and the shadow economy in China or other countries.

Conclusion

Based on the analysis of aforementioned data, it is obvious that the amount of illicit money and gray income related to corruption in China increased year by year from 1993 to 2003, especially in the economically well-developed areas. Corruption and the shadow economy are much more active in Northwest China, where the economic development level is relatively higher, than in Central China and Eastern China. The power of seeking rent is the link that ties corruption and the shadow economy together. This power is held by national public officers and civil servants and becomes a productive factor when they take part in the process of commodity exchange and market competition for land, capital, labor, or other productive factors. But unlike other productive factors, this public power produces nothing. Thus, it is not fair for it to participate in the economic life of the country. The power of seeking rent can be seen as the original incentive for corruption and the shadow economy in China. There is a long way to go for the Chinese government to fight with and control corruption and the corruption-related shadow economy, which is brought to us by the power of seeking rent.

References

Antinori, A. (2012). Organized crime, the mafia, white collar crime, and corruption. In M. Edelbacher, P. Kratcoski, and M. Thiel (eds.), *Financial Crimes: A Threat to Global Security*. Boca Raton, FL: CRC Press, pp. 154–155.

The Opinions of how to apply laws during the process of dealing with corruptions of The Supreme People's Court and the Supreme People's Procuratorate of China on 08.07.2007.

Weiting, H. (1996). *Shadow Economy in China*. China Business Press, 1996, cited in L. Guofeng and W. Yong, Prognosis of shadow economy in China based on EMIMIC model, Modern Finance and Economics, China, Issue No. 9 of 2011.

UN Convention against Corruption. Online resources, from http://www.unodc.org/unodc/en/treaties/CAC/index.html#UNCACfulltext. (Retrieved on May 21, 2014.)

Xiaoli, D. (2011). Grey incomes coming from power of seeking-rent, in *Knowledge Economy* (7) Chongqing; China.

Online Resources

Online news, retrieved on May 6, 2014 from http://www.spp.gov.cn/tt/201403/t20140318_69216.shtml.

Online news, retrieved on May 6, 2014 from http://www.spp.gov.cn/gzbg/201303/t20130316_57131.shtml.

Online news, retrieved on May 6, 2014 from http://www.spp.gov.cn/gzbg/201208/t20120820_2499.shtml.

Online news, retrieved on May 6, 2014 from http://www.spp.gov.cn/gzbg/201208/t20120820_2498.shtml.

Online news, retrieved on May 6, 2014 from http://www.spp.gov.cn/gzbg/201208/t20120820_2497.shtml.

Online news, retrieved on May 6, 2014 from http://www.spp.gov.cn/gzbg/201208/t20120820_2496.shtml.

Online news, retrieved on May 6, 2014 from http://www.spp.gov.cn/gzbg/201208/t20120820_2495.shtml.

Online news, retrieved on May 6, 2014 from http://www.spp.gov.cn/gzbg/201208/t20120820_2494.shtml.

Online news, retrieved on May 6, 2014 from http://www.spp.gov.cn/gzbg/201208/t20120820_2493.shtml.

Online news, retrieved on May 6, 2014 from http://www.spp.gov.cn/gzbg/201208/t20120820_2492.shtml.

Online news, retrieved on May 6, 2014 from http://www.spp.gov.cn/gzbg/200602/t20060222_16375.shtml.

Online news, retrieved on May 6, 2014 from http://www.spp.gov.cn/gzbg/200602/t20060222_16373.shtml.

Online news, retrieved on May 6, 2014 from http://www.spp.gov.cn/gzbg/200602/t20060222_16386.shtml.

Online news, retrieved on May 9, 2014 from http://www.zjjcy.gov.cn/jwgk/gzbg/201401/t20140126_1313864.htm.
Online news, retrieved on May 9, 2014 from http://www.bjjc.gov.cn/bjoweb/gzbg/57374.jhtml.
Online news, retrieved on May 9, 2014 from http://www.hejcy.gov.cn/newsInfo/Default.aspx?NewsInfo_ID=2188&type=.
Online news, retrieved on May 9, 2014 from http://www.tj.jcy.gov.cn/jwgk/gzbg/201403/t20140328_1359832.shtml.
Online news, retrieved on May 9, 2014 from http://www.cqjcy.gov.cn/ygjw/infos/InfoDisplay.asp?InfoID=57.
Online news, retrieved on May 9, 2014 from http://www.sn.jcy.gov.cn/0/1/9/11/10863.htm.
Online news, retrieved on May 9, 2014 from http://www.sx.jcy.gov.cn/gzbg/201101/t20110125_492654.shtml.
Online news, retrieved on May 9, 2014 from http://www.nm.jcy.gov.cn/xcms/newsshow.do?category=2&info=6816.
Online news, retrieved on May 9, 2014 from http://www.xjpeace.cn/html/zqgj/20131127/20131127182231.html.
Online news, retrieved on May 9, 2014 from http://www.gx.jcy.gov.cn/ygjw/jcgzbg/201402/t20140225_1331263.shtml.
Online news, retrieved on May 9, 2014 from http://www.jcrb.com/xztpd/2014zt/201401/2104difanglianghui/jianchagongzuo-baogao/201402/t20140210_1318442.html.
Online news, retrieved on May 9, 2014 from http://www.js.jcy.gov.cn/jianwangfayanren/201401/t1381848_1.shtml.
Online news, retrieved on May 9, 2014 from http://www.ah.jcy.gov.cn/jwgk/gzbg/201402/t20140218_1324525.shtml.
Online news, retrieved on May 9, 2014 from http://www.fj.jcy.gov.cn/Article.aspx?NewsID=78e88413-c70b-42de-93d6-d32c631b4c88.
Online news, retrieved on May 9, 2014 from http://www.hbjc.gov.cn/gzbg/201401/t20140129_1315653.html.
Online news, retrieved on May 9, 2014 from http://www.hn.jcy.gov.cn/xwfb/qwfb/gg/2014/content_41879.html.
Online news, retrieved on May 9, 2014 from http://www.sdjcy.gov.cn/html/2014/mtbd_0120/10336.html.
Online news, retrieved on May 9, 2014 from http://www.gd.jcy.gov.cn/ygjw1/gzbg1/201402/t20140219_1326156.html.
Online news, retrieved on May 9, 2014 from http://www.gz.jcy.gov.cn/jwgk/gzbg/201402/t20140225_1331410.shtml.
Online news, retrieved on May 9, 2014 from http://www.ynjcy.gov.cn/content.aspx?ArticleID=2953.
Online news, retrieved on May 9, 2014 from http://www.sc.jcy.gov.cn/jwgk/gzbg/201402/t20140208_1317808.shtml.
Online news, retrieved on May 9, 2014 from http://www.jcrb.com/xztpd/2014zt/201401/2104difanglianghui/jianchagongzuo-baogao/201402/t20140208_1317895.html.
Online news, retrieved on May 9, 2014 from http://www.jcrb.com/xztpd/2014zt/201401/2104difanglianghui/jianchagongzuo-baogao/201402/t20140210_1318676.html.
Online news, retrieved on May 9, 2014 from http://www.jcrb.com/xztpd/2014zt/201401/2104difanglianghui/jianchagongzuo-baogao/201402/t20140210_1318662.html.
Online news, retrieved on May 9, 2014 from http://www.jcrb.com/xztpd/2014zt/201401/2104difanglianghui/jianchagongzuo-baogao/201402/t20140210_1318740.html.
Online news, retrieved on May 16, 2014 from http://www.guancha.cn/economy/2014_01_20_200873_s.shtml.
Online news, received on May25, 2014 from http://www.jcrb.com/xztpd/2013zt/201312/ffnzch1/index.html.
Online news, received on May 25, 2014 from http://baike.baidu.com/view/477.htm?fr=aladdin.
Online news, retrieved on June 1, 2014 from http://baike.baidu.com/view/60211.htm?fr=aladdin.
Online news, retrieved on June 1, 2014 from http://finance.sina.com.cn/china/20120605/011112220954.shtml.
Chinese Naked Officials Report, Online news, retrieved on June 1, 2014 from http://www.360doc.com/content/13/1015/00/2457585_321507892.shtml.
Online news, retrieved on June 6, 2014 from http://www.chgwy.cn/24337.htm.

13. A Change in Activities of Japanese Organized Criminal Gangs

From Conventional Illegal Activities to Erosion to a Legal Economy

Minoru Yokoyama

Origin of Japanese Indigenous Organized Criminal Gangs

In Japan, there are indigenous organized criminal gangs known as *Yakuza* in foreign countries. Originally, these gangs obtained power by the use of violence or by menacing the people through use of the underground informal economy by establishing intimate corrupt relations with the influential people in business and the government. In this chapter, the development of these criminal gangs will be analyzed, from their early economic activities in the underground economy to their recent infiltration into the legal economy.

Members of Japanese indigenous organized criminal gangs call themselves *yakuza*. The meaning of the word is a "hooligan" or a "worthless scamp" (Yokoyama, 1999, p. 135). Previously, this term was accepted by the people and popularized through the media in popular movies and songs, which characterized the gang members as dropouts from the established society. However, around 1960, the police began to advocate that they should be called *Boryokudan*, a term that literally means a violent group. By using this term, the police intended to warn the ordinary people, who are inclined to sympathize or romanticize with hooligans or worthless scamps, that such individuals were harmful and violent and connected with organized criminal gangs.

Boryokudan are categorized into three groups by their origin. The groups are Bakuto (gamblers), Tekiya (peddlers or stallkeepers), and Gurentai (street hoodlums). Toward the end of the Edo era (1603–1867), Bakuto and Tekiya were formed by outlaws, who dropped out of the feudal caste system under the Tokugawa shogunate.* At that time, Japan witnessed many desperately poor farmers suffering a famine. The desperate people indulged themselves in gambling by the use of Hanafuda, a kind of a game card. Those who could not pay their taxes left their native villages and loitered around a big city such as Edo (the current Tokyo). Some of them became Bakuto bosses, that is, professional bookmakers in gambling. Under the patriarchy controlled by the bosses, Bakuto groups were formed as quasi-families, in which many dropouts from the regular society were supported.

During the Edo era, peddlers traveled to sell commodities at fairs and festivals, or in shrines and temples. The strong-arm protectors for these peddlers who also promoted shows at fairs and festivals were called *Tekiya bosses*. Although the bosses demanded "rent" from Tekiya members, that is, peddlers and stallkeepers, under the patriarchy controlled by the bosses, they were unified by their common worship of Jin-no.†

At the end of the Edo era, many Bakuto and Tekiya bosses were regarded as heroes living in the way of Ninkyo-do, that is, a kind of chivalrous way to beat the strong and to help the weak. The core ethnics of Ninkyo-do were composed of such conventional virtues under Confucianism as Giri (obligation and duty) and Ninjo (empathy and humanness). Especially, the emphasis on Giri made the henchmen feel obligated to have an absolute loyalty to their bosses and their seniors.

Although Tekiya and Bakuto were proud of Ninkyo-do, in reality they lived mainly by depriving ordinary people of money. Bakuto did so by gambling, while Tekiya victimized people by selling commodities of a bad quality, fraudulently, on the streets or at fairs and festivals. Bakuto and Tekiya were parasitic members of the underground informal economy during the feudal era. They shared a subculture that was based on short-term hedonism and contempt for working diligently.

After the Meiji Restoration of 1868, Japan's legal system was modernized, following the examples of western countries. Gambling was now defined as a criminal offense under the Penal Code. The police, however, did not always strictly regulate gambling committed by Bakuto. As Bakuto often solicited idle rich men, they continued to pass themselves off with an image of knights living modestly at the bottom society who did not annoy the diligently working ordinary people.

Even after the Meiji Restoration, unorganized peddlers, stallkeepers, and entertainers continued traveling to join festivals and fairs at various places. With their help, Tekiya bosses had a wide network in the underground.‡ The deviant behaviors committed by Tekiya were more invisible than those by Bakuto.

Economic and political factors contributed both to the survival and to the development of Bakuto and Tekiya during the period from 1868 to 1945. Japan had become industrialized by the middle of the nineteenth century. Newly founded modern companies, especially those engaged in mining, manufacturing, construction, and transportation, needed to employ many laborers at cheap wages.

Bakuto and Tekiya tied up with capitalists and provided the companies with cheap labor forces, which they controlled by the use of violence or threats of its use. In addition, they exploited many laborers as bookmakers for small bets. Around the beginning of the twentieth century, organized labor unions emerged to oppose the exploitation by capitalists. Capitalists often employed Bakuto and Tekiya as strikebreakers.

Under the authoritarian regime for the Showa Emperor, nationalism was prevalent. Bakuto and Tekiya now became more closely affiliated with the established conservative groups. In 1919, they founded a political right-wing association in the Kanto area. In the following year, Bakuto and Tekiya living in the Kansai area organized a similar association in Osaka, and many of its founding members paraded under the protection of police officers. Since Bakuto and Tekiya had been identified as right-wing groups since 1920, they maintained good relations with conservative leaders in the ruling class such as politicians, capitalists, and the military, who drove people into World War II under the name of the Showa Emperor. During this period, we witnessed the advancement of the corrupt

* The top caste was warriors, followed by farmers, craftsmen, and merchants. As warriors depended on the annual rice tax imposed on farmers, the farmers' status was a second high ranking. However, merchants with the last ranking grasped the strong economic power with the development of a monetary economy toward the end of the Edo era. Besides, there were the outcastes, who were compelled to participate in such jobs as butchery and disposition of a dead body. Although Tekiya and Bakuto were outlaws, they were not regarded as the outcaste.

† Jin-no was a Chinese legendary god, who taught people how to farm and how to produce drugs. Jin-no was believed to relieve the diseased by drugs.

‡ During the Edo era, many Tekiya bosses were appointed as secret police officers with the bottom ranking, as they could use the information in the underground to investigate a suspect.

relationship between the police and rightists, including Bakuto and Tekiya.

After the end of World War II in 1945, the authoritarian regime under the Showa Emperor collapsed. Bakuto and Tekiya could not survive by being parasitic with the conservative groups. They had to make the livelihoods by their own ability. During the ensuing chaos, many of Bakuto and Tekiya fell from their positions of power.

Immediately after the war, the Japanese experienced an absolute shortage of the necessities of life. They could hardly survive without buying commodities at black markets, which were opened spontaneously at fields in cities burned by bombing from Boeing B29 Superfortresses. Initially, most black markets were controlled by Koreans and Chinese, who had been taken compulsorily to Japan for slave labor during the war. Immediately after the war, Japan was placed under the control of the General Headquarters (GHQ) of the Allied Powers. GHQ liberated the oppressed Koreans and Chinese. Under the direction of GHQ, the authoritarian system of the national police was disbanded (Yokoyama, 2001, p. 190). In such a chaotic situation, the Koreans and Chinese could participate in many illegal economic activities, especially in black markets, without fear of being rounded up by the police. However, after a short time, they were expelled from the black markets by gangs of young Japanese. The cores of these gangs were ex-soldiers. These groups were called *Gurentai* (street hoodlums).

The surviving Bakuto and Tekiya also extended their territory over new black markets by the use of violence. Therefore, in terms of identifying the groups resorting to violence, it was difficult to distinguish these groups from Gurentai. By 1960, Bakuto, Tekiya, and Gurentai merged together and developed into large-sized gang groups that committed every kind of organized crime by violence or by the threat of violence.* The police categorized all of these groups as Boryokudan, that is, violent groups.

* Many foreigners, especially Koreans expelled from a black market, became members of the Japanese gang group, of whom able-bodied, strong men acquired positions of bosses or licutenants with a high ranking.

The Emergence and Development of Boryokudan

At black markets in Kanagawa Prefecture, several Gurentai groups were rampant. They needed to justify their activities. In 1949, bosses of four Gurentai groups requested Kakuji Inagawa, a professional gambler of 35 years of age without any criminal record, to become their godfather (Masanobu, 1993, p. 70). When he became a godfather of Inagawa-kai, he called himself "Seijyo Inagawa". Although he stepped down from the position of the president in 1985, Inagawa-kai has succeeded in expanding its territory from their headquarters in Tokyo. By the time Kakuji Inagawa stepped down from the position of the president in 1985, Inagawa-kai has succeeded in expanding its territory from their headquarters in Tokyo.

After World War II, the most developed Boryokudan was Yamaguchi-gumi. It was founded with about 50 members in Kobe Harbor around 1915 (Mizoguchi, 1985, p. 47). Their main job was to provide longshoremen workers who provided cheap labor for their customers. In 1941, Kazuo Taoka became the third president of Yamaguchi-gumi. As he had charisma and excellent business ability, under his dictatorship, Yamaguchi-gumi developed from a local Boryokudan in Kobe to the largest Koiki (wide area) Boryokudan. In addition to providing longshoremen, Yamaguchi-gumi earned money from gambling and strong-arm protection. With the backing of funds from rich businessmen, Taoka became well entrenched with many conservative political leaders. His association with corrupted political and business leaders was one of the reasons why Yamaguchi-gumi succeeded in their business.

Another element in the development of Yamaguchi-gumi was their strong manpower organizations. They were equipped with modern high-power weapons, most of which were smuggled into Japan from other countries. Taoka often dispatched his lieutenants and henchmen to west Japan to take over some territory, or to interfere in a struggle between local Boryokudan groups. Thus, several severe fights erupted. The most serious case was the fight in Bettupu, a tourist city, that occurred in 1957.† In addition, the severe struggle between Boryokudan in Hiroshima that lasted from 1950 to 1972 caused much bloodshed. As a result, many local Boryokudan groups in western Japan became subordinates of Yamaguchi-gumi.

† Ishii-gumi, a subordinate Boryokudan group of Yamaguchi-gumi, invaded the territory ruled by Ida-gumi in Bettupu. Both fought to acquire concessions for the 1957 exposition. Over 400 members of both Boruyokudan groups holding pistols and swords walked around for fighting in the center of Bettupu. Their activities were not effectively suppressed by 521 police officers affiliated with the Oita Prefecture Police.

Paralleled with it, Yamaguchi-gumi began to participate in new businesses, such as construction and loans. As a result, the foundation for legal businesses was established. They were the most successful in the entertainment business, in which Yamaguchi-gumi worked as promoters and as providers of security. With the development of their erosion into new businesses, Taoka succeeded in adopting new measures to prevent being investigated and arrested by the police. In 1962, he divided his lieutenants into two groups: managers of the legal enterprises and directors of "fighting soldiers" (Mizoguchi, 1985, p. 74). The former were prohibited from having their own soldiers, although they continued to conduct their business by the use of Yamaguchi-gumi's violence as the last resort and only when considered necessary. After the example of Yamaguchi-gumi, Boryokudan changed from groups respecting the ethics of Ninkyo-do to the modern organized gangs with goals similar to companies in the capitalistic economy, that is, to earn as much money as possible.

One of three Koiki Boryokudan is Sumiyoshi-kai. In the early Meiji era, a local Bakuto group in Tokyo founded Sumiyoshi-ikka. In 1958, a total of 28 groups of Bakuto, Tekiya, and Gurentai in the Kanto Plain, including Tokyo, formed a new organization by the advocacy of the third president of Sumiyoshi-ikka, from which Sumiyoshi-kai was developed. In contrast with Yamaguchi-gumi and Inagawa-kai, Sumiyoshi-kai adopted a conglomerate structure consisting of powerful Boryokudan groups. Sumiyoshi-kai is independent from Yamaguchi-gumi, although in 1996 the fifth president of Yamaguchi-gumi and the third president of Ingawawa-kai held a "meeting" to exchange a cup of Sake, a Japanese liquor, in order to establish the equal quasi-brotherhood relations.*

* Inagawa-kai had to establish the quasi-sibling relation with Yamaguchi-gumi in order to prevent their territory from being invaded by Yamaguchi-gumi.

Close Ties of Boryokudan with Rightist Political Groups during the 1960s

GHQ changed the policy of democratizing Japan soon after the Cold War against socialist countries started. Under the regime of conservative parties, the police gradually resumed strong power. The police were worried about the leftists' activities to overthrow the national government supporting the capitalistic economy. Boryokudan and the successors to Bakuto and Tekiya were still affiliated with rightist political groups. During a political crisis in 1960, Yoshio Kodama, a top fixer in the underground triangle, that is, rightist politicians, Boryokudan and Sokaiya (hoodlum at the general meeting of stockholders) worked for the conservative government. He planned to organize Boryokudan members as guards against leftists who were planning on protesting the visit of the president of the United States. This was done in order to supplement the legitimate police power. In such a political climate, the police often overlooked the illegal activities of Boryokudan, as they performed their mandated activities in favor of the right-wing political organization (Yokoyama, 2004, p. 318).

Beginning of Stricter Regulations of Boryokudan by the Police

Political tension ceased in Japan after 1960. The national government no longer needed the help of Boryokudan. On the contrary, it had to respond to the public opinion against violence, especially such visible violence caused by Boryokudan. In addition, a significant increase of juvenile delinquency was evident around 1964, and violent offenses by juveniles drew the attention of the public as well as the government. (Yokoyama, 2002, p. 329). In the 1960s, many Boryokudan members enjoyed the conspicuous consumption of material things that members in the leisure class possessed. Youngsters admiring their luxurious life became henchmen of Boryokudan (Yokoyama, 2000, p. 3). Thus, Boryokudan could succeed in recruiting many juveniles who belonged to the first baby-boomer generation and were willing to drop out of normal social life to join the Boryokudan. The total number of Boryokudan members reached a peak in 1963.†

People strongly felt the menace of the Boryokudan. In the upsurge of public opinion against violence, especially that by Boryokudan, the National Police Agency

† By the research of Criminal Investigation Bureau of the National Police Agency, the total number of Boryokudan members increased from 92,860 in 1958 to 184,091 in 1963, at which they belonged to 5,216 Boryokudan groups (White Paper on Police, 1989, p. 15). By the way, the police could count the number of the members individually as they had many informants in Boryokudan.

carried out a strategy against Boryokudan by mobilizing all prefectural police forces in 1964. As a result of this strategy, referred to as "the strategy to catch the top" many bosses and lieutenant with high ranking were arrested by the police.*

By 1970, many bosses and gang members who were arrested around 1964 were discharged from prison. As they began to reconstruct their Boryokudan, the police started the second strategy to catch the top in 1970 and the third strategy in 1975. However, the police failed to arrest many bosses and lieutenants, because they had learned how to commit offenses indirectly and in a sophisticated way even though they still were the leaders of their Boryokudan.

Due to the continuous police investigations and arrests after 1964, many small-sized Boryokudan could hardly perform their illegal activities to collect money. These Boryokudan were either dissolved or absorbed by three Koiki (wide-area) Boryokudan organizations, that is, the Yamaguchi-gumi, the Sumiyoshi-kai, and the Inagawa-kai.†

After the severe regulations under "the strategy to catch the top" in 1964, it was difficult for Boryokudan to collect money by gambling, especially conventional gambling by the use of Hanafuda. Many small-sized local Boryokudan depending on gambling were dissolved or absorbed by Koiki Boryokudan. Since 1970, the most important source of revenue of Boryokudan is estimated to be the sale of methamphetamine stimulant drugs.‡ Boryokudan smuggle stimulant drugs from the neighboring countries into Japan.§ Through their underground network, they retail the drugs to make a great deal of profit.¶

In around 1985, "in-fighting" between Boryokudan increased, and gun fighting often occurred.** In the late 1980s, Japan enjoyed a "bubble economy," and Boryokudan actively eroded, infiltrated the established economic fields. At that time, most of corporations had a lot of surplus money, which they used for buying land. To assist in the purchase of a large space of land, they employed a "Jiageya," a kind of the land shark. Jiageya used various methods to persuade land owners to sell their land. In case Jiageya failed to persuade the landowners to sell, they often employed Boryokudan members to destroy the house that was built on the land (Yokoyama, 2000, p. 11). This visible violence provoked indignation against Boryokudan. In such a situation, the movement to expel Boryokudan from the community surged up. For example, the movement against Ichiriki-ikka, a subordinate Boryokudan of Yamaguchi-gumi, drew great attention in 1986 when a lawyer, a leader of the expelled Boryokudan movement, was stabbed by a member of Ichiriki-ikka in 1987. However, the citizenry was not dissuaded, and the people were successful in expelling Boryokudan from their community. In 1991, when the "bubble economy" burst, the *Law to Cope with Boryokudan* was enacted to prevent and suppress injurious "demand" behaviors of Boryokudan members and to expel an office of Boryokudan from the community.

* Police arrested Kakuji Inagawa in 1965 on the charge of bookmaking in gambling by the use of Hanafuda at Hakone, which many bosses of Boryokudan joined. On the other hand, they failed to arrest Kazuo Taoka, a rational godfather of Yamaguchi-gumi, for any offense.

† The rate of members affiliating with these three Koiki Boryokudan among all Boryokudan increased from 21.8% in 1979 to 39.9% in 1988, although the total number of Boryokudan members decreased from 106,754 to 66,552 for the same period (White Paper on Police, 1989, p. 17).

‡ By the research of the police in February 1989, the sale of the stimulant drugs amounted to 34.8% of all annual revenue of Boryokudan (White Paper on Police, 1989, p. 46).

§ Soon after World War II, we witnessed the epidemic of stimulant drugs. By the severe roundup by the police, factories to produce stimulant drugs moved to foreign neighboring countries.

¶ We witness a phenomenon of severe criminalization to eradicate the drug abuse. However, the police cannot regulate illegal drugs, especially stimulant drugs, efficiently, because they can rarely expose the system for smuggling and retailing the drugs controlled by Boryokudan.

** After the death of Kazuo Taoka in 1981, Yamaguchi-gumi was split into two groups through the quarrel about the succession to the position of a godfather. In 1985, the documented fighting reached 293 (White Paper on Police, 1989, p. 2).

Exposure of Corrupt Relations between Boryokudan and Conservative Politicians

Corrupt relation between Boryokudan and conservative leaders in the ruling class, which the police, the public prosecutors, and the mass media rarely exposed, continued even after World War II.†† However, in the United States, a big scandal, the Lockheed scandal, was exposed in 1976. The Lockheed Company gave a lot of money to influential politicians and the executive members of airline companies in such countries as Japan, Italy, and Turkey. On February 5, 1976, the *Asahi Newspaper* reported that Lockheed paid $7,080,500 USD and $3,220,300 USD to the Yoshio Kodama and

†† The Special Investigation Department of three public prosecutor offices is responsible for investigating a big scandal in the political and economic field.

Chapter 13

the Marubeni Trading Company, respectively, in order to sell their aircrafts to all Nippon airlines. After an investigation by the special investigation department of Tokyo Public Prosecutors' Office, a total of 17 suspects, including Yoshio Kodama and Kakuei Tanaka, a former prime minister, were prosecuted.* In this scandal, Yoshio Kodama, an authoritarian fixer in the underground groups including Boryokudan, had corrupt relation with influential conservative politicians and the top executives of major companies. After the death of Kodama, Boryokudan activated their "business" without control of an influential political fixer.

One of three main underground groups was Sokaiya (hoodlums at general meeting of stockholders). They hold a small number of stocks in many companies to get the positions of stockholders. By abusing the privilege as stockholders, they plot to receive or extort money or some interests from companies by every means available, especially by causing trouble at the *Sokai* meeting, that is, the general meeting of stockholders. Every time the scandal caused by Sokaiya was exposed, the regulations against their activities were strengthened. Therefore, Sokaiya decided to give up their conventional activities and became a consultant for Boryokudan.† By the use of highly sophisticated techniques and knowledge of professionals such as Sokaiya, and its technicians and lawyers, Boryokudan was able to conduct the "business" by "inside trading" and by taking over companies with large sums of laundered money, and thus Boryokudan was able to gain a firm foundation in the established economic fields (Yokoyama, 2000, p. 9). One of main purposes of the *Law to Cope with Boryokudan* passed in 1991 was to suppress their intervention into citizens' activities in the established economic fields through the threat or actual use of violence.

* Kakuei Tanaka was charged with receiving a bribe of $4,000,000 USD, which Lockheed offered through the mediation of Marubeni.

† By the estimation of the police, at the end of 1996, those who continued to work as Sokaiya amounted to about 1000, of which 10% were affiliated with Boryokudan (Yokoyama, 2003, p. 74).

Provisions of the 1991 Law to Cope with Boryokudan

In Japan, the freedom of association is guaranteed under Article 29 of the Constitution of 1946. Therefore, even Boryokudan groups can exist, although several groups such as Tosei-kai and Inagawa-kai were once ordered to dissolve under the Ordinance to Regulate Groups of 1949 (White Paper on Police in 1989, p. 10). The Law to Cope with Boryokudan in 1991 has no prescription to order the dissolution of Boryokudan.

The law prescribes the definition of Boryokudan as a group, which is prone to facilitate their members to carry out violent illegal behavior collectively and repeatedly (Paragraph 2 of Article 2). The prefecture Public Safety Commission can designate a Boryokudan as Shitei Boryokudan in cases in which the group is composed of over a certain number of members with a criminal career and has a hierarchy of members under a boss.‡ The law purposes to control 11 injurious "demand" behaviors to ordinary people conducted by members of the Shitei Boryokudan, which were not regulated efficiently under the previous criminal laws.§ These members were prohibited from committing such minor threatening "demand" behavior as extorting money by taking advantage of someone's weakness and demanding a gift injuriously.¶ In case a member of Shitei Boryokudan conducts an injurious "demand" behavior, the Public Safety Commission can issue a conjunction, a stop order, to him. If he is prone to conduct injurious "demand" behavior repeatedly, the commission can issue a recurrence prevention order valid for within 1 year. If the violator neglects these orders, he can be imposed criminal punishment. In addition, the commission can give a Shitei Boryokudan group an order not to use an office in case the group is involved in a struggle with another Boryokudan group.

Under the Law to Cope with Boryokudan, the Public Safety Commission is obligated to give aid to victims of an injurious "demand" behavior. To realize the purposes of the law, the *Center to Promote Movement to Eliminate Boryokudan* was established.

‡ The Shitei Boryokudan is designated in case the Boryokudan aims in substance to permit its members to use its power in order to earn money for its members to make their living, to accumulate their property, and to perform their business.

§ In case a Boryokudan member demanded money softly by showing a badge of his Boryokudan, the police could hardly arrest him for extortion or intimidation.

¶ By several revisions of the law, the prohibited demand activities were expanded.

Exposure of the Tokyo Sagawa Kyubin Scandal in 1992

The Liberal Democratic Party (LDP), composed of many conservative politicians, monopolized the political power in Japan since 1955. The politicians affiliating with LDP needed to have a lot of money for the election campaign. Therefore, they were prone to be involved in a scandal of receiving a bribe, of which the scandal was investigated by the special investigation department of the Public Prosecutors' Office and the police.

In 1992, the mass media reported the Tokyo Sagawa Kyubin Scandal, which occurred in 1987 in which influential rightist politicians of LDP and Boryokudan were involved (Yokoyama, 2007, p. 173). The exposure of the scandal in 1992 resulted in an influential politician of LDP, Shin Kanemaru, resigning from the Diet, after it was discovered that he received 50 million yen illegally as political contributions from Tokyo Sagawa Kyubin.

In 1987, a small right-wing group drove a campaign car around the Diet building every day applauding Noboru Takeshita, a candidate for prime minister affiliated with LDP, using a loud speaker. The purpose of this campaign was to give negative fame to Takeshita and to make people know about his corrupt relations with the underground. Then, by the intervention of a president of Tokyo Sawaga Kyubin, Takeshita met with Susumu Ishii, the second president of Inagawa-kai, and with Shin Kanemaru, an influential supporter of Takeshita, in order to make this group stop the campaign against him. By the pressure from a "godfather" of Inagawa-kai, the group stopped the campaign immediately. Takeshita succeeded in being elected a prime minister in November 1987.

After the exposure of this scandal, LDP lost political power in 1993* (Yokoyama, 2005, p. 36). With this change in the political climate, the police were able to get rid of the corruptive relations with Boryokudan and began to regulate activities by Boryokudan under the Law to Cope with Boryokudan.

* Since 1993, we have had the coalition government composed mainly of LPD.

Immediate Effects of the Law to Cope with Boryokudan

The Law to Cope with Boryokudan was enforced in March 1992. The following year, the Law to Cope with Boryokudan was revised, and the scope of what constituted an injurious "demand" behavior was expanded. Under this revised law, members of Boryokudan are given some aid in case they wish to leave their Boryokudan. Such coercive activities as cutting a little finger off as a token of apology or tattooing a juvenile are prohibited.† In addition, Shitei Boryokudan members are prohibited from coercing a juvenile to join their group. This revision of the law purposed to decrease the manpower of Shitei Boryokudan.

The total number of dissolved Boryokudan groups increased from 80 (1131 members) in 1990 to 131 (1430 members) in 1991 and to 158 (2051 members) in 1992 (White Paper on Police, 1994, p. 148). In March, 1993, the Public Safety Commission designated 18 Boryokudan, including three Koiki Boryokudan as Shitei Boryokudan (White Paper on Police, 1993, p. 35).‡ In 1994, the total number of Shitei

Boryokudan amounted to 24 and the total number of Boryokudan members amounted to about 52,900, of which 82.0% were affiliated to Shitei Boryokudan (White Paper on Police, 1994, p. 161).

After the rigid enforcement of the Law to Cope with Boryokudan, the Public Safety Commission began to issue an order to members of Shitei Boryokudan. In 1993, the commission issued 610 stop orders, of which 54.9% were against violent "demand" behavior to collect money, followed by 43.1% of the interference in member's secession from Boryokudan and for using coercive methods to force people to join Boryokudan (White Paper on Police, 1994, pp. 161–164). In addition, the commission issued 35 recurrence prevention orders.

† It would be difficult for a former member of Boryokudan to rehabilitate himself into the community if he lost his little finger and had a tattoo.

‡ Four Boryokudan designated Shitei Boryokudan on June and July in 1992 sued the public safety commission for the withdrawal of its decision to designate them as Shitei Boryokudan. The courts judged that this designation did not offend the freedom for associations under the Constitution (White Paper on Police, 1996, p. 207). The main reason why the Law to Cope with Boryokudan is constitutional is that it neither prescribes the direct limit to activities of Boryokudan nor the dissolution of Boryokudan.

According to the Law to Cope with Boryokudan, the Public Safety Commission is obligated to redesignate (reclassify) Shitei Boryokudan every 3 years. In 1995, the commission redesignated 15 Boryokudan, including three Koiki Boryokudan, as Shitei Boryokudan (White Paper on Police, 1996, p. 206). Since then, many large-sized Boryokudan, including three Koiki Boryokudan, have been redesignated as Shitei Boryokudan.

Strengthening Regulations against Shitei Boryokudan

In 1997, the Law to Cope with Boryokudan was revised. Under the revised law, the collection of debt in violent words and behavior is added as an injurious "demand" behavior. The Public Safety Commission can issue a recurrence prevention order to prevent violent "demand" behavior connected to the business of Shitei Boryokudan. In addition, those who have a special relation with a member of Shitei Boryokudan are prohibited from conducting an injurious "demand" behavior by using the power of their related Shitei Boryokudan.

In the new millennium, our country has put an emphasis on the establishment of measures against organized crimes. In 2003, the Cabinet Meeting on the Measures against Crimes issued the Action Plan to Realize a Strong Society against Crimes. One of the purposes of this plan is to protect our society and economy from organized crimes. To realize this purpose, the National Police Agency established the Organized Crime Department in the Criminal Investigation Bureau. The department has three divisions. These are devoted to planning and analysis, coping with Boryokudan, and coping with drugs and guns. In addition, there are administrators in charge of international investigation. Under this new system, the police began operations to cope with organized crimes comprehensively.

In 2004, the Law to Cope with Boryokudan was again revised to make a boss of Shitei Boryokudan liable for damages which a member of his Shitei Boryokudan causes. This revision contributed to a decrease in the use of weapons among Boryokudan groups.

In 2008, the Law to Cope with Boryokudan was amended. Under the amended law, violent "demand" behavior against the government is regulated. The obstruction of a victim's claim for damages is prohibited. The Public Safety Commission can issue an order to a member of Shitei Boryokudan not to give money and commodities to another member who finishes serving imprisonment for committing a certain kind of a violent crime. A boss of Shitei Boryokudan is liable for damages caused by his henchmen's behavior related to collection of a fund to show the power of his Shitei Boryokudan. In addition, national and local governments are obliged to take the necessary measures to prevent a member of Shitei Boryokudan and a corporation affiliated with it from participating in a bid. Corporations are obliged to take measures to prevent damages caused by an injurious "demand" behavior. The revised law tries to stop a Boryokudan member from acquiring undue profit through their business. National and local governments must give information, advice, and guidance to corporations, in order to facilitate the latter's voluntary movement to exclude violent activities by a Boryokudan member.

In 2012, the Law to Cope with Boryokudan was revised. One of the purposes for the revision is to prevent citizens from suffering the damages by a struggle between Boryokudan groups. The Public Safety Commission can designate Boryokudan groups as the Federation of Shitei Boryokudan if most of member groups are Shitei Boryokudan. In addition, the Public Safety Commission can designate a Shitei Boryokudan as a "Specific Dangerous Shitei Boryokudan" in cases in which members of the Shitei Boryokudan do violent behavior by the use of a weapon to cause serious damage to a person's life and body and in cases in which they repeatedly conduct the violent behavior. The Public Safety Commission can designate the area where they are prone to repeatedly do violence as the "Area for Lookout." Members of Specific Dangerous Shitei Boryokudan are prohibited from demanding an interview with or telephoning a citizen or loitering around his or her house or office in the Area for Lookout in order to conduct the violent "demand" behavior. In case they perform an injurious "demand" behavior in the Area for Lookout, they can be imposed a fine directly without being issued of a stop order.

Under this revised law, the Public Safety Commission can designate most dangerous Shitei Boryokudan as Specific Struggle Shitei Boryokudan in cases in which this Boryokudan is prone to give serious damage to citizen's life and body by involving them in a struggle. Members of Specific Struggle Shitei Boryokudan are arrested immediately in cases in which they conduct such a behavior in the Area for Lookout as entering a Boryokudan office, opening a new office, chasing a member of the rival Boryokudan, or having over five members of their Boryokudan gather.

Another purpose of the revised law of 2012 is to remove an office of Shitei Boryokudan from the community. An organization designated by the Public Safety Commission as the Center to Promote Movement to Eliminate Boryokudan can sue for the removal of an office of Boryokudan with the support of the community residents. In addition, the criminal punishment imposed for an offense of the Law to Cope with Boryokudan was increased.

At a local level, too, the legal system to cope with Boryokudan has been improved since 2004. For the first time in 2004, Hiroshima Prefecture and Hiroshima City enacted an ordinance prescribing that a member of Shitei Boryokudan and his relatives are not qualified to enter the prefectural or municipal apartment. Under the Ordinance on Life Safety in Toshima Ward, enforced in 2009, a member of Boryokudan is excluded from a transaction of real estate. In the same year, the Saga Prefecture Assembly enacted the Ordinance to Prevent the Establishment of Boryokudan's Office.

In April 2010, the first comprehensive Ordinance to Exclude Boryokudan was enforced in Fukuoka Prefecture. This ordinance has such prescriptions as the prohibition of a Boryokudan member from contacting a citizen by showing power of his Boryokudan, the exclusion of a Boryokudan member from public works, and the protection of a person who may be inflicted injury by Boryokudan. By the end of 2011, all prefectures had a similar comprehensive ordinance to exclude Boryokudan. In addition, the ordinances are revised toward criminalization of Boryokudan activities and regulating the activities of a Boryokudan member more comprehensively and minutely. At present, Boryokudan members are finding it more and more difficult to operate in a community setting.

The situation for Boryokudan has changed drastically since the enforcement of the Law to Cope with Boryokudan in March 1992. This is illustrated by the use of the formal data gathered by the police.

Changes in Boryokudan Groups and Members

At the end of 1991, the total number of Boryokudan members amounted to 91,000 of which 17,200 or 18.9% were semimembers* (White Paper on Police, 1992, p. 73). As the regulation under the Law to Cope with Boryokudan had become more severe, the number of members decreased to 58,600 in 2013 (White Paper on Police, 2014, p. 122). Formal Boryokudan members dropped from 73,800 in 1991 to 25,600 in 2013. On the other hand, the semimembers increased from 17,200 to 33,000 during the same period. The severe regulations under the Law to Cope with Boryokudan forced many formal members of Boryokudan to leave. If they do not find a good stable job, in the formal economy, they earn their livelihood as a semimember. In addition, Boryokudan had diversified its way to collect money. In this way, many new persons began to support the Boryokudan, indirectly. The police referred to these supporters as semimembers.†

Japan has become an older-aged society, as the percent of the total population over 65 years of age amounted to 25% in 2013. The phenomenon of aging also contributes to the decrease in persons affiliating with Boryokudan. At present, Japanese youngsters have grown tired of the overprotection. They do not like to be trained as a Boryokudan member under the conventional apprentice system. In addition, the Boryokudan are prohibited by law from tempting a youngster to join the Boryokudan. Therefore, the Boryokudan has failed to recruit many new members, especially younger persons. Another factor is that the age composition in Boryokudan is also higher than the general population. This is another factor that makes the Boryokudan unattractive to younger persons.

The total number of Shitei Boryokudan designated under the Law to Cope with Boryokudan changed from 24 in April 1994 to 21 in June 2014. Of 21 Shitei Boryokudan, 19 are seen on the list in 1994.‡ Although the "godfather" changed in many of these Shitei Boryokudan, they continue to maintain their organizations in spite of the decrease in members.

The total number of members affiliating with Yamaguchi-gumi decreased from 23,100 in 1994 to

* Boryokudan have a hierarchy, in which a boss has a top position followed by lieutenants and henchmen. A semimember is a person having some relation with Boryokudan who conducts violent illegal behavior by showing power of the related Boryokudan and who supports the maintenance of the Boryokudan in such a way as supplying money and weapons.

† In 2007, NHK broadcasted a special feature entitled on "Yakuza Money." By this TV program, we knew that a secondary subordinate group of Yamaguchi-gumi employed several professional traders in stock transactions by the use of IT (Itakura, 2011, p. 275). Such traders are also regarded as semimembers of Boryokudan.

‡ In 2013, 13 Boryokudan were designated as Shitei Boryokudan eight times since 1992 (White Paper on Police, 2014, p. 123).

11,600 in 2014, while members of other Boryokudan dropped more drastically. Yamaguchi-gumi had expanded their territory as far as to East Japan. At present, Boryokudan, except for a few Boryokudan such as Sumiyoshi-kai and Kodo-kai, keeps the quasi-sibling relation with Yamaguchi-gumi through performing a rite of exchanging a cup of Sake.

Currently, the main target of regulation by the police is activities of Yamaguchi-gumi, especially Kodo-kai, of which the first president became the sixth godfather of Yamaguchi-gumi.* In 2012, the police arrested 23 bosses of the top subordinate group of Yamaguchi-gumi and 5 bosses and 27 lieutenants of the top subordinate group of Kodo-kai† (White Paper on Police, 2013, p. 118). In the severe confrontation, the police got rid of the corrupt relations with Boryokudan completely, although a police officer in charge of coping with Boryokudan was occasionally corrupted by Boryokudan.

* Kodo-kai, of which the headquarters is located in Nagoya City, has a strong hostility to the police. Through strong control inside the organization it keeps secrecy. In case its member is interrogated by a detective, he keeps silence completely. On the other hand, it collects information about police officers in charge of coping with Boryokudan, their relatives and their residence, by which it pressures the police.

† A large-sized Boryokudan composes of some stratum of subordinate groups. The lower groups have obligation to pay the membership fee to their upper Boryokudan. Through this system Koiki Boryokudan collect a gigantic amount of money without fear of being rounded up by the police.

Struggle between Boryokudan

Under the Law to Cope with Boryokudan, the Public Safety Commission can give the Shitei Boryokudan an order not to use an office in case the Boryokudan is involved in a struggle with another Boryokudan. In addition, since 2004, a boss of Shitei Boryokudan has liability for damages which a member of his Shitei Boryokudan causes. Therefore, the Shitei Boryokudan refrains from fighting with another Boryokudan. However, for a few years after 2010, some Boryokudan groups in North Kyushu fought each other severely. In December 2012, Kodo-kai was designated as a Specific Dangerous Shitei Boryokudan.‡ In addition, Dojin-kai and Kyushu Seido-kai were designated as Specific Struggle Shitei Boryokudan.§

To reduce damages from the struggle between Boryokudan, the police endeavor to forfeit weapons, especially guns, from Boryokudan. Thus, the total number of guns confiscated from Boryokudan members amounted to 1767 in 1985 (White Paper on Police, 1992, p. 75) but continued to decrease drastically to 74 in 2013 (White Paper on Police, 2014, p. 133). The police estimate that the Boryokudan had smuggled a large number of guns. However, they generally do not find these guns even in cases when they round up suspects in the office of Boryokudan. The Boryokudan conceal guns in sophisticated ways, which they keep secret. With the more severe regulations, the activities of Boryokudan have become very difficult to detect. Boryokudan tends to become a secret organization in the underground, although the place of their office is known.¶

‡ Kodo-kai is the largest Boryokudan in North Kyushu. It has strong hostility towards the police as a struggling group. Its members caused troubles against citizens such as shooting at a company and a leader of the movement to expel Boryokudan.

§ In 2006, Kyushu Seido-kai split into two groups on the problem of successor of the president of Dojin-kai. Since 2006, Dojin-kai and Kyushu Seido-kai fought each other severely. In 2007, the president of Dojin-kai was shot to death. By the struggle between both Boryokudan, a total of nine persons including one innocent citizen were killed. After the designation as the Specific Struggle Shitei Boryokudan, both Boryokudan stopped the struggle. Then, in June 2014, the Public Safety Commission decided not to designate them as the Specific Struggle Shitei Boryokudan again.

¶ Before 1992, the Boryokudan hung a signboard, on which its name was written. Although the signboard disappeared, we know the place of an office of Boryokudan.

Change in Revenue of Boryokudan

In 1997, the total number of Boryokudan members arrested by the police amounted to 32,109, of which 14,405 or 44.9% were on charges of a conventional offense to collect money (White Paper on Police, 2002, p. 197). Of all arrested members, 7804 were arrested for an offense violating the Stimulant Drug Control Law, followed by 2638 for intimidation, 1728 for gambling, and 2235 for illegal bookmaking in such legal gambling events such as bicycle racing, horse racing, and boat racing. On the other hand, in 2013 the total number of Boryokudan members arrested by the police dropped to 22,861, of which 7,478 or 32.7% were on charges of a conventional offense to collect money (White Paper on Police, 2014, p. 124). Those arrested for gambling and the illegal bookmaking in legal gambling dropped drastically to 294 and 55, respectively.* As those arrested for an offense of the Stimulant Drug Control Law and for intimidation amounted to 7478 and 6045, respectively, the sale of a smuggled stimulant drug† and the arm-strong protection as a bouncer‡ seem to be important revenues for Boryokudan.

Boryokudan seems to divert the measures to collect money by erosion to the legal economic activities. According to the police, the Boryokudan members commit such a sophisticated offense as the intimidation and violent demand to a company and a government and the illegal reception of public benefits (White Paper on Police, 2014, p. 126). Recently, the bank transfer scam is prevalent in which many Boryokudan seem to participate.§ In addition, Boryokudan members commit such economic crimes as offenses violating the Law on Money Lending Business and the Law on Waste Disposal and Public Cleansing.

Previously, the Boryokudan members rarely committed theft and robbery, as they looked at such offenses with contempt. However, we now witness more Boryokudan members committing theft and a robbery, because they became too poor to maintain their livelihood while still paying a membership fee to their Boryokudan. This is becoming a serious social problem as many of these crimes are committed by elderly persons (Yokoyama, 2014).

* Although gambling by the use of Hanafuda and illegal bookmaking in legal gambling wane, gambling such as Pachinko (a pinball game) and PC games are prevalent. Therefore, about 5% of all adults seem to be gambling addicts according to the research by the Ministry of Health, Labor and Welfare, although a casino is not legalized (*Nihon Keizai Newspaper* on August 21, 2014).

† In 2013, the total number of persons arrested for smuggling stimulant drugs amounted to 160, of which 30 and 113 were Boryokudan members and visiting foreigners, respectively (White Paper on Police, 2014, p. 131).

‡ In 2013, the total number of the issues of a stop order and a recurrence prevention order amounted to 1747, of which 168 and 285 were issued for demand of the protection money and for the strong-armed protection, respectively (White Paper on Police, 2014, p. 127).

§ Professional scam groups invented this kind of fraud. First, a swindler calls an elderly person and informs him or her that his or her relative such as a child or a grandchild is involved in a trouble such as a traffic accident. The swindler asks him or her to transfer a lot of money in order to solve this trouble. If he or she transfers money into an account at a bank, a person asked by the swindler withdraws it from the account. It is very hard for the police to catch the swindler, because he or she does not appear to receive the money. The police estimate that many Boryokudan also commit the bank transfer scam.

Severe Regulations of Money Collected Illegally by Boryokudan

The police have strengthened the regulation on money collected illegally by Boryokudan. The important measures are for money laundering. This type of law was first advocated by UN Convention against Illicit Traffic in Narcotic Drugs and Psychotropic Substances in December of 1988, just after the end of the Cold War between the east and the west.

Under the international pressure, the Law Concerning Special Provisions for the Narcotics and Psychotropics Control Law was enacted in 1991, by which the concealment and reception of proceeds earned by the illegal trade in drugs such as narcotics and stimulant drugs was criminalized, in addition to the forfeiture of the proceeds gained from these illegal activities. In 1999, the Law to Punish Organized Crimes and to Control of Crime Proceeds was enacted, under which the laundering of money earned by other illegal activities than the illegal trade in drugs is criminalized.

In 2007, the Law to Prevent Transfer of Criminal Proceeds was enacted, under which all financial organizations, including a bank and a stock company, are obligated to check the identification of their customers, to preserve all record on the trade with customers, and to report about a suspicious trade to the Financial Intelligence Unit.¶ Under these laws, the police have strengthened their regulation against the transfer and the laundering of proceeds earned by Boryokudan.

At present, all financial organizations are prohibited from receiving money from Boryokudan members and financing to them. In case these organizations do not perform their duty, they are severely criticized. With the confrontation of severe regulation by the police and the upsurge of the Movement to Eliminate Boryokudan in the community, conventional crimes by Boryokudan members, especially those committed by the elderly, seemed to wane.

¶ In 1990, the Ministry of Finance requested financial organizations to check the identification of their customers. In 2000, the Financial Intelligence Unit was established. In 2007, FIU was transferred from Financial Services Agency to National Public Safety Commission. After this transfer the police took the initiative in regulation of proceeds earned by illegal activities.

Conclusion

Before the enforcement of the Law to Cope with Boryokudan in 1992, Boryokudan (crime syndicate) enjoyed prosperity, especially the Yamaguchi-gumi, who succeeded in collecting a lot of money by eroding (infiltrating) into the legal economic fields. This organization got rid of its dependence on such conventional crimes as gambling and concentrated more on economic crimes. After 1992, many local Boryokudan were absorbed by three Koiki Boryokudan organizations. These Boryokudan, especially Yamaguchi-gumi, had established a monopoly over the proceeds in the underground. In addition, their activities to collect money were diversified and performed in many sophisticated ways. The police are expected to suppress such complicated invisible activities of Boryokudan although it is very difficult.

Currently, Boryokudan cannot support the livelihood of its elderly member, and this downfall of revenue and the severe regulations of the laws passed to combat organized crime have forced members to leave their Boryokudan. Now, the police are required to treat them under the rehabilitation model. The police established the Council to Cope with Social Rehabilitation together with the Center to Promote Movement to Eliminate Boryokudan and other organizations in order to give guidance and advice to any individual who wants to secede from their Boryokudan (White Paper on Police, 2014, p. 129). Since April 2013, the police and the probation and parole office have shared the information about the parolees who have secedes from their Boryokudan during their imprisonment term. Both begin to support them in such a way as giving guidance, advice, and help to find a job in order to prevent them from rejoining their Boryokudan.

References

Itakura, H. (2011). Measures to cope with Boryokudan from standpoint of news reporter (written in Japanese). *Security Science Review*, 13: 272–281.

Masanobu, T. (1993). *Last Gurentai* (written in Japanese). Tokyo, Japan: Sanichi-shobo.

Mizoguchi, A. (1985). *Document of yamaguchi-gumi—Blood and Fighting* [written in Japanese]. Tokyo: Sanichi-shobo.

National Police Agency (1989). White paper on police in 1989 (written in Japanese). Tokyo: Printing Bureau of the Ministry of Finance.

National Police Agency (1992). White paper on police in 1992 (written in Japanese). Tokyo: Printing Bureau of the Ministry of Finance.

National Police Agency (1993). White paper on police in 1993 (written in Japanese). Tokyo: Printing Bureau of the Ministry of Finance.

National Police Agency (1994). White paper on police in 1994 (written in Japanese). Tokyo: Printing Bureau of the Ministry of Finance.

National Police Agency (1996). White paper on police in 1996 (written in Japanese). Tokyo: Printing Bureau of the Ministry of Finance.

National Police Agency (2002). White paper on police in 2002 (written in Japanese). Tokyo: Printing Bureau of the Ministry of Finance.

National Public Safety Commission and National Police Agency (2013). White paper on police in 2013 (written in Japanese). Tokyo: Nikkei Printing.

National Public Safety Commission and National Police Agency (2014). White paper on police in 2014 (written in Japanese). Tokyo: Gyosei.

Yokoyama, M. (1999). Trends of organized crime by Boryokudan in Japan. In S. Einstein and M. Amir (eds.), *Organized Crime: Uncertainties and Dilemmas*. Chicago, IL: The Office of International Criminal Justice, The University of Illinois at Chicago, pp. 135–154.

Yokoyama, M. (2000). Change in Japanese organized crime and enforcement of the Law to Cope with Boryokudan in 1992. *Kokugakuin Journal of Law and Politics*, 38(3): 1–33.

Yokoyama, M. (2001). Analysis of Japanese police from the viewpoint of democracy. In S. Einstein and M. Amir (eds.), *Policing Security and Democracy: Theory and Practice*. Huntsville, TX: The Office of International Criminal Justice, Inc., pp. 187–209.

Yokoyama, M. (2002). Juvenile justice and juvenile crime: An overview of Japan. In Winterdyk, J. (ed.), *Juvenile Justice Systems—International Perspectives*, 2nd edn. Toronto, Ontario, Canada: Canadian Scholars' Press, Inc., pp. 321–352.

Yokoyama, M. (2003). Analysis of corruption by Sokaiya (Hoodlums at General Meeting of Stockholders) in Japan. *Kokugakuin Journal of Law and Politics*, 40(4): 59–86.

Yokoyama, M. (2004). Structural corruption and individual corruption in Japanese Police. In M. Amir and S. Einstein (eds.), *Police corruption: Challenges for Developed Countries: Comparative Issues and Commissions of Inquiry*. Huntsville, TX: The Office of International Criminal Justice, Inc., pp. 309–351.

Yokoyama, M. (2005). Analysis of political corruption in Japan. *Kokugakuin Journal of Law and Politics*, 42(4): 1–49.

Yokoyama, M. (2007). Policing the right wing violence during last two decades in Japan. *EuroCriminology*, 20/21: 171–197. Lodz University Press, Lodz, Poland.

Yokoyama, M. (2014). Increase in crimes committed in Japan by elderly people and the way they are treated in criminal justice. In E. W. Plywaczewski (ed.), *Current Problems of the Penal Law and the Criminology No. 6*. Warszawa, Poland: Wolters Kluwer Polska Sp. zoo.o., pp. 790–803.

14. An Analysis Regarding the Roma Community from Romania

Soria-Maria Cofan

Introduction

With the "Fall of the Iron Curtain" in the early 1990s, Western Europe has faced waves of citizens coming from the former communist countries, including Romania, in search of a better life. This migration phenomenon increased in Romania's case by the adheration to the European Union (EU) in 2007, and with it, the free movement of its citizens in the member states constituted and constitutes a significant social and economic pressure for European governments. Among those citizens, we can include Roma, regardless of their country of origin (Romania, Bulgaria, Hungary, or another country).

In this study, we have used demographic data collected by the National Institute of Statistics from Romania's population census from 1930, 1956, 1966, 1977, 1992, 2002, and 2011.* In order to depict the historical and cultural image of Roma, we used studies and books published by historians, linguists, and anthropologists. For evoking the current situation of Roma in Romania today, we used information published on Soros Romanian Foundation website,† Romanian and European legislation, and data collected directly from lawmen through interviews. State authority representatives, with responsibilities in the field of Roma integration and monitoring national strategies to address this issue, were involved in this study. We also mention that, in accordance with Article 7, paragraph 1 of Law 677/2001 on the protection of individuals with regard to the processing of personal data and on the free movement of such data,‡ in Romania no public institution either collects data on ethnicity of the Romanian citizens or keeps such data, except in accordance with paragraph 2 of the same article of the law, stating exceptions to the prohibitions set out in paragraph 1. In other words, none of the accessed public institutions with responsibilities in the integration of Romanian Roma were able to provide data sets on the level of training,

* Demographic data collected by the National Institute of Statistics at Romania's population censuses from 1930, 1956, 1966, 1977, 1992, 2002, and 2011, and are available at: http://www.insse.ro/cms/files/RPL2002INS/vol4/titluriv4.htm and http://www.recensamantromania.ro/rezultate-2/.

† Studies are available at: http://www.soros.ro/?q=publicatii.

‡ Law 677/2001 on the protection of individuals with regard to the processing of personal data and on the free movement of such data, published in Official Monitor No. 790 of December 12, 2001.

employment, standard of living, houses owned, or crime and victimization among Roma (Joja, 1966).

Declaring ethnicity to the census is a personal choice and not an obligation of citizens, since Romania has taken into national law the provisions of Directive CE95/46/1995 of European Parliament and the Council on the protection of individuals regarding the processing of personal data and on the free movement of such data.* *The ideas expressed in this study reflect the personal opinion of the author and do not represent the official position of any institution of Romania or the Romanian state.*

In conducting this study, we used the following analytical techniques:

- The three-order polynomial function, for viewing trends
- Geospatial analysis using GeoMedia Professional software for thematic visualization
- Profile analysis
- Comparative analysis to draw conclusions based on multisource data

* Directive CE95/46/1995 of European Parliament and the Council on the protection of individuals regarding the processing of personal data and on the free movement of such data, available at http://eur-lex.europa.eu/LexUriServ/LexUriServ.do?uri=CELEX:31995L0046:en:HTML.

Historical View on Roma

Before outlining, even broadly, some defining aspects of Roma history, there is a need for clarification on the very name this ethnicity carries. In Romania, until the 1990s, the name they called themselves and that assigned by the Romanian population was *Gypsy*, a term that has become pejorative and has been replaced by the word *Roma*. *The Romanian Encyclopedic Dictionary* (Joja, 1966) published by the Romanian Academy defines the word *Gypsy* as follows:

> **Gypsy** is the name given to the ethnic group, native from the northwestern India. Their language belongs to the family of Indo-European languages. Since the 5th century they migrated to Iran and Mediterranean Asia, and the Byzantine Empire (9th century), from where, between 10th and 14th centuries have entered south-eastern and central Europe, and in the North of Africa. In the 15th century they entered Western Europe (especially in the Iberian Peninsula), and in the 19th century in the Americas. They are first time mentioned on the Romanian territory in the 14th century. In the Middle Ages, most Gypsies from the Romanian Countries were slaves (royal, boyar and monastic), their main occupations being those of coppersmiths, blacksmiths, goldsmiths, rudar, tinsmiths, singers, etc. In 1844 in Moldavia and in 1847 in the Romanian Country, royal and monastic Gypsies were emancipated, and in 1855 in Moldavia and in 1856 the Romanian Country the boyar ones. The society development has led to changes in the Gypsies lifestyle, their nomadism reluctantly made way for sedentary life and integration in all fields of society. Gypsy folklore has a rich treasure (literature, music and dance), which in some countries has been assimilated by the national one, or influenced it.

The *Explanatory Dictionary of the Romanian Language* (Romanian Academy, Institute of Linguistics, 1998) published by the Romanian Academy, Institute of Linguistics “Iorgu Iordan” offers the following explanation for the word Gypsy:

> **Gypsy**—1. individual who is part of a population originating in India and widespread in most European countries, living in some parts still in semi-nomadic state; 2. Epithet given to brunette person; 3. Epithet given to a person with bad habits.

In the United Kingdom, we meet them as the *romanichal* and *gypsy*, as in the United States, Canada, and Australia. In Spain and southern France, they bear the name *calé* (black), *kaale* in Finland, *sinti* in Germany, and *manouches* in the rest of France (Fraser, 1998, pp. 14–15).

Alexandre Paspati, in his work *Studies on Gypsies*,† published in Constantinople in 1870, stated that “the true history of the Gypsy race is in their idiom study.” In the European Romani languages, the Gypsies will call themselves *rom*, in the Armenian dialect, *lom*, and in the Syrian and Persian, *dom*. Sir Angus Fraser mentions in his book *The Gypsies*, “Roma word has no connection with Romania, but literally translates with human or man.”‡

For many centuries of Roma history, we hardly find historical records and these often are made by people outside the ethnic group. Linguistic (Gjerdman and şi Ljungberg, 1963; Paspati, 1870; Sampson, 1926) and anthropological studies (Pittard, 1932) place the origins

† Paspati, A., cited by Fraser A. in his book *The Gypsies*, Humanitas, Bucharest, 1998. p. 18.

‡ Fraser, A., op. cit. p. 15.

of the Roma in the northwest or central India. There are two theories that dominate the twentieth century on Roma migration from India. One is that in the ninth century AD, they migrated from northwest India to Iran and from there across Europe (Sampson, 1927), and the second claims that around the year 250 BC proto-Gypsies migrated from central to northwestern India and from there to Iran and Europe (Sir Ralph Turner) (Turner, 1926, 1927). American researcher Terrence Kaufmann (Kaufmann, 1984) links Roma migration from northwest India to Persia to Alexander the Great's incursions into this area in the years 327–326 BC.

Eugène Pittard turned his anthropometric studies on Roma populations in the Balkans, its results seeing the light of printing in the 1930s. He concludes in his study *Les Tziganes ou Bohemiens** that they exceed the European average height, giving them "a very honorable place in the human body aesthetics. Among them are often very handsome men and beautiful women. Their olive skin, pitch black hair, straight and well shaped nose, white teeth, wide eyes with dark brown color, with a vivid expression or languorous, overall suppleness of their posture and harmony of their movements put them in terms of physical beauty, well above many of the European nations."

In Iran, we find a record of the Arabian historian Hamza of Ispahan† (950 AD) mentioning that the monarch Bahram Gur (reigned until 438 AD), having decided that his subjects will work half the day, with the rest of the day spent together eating and drinking in the sound of music, met a group that was drinking wine without listening to music. When asked why they did not accompany their party with music, they said they had tried to find a fiddler, but this was not possible. In this context, Bahram Gur asked the king of India to send 12,000 fiddlers, which were spread to all corners of the Persian kingdom. An Arab historian also notes that "the descendants of those fiddlers are still in Persia and make Zott population"‡ (*zotti*, plural *zot*, Persian name for Gypsies).

The national Persian poem Sah-Name (Book of Kings) of the poet Ferdowsi describes in 60,000 verses the country's history (year 1010). The poem mentions Bahram Gur's request to the Indian King Shangul to send fiddlers and artists to Persia. Bahram Gur gave to the 10,000 Lurs§ received, men and women, grains, cattle, and donkeys and sent them to the kingdom provinces to work as farmers and at the same time to make music. In a year, the Lurs ate everything the king gave them, falling under his rebuke "then banished them, ordering to upload their entire fortune on the backs of the donkeys and to sustain themselves from their songs and jingle of the bows, and every year to walk through the country and sing for the delight of the rich and the poor. According to this mandate the Lurs are still walking through the world today, looking for work, seeking companionship of the dogs and wolves, stealing at the high road in daylight and at night."¶

It seems that the Roma migrated from Persia to Armenia, the Byzantine Empire, the Balkans, and into entire Europe.**

* Pittard, E. cited by Fraser, A. in his book *The Gypsies*, Humanitas, Bucharest, 1998, pp. 30–31.

† Fraser, A., op.cit., pp. 42–43.

‡ Hamza of Ispahan quoted by Fraser, A., op.cit., p. 42.

§ *Luri*, or *luli*—Persian name for Gypsies.

¶ Quote mentioned in A. Fraser, *The Gypsies*, p. 43. Original quote and the translation appears in Harriot (1830).

** Fraser, A., op.cit., pp. 50–51, 55–70.

The Roma Situation in Romania

The first documentary attestation of the Roma presence in Romania dates back to 1385 when, in a document issued by the ruler Dan I, it mentioned the donation of 40 families of Gypsy slaves to the Tismana Monastery. Other documents of the time record donations of families of Gypsy slaves to Cozia Monastery in Wallachia and Bistrita Monastery in Moldavia. The Roma arrived in Romania from the Byzantine Empire; they acquired great economic importance for the rulers of the time, and in order to prevent them from running, their nomadic existence being notorious were transformed into slaves. Each Gypsy without an owner was declared state property (Gheorghe, 1983; Panaitescu, 1941). They were valued as blacksmiths, craftsmen producing objects of copper and tin, animal dealers, itinerant merchants, singers, dancers, and so on. From this point of view, they were complementary to Romanian population, which consisted mostly of peasants, farmers, and shepherds. Unlike the countries of Western Europe, where crafts were controlled by guilds, the Roma found in Romania a development economic segment uncovered that they exploited. Their slave status has not changed for more than five centuries.

We can thus conclude that Roma were accepted into the social structure of the Romanian Principalities, on the lowest social stage of it, and because they were sedentarized by linking to certain lands (boyar, monastic) and prevented from migrating, their presence in Romania was quite numerous. However, they did not receive very good treatment from their masters who, although they had not the right of life and death over their slaves, could punish or imprison them and sell and divide their families. Any Romanian, man or woman, who married a gypsy, became in turn a slave (Kogălniceanu, 1837).

In Transylvania, Roma's status varied from slaves to royal serfs, who were free, their only obligation being to pay tribute to the king. In the eighteenth century, in Transylvania, Habsburg emperors imposed measures to abolish the nomadic behavior of the Roma. They were forced to settle in one place, their horses and carts were confiscated, and they had the right to move from one place to another only with special permission. They were not allowed to wear their traditional garments or to use their traditional language. They were forced to work in agriculture, their children to go to school, and marriages between Romas were prohibited. After the disappearance of monarchs who have imposed these measures, Roma returned to their traditional lifestyle (Voicu and Tufiş, 2008, p. 7).

Around the time of the revolutionary movement from 1848, Roma have gained the status of free people. M. Voicu and C. Tufiş mention in the study *Roma—life stories** that Roma emancipation had, paradoxically, the effect of worsening their situation. Some have migrated to European countries and others settled on the periphery of Romanian cities, continuing to practice their traditional crafts. Roma emancipation coincided with the second wave of Roma migration to Western European countries.

The Second World War brought to the Romanian Roma the Nazi persecution, culminating in 1942 with the deportation to Transnistria by the Marshal Antonescu regime of an estimated number of 25,000 Roma (Achim, 1998), with a mortality rate of more than 50%.

During the communist period (1948–1989), a series of measures were taken aimed to remove any social and economic disparities in the Romanian society, without any positive discrimination to Roma population. These included compulsory and free education for everyone, urban systematization with effects in dissolution of the peripheric slums of the cities, and the obligation to hold a job. The state built buildings where Roma received comfortable houses, with current water, sewerage, and heating. In this way, unhealthy districts, traditionally inhabited by Roma, disappeared. The State policy of full employment of labor had effects on the Roma, but they often avoiding formal employment.† Men occupied unqualified worker's positions and were employees in sanitation or in the oil industry, or doing jobs that did not require specialization, while women occupied cleaning ladies positions. Although free access to education for all Romanian citizens was opened, including the high school level, the school dropout rate among Roma was the highest. They preferred practicing ancestral crafts inherited from their parents rather than going to school (O'Grady and Tarnovschi, n.d.).

In rural areas, Roma were used as raw labor force by state farms, since they don't have their own means of production (arable land, agricultural equipment or animals). Those who did not know a craft used to work as day laborers, having no source of steady income and not paying taxes and also did not benefit from the right to old age pensions.

Another aspect of the communist policies beneficial to the Roma was encouraging the birth rate, and financial assistance (allowances) offered to families with numerous children. Through Decree 770/1966 regulating the interruption of pregnancy, abortion was prohibited by law for females under 45 years of age having less than four children and could only be done in exceptional circumstances, in hospital units, under the control of regional commissions (Decree, 770/1966). At the same time, unmarried and childless couples were required to pay additional fees, and divorces were continually being discouraged. As Roma women had an increased rate of birth, compared to Romanian women, social welfare income for them was significant, but it only provided families means to survive, not for individual development.

Although the communist regime pursued a policy of forced leveling of living and educational differences among the population, favorable to the raising the status of the members from the poor and the poorest social classes of the society, such as the Roma, they did not make the leap the authorities expected, preferring their traditional lifestyle. This only served to deepen their social exclusion and worsen the problems they face, including illiteracy, poverty, poor health, unsanitary housing, and subsistence from the informal economy market (Voicu, 2007).

After the "Fall of the Communist Bloc" (1989), Roma members redefined their identity, calling themselves Roma. NGOs, political parties, and specialized associations appeared to promote their interests (Tarnovschi, 2012), but social disparities, both among the general population and ethnic members, deepened. Most of them are living in poverty, but a small number reach

* Voicu, M., Tufiş, C., op. cit. p. 8.

† Voicu, M., Tufiş, C., op. cit., p. 9.

economic prosperity, displaying high living standards, luxury cars, and turret houses. In the 1990s, in the Romanian industry decline context, the first employees to be made redundant were the Roma, who occupied unqualified workers positions (Voicu and Tufiş, 2008). Lack of skills and employers' prejudices prevented socioprofessional reintegration of the Roma in the formal economy, thus favoring slippage of members of this ethnic group into the informal economy. Following the dissolution of cooperative and state ownership, in rural areas, the Roma continue to work in agriculture as day laborers without formal labor contracts. Lack of formal contracts of employment, of identity documents, and ownership of land and houses on the one hand, and extending the influence of ethnic traditions (e.g., early marriage) and malformed conformity to community rules (as their's Stabor) on the other hand, fed isolation and self-isolation trends, which help keep the members of the Roma community outside the social security system, health benefits, and pensions, often preventing them access to education and a life in accordance with European state standards (Cacc et al., 2010).

The first groups of Roma who arrived in Germany came from Romanian regions, traditionally inhabited by ethnic Germans (Sibiu, Brasov, Timisoara, Sighisoara), following the Swabians massive migration from Transylvania and Banat to the German territories (in the 1970s–1990s) (Liéjois, 2009). These groups were the subject of adverse reactions of the communities from the states in which they emigrated, representing a socioeconomic problem for the government. European national authorities have developed programs to integrate Roma migrants. Simultaneously, after the 1990s, other policies have been developed, some synonymous with expulsion. We mention the convention signed in 1992 between Germany and Romania, known in the media under the name *Zigeuner Protocol*, to repatriate Roma of Romanian nationality. A similar agreement was signed between Romania and the French Government in 1994, for repatriation of people to whom asylum applications have been denied and thus are illegally staying. These bilateral practices continue.

After Romania's integration into the EU, we witnessed a new wave of Roma migration in the Western European countries. This situation has generated numerous debates at the European level, in reference to the status that should be associated to them. Should they be regarded as migrants, migrant workers, refugees, asylum seekers, displaced people, or stateless people? (Liéjois, 2009) This wave of Roma migration originating from the Balkan countries has become a major political issue on the agenda of the developed European governments, the European Council, and the United Nations High Commissioner for Refugees. In the present socioeconomic situation of Roma who emigrated to EU countries, the existence of xenophobic attacks against them and violent (Article, 2014; N. Ireland thugs drive Gypsies, 2009; Roma, 2014) manifestations, involving racist attitudes and rejection behaviors, have frequently been reported.

Another phenomenon encountered in Romanian Roma families is that they migrate in groups from the same village or from the same region to the same cities or regions of a foreign country (Belgium, France, Germany, or Great Britain), thus restoring their family group from their native place (Giurca et al., 2012).

Demographic Aspects of the Roma Population in Romania

Romania demographic development from 1930 to 2011 reveals an increasing population until the 1990s, and then we witness a decline in population, from one census to another (Figure 14.1).

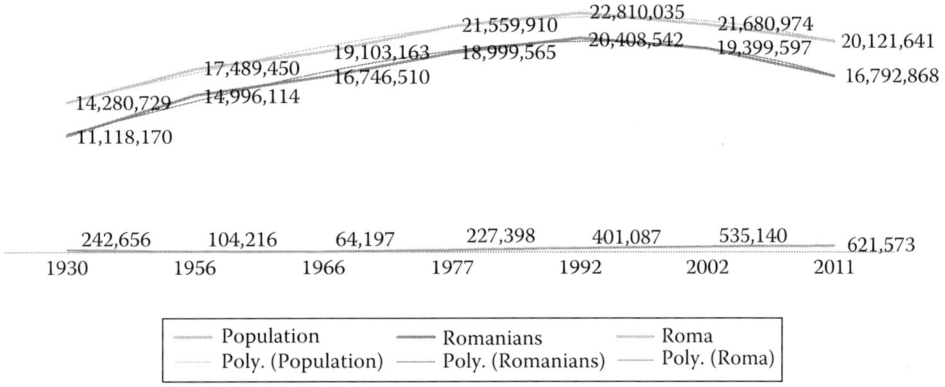

FIGURE 14.1 Demographic evolution in Romania, between 1930 and 2011.

The Romanian percentages that declare themselves Roma decreased until the 1966 census, when it reached the minimum rate of 0.34% from the total population, and then we witness a constant increase of this percentage, with a maximum in the 2011 census, when more than 3% of the population declared Roma (Figure 14.2).*

	Population	Romanians	Roma	Other Ethnic Groups	% Roma
1930	14,280,729	11,118,170	242,656	2,919,903	1.70
1956	17,489,450	14,996,114	104,216	2,389,120	0.60
1966	19,103,163	16,746,510	64,197	2,292,456	0.34
1977	21,559,910	18,999,565	227,398	2,332,947	1.05
1992	22,810,035	20,408,542	401,087	2,000,406	1.76
2002	21,680,974	19,399,597	535,140	1,746,237	2.47
2011	20,121,641	16,792,868	621,573	2,707,200	3.09

The 2011 census shows an ethnic profile of the Romanian citizens as in the chart: the majority of the population declares themselves to be of Romanian ethnicity (84%), while 6% declares themselves to be Hungarians, 3% declares themselves to be, and only 1% as ethnic Armenians, Bulgarians, Csángós, Czech, Chinese, Croatian, Hebrew, German, Greek, Italian, Macedonian, Polish, Russian-Lipovans, Serbs, Slovaks, Tatars, Turks, Ukrainians, and other nationalities. For 6% of the censed population, there was no available information regarding their ethnicity.

As it can be seen in Figure 14.3, the counties of Romania with the highest rate of declared Roma are Mures (8523 Roma per 100,000 inhabitants) and Calarasi (7480 Roma per 100,000 inhabitants), followed by Salaj (6687 Roma per 100,000 inhabitants) and Bihor (6020 Roma per 100,000 inhabitants), while the lowest rate of the Roma population is registered in Bucharest (1273 Roma per 100,000 inhabitants).

In the study A Social Map of Roma Communities (Sandu, 2005) conducted by the Romanian Government and the World Bank in 2005, the number of Roma in Romania was estimated at 730,174 people (minimum estimation), 851,048 people (medium estimation), and 970,000 people (maximum estimation). In the Communication *An EU Framework for National Roma Integration Strategies up to 2020*, the European Commission estimates, based on Council of Europe, that in Romania, there lived 1.2 million Roma (minimum estimation), 2.4 million Roma (maximum estimation), and 1.85 million Roma (average estimate), which would represent 8.32% of the total population of Romania.

* Data source for the 1930–2011 censuses: National Institute of Statistics. Data available at: http://www.insse.ro/cms/files/RPL2002INS/vol4/titluriv4.htm.

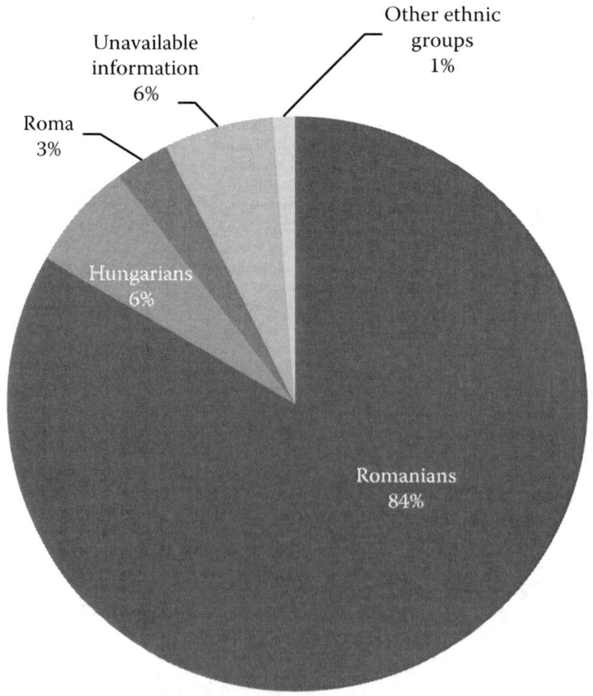

FIGURE 14.2 Ethnic profile of the Romanian population at the population census from 2011. (Data from National Institute of Statistics, http://www.recensamantromania.ro/rezultate-2/ Accessed January 25, 2014.)

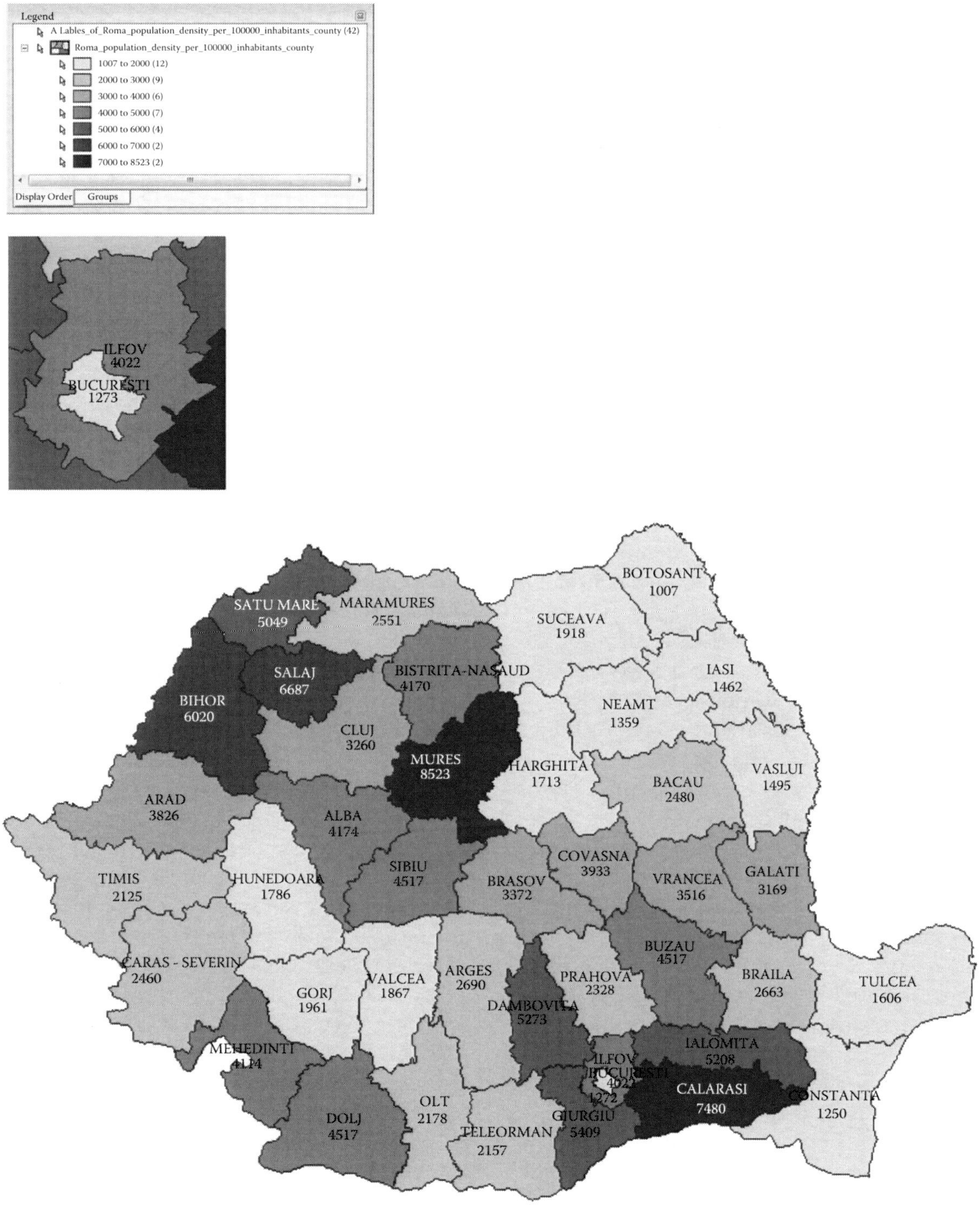

FIGURE 14.3 County distribution of Roma declared population density in Romania, per 100,000 inhabitants, according to Census 2011.

Romanian public perception of the proportion of Roma is most often associated with the issues facing the local community (theft, conflicts, violence). In turn, the perception of local issues is influenced on the one hand by the personal perspective (education, values, or attitudes) and on the other hand by the quality of life in the area.

Based on the Roma presence association with problems in the neighborhood, we come to the level of tolerance for different people in terms of ethnicity and religious beliefs. Previous studies have shown that the level of tolerance is the expression of the social and economic development level of a nation (Inglahart, 1997). The higher the standard of living in the society and more frequent the interactions with different individuals concerning ethnicity and race, the less discriminatory behavior and intolerance to diversity occurs in the society. The survey results in the early 1990s show a high ethnic intolerance among the population in Romania, with over 70% of Romanian being unwilling to have Roma neighbors (Zamfir and Preda, 2002). These results are reinforced by the emergence of tensions and conflicts (Lynch Law, 1994) between Romanian and Roma populations in localities where Roma lived in compact communities, because of the dissatisfaction arising from their behavior and lifestyle, which is different from the majority population (Major Ethnic Conflicts Between Gypsies, Hungarian and Romanian n.d.; The conflicts from Hădăreni, n.d.). Studies also show that the Romanian's intolerance to the Roma's presence decreased significantly during the period 1993–2006, from 72% to 36% (Bădescu et al., 2007). The causes of such a change may reside in the increase of the living standards and the development of a democratic Romanian society.

Considerations of Roma Participation in the Informal Economy

Economic activities carried out by the Roma are extremely varied and variable, the features of which being determined by their clan organization and nomadic life, as ethnocultural ancient landmarks. There are families engaged in survival from one day to another, where bartering is an important activity, while others are investing not only in luxury cars (that would give them the appearance of prosperity) but also in real estate and financial investments. Their occupations take traditional forms, ordinary family members never being limited to a single economic activity, much less to a single profession. Family multieconomic activity is a general rule. Roma groups are founded on ethnic criteria and are traditionally based on trades, seen as specializations, characteristic to that group such as florists, brick makers, coppersmiths, ursari, boiler makers, tinsmiths, blacksmiths, fiddlers, circus peddlers, horse traders, peddlers, fortune tellers, goldsmiths, car dealers, wicker baskets manufacturers, or crafts producers.

Another aspect worth mentioning is that the trades practiced from ancient times have not changed, and their economic activities have not been able to integrate into modern industries. Thus, Roma can be encountered as day laborers in agriculture, harvesting fruits and vegetables, showing a true symbiosis with rural life, especially in areas where modern machinery cannot be used.

The decision of Roma families to move to a new region for economic purposes, the community decide to settle, is based on the preexisting balance between Roma families already established in the region and the local economic potential (formal and informal). Throughout the active existence of an individual, one finds his own ability to learn through observation and early participation in the group activities, a body of knowledge based on dexterity, adaptability, ingenuity, and economy of production means. Practicing an occupation success is not due to professional specialization as a guarantor of economic insertion in a modern society but to the ability to adapt to the local environment and make the best use of opportunities. Thus, by mimetism, the individual acquires in the family and then in the community the ability to make working a combination of economic subsistence solutions, based on identifying the needs of the majority in certain places and times. One must be able to mobilize the local material resources, the cheaper and more easily available the better, in order to fulfill local demand for the services provided.

A family can engage throughout a year in a series of activities, such as artisans/fiddlers at local festivals, selling from door to door, providing small local services, provision of seasonal work (in agriculture, gathering fruits, medicinal plants, forest fruit), collecting waste (scrap metal, bottles, paper), dealing in resale items, or even begging. Roma women involve children from an early age in selling and bartering activities, not only to arouse compassion from the customers, but primarily to help children acquire an early sense for commercial transactions. In the family and family groups, there is an obvious division of tasks between the members, a prerogative of the subsistence economy, to meet as closely as possible the identified needs of the local communities where Roma live. The whole family helps to achieve the same objective, which is to ensure family subsistence, using ancestral knowledge acquired in many forms of transactions with the local environment. These activities are characterized by an attitude of mutual self-help among the members of the family group, a traditional value of the Roma.

The sale and resale of goods (of different origins, legal/illegal) is the most visible activity, all Roma families make more or less use of this method of subsistence. More than a precise activity, this way of making a living is rather an attitude and a general goal for Roma. These transactions in many cases go outside state fiscal control, belonging to the informal economy.

Some crafts, including tin manufacture, making buckets and copper boilers, manufacturing high-quality metal objects, repairing of old metal objects, artisanal aging of industrial manufactured objects, and adjustment of industrial metal pieces (Humeau, 1995), brought Roma fame among other craftsmen and distinguished them from other groups of the same ethnicity as historically recognized groups. Such concerns also generate happy stories told in Roma communities, identify true best practices for other Roma family groups, and create positive precedent integration and subsistence to legal compliance.

Case Study: A Roma Community in the Region Brahasesti–Toflea, Galati County*

* All information presented in the case study were collected by direct interview from the Brahasesti mayor and Brahasesti Hall website, available at: http://www.primariabrahasesti.ro/.

In the north of the county of Galati, about 35 km from the city of Tecuci, is located Brahasesti commune comprising of two villages, Toflea and Brahasesti, with the highest density of Roma in Romania. Voting population rises to 9700 inhabitants, of whom 5800 are Roma ethnic population, approximately 1500–1700 families (average family includes 6 members) of sedentary Ursari category, without a traditional port. In secondary schools, there are more than 1500 pupils registered, 850 in the School of Toflea (composition 100% Roma) and 650 in the School of Brahasesti (composition 60% Roma).

The mayor of the commune says that this is a different commune. Since ancient times, community men have mastered the art of metalworking. By the 1990s in Toflea, handmade items were produced, including chisels for carving, tool kits, drills for wood railway sleepers, castings, and aluminum cauldrons. The craft still exists today, and any metal part could be reproduced manually by the ancestral technological process. Before the 1990s, almost all men were working legally in nearby cities, 90% of them working in foundries and forges, gaining fame for being good toolmakers. Hundreds of thousands of railway drills were handmade in Toflea, due to contracts with Romanian Railways.

In terms of education, during the communist era no more than 10 local residents with high school diplomas and 5 with university degrees lived in the region. Roma girls used to complete only secondary school education, a small percentage of them having less than five primary classes. Early marriages are not a tradition in the area, and the minimum age for marriage is considered 16 years.

After the 1990s, we witnessed trade liberalization. Many locals were launched in trade businesses and set up companies that either sell the goods they produce or resell products. By 2000, the local education level increased to 10 primary classes, many following professional schools. In 2004, Roma elders in the area established the *Toflea Foundation*, which in 2008 began to bear fruit. One of the foundation's success is the support they offer for the training process of the Roma, by providing scholarships for continuing their secondary and university education (in 2013, there were about 360 scholars). Currently, 60 of the Roma residents have completed university studies, 100 are students in the country's university centers, and 300 are following high school. The mayor of the commune considers that at the primary education level (grades 1–8), the school dropout rate among Roma is about 20% and is caused by the poverty. If young people reach high school, school dropout becomes rare.

In the Brahasesti commune, *Second Chance* project runs for those locals who were not able to complete their studies at the proper time. In this project, 110 Roma are completing high school and more than 200 are enrolled in secondary school.

Both in Brahasesti and in Toflea, there is a dispensary; the one in Toflea has very good conditions, while Brahasesti dispensary requires rehabilitation. In 2012, there were 200 births in Roma families. Migration for better employment and education is present in the Brahasesti commune, around 10% of the population going to Great Britain.

Besides metalworking activities, Brahasesti commune ethnics have also artistic concerns, carrying on the ancestral tradition of fiddler music. The village has a folk band called *Burning Bush*, which used to attend even religious rituals. The Brahasesti community has future projects, investment in education being the main priority. The mayor speaks enthusiastically about their development projects in agriculture, services and agrotourism and, along with agrotourism, the conservation of ancient metalworking crafts that brought them fame. He said with confidence that inhabitants' businesses are 100% legal, all being contributors to the state budget.

The story of the Roma community in Brahasesti commune proves that it is possible to talk about successful integration of the Roma in Romania, the key of the whole process being serious investment in education and personal effort to overcome one's condition.

Initiatives to Manage Problem Roma Communities

Roma are often presented by the authorities, both nationally and internationally as a "problem" with various negative implications, including poverty, illiteracy, crime, poor health, nomadism, and participation in the informal economy. They are often the object of exclusive treatment such as xenophobic, racist, and discriminatory behavior from the majority population (Liegeois, 2009).

Over time, states naturalized, tried to socially integrate Roma, and sought to have them adopt the style and values of the majority population. This was successful with a small percentage. Roma do not have a caste of priests, do not hold a recognized standard language, have no written texts to ensure the transmission of beliefs, and have no moral code or guardians of ethnic traditions. They have a culture specificity shaped by a multitude of factors over history, pursue a nomadic lifestyle, and exist on the outskirts of modern societies. However, it is obvious that their identity was kept quite distinct of the majority populations they live among (Sir Angus Fraser, 1992).*

The senator Pierre-Etienne Flandin, in the statement of reasons for the promotion of the Law of July 16, 1912 (Loi du 16 Juillet, 1912) against nomadism in France, during a meeting of the Senate held on March 10, 1911, summarizes the so-called "Roma problem" as follows: "head of family pretends himself as practicing basket maker craft, upholsterer, tinsmith, but in reality the tribe lives begging... and more than that from robbery, which comes to be added to hunting and fishing poaching. These nomads live on our territory as in a conquered land, refusing to know neither hygiene rules, nor our civil law provisions, showing contempt for our criminal laws and tax laws."

Improvement of the Roma situation has become a priority in the EU. The "Europe 2020" (http://ec.europa.eu/eu2020/pdf/COMPLET%20EN%20BARROSO%20%20%20007%20-%20Europe%202020%20-%20EN%20version.pdf) strategy defined the European framework for smart, sustainable, and inclusive growth. This strategic framework excludes economic and social marginalization of the Roma, the largest European ethnic group, which would include an estimated 10–12 million individuals. In this respect, it was developed as *"An EU framework for national Roma integration strategies up to 2020" (http://eur-lex.europa.eu/legal-content/en/ALL/;ELX_SESSIONID=MS1vTt1cxTpppkChhvjyBy8T39828DtTqrphvLdcKXZy0VMQyBYY!-764833830?uri=CELEX:52011DC0173)*, normative transposed to national strategic document: "Government Strategy for Inclusion of Romanian Citizens Belonging to the Roma Minority, for the Period 2012–2020" (http://www.anr.gov.ro/docs/MO6bis.pdf).

These strategic documents structure the authorities' efforts to improve the Roma situation on the levels of education, employment, health, housing, culture, and social infrastructure.

One of the implemented measures in the public institutions, facilitate access to public information of Roma community members is the recruitment of Roma in public places. Thus, at the counties level, there were created County Offices for Roma, and the municipalities have recruited Roma advisors. One hundred sixty Roma policemen currently work in the Romanian Police, including 43 police officers and 117 police agents.†

Since 2007, with Romania's admission to the EU, member states have reported increased crime involving Romanian citizens. As an intergovernmental agreement, Romanian policemen were sent to law enforcement agencies from the countries facing Romanian origin crime, to prompt the management of criminal cases involving Romanian citizens. The situation in the last 4 years regarding the involvement of the Romanian police officers to sustain judicial investigations at the request of the respective states, by participating to investigative activities in the applicant countries, is shown in Table 14.1.

Table 14.1 Romanian Police Officers Participating in Investigative Activities in Other Countries: 2010–2013

Countries	2010	2011	2012	2013
Austria			2	2
Belgium				6
Denmark		1		2
Finland			1	2
France	10	27	68	46
Germany				10
Great Britain		2	13	13
Italy		4	3	4
Netherlands		3		
Poland			2	
Sweden				2
Switzerland				4
Total policemen	**10**	**37**	**92**	**91**

* Fraser, A., op. cit., p. 54.

† *Source*: Romanian Police.

Member states' requests for Romanian police officers were made to prevent and combat crimes involving Romanian citizens (as perpetrators or as victims), small criminality combat on the streets of Paris (especially around winter holidays) in 2010; to combat proliferation of burglary, robbery, pick-pocketing, and luggage thefts in 2011; to prevent and combat begging, bankcard fraud, cybercrime, human trafficking, theft from railway infrastructure, and association to organized crimes groups to break the law in 2012; and to combat thefts (pick-pocketing, burglaries, shoplifting, from ATM, metal components from railway infrastructure), robbery, prostitution, pimping, computer crimes (especially those related to electronic payment methods), serious crimes copper theft, street deceit (fraudulent exchange, *Maradona** method, etc.), association to organized groups to commit crimes, illegal residence, and false concerning identity in 2013.

* The *Maradona* method consists in the usurpation of an official position (police, tax controller) and the simulation of a routine control for currency counterfeit identification. The victim is requested to display the identification documents and money to control, during which criminals steal some money and/or other valuable goods from the victim.

Conclusion

Despite the development of national strategies to improve the situation of Roma, the first in 2001, revised in 2006 and expired in 2011, and the second developed in 2012, in line with *An EU Framework for National Roma Integration Strategies up to 2020*, the establishment of the National Agency for Roma in 2004, as the state body specialized in developing national policies to protect the rights of the Roma minority and the activation of numerous NGOs with activity purpose the protection of Roma community values, the Roma population of Romania is still in a situation of vulnerability. Strategic documents remain only partially effective in the face of the poverty realities and lack of education of most of Romanian Roma representatives (Moisă, 2013).

Successful cases among Roma are still rare, with most of them struggling to subsist using rudimentary means with no future. The Roma community participates only to a small extent in the formal economy because of their lack of education (25% of them are illiterate (Tarnovschi et al., 2011)) and professional qualifications, and the prejudice and discriminatory attitudes toward them are still manifested by some employers. Most of the Roma work in agriculture, construction, and industry in positions that do not require expertise. Their unemployment rates remain at high levels.

Romania does not have any relevant data concerning the number and the geographical distribution of Roma citizens, nor on the real issues they are facing, including their levels of education, health, employment, and housing. Without state authorities' responsible commitment to collect such structured data, it will be impossible to outline a situational picture close to reality regarding the scale of the problems these community members are facing, and without a pertinent radiography of the Roma situation, however difficult it might be, government measures will remain just a formality and the resources invested without any long-term effects.

Annually, Romania incurs losses of 202–675 million euros (World Bank, 2010) as a consequence of the fact that Roma are not integrated and in their vast majority remain an unproductive segment of the population operating in the area of the informal economy.

References

Bădescu, G., Grigoraş, V., Rughiniş, C., Voicu, M., Voicu, O. (2007). *Roma inclusion barometer*, Open Society Foundation, Bucharest, Romania. Available at: http://www.fundatia.ro/?q=barometrul-incluziunii-romilor-2007. (Accessed January 25, 2014.)

Fraser, A. (1998). *The Gypsies*, Humanitas Publishing House, Bucharest, Romania, pp. 14–15, 18, 30–31, 42–43, 50–51, 55–70.

Gheorghe, N. (1983). Origin of Roma's slavery in Romanian principalities, *Roma*, 7(1):12–27.

Gjerdman, O., Ljungberg, E. (1963). *The Language of the Swedish Coppersmith Gypsy Johan Dimitri Taikon*, Lundequist, Uppsala, Sweden.

Harriot, J.S. (1830). Observations on the oriental origin of the Romnichal, *Transactions of the Royal Asiatic Society*, 2: 518–558.

Humeau, J.B. (1995). *Tsiganes en France. De l'assignation au droit d'habiter*, L'Harmatan., Cambridge University Press, Cambridge.

Inglahart, R. (1997). *Modernization and Postmodernization: Cultural, Economic and Political Change in 43 Societies*, Princeton University Press, Princeton, NJ.

Joja, A. (1966). *Romanian Encyclopedic Dictionary*, Politic Publishing House, Bucharest IV, Romania, p. 754.

Kaufmann, T. (1984). Explorations in protoGypsy, Communication presented on the occasion of the *6th Roundtable analysis of South Asian Languages*, Austin, TX, p. 42.

Kogălniceanu, M. (1837). Esquisse sur L'histoire, les Moeurs et la Langue des Cigains, Connus en France sous le Nom de Bohémiens, Berlin, Germany.

O'Grady, C., Tarnovschi, D., Roma from Romania, p. 9. Available at: http://www.ardor.org.ro/content/ro/Romii_din_Romania.pdf. (Accessed January 25, 2014.)

Panaitescu, P. (1941). The gypsies in Walachia and Moldova: A chapter of economic history, *JGLS* 3(20): 58–72.

Paspati, A. (1870). *Etudes sur les Tchinghianés*, Antoine Koroméla, Constantinopol.

Pittard, E. (1932). *Les Tziganes ou Bohemiens*, Société Générale d'Imprimerie, Geneva, Switzerland.

Romanian Academy, Institute of Linguistics. (1998). Iorgu Iordan, *DEX Romanian Explanatory Dictionary*, 2nd edn., p. 1126, Encyclopedic Universe Publishing House, Bucharest, Romania.

Sampson, J. (1926). *The Dialect of the Gypsies of Wales*, Clarendon Press, Oxford, UK.

Sandu, D. (2005). Roma communities in Romania. A map of community poverty through the survey PROROMI, World Bank, Bucharest. Available at: http://www.anr.gov.ro/docs/statistici/PROROMI__Comunitatile_de_Romi_din_Romania_187.pdf. (Accessed January 25, 2014.)

Tarnovschi, D., Preoteasa, A., Serban, M. (2011). *Roma Situation in 2011. Between Social Inclusion and Migration*, Dobrogea Publishing House, Constanta, Romania, p. 37. Available at: http://www.fundatia.ro/?q=situa%C8%9Bia-romilor-%C3%AEn-2011-%C3%AEntre-incluziune-social%C4%83-%C5%9Fi-migra%C8%9Bie-1. (Accessed January 25, 2014.)

Turner, R. (1926). The position of Romani in Indo-Aryan, *JGLS*, 5(3): 145–189.

Voicu, M., Tufiş, C. (2008). *Roma Life Stories*, Soros Foundation, Bucharest, Romania, pp. 7–9, 11. Available at: http://www.fundatia.ro/?q=romii-pove%C8%99ti-de-via%C8%9B%C4%83-0. (Accessed January 25, 2014.)

Zamfir, C., Preda, M. (2002). *Roma in România*, Expert Publishing House, Bucharest, Romania.

Normative Acts

An EU Framework for National Roma Integration Strategies up to 2020. Available at: http://eur-lex.europa.eu/legal-content/en/ALL/;ELX_SESSIONID=MS1vTt1cxTpppkChhvjyBy8T39828DtTqrphvLdcKXZy0VMQyBYY!-764833830?uri=CELEX:52011DC0173. (Accessed January 25, 2014.)

Decree 770/1966 regulating the interruption of pregnancy. Available at: http://www.lege-online.ro/lr-DECRET-770%20-1966-(177).html. (Accessed January 25, 2014.)

Europe 2020 Strategy. Available at: http://ec.europa.eu/eu2020/pdf/COMPLET%20EN%20BARROSO%20%20%20007%20-%20Europe%202020%20-%20EN%20version.pdf. (Accessed January 25, 2014.)

Government Strategy for inclusion of Romanian citizens belonging to the Roma minority, for the period 2012–2020. Available at: http://www.anr.gov.ro/docs/MO6bis.pdf. (Accessed January 25, 2014.)

Loi du 16 Juillet 1912. Available at: http://histoire.comze.com/etrangers16juillet1912.pdf. (Accessed January 25, 2014.)

Web Data Sources

Article *Romanian beggar, stoned by many young people in Stockholm*, April 3, 2014. Available at: http://www.antena3.ro/externe/cersetoare-romanca-atacata-cu-pietre-de-mai-multi-tineri-in-stockholm-249262.html. (Accessed January 25, 2014.)

Lynch Law: Violence against Roma in Romania, Human Rights Watch/Helsinki November 2, 1994, Vol. 6, No. 17. Available at: http://www.hrw.org/reports/pdfs/r/romania/romania94n.pdf. (Accessed January 25, 2014.)

Major ethnic conflicts between Gypsies, Hungarian and Romanian. Available at: http://verticalnews.ro/marile-conflicte-interetnice-intre-tigani-unguri-si-romani/. (Accessed January 25, 2014.)

N. Ireland thugs drive Gypsies from homes, June 17, 2009. Available at: http://www.nbcnews.com/id/31416283/ns/world_news-europe/t/n-ireland-thugs-drive-gypsies-homes/#.U7MfB_l_uRY. (Accessed January 25, 2014.)

Roma boy left unconscious after being savagely beaten and tortured during vigilante attack in Paris suburb, June 17, 2014. Available at: http://www.independent.co.uk/news/world/europe/roma-boy-left-unconscious-after-being-savagely-beaten-and-tortured-during-vigilante-attack-in-paris-suburb-9544346.html. (Accessed January 25, 2014.)

The conflicts from Hădăreni. Available at: http://ro.wikipedia.org/wiki/Ciocnirile_de_la_H%C4%83d%C4%83reni. (Accessed January 25, 2014.)

15. Hells Angels in the Shadow Economy

Petter Gottschalk

Introduction

Hells Angels (HA) is a criminal matrix organization. The vertical axis of the organization is characterized by a legal men's club of individuals interested in a brotherhood linked to Harley Davidson motorcycles. The horizontal axis of the organization is characterized by illegal activities organized by individuals in the club. Money from illegal activities such as drug dealing and human trafficking can be laundered in legal enterprises owned by club members. Money laundering instruments include tattoo studios and construction companies owned by members of Hells Angels Motorcycle Club (HAMC). This chapter describes HAMC activities and the case of Gjensidige Insurance Company in Norway seeking repayment from HAMC members after a bomb attack several years ago.

Hells Angels MC

A distinction must be made between noncriminalized and criminalized bikers. The latter outlaw bikers are typically motorcycle club (MC) members referring to themselves as "1 percenters." Among the criminal biker clubs, we find HA, Outlaws, Bandidos, Pagan, black Pistons, Mongols, and Coffin Cheaters. The most well known is HAMC, which is in charge of many criminal business enterprises all over the world. The trademark of HA is almost as well known as Coca Cola, McDonalds, and Nike across the world.

Lavigne (1996, p. 1) described criminal bikers in this way:

> The darkness of crime lies not in its villainy or horror, but in the souls of those who choose to live their lives in the abyss. A man who toils from youth to old age to violate the line that divides civilization from wilderness, who proclaims he is not of society, but an outsider sworn to break its laws and rules, yet who readily seeks refuge in its lenient legal system, embraces its judicial paternalism and gains substance from its moral weakness; whose very existence as an outlaw is defined by society's being, is but a shadow of the real world, bereft of freedom and doomed to tag along in society's wake (p. 1).

As a shadow of the real world, criminal bikers participate in and organize the shadow economy. Some of the profit is kept in the shadow economy for consumption. Some of the profit is laundered into the legal economy for investments in tattoo studios, construction companies, restaurants, hotels, and other enterprises both nationally and internationally.

When looking back at history of HAMC, it all started in 1948 (http://www.wikipedia.org—search HA):

> The Hells Angels were originally formed in 1948 in Fontana, California through an amalgamation of former members from different motorcycle clubs, such as The Pissed Off Bastards of Bloomington. The Hells Angels website denies the suggestion that any misfit or malcontent troops are connected with the motorcycle club. However, the website notes that the name was suggested by Arvid Olsen, an associate of the founders, who had served in the Flying Tigers "Hells Angels" squadron in China during World War II. The name "Hells Angels" was believed to have been inspired by the common historical use, in both World War I and World War II, to name squadrons or other fighting groups by fierce, death-defying name.

HAMC has grown to several thousand members worldwide. Over the years, studies of HAMC have repeatedly shown that running an outlaw club costs money and the money is earned by organized crime (Quinn and Koch, 2003; Rassel and Komarrnicki, 2007). There are 100 HAMC members in Norway, which is a small Scandinavian country of five million inhabitants. Seventy-five out of 100 members in Norway have been convicted to jail sentences once or more times for criminal activities.

In Scandinavia, a war on organized drug crime broke out two decades ago. Consequences of this war can be found today in the rivalry between Gjensidige Insurance Company and one of the chapters of HAMC in Norway. The gang war involved HA and Bandidos (http://www.wikipedia.org—search HA):

> A gang war over drugs and turf between the Hells Angels and the Bandidos, known as the "Great Nordic Biker War", raged from 1994 until 1997 and ran across Norway, Sweden, Denmark and even parts of Finland and Estonia. By the end of the war, machine guns, hand grenades, rocket launchers and car bombs had been used as weapons, resulting in 11 murders, 74 attempted murders, and 96 wounded members of the involved motorcycle clubs. This led to fierce response from law enforcement and legislators, primarily in Denmark. A law was passed that banned motorcycle clubs from owning or renting property for their club activities. The law has subsequently been repealed on constitutional grounds.

One of the bombs that exploded during the "Great Nordic Biker War" in 1997 represents the historical background of the continuing dispute between a municipality, a police station, an insurance company, and a club.

Hells Angels Clubhouse

After the bomb exploded in the city of Drammen outside Oslo in Norway in 1997, police investigations concluded that the bomb was placed outside the Bandidos clubhouse by members of HAMC. Several HAMC members were convicted to jail sentences. Furthermore, Gjensidige Insurance Company, which had insured the destroyed buildings, paid close to $100 million USD to the owners of the buildings. After several court sentences against HAMC members, Gjensidige sought repayment from those members. The members did not pay, but Gjensidige found out that they owned shares in a clubhouse outside the city of Hamar. Gjensidige got a majority pledge in the clubhouse based on the debts of these members. Still, in 2014, however, Gjensidige has this pledge without taking any actions to retrieve the money (Brandås, 2011; Holmlund, 2011a,b).

Gjensidige has argued that their role is to retrieve money lost in insurance payments because of the Drammen bomb. They say that forcing HA out of the clubhouse does not make sense for three main reasons. First, the value of the clubhouse is less than a million dollars, while they lost a hundred million dollars. Second, the efforts and costs involved in throwing HA members out will probably exceed the benefits for Gjensidige. Third, it is not the responsibility of a business firm to get involved in law enforcement, even if it is a matter of serious organized crime where the firm might make a difference.

The small town of Ringsaker where the clubhouse is located would very much like to get rid of the HA chapter. They see Gjensidige's pledge as a golden opportunity to get rid of the criminals. All politicians in the town have encouraged Gjensidige to use their economic and legal force to throw HA members out of the house and then sell it on the open market to a noncriminal organization.

Similarly, local police in Ringsaker would also very much like to get some help from Gjensidige to get rid of the club, the members, and the associated criminal activity in drugs, prostitution, and violence.

Police officers can observe young prospects and hangarounds being attracted to and willing to work for HA.

Therefore, the current situation at the time of writing this chapter in 2014 is like it has been for several years: Gjensidige has decided to give the HAMC house pledge for free to the town of Ringsaker close to the city of Hamar. This will allow the city to foreclose on the HA and get them out of the community while relieving Gjensidige of what they expect to be a costly legal bill. However, the town council does not think it is that simple, so they have turned down the offer.

There seem to be no new developments emerging in 2014. Local police would like the insurance company and the city council to do more to get rid of HAMC, city council would like the insurance company and the local police to do more, and insurance company would like the local police and the city council to do more.

Hells Angels Business

Based on court rulings for convicted HA members in Norway, it is clear that they are involved in a number of illegal as well as legal business activities. They run a multimillion-dollar business network and protect their territorial stake on organized crime. Many HA use nominees—trusted associates who register companies in their names—to hide business assets.

Globally, HAMC makes money in prostitution, drug manufacturing, dealing and smuggling, extortion, auto theft, weapons dealing, and human trafficking. They are hard to arrest and convict because it is a very tightly knit organization and difficult to infiltrate. Club members are known by the public as being fearsome, short tempered, and often involved in criminal activity, despite efforts of local club chapters to perform good works in the community. Law enforcement keeps close tabs on the HA and other motorcycle-centered organizations. Police say the bikers often resort to murder to eliminate rivals who threaten their profitable criminal enterprises (Parker, 2012).

Despite outlaw image, HA sues often. Fritz Clapp, a lawyer practicing intellectual property law, represents the interests of a group not commonly associated with intellectual property, the HAMC. His main role is not as a bulldog criminal defense counsel for the notorious group but as a civilized advocate in its relentless battle to protect its many registered trademarks (Kovaleski, 2013):

> Just in the past seven years, the Hells Angels have brought more than a dozen cases in federal court, alleging infringement on apparel, jewelry, posters and yo-yos. The group has also challenged Internet domain names and a Hollywood movie – all for borrowing the motorcycle club's name and insignias. The defendants have been large, well-known corporations like Toys "R" Us, Alexander McQueen, Amazon, Saks, Zappos, Walt Disney and Marvel Comics. And they have included a rapper's clothing company, Dillard's and a teenage girl who was selling embroidered patches on eBay with a design resembling the group's "Death Head" logo.

The business of HA in Norway is organized from seven chapters across the country: Trondheim, Oslo, Stavanger, Hamar, Skien, Tromsø, Drammen, and Bergen. HA is affiliated with other criminal coalitions. The clubs under the domain of the HA are in the majority and have a much more stable membership than the clubs belonging to Bandidos and Outlaws: more than 90% of the other one percenter clubs in Norway support HA, according to a report on "The Norwegian police force's efforts to combat outlaw motorcycle gangs, 2011 to 2015" (Police, 2010).

HAMC in Norway control the chain of tattoo parlors of Tattoo World and House of Pain (Police, 2010). While tattoo symbols are important on body parts of members, tattoo business is also important to the club. Business practice and competitive forces in the tattoo area is very different from other business sectors. Threats and money laundering are elements found in the tattoo business.

It is very humiliating for club members to have their "colors" confiscated. The uniform is a form of communication both internally and externally. The main message is one for all, all for one, and aggression—a message that in practice has significant impact toward independent business competitors. The club logos worn on the members' jackets are borrowed from the club. In other words, the members do not own the logo and have to return it if they withdraw from or are excluded from the club (Police, 2010). It is business attire used in organized crime to be on top of criminal enterprises.

Several of the club premises in Norway provide living quarters for members and registered business addresses for their companies. The club is pragmatic enough to realize that open warfare is bad for business, and to date, the market is sufficiently profitable for all parties. Tattoo World in Norway is currently owned and managed by Leif Ivar Kristiansen ("Leifen"), HA's president in Norway. The company's registered business address is the same as that for the HA's premises in Trondheim. House of Pain on the island of Stord and in the city of Arendal is owned by HA member Vemund Sæterstøl, who is a member of the Oslo chapter (Police, 2010).

In an interview when confronted with the question whether he was the president of HAMC Norway and hence top executive in Norway, Kristiansen replied in the daily newspaper *Aftenposten*, "I don't answer such questions. This is my secret. All my business activity occurs within my personal enterprise. It has nothing to do with HA. Such allegations build on stupidity, but it does not provoke me."

The leaders in HAMC are a special brand of entrepreneurs who consider the laws in society as not valid neither for themselves nor for their business activities. In Canadian criminal intelligence report, it was stated that "without making light of their propensity for extreme violence – augmented by loyalty to the club's name – members of the Hells Angels continue to lack in criminal business savvy," and "they have proven themselves to be an available source of 'muscle' either for their own endeavors or for other criminal organizations. They are preoccupied with the supremacy of their name within the criminal biker sub-culture."

In Amsterdam in the Netherland, HA is running much of the operations in the red light district. The MC owns restaurants and gambling casinos, and they run the prostitution and drug business. Since HA has full control of the situation, there is not much public crime in the district. Therefore, Dutch police seem satisfied with the situation although they know it is wrong. Dutch police know that many of the major drug deals for Europe are settled in the red light district, where HA is in charge.

Business Characteristics

Understanding both similarities and differences between criminal business enterprises and between criminal and legal business enterprises is critical in successful policing of organized MC crime. Each organized crime organization has its own individual business interests, which can include drug trafficking, racketeering, money laundering, prostitution, gambling, loan shark activities, and other illegal activities. According to Jamala (2011), HA finds business interest in many illegal activities such as trafficking of drugs and stolen goods, extortion, and violent crime. According to the police, HAMC make millions of dollars off their business interests and invest the profits in legal activities as well as in criminal resorts.

Some of the differences between legal and criminal business enterprises are listed in Table 15.1. HAMC has a number of rules to which members have to obey strictly, while legal businesses are managed by goals. Criminal activities are organized either in the matrix or in the network shape, where some individuals are more central than others. Legal activities are organized in a hierarchy, which looks like a pyramid, where there are a few executives at the top and many workers at the bottom.

Like many exclusive and closed organizations, HA maintains a great deal of secrecy involving how to become a member. Candidates should never have applied to be a police officer or prison guard and not be a child molester. Members must be white. The road to full membership has several phases and can last for years. First, candidates are hang-arounds, a status that allows prospective members to attend some club events. Next, a candidate can become an associate, if members take interest in the person. Further on, a candidate can become a prospect. This status is full acknowledgment that an individual is in the pipeline for consideration. The person may participate in club

Table 15.1 Comparison of Criminal and Legal Business Enterprises

Characteristics	Criminal Business Organization	Legal Business Organization
Management	Managed by rules	Managed by goals
Organization	Matrix and network	Hierarchy and pyramid
Recruitment	Friendship and record	Market and CV
Leadership	Control of activities	Control of information
Relationships	Tight brotherhood	Loose colleagues
Finance	Cash transfer	Bank transfer
Marketing	Corruption and threats	Advertising and promotion

activities, but has no voting privileges. Finally, successful prospects graduate to the status of full member or full-patch. Full-patch—or being patched—refers to the fact that the member now has the right to wear all the sanctioned jacket patches, including HA death head logo (Parker, 2012).

Compared to HA recruitment, joining a legal business enterprise is a straightforward process. Candidates apply for a vacant position, and the best candidate gets the job.

Leadership in criminal organizations is characterized by control of activities, where rules and regulations in the club determine whether members should be rewarded or punished. Leadership in legal organizations is characterized by control of information and motivation of employees.

Relationships among members of a criminal organization are tight, often like a brotherhood. Colleagues in a business enterprise are loosely associated with each other.

Much of the funds in criminal business organizations are held in cash, while legal business organizations use banks.

Finally in Table 15.1, influencing the market, competitors, and customers is by means of corruption and threat by criminal units, while legal units apply advertising and other promotional activities.

Corporate Responsibility

Gjensidige Insurance is a legal organization, while HAMC is a criminal organization. When two such organizations meet, it is interesting to note to what extent a legal organization is willing to contribute to policing an illegal organization. With a majority pledge in the HA house, Gjensidige can make a difference for the police. The extent to which a legal organization contributes in society, is labeled corporate social responsibility (CSR). CSR is a concept related to the behavior and conduct of corporations and those who are associated with them. During the best of times, it is a concept adopted and taken for granted. During the worst of times, however, CSR becomes a threatening concept to most business as well as public organizations (Jayasuriya, 2006). CSR is a set of voluntary corporate actions designed to improve corporate actions. These corporate actions not required by the law attempt to further some social good and extend beyond the explicit transactional interests of the firm. The voluntary nature of CSR means that these activities can be viewed as gifts or grants from the corporation to various stakeholder groups (Godfrey et al., 2009).

Basu and Palazzo (2008) define CSR as the process by which managers within an organization think about and discuss relationships with stakeholders as well as their roles in relation to the common good, along with their behavioral disposition with respect to the fulfillment and achievement of these roles and relationships. It is an intrinsic part of an organization's character, with the potential to discriminate it from other organizations that might adopt different types of processes.

CSR is a concept by which business enterprises integrate the principles of social and environmental responsibility in their operations as well as in the way they interact with their stakeholders. This definition shows two perspectives. First, social and environment responsibility in their operations requires internal change processes to integrate the principles into business operations. Second, interactions with stakeholders require stakeholder engagement (Zollo et al., 2009).

The concept of CSR developed as a reaction against the classical and neoclassical recommendations from economics, where rational decision-making and free markets are concentrated solely on profits. This narrow economic view has been questioned due to inconsistencies with the economic model and the evidence of unethical business practices. These problems have led to the realization that organizations should also be accountable for the social and environmental consequences of their activities (Mostovicz et al., 2009).

Levels of Responsibility

Gottschalk (2013) introduced the stages of growth model to describe the levels of CSR. Depending on the level in this model, Gjensidige will or will not contribute further to expel HAMC members from the clubhouse outside Hamar in Norway.

These are the four stages as defined by Gottschalk (2013):

1. *Business stage of profit maximization for owners within the corporate mission.* At this basic maturity level, the company is only concerned with itself and its owners. In addition, the company is out to please customers. The only responsibility corporations have is that of maximizing profits to

shareholders while engaging in open and free competition, without deception and fraud (Adeyey, 2011). The decision about what to do about HA is strictly based on a financial cost–benefit analysis of this particular decision. In financial terms, there is less than $1 million USD in benefits to be expected, while the internal and external costs of court proceedings and lawyers will far exceed this amount.

2. *Function stage of establishing a function for CSR in the company.* At this second maturity level, business executives have understood that they need to address company relationships with the outside world in a professional way. Out of necessity and external expectations, a CSR function is established within the company staffed with individuals who have a business perspective. The decision about what to do about HA is based on a communication perspective, where the insurance firm is willing to help others to reach their goals. Managers are willing to inform the police and local municipality about the firm's involvement and claims against HA at Ringsaker outside Hamar in Norway.
3. *Resource stage of resource mobilization for potential threats and opportunities.* At this level, we find a complete yet passive form of CSR. It represents a reactive strategy where the company has mobilized resources for cases of emergency. The company is prepared for crisis management as well as opportunity exploration and exploitation. Opportunities may emerge where corporate executives will implement opportunistic behavior to gain from opportunities in terms of strengthening corporate reputation (Zollo et al., 2009). This third level of maturity is where we find Gjensidige insurance company in 2014. The firm has expressed willingness to help the municipality with legal resources as well as transfer of ownership rights to the municipality. Firm resources are made available to enable the municipality and the police to throw HA members out of the house based on legal prosecution and ownership action.
4. *Contribution stage of proactive involvement in society.* At this final maturity stage, corporate executives as well as all other organizational members perceive their business as part of a greater course of society. They take on a comprehensive and active responsibility in the local as well as national and global society. They look for opportunities in society where the company can make a difference (Mostovicz et al., 2009). Again we return to the example of the Norwegian insurance company that has a claim in the clubhouse of HA. While the claim has insignificant monetary value that was almost impossible to retrieve, the claim can help both municipality and police to fight organized crime in society. At this level of CSR, short-term loss to the company can be acceptable for the long-term good of society. CSR at this level is a long-term commitment to society. Evidence is emerging that long-term citizen commitment on the part of the company does not at all have to harm corporate profitability neither in the short term nor in the long term.

Conclusion

HA in the shadow economy is involved in a number of black markets. Goods and services are traded illegally. The key distinction of a black market trade is that the transaction itself is illegal. It is not just a matter of tax evasion. While the shadow economy in general is concerned with all business activities where national income tax laws are violated, the black market or underground economy is concerned with transactions that are forced to operate outside the formal economy. The black market is distinct from the gray market, in which commodities are distributed through channels that, while legal, are unofficial, unauthorized, or unintended by legal enterprises. HAMC is one of the main operators on black markets in the underground economy in Norway.

Fighting organized crime groups such as HAMC requires not only law enforcement agencies to work efficiently and effectively but also legal business enterprises need to contribute wherever they can. In this chapter, contribution is conceptualized in terms of CSR. Four levels of CSR were defined. Norwegian insurance company Gjensidige was found on level 3, where the firm has expressed willingness to help the municipality with legal resources as well as transfer of ownership rights. If Gjensidige moves to level 4, then the firm can make a more important impact in the fight against organized crime.

References

Adeyeye, A. (2011). Universal standards in CSR: Are we prepared? *Corporate Governance*, 11(1), 107–119.

Basu, K. and Palazzo, G. (2008). Corporate social responsibility: A process model of sensemaking, *Academy of Management Review*, 33(1), 122–136.

Brandås, F. (2011). Gjensidige nøler med å kaste ut Hells Angels (Gjensidige reluctant to throw out Hells Angels), daily newspaper *Hamar Arbeiderblad*. http://www.h-a.no, published March 26, 2011.

Godfrey, P.C., Merill, C.B., and Hansen, J.M. (2009). The relationship between corporate social responsibility and shareholder value: An empirical test of the risk management hypothesis, *Strategic Management Journal*, 30(4), 425–445.

Gottschalk, P. (2013). Limits to corporate social responsibility: The case of Gjensidige Insurance Company and Hells Angels Motorcycle Club, *Corporate Reputation Review*, 16(3), 177–186.

Holmlund, J.A. (2011a). Vil ha kommunen som medeier i klubben (Wants the municipality as partly owner of club), daily newspaper *Hamar Arbeiderblad*. http://www.h-a.no, published April 5, 2011.

Holmlund, J.A. (2011b). Rådmann vil tilgi (Chairman will forgive), daily newspaper *Hamar Arbeiderblad*. http://www.h-a.no, published May 21, 2011.

Jamala. (2011). Hells Angels, Study mode, http://www.studymode.com/essays/Hells-Angels-585034.html. (Accessed April 11, 2012.)

Jayasuriya, D. (2006). Auditors in a changing regulatory environment, *Journal of Financial Crime*, 13(1), 51–55.

Kovaleski, S.F. (2013). Despite outlaw image, Hells Angels sue often, *The New York Times*. http://www.cnbc.com/id/101235239, published November 29, 2013.

Lavigne, Y. (1996). *Hells Angels: Into the Abyss*, Harper Paperbacks/Harper Collins Publishers, New York.

Mostovicz, I., Kakabadse, N., and Kakabadse, A. (2009). CSR: The role of leadership in driving ethical outcomes, *Corporate Governance*, 9(4), 448–460.

Parker, A. (2012). How the Hells Angels motorcycle club works, How stuff works. http://auto.howstuffworks.com/hells-angels5.htm. (Accessed April 11, 2012.)

Police. (2010). The Norwegian Police Force's efforts to combat outlaw motorcycle gangs, 2011 to 2015, Norwegian Police Directorate, Oslo, Norway. https://www.politi.no/vedlegg/rapport/Vedlegg_1473.pdf. (Accessed April 11, 2012.)

Quinn, J. and Koch, D.S. (2003). The nature of criminality within one-percent motorcycle clubs, *Deviant Behavior: An Interdisciplinary Journal*, 24(3), 281–305.

Rassel, J. and Komarnicki, J. (2007). Gangs ranked: Crazy dragons head list of Alberta crime threats, *Calgary Herald*, Saturday, July 21, 2007. http://www.canada.com/story.html?id=5f440d79-5e53-4a57-b03d-11be2f2ebff1.

Zollo, M., Minoja, M., Casanova, L., Hockerts, K., Neergaard, P., Schneider, S.C., and Tencati, A. (2009). Towards an internal change management perspective of CSR: Evidence from project RESPONSE on the sources of cognitive alignment between managers and their stakeholders, and their implications for social performance, *Corporate Governance*, 9 (4), 355–372.

16. A Discourse on the Gray Economy, Corruption, and Organized Crime in Slovenia

Katja Eman, Tine Furdi, Rok Hacin, and Bojan Dobovšek

Introduction

The year 2008 represents the beginning of the economic crisis in Europe when people slowly began to drift into the *shadow* economy and illegal activities. Ever since its independence, Slovenia, similar to other countries, has been witnessing ever more complex developments due to changes in the socioeconomic field and in the area of general human values, which influence changes in society as well as in criminal activities (Schneider, 2014). The economy, corruption, and organized crime, which are closely intertwined with the first two phenomena, are also a result of political changes (e.g., instability), economic deregulation, frequent migrations, and insecurities in the labor market.

The purpose of this chapter is to present an overview of organized crime, corruption, and the *gray* economy in Slovenia and identify specificities of the selected types of crime by analyzing statistical data and applying the crime mapping methodology. The authors find that all three analyzed types of crime have recently been increasing. In addition, they observe specificities in terms of the geographical location of analyzed phenomena, since corruption offenses tend to be most frequent in Ljubljana and Maribor, the two largest Slovene cities, while organized crime is more evenly dispersed across Slovenia's territory, even though it is more frequent in the vicinity of major transportation routes (motorway network) and national borders. In the final section of this chapter, the authors discuss potential proposals aimed at responding to identified specificities of analyzed types of crime in Slovenia.

As Pečar (1996) states, crime always reflects the general social conditions, and organized crime, corruption, and the gray economy are no exceptions. Due to political changes (e.g., instability), economic deregulation, frequent migrations, and insecurities in the labor market, the growth of informal economy and self-employment represents an ever more common phenomenon in today's neoliberal society. Decreasing social transfers and (low) tax morality should also be added to the aforementioned underlying causes. According to the Shadow Economy in Europe 2013 report, the gray economy is worth more than

2.15 trillion euros and causes tremendous problems to national governments that try to balance budgets by "avoiding tax increases and benefit cuts that can hamper economic recovery" (Schneider, 2014, p. 3). In transition countries in southeastern Europe, the gray economy amounts to approximately 30% of the size of the official economy, and Slovenia is no exception. Apart from decreased spending and increased taxes, Schneider (2014, p. 7) also emphasizes the following four main factors of the gray economy: (1) savings, (2) lack of a "guilty conscience," (3) low risk of detection, and (4) ease of participation.

Characteristics of Slovenia

Slovenia is a parliamentary democracy, placed at the very top of the scale of economically developed transition countries, with a long tradition in mining and other industrial sectors (which are currently being modernized) and well-developed service sectors. Farming and livestock production are slightly less important, as only about 20% of the country's territory, which amounts to 20,273 km^2 in total, are cultivated. Nevertheless, the number of agricultural holdings focusing on organic farming has recently been increasing. Over two-thirds of the country's territory is covered by forests; however, the share of land dedicated to roads is growing. Slovenia endeavors to achieve sustainable development targets and increase the production and efficient use of renewable energy; in addition, it has recently restructured its waste management policy and increased the share of recycled waste (Hren et al., 2011).

The change in the economic system and the general economic development observed after Slovenia's independence contributed to substantial changes in the Slovene economy after 1991,* since GDP has been increasing since 1993. The highest economic growth was recorded in the period of outstanding economic boom, particularly in 2007, when GDP rose by 6.9% in real terms. In 2009, which was marked by the great economic crisis affecting a considerable part of the developed world, the GDP dropped by 8.1% in real terms, while economic growth was again recorded as early as in 2010, albeit it only reached 1.2%. The state sector represents an important part of Slovenia's economy, which has been recording a financial deficit since 1995 (a significant share of such deficit can be attributed to the manner in which transactions related to the reimbursement of property forfeited after WWII and the completion of denationalization procedures were entered into the bookkeeping system). However, due to the economic crisis, the state sectors' deficit increased significantly in 2009, when it amounted to 6% of the national GDP. In addition, the debt of the Republic of Slovenia also increased. In fact, the national debt was gradually rising before 2004 and Slovenia's accession to the European Union (EU), when it amounted to 27% of the GDP, after which it had been decreasing until the end of 2008. In 2009, the national debt rose by a whopping 35% due to the economic crisis and amounted to 12,449 million euros (Statistical Office of the Republic of Slovenia, 2010).

Centralization of activities and services in the very heart of the country, that is, in Ljubljana, the capital, is typical of Slovenia. In 1995, Slovenia's territory was divided into 147 municipalities on the local level (there were 211 municipalities in 2010). However, the level of economic development is not the same in all Slovene regions. In terms of regional GDP per capita, the Osrednjeslovenska region† (Central Slovenia region) stands out the most. On the other hand, the Pomurska region records the lowest share of GDP per capita. Despite the disparity of financial conditions in the country, Slovene households were among the most economical in the EU after 2005, as they manage to save 15% of their disposable income on average (Hren et al., 2011).

Apart from the financial crisis and high level of unemployment, which have been pestering the country since 2011, the issue that the Slovene public has been drawing attention to primarily refers to the impact of politicians and other "political games," such as corruption has had on the economy and other fields. Politicians, serving their own interests, were acquiring necessary power both in economic (increase of taxes and goods available on the market, decrease of salaries)

* The structure of the economy changed significantly; the share of agricultural activities in the GDP decreased by more than 50%, that is, from 5.7% of the GDP in 1991 to 2.4% in 2010; the share of industry and construction dropped from 44% of the GDP in 1991 to 31% in 2010, while the share of services increased substantially, that is, from 50% in 1991 to 67% in 2010 (Hren et al., 2011, pp. 51–52).

† After 1995, the Osrednjeslovenska region has been increasing its lead with respect to the average GDP. In 2008, it recorded a 42% higher GDP per capita in comparison with the Slovene average (Hren et al., 2011, p. 53).

and legal terms (the adoption of legal acts benefiting individuals and taking advantage of legal loopholes), as well as by exploiting recession to accumulate financial resources and causing instability in the country. Slovenia is thus witnessing important changes in companies' management and an extremely heated response from the public with respect to the conduct of managers before their replacement. It was, in fact, the mere pressure exerted by the public that brought economic crime among politicians to an end, since the public could no longer bear corruptive conduct and false promises, in particular (with respect to employment, decreasing taxes, and lowering the price of goods). Politically motivated staffing and numerous changes in managerial positions, which can be observed before and after the handover of power to another political party, are particularly alarming. An overview of research in the field of crime shows that systemic corruption is a crucial issue in Slovenia. It is reflected in the inability to control elites, in the period of uncontrolled privatization, and in relation to the financial and economic crime, whereby organized crime also contributes its share of corruption.

In this chapter, the authors present an overview of organized crime, corruption, and the gray economy in Slovenia and identify the specificities of selected types of crime by analyzing statistical data and applying the crime mapping methodology.

Organized Crime

Slovenia boasts of a unique geographical position between Western and Eastern Europe and the north–south border. Slovenia is renowned for its diversity, as it combines different landscapes from Alpine and Dinaric to Pannonian and Karstic. It is also a transit country for (organized) criminal groups, which merely store their "precious cargo" on its territory or, most often, simply carry it through the country via the so-called Balkan drugs route. Due to the aforementioned facts affecting the economy, Slovenia cannot avoid risks and threats posed by organized crime, which has been penetrating different economic sectors and destabilizing the country's system in the past decade, despite the fact that Slovenia has been a member of the EU for 10 years and is actively cooperating with Europol and other investigating bodies.

Organized criminal groups are characterized by their formalized structure (particularly in the field of criminal entrepreneurship), while the generation of money through illegal activities is their primary goal. They maintain their position in society through threats, violence, bribery of state officials, and extortion and have a significant influence on people, local communities, regions, or entire states (Federal Bureau of Investigation, 2014). According to the Council of Europe, the sphere of organized crime includes "illegal activities carried out by a structured group of three or more persons, existing for a period of time and acting in concert with the aim of committing serious crimes through the use of threats, violence, corruption, or other means in order to obtain, directly or indirectly, financial or other material benefits" (Dobovšek, 2012, p. 37).

Due to the rapid development of technologies and changing legislation, the activities of organized crime differed through the years. Šorli (1998) defines organized crime as an "activity with which criminal groups commit criminal offenses in an entrepreneurial manner and expressly use violence, threats of violence and (or) corruption to achieve their goals" (Dobovšek, 2012, p. 41), which clearly indicates its link to the economy. Finckenauer and Veronim (2001), who are of a similar opinion, take it a step further and define organized crime as an act committed by criminal groups that operate for longer periods of time by conducting criminal activities for which they systematically use elements of violence and corruption. Such criminal groups are also capable of causing economic, physical, psychological, and social damage. The greater their ability to cause damage, the more serious the threat they pose to the entire society (Klaus, 2011).

Organized crime is a "modern phenomenon that manifests itself as the fifth branch of power." Apart from the standard three branches of power, that is, legislative, executive, and judicial powers, as well as the media, which have often been analyzed and declared the fourth branch of power, global processes are ever more often subject to the struggle for world supremacy by organized crime groups, which represent the fifth, completely independent, branch of power. Organized crime appears as a source of threat to two fundamental functions of the state, that is, the collection of taxes and the use of force. The means that criminal organizations have at their disposal today enable them to destroy countries' economies and devalue social values. In order to define this phenomenon, Dobovšek (2012, p. 43) lists key elements of organized crime, which include "power; profit; premeditated crime; structured organisational scheme; self-preservation; success; access to goods through crime; continued activity; secrecy of operation; control; corruption; complex detection; efforts to obtain immunity; intimidation and the use of force; non-impulsiveness."

Table 16.1 shows that the police in Slovenia deal with 230 criminal offenses related to organized crime groups on average, out of which drug trafficking and grand theft are the most prominent. The share of fraud and firearms trafficking is also high. However, it must be stressed that the given data include offenses that were detected and recorded by the police, whereby parts of organized crime remain in the gray area, as they are never detected and processed.

Slovenia is influenced by criminal activities conducted on the main Balkan route, where drug trafficking (Dobovšek, 2012) and trafficking in human beings represent the most prominent offenses. At the same time, the free movement of goods into Central Europe is also increasing due to the abolition of customs duties between European countries. An increase of crime was also recorded particularly with respect to the smuggling of migrants from countries that are currently undergoing different types of "revolutions" and changes (e.g., in Syria). The emergence of links between organized crime and gray economy in individual countries was also detected, as individual infamous cases of corruption and business fraud have recently been made public (e.g., the Balkan Warrior drug case, the Patria bribery case, the NKBM bank fraud case).

Characteristics of Organized Crime can be summarized as follows:

- The main purpose of organized crime is to commit criminal offenses in order to acquire power and generate profits.
- Organized crime is an integral part of the most serious forms of crime, since individuals come together in a structured organization whose illegal activities damage the state system.
- It is the organization that creates its own rules within its internal structure, which reflect its operation (secrecy, tasks, etc.)—experts have identified the bureaucratic corporatist model and the patrimonial model (the latter is typical of Slovenia, as organizations are based on family ties).
- Organized crime differs in its operation—apart from classic types of crime (e.g., prostitution, drugs), it also includes more complex forms of entrepreneurial crime and the crime of political elites, which is nowadays most often observed in transition countries, while individual forms are also present in Slovenia.
- Organized crime is nowadays extremely active in the field of corruption and extortion with the aim of achieving a certain goal or purpose—through corruption, it is penetrating all spheres of the state system (e.g., politics, police, courts).

Table 16.1 Criminal Offenses of Organized Crime in Slovenia during the 2008–2013 Period

	2008	2009	2010	2011	2012	2013
Manslaughter	0	0	0	1	0	0
Illegal crossing of state borders or state territory	0	4	12	2	0	18
Illicit manufacturing of or trafficking in firearms and explosives	10	17	3	4	0	2
Abuse of prostitution	3	0	0	0	0	1
Illicit manufacturing of and trafficking in narcotic drugs, illicit substances in sports, and drug precursors	96	345	79	164	78	141
Grand theft	5	38	44	37	25	32
Robbery	22	1	0	0	0	0
Fraud	30	18	23	24	23	21
Extortion	1	19	11	10	6	7
Total	**167**	**442**	**172**	**242**	**132**	**222**

Source: General Police Directorate, Planning and Analysis Section, 2013.

- Organized crime activities are noticeably shifting from local, regional, and national levels to the transnational level, which fosters the cooperation between and further intertwining of new criminal networks around the world.
- Money laundering is an important element of organized crime, as it enables criminal organizations to transform proceeds of crime into legitimate money while causing damage to the state.

Corruption

Corruption represents an important issue and a threat to modern society, as it continues to avoid preventive mechanisms despite constant efforts aimed at reducing its existence and impacts. Each corruptive activity has two sides, the briber and the bribed, whereby both sides benefit from such an activity (Dobovšek, 2012). Due to the nature of this phenomenon, it is possible to presume that there is an extensive gray area of corruption. Offenses that remain undetected and consequently affect the functioning of the entire state can be observed in the state's economic situation (poverty and the rise of organized crime), social aspects (unemployment), as well as in an unjust and discriminatory division of citizens (privileges and informal networks within the system).

Corrupt political interests arise with a view to obtain greater personal property, whereby different corrupt methods are used to shift the entire burden on citizens' shoulders. This causes "ostensible" damage to the people (e.g., by increasing taxes), as politicians attempt to cover their corruption offenses by adopting legitimate legal acts. However, by doing so, they harm the interests of the state, thus contributing to the decrease of trust in politics, political elites, and political parties (Dobovšek and Miklavčič, 2010).* Consequently, the level of mistrust is then also transferred to other authorities of formal social control.

Corruption stands for any type of violation due conduct, the main purpose of which is to obtain benefit for oneself or for a third party. In Slovenia, the official definition of corruption can be found in Article 18 of the Integrity and Prevention of Corruption Act† (2011). It states: "Any violation of due conduct by officials and responsible persons in the public or private sector, as well as the conduct of persons initiating such violations or of persons benefiting from them, for the purpose of undue benefit promised, offered or given directly or indirectly, or for the purpose of undue benefit demanded, accepted or expected for one's own advantage or to the advantage of any other person" constitutes corruption.

The problem of corruption in Slovenia is mainly reflected in the inability of investigators to determine the extent of corruption. According to the Commission for the Prevention of Corruption‡ (2013), the most

* In Slovenia, such examples can be observed in the more prominent news reports focusing on individual politicians involved in approving or authorizing business deals with suppliers bidding in procurement procedures, who belong to their own circles, and signing different contracts (for obtaining an illegal loan or project funds). The involvement of politicians in criminal networks characterized by transnational crime and the awarding of business deals could also be emphasized (the Patria case, suspicious dealings in the TEŠ6 case [construction of a new thermal power plant facility], etc.).

† Apart from the Integrity and Prevention of Corruption Act (2011), the area of corruption and its prevention is also regulated by the Prevention of Corruption Act (2004), Rules of Procedure of the Commission for the Prevention of Corruption (2012), Resolution on the Prevention of Corruption in the Republic of Slovenia (2006), Rules on Limitations and Duties Imposed upon Public Officials with Respect to Receiving Gifts (2010), and the Incompatibility of Holding Public Office with Profitable Activity Act (1992). The field of corruption is also regulated by numerous international acts signed by the Republic of Slovenia: (1) Convention on Combating Bribery of Foreign Public Officials in International Business Transactions (OECD, 1997); (2) United Nations Convention on Transnational Organised Crime (UN, 2000); (3) United Nations Convention against Corruption (UN, 2003); (4) Convention Drawn up on the Basis of Article K.3 (2) (c) of the Treaty on European Union on the Fight Against Corruption Involving Officials of the European Communities or Officials of Member States of the European Union (EU, 2000); (5) Civil Law Convention on Corruption (Council of Europe, 1999a); and (6) Criminal Law Convention on Corruption (Council of Europe, 1999b).

‡ The CPC assumes the role of the principal actor in the fight against corruption; its functioning is not merely repressive, since it also endeavors to prevent corruption through its research activities. In doing so, the CPC cooperates with numerous nongovernmental and civil society organizations, such as Društvo Integriteta—Transparency International Slovenia. In carrying out research activities related to the detection of corruption and in-depth studies of the concept of corruption as such, the CPC has also been successfully cooperating with the Faculty of Criminal Justice and Security of the University of Maribor and the Faculty of Law of the University of Maribor. Furthermore, the CPC cooperates with the Slovene Information Commissioner in the field of access to public information and with the Slovene Human Rights Ombudsman in the field of protection of human rights and fundamental freedoms. Since 2011, the CPC has been conducting the majority of investigations in the fields related to the political system and justice (CPC, 2013; Dimc, 2012, pp. 23–25).

frequent causes of corruption in Slovenia include weaknesses identified in the management of organizations and conduct of procedures, lack of control, lack of adequate ethical standards, lack of appropriate education and training of employees, inconsistent and unjust sanctioning of violations in society and/or organizations, abuse of the freedom of choice, and poor exchange of information. A substantial gap between the officially identified corruption and its perception by the citizens appears to be a specific issue in Slovenia. The Commission for the Prevention of Corruption (henceforth CPC) finds that the level of corruption exceeds official statistical data; however, it still does not amount to the level identified by public opinion polls. It also observes the mutual links between corruption and other criminal activities, and the constant presence of an international dimension (CPC, 2013).

Dimc (2012, pp. 20–22) states that independent international indicators, unlike national ones, point to the fact that the level of corruption in Slovenia is stagnating or that it is not increasing. According to CPC's assessments, the extent of damage caused by corruption in the Republic of Slovenia ranges between 1.5% and 2% of GDP, which amounts to between 531 and 708 million EUR. In the framework of Transparency International's* Corruption Perception Index, which indicates the experts' perception of corruption in the public sector and politics, Slovenia ranked 43rd in 2013 (it held 37th place in 2012). Results show that corruption is perceived as a serious problem in the country and that its people distrust political and judicial institutions responsible for the prevention of corruption. Respondents defined political parties, the parliament, judiciary, public administration, and the media as institutions in which they perceived the strongest presence of corruption (Transparency International, 2013).

In 2013, Ernst & Young, the American financial agency, published results of a research study that saw the participation of 3459 enterprises from 36 countries (22 of which were EU member states) involved in corruption. Slovenia was identified as the country with the highest level of corruption in the European Union. Most irregularities were detected with respect to the publication of enterprises' business results and giving bribes as part of a regular business practice (Ernst & Young, 2013).

In May 2013, GRECO (Group of States against Corruption)† issued a report in which it recognizes improvements with respect to integrity rules for members of parliament, judges, and prosecutors in the Republic of Slovenia. Furthermore, the report acknowledges positive features of the newly introduced Internet-based system for reporting corruption. At the same time, however, the report states that the education and training of public officials in the field of integrity and conflicts of interest is insufficient. The report also points to an inadequate implementation of the legal framework in the field of corruption prevention (Council of Europe, 2013).

Table 16.2 presents criminal offenses with elements of corruption that were committed in Slovenia between 2008 and 2013, as categorized in the Criminal Code of the Republic of Slovenia (KZ-1, 2012).

Table 16.2 clearly shows that the number of corruption offenses was increasing in the 2008–2013 period and that it reached its peak in 2010. It is possible to observe that the number of corruption offenses grew by almost one-third between 2008 and 2010, followed by an almost two-thirds decrease between 2010 and 2012, and increased again in 2013. The abuse of office or official privileges, as well as giving or accepting bribes, are the most common types of corruption. The lowest number of corruption offenses are recorded with respect to obstructing the freedom of choice and accepting bribes during elections or ballot. On the basis of such data, one may conclude that the perpetrators of corruption offenses mostly include people in certain positions, who attempt to influence certain procedures and decisions, and not those who try to acquire a given position by influencing elections or ballot.

Official statistical data show an increase in corruption offenses in the Republic of Slovenia, which is in direct contrast with statements made by international organizations claiming that the level of corruption in Slovenia is stagnating. Results of national public opinion polls also demonstrate the spread of corruption and the general distrust of the public toward political parties and public institutions. The main reasons for the growth of detected corruption offenses can be found

* Transparency International (TI) is one of the leading nongovernmental organizations dealing with the analysis and suppression of corruption. It publishes renowned annual statistics reports, which indicate the level of corruption in individual countries around the globe (Meško, 2009).

† GRECO is a body of the Council of Europe whose objective is to improve the capacity of its members to fight corruption by monitoring their compliance with anticorruption standards. It helps its member states to identify deficiencies in national anticorruption policies prompting the necessary legislative, institutional, and practical reforms. GRECO currently comprises 48 European states and the United States (Council of Europe, 2013).

Table 16.2 Corruption Offenses in Slovenia during the 2008–2013 Period

	2008	2009	2010	2011	2012	2013
Giving gifts for illegal intervention	1	6	4	0	0	1
Giving bribes	4	6	27	8	6	16
Taking bribes	12	20	25	12	5	9
Obstruction of freedom of choice	1	0	3	0	1	0
Unauthorized giving of gifts	2	2	3	4	1	8
Unauthorized acceptance of gifts	10	3	3	5	2	13
Accepting benefits for illegal intermediation	7	9	4	3	2	3
Acceptance of bribe during the election or ballot	0	0	2	0	0	0
Abuse of office or official privileges	159	134	198	75	84	212
Total	196	180	269	108	101	262

Source: General Police Directorate, Planning and Analysis Section, 2013.

in: better equipment of law enforcement authorities for detecting corruption offenses; less efficient operation of perpetrators giving or accepting bribes; successful suppression of corruption by law enforcement authorities; and reduced fear of consequences resulting from the reporting of corruption (slow functioning of courts and short criminal sanctions for corruption offenses).

In Slovenia, corruption can be linked to organized crime, as the issue of corruption appears on a systemic level where the perpetrators of corruption offenses are persons holding a political or other position that provides them with a certain degree of immunity and protection against consequences. In addition, corruption has a direct impact on the extent of gray economy, since entrepreneurs find themselves in a hopeless position if they lack resources that would enable them to "successfully obtain" business deals.

The Gray Economy

The *gray economy* is defined as the generation of revenues on the basis of legitimate or legal activities or on the basis of illegitimate or illegal activities without paying any taxes. Nastav (2009) stresses that the production of goods and services in an individual country serves as the main criterion for defining the strength and size of its economy, which is known as gross domestic product (GDP). According to all economic rules, the GDP should comprise the entire production in a given space and time, however, a certain part of production in an individual country has always avoided official records and remained hidden and uncontrolled. This phenomenon is most often known as the gray economy, while the term illegal economy is also in use. Dobovšek and Kuhar (2009, p. 64) list the types of gray economy, which also include underground economy, shadow economy, black economy, parallel economy, and the black market (Black Economy, 2007). The field of the gray economy is not only extremely vast but also quite diverse, as it can be observed in commercial and noncommercial sectors, as well as in legal and illegal activities.

Nastav (2009, p. 28), similar to Dallago (1990, p. 150), believes that there are four factors contributing to the functioning of a gray economy: (1) technology, (2) cost structure, (3) national regulatory framework, and (4) flexibility. Even though the causes for the emergence of the gray economy include diverse factors, which differ from one another in time and space, researchers (Kyle, 2001; Schneider and Enste, 2002; Williams, 2004; Choi and Thum, 2005; Nastav, 2009) categorize these into the following groups: (1) high tax burdens (taxes and other contributions); (2) different crisis conditions in the economy (economic crisis and irregularities found in the functioning of a state); (3) frequent and cumbersome administrative barriers, that is, bureaucratization (excessively long and complex procedures and high standards); (4) inefficiency of control systems in the field of detection and prosecution of illegal (gray) production; (5) corruption; (6) poorly functioning system of pension, health, and unemployment insurance (poorly functioning systems and inefficient control and sanctioning of violations); and (7) desire to claim social assistance in an unjustified manner (insufficient income and unregulated systems, social assistance in cash and social transfers for the unemployed).

The consequences of the gray economy can be split into two parts: *negative consequences* (the loss of a state's tax revenues; reduced efficiency of the economy resulting from the fact that enterprises are focused on avoiding administrative burdens instead of increasing their productivity; suppression of opportunities for the development of the human factor; inadequate or low-quality products and services); and *positive consequences* (lower prices for goods and services due to unissued invoices and undeclared taxes; employment, source of income, and subsistence; absence of complex bureaucracy).

The actors are the ones who work in the gray economy, that is, suppliers of goods and providers of services, and those who buy products and services that were produced or provided in the gray economy. Actors operating in the field of the gray economy typically include individuals with lower income; the unemployed (regardless of their gender or age); youth in full-time education (extending the time of third-level education, high dropout rates at faculties, etc.); working age population, which, however, is not in employment (housewives, pensioners, and other nonworking groups); registered unemployed persons; and employed and self-employed persons. The European Commission report (2007) states that there are twice as many men dealing with the gray economy than women and that almost half of them fall into the 15–24 age bracket. Results also indicate that the participation in gray economy is decreasing with age. Researchers (Tanzi, 1982; Dobovšek and Kuhar, 2009; Nastav, 2009) categorize the perpetrators of offenses related to the gray economy into four sectors: (1) households,[*] (2) informal sector,[†] (3) illegal sector,[‡] and (4) crime sector.[§]

The gray economy is a phenomenon that includes a range of activities,[¶] which are present in all countries, including in the Republic of Slovenia. The causes of gray economy in Slovenia include the acquisition of monetary benefits, excessive administrative barriers, high tax burdens, and the desire to exercise the right to social assistance in an unjustified manner (Dobovšek and Kuhar, 2009; Nastav, 2009). However, the labor market characterized by a high degree of inflexibility also contributes its share of causes for the emergence of gray economy (Slovenia is attempting to combat the lack of flexibility by adopting provisions contained in the Prevention of Undeclared Work and Employment Act, 2012, the Employment Relationships Act, 2013, and the Labor Market Regulation Act, 2013). Also, "In Slovenia, the otherwise typical economic sectors (that appear in other research studies) are also important in terms of gray economy: agriculture, processing activities, construction, trade in and repair of motor vehicles, hospitality sector, education and other public, collective and personal services" (Nastav, 2009, p. 5).

The Republic of Slovenia is witnessing the actualization of the theoretical model of gray economy developed by Choi and Thum (2005). According to this model, corruption in the formal sector leads to an increase in the gray economy. In the past few years, Slovenia has witnessed several cases of corruption in high-level political and economic circles; at the same time, it was dealing with increasing levels of the gray economy among its population (in 2009, the gray economy in Slovenia ranged between 15% and 20%, while in 2013, it had already reached 23% of the GDP) (Nastav, 2009; Schneider and Enste, 2013).

In Slovenia, the consequences of the gray economy can also be divided into negative and positive ones. Negative consequences of the gray economy can be observed in the loss of the country's tax revenues (loss of revenues originating in labor tax, social security contributions, consumption tax, income tax, and capital

[*] This sector produces goods and services and uses them at the same time. Tanzi (1982) states that it is difficult to measure this sector, as it does not trade in goods.

[†] This sector consists of small-scale producers and their employees, which can sell their products and services (Dobovšek and Kuhar, 2009).

[‡] This sector comprises activities that include tax evasion, avoidance of statutory provisions, and other types of tax fraud (Tanzi, 1982).

[§] This sector typically involves illegal and illegitimate production and distribution (e.g., theft, manufacturing of and trafficking of drugs, prostitution, and trafficking of human beings).

[¶] Glas (1991) lists the following activities in the field of the gray economy: undeclared and thus untaxed work (usually paid in cash); smuggling; illegal gambling; employment without the required work permit; illicit trade of drugs, tobacco, and alcohol products; barter trading; work and repairs carried out by individuals themselves; issuing of excessively high invoices for business expenses; the use of work materials and tools for private benefits; illegal prostitution; work and pay while receiving sickness or unemployment benefits; production of own fruit, vegetables, and other produce and their sale; usurious money lending; performance of undeclared economic activity or economic activity declared in a lesser extent than it is actually performed; illicit trade in real-estate and other goods and services, the income of which is not declared to tax authorities; tips not declared to tax authorities; stealing from customers and staff; landlord tax evasion, etc.

gains or corporation tax), reduced efficiency of economy, suppression of opportunities for the development of the human factor, and inadequate, poor-quality, or low-quality products. Positive consequences of the gray economy can be found in additional income of individuals, which leads to higher purchasing power and prosperity of the population, higher levels of employment, and the emergence of small entrepreneurs or the development of business ideas (Nastav, 2009).

Despite the fact that a substantial share of cases involve corruption, the gray economy, and even organized crime are never detected and recorded, the authors attempt to identify the main features and predominant locations (or trends) of the aforementioned phenomena in the territory of the Republic of Slovenia by drawing up a map that indicates the spatial distribution of analyzed types of crime.

Analysis of Organized Crime, Corruption, and the Gray Economy in Slovenia

In this section, organized crime and corruption are examined on the basis of a statistical data analysis (Graph 16.1) and the graphic presentation of *criminal offenses of organized crime** (manslaughter, illegal crossing of state borders or state territory, illicit manufacturing of or trafficking in firearms and explosives, abuse of prostitution, illicit manufacturing of and trafficking in narcotic drugs, illicit substances in sports and drug precursors, grand theft, robbery, fraud, and extortion) and *corruption criminal offenses* (giving gifts for illegal intervention, giving bribes, taking bribes, obstruction of freedom of choice, unauthorized giving of gifts, unauthorized acceptance of gifts, accepting benefits for illegal intermediation, acceptance of bribe during the election or ballot, and abuse of office or official privileges) in the period between 2008 and 2013. Graph 16.1 shows the distribution of criminal offenses of organized crime and corruption during the 2008–2013 period. The gray economy phenomenon cannot be depicted on the basis of the criminal offenses' records, which is why findings related to the gray economy are presented in a descriptive manner.

Graph 16.1 shows the distribution of criminal offenses of organized crime and corruption between 2008 and 2013. It is clear that the number of detected organized crime offenses in 2009, 2011, and 2012 is higher than the detected corruption offenses. Organized crime offenses reached their peak in 2009, while the highest number of corruption offenses was recorded in 2010. Both groups of criminal offenses saw an increase in the number of detected offenses between 2008 and 2013. The previous graph shows a decrease of both types of offenses until 2012, which was followed by a sharp increase in 2013. It has to be stressed that due to the consequences of the economic crisis, which could be observed at all levels of formal social control, the Republic of Slovenia has been intensifying its control and the prosecution of corruption, organized crime, and particularly undeclared work, as well as other types of gray economy activities since 2010 and 2011. The results of this intensification of control could also be reflected in the increase of police statistics.

A graphic presentation of the distribution of organized crime and corruption offenses is shown in Figures 16.1 and 16.2.

Results obtained through the analysis of data regarding organized crime offenses from the database

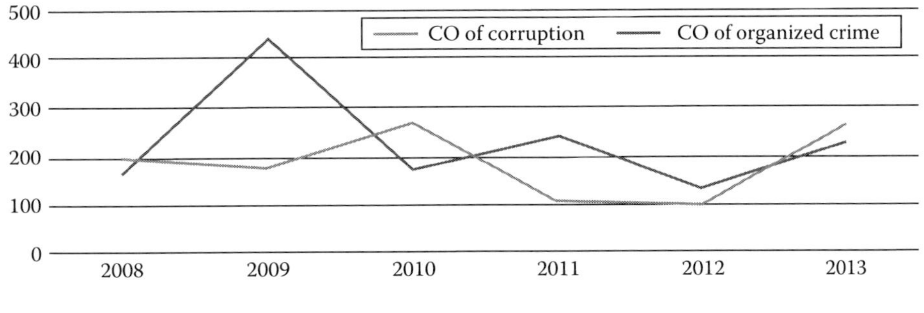

GRAPH 16.1 Distribution of criminal offenses of organized crime and corruption. CO, criminal offense.

* Out of all types of criminal offenses listed earlier, only those that are defined as consequences of organized crime in the Criminal Code of the Republic of Slovenia are shown on crime maps.

Chapter 16

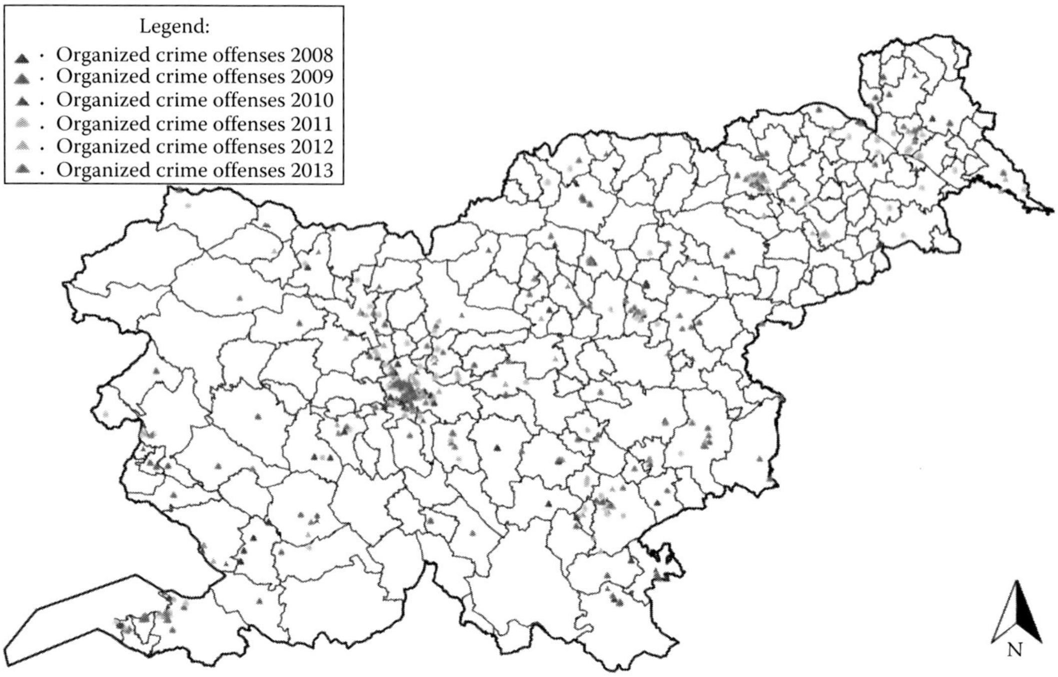

FIGURE 16.1 Concentration of organized crime offenses in Slovenia between 2008 and 2013. (From the General Police Directorate, 2013.)

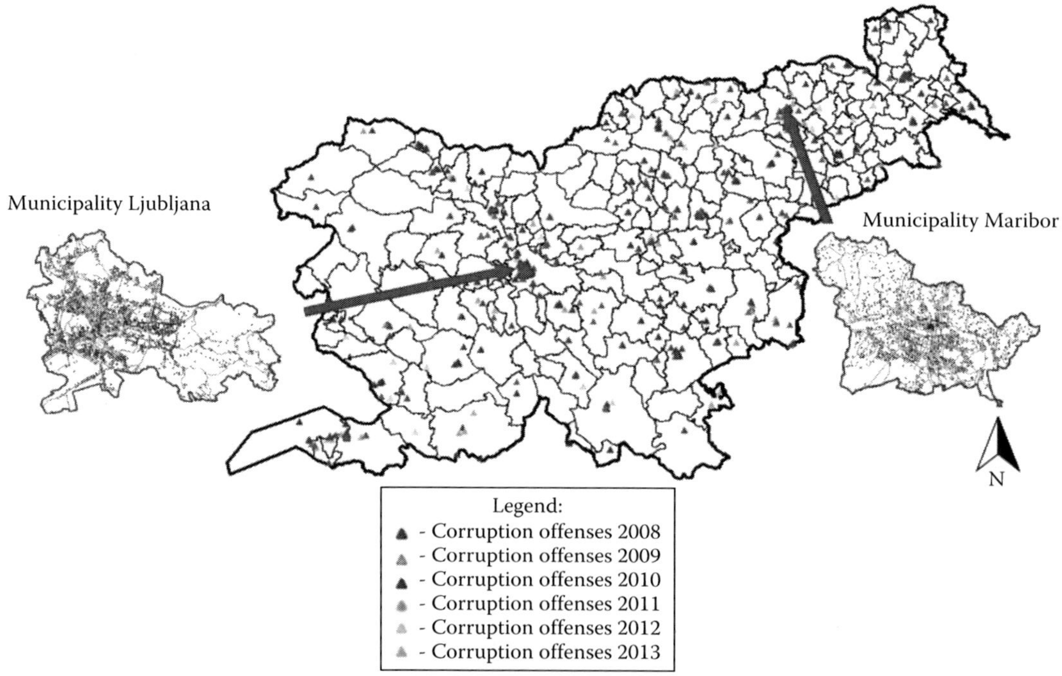

FIGURE 16.2 Concentration of corruption offenses in Slovenia between 2008 and 2013. (From the General Police Directorate, 2013.)

containing geolocations of offenses in the 2008–2013 period demonstrate that two offenses, that is, fraud (30) and robbery (22), were particularly prominent in 2008. These two offenses also depict a crime pattern that involves a larger number of offenses along the main transport routes leading from the southwestern part of Slovenia (Primorska region) toward Central Slovenia and from the northern part of Slovenia into the area of Ljubljana and then toward the southeast national border. The highest level of crime was identified in the area of the Ljubljana Police Directorate (PD), where the abuse of prostitution (3) was the most outstanding criminal offense, as it was detected most frequently in 2008.

In 2009, the number of criminal offenses was the highest in comparison with the remaining period, since a total of 442 criminal offenses were recorded. The most prominent criminal offenses include extortion (19), illicit manufacturing of and trafficking in narcotic drugs (345), and illicit manufacturing of or trafficking in firearms (17). These offenses were most often committed in the southwestern part of Slovenia (primarily along the border and in the coastal area) and in the southeastern part of Slovenia (in the area of the Maribor PD and in border towns covered by the Murska Sobota PD). The area of the Ljubljana PD is also worth mentioning, as it records the highest number of drug-related criminal offenses.

In 2011, grand theft (44) was the most common criminal offense, which appears in the northern part of Slovenia, moves to the central urban part of the Ljubljana PD area, and is then evenly distributed along the northwestern and southeastern parts of Slovenia. Extortion and illicit manufacturing of and trafficking in firearms represent the predominant criminal offenses in the Primorska region, particularly along the border with Italy. The year 2011 was a specific year, since manslaughter committed in the Ljubljana PD area appears for the first time in the analyzed period. Apart from that, the criminal offenses involving illicit drug trafficking in the area of larger towns (Koper, Ljubljana, Novo Mesto, Celje, and Murska Sobota) and grand theft emerging along the major transport routes in Central Slovenia are also rather distinctive. The earlier map demonstrates that the comparison between 2010 and 2011 reveals a shift in the location of organized crime offenses, as these moved from the northeastern part of Slovenia (from the Maribor PD toward the entire area of the Murska Sobota PD), and an increase in crime in the central part of the Ljubljana PD area.

In 2012, the level of crime was at its lowest, with 132 criminal offenses recorded. Figure 16.1 shows that crime is spreading and shifting from the central part of Slovenia toward its northwestern part (extortion and illicit manufacturing of and trafficking in narcotic drugs are prevailing). The year 2012 is a rather interesting year, since a higher concentration of criminal offenses in a single area, that is, in the Ljubljana and Maribor Police Directorates, can be observed, which include elevated numbers of fraud and illicit manufacturing of and trafficking in narcotic drugs.

The year 2013 is also specific, as crime is spreading from Central Slovenia to the upper northwestern part of Slovenia, where criminal offenses are then dispersed around the entire area of the Celje, Novo Mesto, and Maribor PD. Most prominent criminal offenses include illicit manufacturing of and trafficking in narcotic drugs, fraud, and illegal crossing of state borders or state territory. This year is also is marked by the reemergence of the abuse of prostitution, which occurs in the border area of the Murska Sobota PD.

It can be concluded that the illicit manufacturing of and trafficking in narcotic drugs represents the most significant and serious issue, since the analysis of this type of crime shows that it is evenly distributed across the entire territory of Slovenia. In this context, the so-called Balkan route should also be mentioned, as it enables the movement of different "goods" from other countries, whereby Slovenia normally holds the status of a transit country, even though it is also increasingly becoming a country of destination. Results show that the illegal crossing of state borders or state territory is increasing. The same holds true for grand theft, which most often occurs along major transportation routes (north–south and east–west motorway routes) and involves organized crime groups of Bulgarian, Romanian, and Hungarian origin (the Roma are also often involved) that conduct their activities close to larger cities.

Figure 16.2 shows the concentration of corruption offenses in two of the largest Slovene cities, that is, Ljubljana (the capital and administrative center of the Osrednjeslovenska [Central Slovenia] region) and Maribor (the administrative center of the Podravska region). Higher concentrations of corruption offenses can also be observed in towns acting as administrative centers of other Slovene regions (Koper in the Primorska region, Kranj in the Gorenjska region, Slovenj Gradec in the Koroška region, Krško in the Posavje region, Novo Mesto in the Dolenjska region, Murska Sobota in the Prekmurje region, Trbovlje in the Zasavje region, and Celje in the Savinjska region). The findings of an in-depth analysis of corruption offenses in Ljubljana and Maribor show that these criminal offenses are concentrated in city centers. This is not surprising, as official statistical data show that the most common type of corruption involves the abuse of office or official privileges and giving or taking bribes, and the majority of administrative bodies and business organizations in Ljubljana and Maribor are actually based in buildings located in city centers.

By analyzing individual types of criminal offenses, the authors of this chapter identified the most common perpetrators of corruption offenses in Ljubljana: (1) abuse of office or official privileges (local community body, government office, ministry, hospital, court, prosecutor's office, and the police), (2) unauthorized acceptance of gifts (National Bureau of Investigation), and (3) accepting benefits for illegal intermediation (the police). Furthermore, the authors found that the most common form of giving or taking bribes involves cash and securities. The same analytical method was then applied to criminal offenses committed in the municipality of Maribor, which yielded the following results: (1) abuse of office or official privileges (prosecutor's office, court, local community body, secondary vocational school, and professional college), (2) unauthorized acceptance and unauthorized giving of gifts (administrative body), and (3) giving or taking bribes (government offices and administrative body). It was also determined that the most common form of giving or taking bribes involved cash transactions. A comparison of the two analyses shows that the situation is quite similar in both cities, since the most common perpetrators of corruption offenses include local community bodies, government offices, prosecutor's offices, and courts, while the most common form of giving or taking bribes involves cash transactions.

The emergence of the economic crisis in Slovenia has revealed numerous examples of poor management in state-owned companies and within the government as such. An overview of factors contributing to the emergence of the gray economy shows that the following factors are particularly prominent in Slovenia: (1) high tax burdens (Slovenia has the highest taxes in comparison with other EU member states), (2) crisis conditions in the field of economy, (3) numerous and substantial administrative barriers, (4) problems related to the implementation of (criminal law) legislation and consequently to the detection and prosecution of illegal activities, (5) corruption, (6) poorly functioning system of pension and health insurance, and (7) unregulated system of social assistance in cash and social transfers for the unemployed.

In the recent period, a campaign launched by the tax administration of the Republic of Slovenia proved to be one of the most successful responses against the gray economy in Slovenia. The tax administration called upon customers in catering establishments and bars to take a photograph of the invoice they received and send it to tax authorities, which then verified whether individual invoices had been recorded in the system and thus appropriately taxed. Tax evasion in the hospitality sector is (was) one of the more significant issues in the field of gray economy in Slovenia. The performance of control and inspection activities in enterprises aimed at prosecuting undeclared work, during which the police checked employees and activities of small-scale bakers and confectioners across Slovenia, as well as the activities of undeclared car repair shops, proved to be much less successful.

Discussion

In transition countries, which also include Slovenia, the gray economy is linked to corruption in the broadest sense of the word, which is why both of these phenomena require a coordinated and mutual response. One should also not forget the involvement of organized crime, since both gray economy and corruption represent its source or method for generating substantial profits. All three types of illegal conduct threaten the long-term stability of countries (tax transfers), democracy and the rule of law, authorities carrying out formal social control (primarily the criminal law system), other institutions responsible for supervising and, in particular, preventing the gray economy and corruption, as well as the system of values and morality, where integrity and honesty hold a particularly important position. Due to the fact that the aforementioned phenomena are closely linked to the economy, where they cause the suppression of economic development, Miklavčič and Dobovšek (2014, p. 17) emphasize that the civil society's trust into the state and its institutions is decreasing.

Activities for the prevention or reduction of the gray economy in Slovenia are focusing on two fundamental tasks: (1) elimination of causes for the emergence of gray economy and (2) intensified detection and sanctioning of persons participating in gray economy (Omerzu and Starc, 2001). The state attempts to eliminate causes for the emergence of gray economy by rationalizing the system of social transfers and introducing more appropriate policies enabling individuals to move from gray economy into official economy (Dobovšek and Kuhar, 2009; Nastav, 2009). The second task, which involves intensified detection and sanctioning of people participating in gray economy, is implemented by supervising authorities (labor and market inspectorates, tax administration, the police, the Commission of the Government of the Republic of Slovenia for the Detection and Prevention of Undeclared Work and Employment, and other inspection services) (Prevention of Undeclared Work and Employment Act, 2012). Police powers with respect to reducing the extent of the gray economy include indirect control or prevention of undeclared work and employment, as well as different possibilities of the criminal police for detecting the gray economy in the scope of investigations related to economic and organized crime (Dobovšek and Kuhar, 2009), and corruption.

Positive changes brought about by the amendments to the Integrity and Prevention of Corruption Act (2011) can be observed in the following improvements.

The transformation of the CPC into a minor offense authority, the obligation imposed on public institutions concerning the implementation of regular integrity plans, the regulation of lobbying (obligatory registration of lobbyists and transparent access to public institutions and persons that are required to announce lobbyists' visits), the protection of individuals who report corruption offenses; the online application entitled Supervizor,* and the duty of the CPC to report directly to the Slovene parliament (in the past, the CPC reported to a special parliamentary commission), which decreases the possibility to exert political influence upon it (Integrity and Prevention of Corruption Act, 2011; Dimc, 2012, pp. 23–25).

Slovenia has recently witnessed tremendous changes in the cooperation between different institutions, which enables them to exchange infinite quantities of information and establish an important liaison between security bodies performing everyday operational tasks in the field of organized crime. It recorded an increase in the efficiency of operations and particularly in the speed with which Slovene courts deal with individual cases on a daily basis (the Judiciary of the Republic of Slovenia [*Sodstvo Republike Slovenije*], 2013). Important activities aimed at encouraging the general public to report such criminal offenses and raising its awareness in this field have also been launched, since public pressure is one of the well-known methods for combating organized crime.

By adopting and adjusting European regulations and legal acts, Slovenia made an important step in the fight against corruption and economic crime, which can be found both in the public and in the private sector (different enterprises involved in substantial tax evasion cases). The area of gray economy remains a completely different matter. Slovenia saw the development and upgrading of different new fields of work within the police, such as the National Bureau of Investigation, the implementation of the improved Schengen Information System in the field of customs, intensified international cooperation (the Police [*Policija*], 2013), the publication of the tax administration's list of taxable persons who owe higher amounts of unpaid taxes to the state (Tax Administration of the Republic of Slovenia *Davčna uprava Republike Slovenije*, 2013), intensified work of different other institutions, such as the CPC and the media. Apart from education and awareness-raising activities and a clear message sent by the civil society to the holders of power stating that Slovenia should exercise zero tolerance for such illegal conduct, competent authorities should also pay greater attention to financial flows and the origin of property belonging to certain individuals, examine information obtained by investigative journalists more carefully, invest more efforts into increasing integrity levels both in public and in the private sector, increase the intensity and frequency of control over institutions and enterprises, adopt legal acts that would eliminate weaknesses identified in the operation of state bodies, reduce bureaucratization, and enable an increase in economic growth that would consequently contribute to the decrease in illegal activities both among individuals (undeclared work) and at higher levels (corruption and tax evasion).

* Supervizor is an online service (http://supervizor.kpk-rs.si) that enables the general public, the media, experts, and state authorities to obtain an insight into the expenditures of public bodies for the acquisition of goods and services (Commission for the Prevention of Corruption, 2013).

References

Choi, J. and Thum, M. (2005). Corruption and the shadow economy. *International Economic Review*, 46(3), 817–836.

Council of Europe. (2013). Group of States against corruption. Available at: http://www.coe.int/t/dghl/monitoring/greco/news/News(20130530)Eval4Slovenia_en.asp.

Dallago, B. (1990). *The Irregular Economy*. Aldershot, UK: Dartmouth.

Davčna uprava Republike Slovenije. (2013). Seznami davčnih zavezancev. Available at: http://www.durs.gov.si/si/storitve/seznami_davcnih_zavezancev/.

Dimc, M. (2012). Korupcija. In V.S. Habič (ur.), *Nacionalni sistem integritete v Sloveniji* (pp. 20–22). Ljubljana, Slovenia: Narodna in univerzitetna knjižnica.

Dobovšek, B. (2012a). *Korupcija v tranziciji*. Ljubljana, Slovenia: Fakulteta za varnostne vede.

Dobovšek, B. (2012b). *Transnacionalna kriminaliteta: študijsko gradivo*. Ljubljana, Slovenia: Fakulteta za varnostne vede.

Dobovšek, B. and Miklavčič, K. (2010). Korupcija v politiki: Razvojni pristop k preventivi. Accessed at: http://www.fvv.uni-mb.si/dv2010/zbornik/preprecevanje_korupcije/Miklavcic_Dobovsek.pdf.

Ernst & Young. (2013). Navigating today's complex business risks. Available at: http://www.ey.com/Publication/vwLUAssets/Navigating_todays_complex_business_risks/$FILE/Navigating_todays_complex_business_risks.pdf.

Federal Bureau of Investigation. (2014). Reports and publications. Available at: http://www.fbi.gov/stats-services/publications.

Finckenauer, J. and Voronin, Y. (2001). The Threat of Russian Organized Crime. Washington, DC: National Institute of Justice.

Glas, M. (1991). *Siva ekonomija v svetu in slovenskem gospodarstvu*. Ljubljana, Slovenia: Univerza v Ljubljani: Ekonomska fakulteta.

Hren, K., Čirjaković, J., Korenič, R., Kralj, A., Peceli, S., Grabnar Repovž, I., Stražišar, N. in Štemberger, P. (2011). Sloveniji za 20. rojstni dan-Slovenski statistiki. Available at: http://www.stat.si/Brdo2011/doc/SLO-20-let.pdf.

Meško, K. (2009). *Preventivni vidik ukrepov proti korupciji*. Ljubljana, Solvenia: Fakulteta za varnostne vede.

Nastav, B. (2009). Siva ekonomija v Sloveniji: merjenje, vzroki in posledice (Doktorska disertacija). Ljubljana, Solvenia: Ekonomska fakulteta.

Omerzu, B. in Starc, M. (2001). Negativni vplivi sive ekonomije na varnost ljudi, premoženja in okolja. In Pagon, M. (Ed.), *Dnevi varstvoslovja* (pp. 209–221). Bled: Visoka policijsko-varnostna šola.

Organisation for Economic Co-operation and Development (OECD). (1997). Konvencija o boju proti podkupovanju tujih javnih uslužbencev v mednarodnem poslovanju. Available at: https://www.kpk-rs.si/upload/datoteke/Konvencija%20o%20boju%20proti%20podkupovanju%20tujih%20JU.pdf.

Pečar, J. (1996). Podjetniška kriminaliteta. *Revija za kriminalistiko in kriminologijo*, 47(3), 203–212.

Policija. (2013a). Letna poročila o delu policije. Available at: http://www.policija.si/index.php/statistika.

Policija. (2013b). *Mednarodno sodelovanje*. Available at: http://www.policija.si/index.php/mednarodno-sodelovanje/sirene.

Schneider, F. (2014). The shadow economy in Europe 2013. Available at: http://www.atkearney.com/financial-institutions/featured-article/-/asset_publisher/j8IucAqMqEhB/content/the-shadow-economy-in-europe-2013/10192.

Schneider, F. in Enste, H. (2013). *The Shadow Economy and International Survey*. Cambridge, UK: Cambridge University Press.

Sodstvo Republike Slovenije. (2013). Statistika in letna poročila. Available at: http://www.sodisce.si/sodna_uprava/statistika_in_letna_porocila/.

Šorli, M. (1998). Pravna problematika nekaterih vrst organiziranega kriminala v Sloveniji. In V.R. Bohinjc (ed.), *Dnevi slovenskih pravnikov* (pp. 922–928). Ljubljana, Solvenia: Gospodarski vestnik.

Statistični urad Republike Slovenije. (2010). Popravki zajetja BDP in siva ekonomija, Slovenija 2010. Available at: http://www.stat.si/novica_prikazi.aspx?id=5588.

Tanzi, V. (1982). *The Underground Economy in the United States and Abroad*. Lexington, KY: Lexington Books.

Transparency International. (2013). Slovenia. Available at: http://www.transparency.org/gcb2013/country/?country=slovenia.

Williams, C. (2004). *Cash-in-Hand Work: The Underground Sector and the Hidden Economy of Favours*. Hampshire, UK: Palgrave McMillan.

17. The Informal Economy in the United States

Size, Determinants, and Comparisons

David G. Baker

Introduction

No area is as finely calibrated as the economy. Employment, production, and money supply are specified in multiple ways and are measured in quarterly, monthly, weekly, and, in some cases, daily intervals. The measures indicate the strength of a national economy and the well-being of various constituent groups. Good *numbers* can mean the difference between popularity of an incumbent executive and can even spell victory or defeat in an election. Not included in most cases in this myriad of figures is the informal economy. The exclusion is significant in the sense that only with its inclusion is the national economy fully described or specified. But as importantly, without the inclusion of the informal economy, the relative position and health of industries, groups, and individuals is not fully known. This chapter seeks to partially fill this void for the U.S. economy, first by defining the informal economy and then by estimating its components. Next, the foci are upon the determinants of this economy and upon the comparison of the U.S. informal economy with those of other nations in the industrialized world.

Definition of Informal Economy

The simplest definition of the informal economy is the difference between actual individual and corporate income and reported income levels. This difference is a result of underreporting income and/or overstating deductions. In the eyes of the U.S. Internal Revenue Service (IRS), the practice of deliberate or unintentional underreporting or inflation of deductions constitutes tax evasion. The growing complexity of U.S. income taxation law increases the possibility of both intentional and unintentional forms of evasion. This growing complexity is fueled by the heavy use of tax expenditures in the U.S. budget. In order to avoid debates that surround unpopular tax increases, policy makers have increasingly favored funding many programs through tax deductions rather than outright expenditures. The fiscal incidence of these two funding routes is nearly identical, but the tax expenditure route results in increasing taxation law complexity. Figure 17.1 illustrates the exponential growth in tax code, regulations, and rulings. Note that in the short period between 2001 and 2003, there is greater than 20% increase in tax rules. The reality of divided government and increasing partisan polarization in recent years do not bode well for those who would advocate reversing this trend.

Before proceeding to discuss the size of the informal economy, the character of this income requires

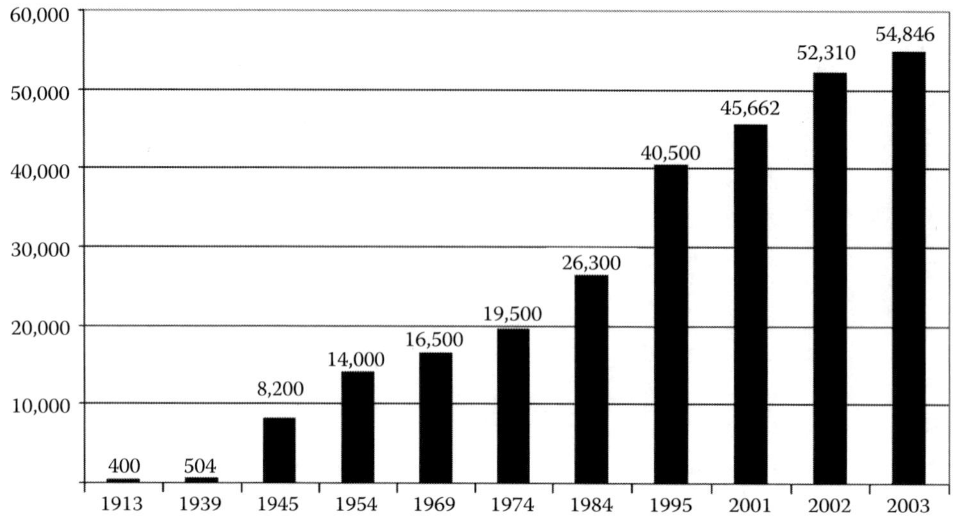

FIGURE 17.1 Total pages of Federal Tax Rules (includes the tax code, tax regulations, and various IRS). (From CCH Inc., Number of pages in the CCH Standard Federal Tax Reporter, www.cch.com.)

specification. Part of the difference between actual and reported individual and corporate income is income legally earned but underreported. The fact that there are criminal and/or civil penalties attached to underreporting income or overstating deductions does not alter the fact that this income is gained through legal activities. Another part of the informal economy in the United States is income gained through illegal activities, which in most cases is not reported. In the next section, estimates of both parts are offered.

The Size of the U.S. Informal Economy

It is challenging to measure the size of the informal economy in that much of the behavior that drives it is illegal. According to Richard Cebula and Edgar Feige, the best method of estimating the size of the informal economy is to use the IRS's own Taxpayer Compliance Measurement Program (TCMP) (Feige and Cebula, 2011). They justify this selection by citing J. Slemrod who characterizes the TCMP as "the most careful and comprehensive estimates of the extent and nature of tax noncompliance anywhere in the world" (Slemrod, 2007). The problem of using TCMP as the exclusive estimate of the informal economy is twofold. First, this process is not employed annually and therefore cannot provide a dynamic indication growth of the informal economy relative to the formal economy or the gross domestic product (GDP). Second, TCMP measures the tax gap between the revenues collected and the revenues due from all legal economic activity. That is, it does not encompass illegal activity. For this reason some economists have used the general currency ratio (GCR) to estimate all economic activity, legal and illegal. It is beyond the scope of this paper to lay out this method except to say that the use of the GCR rests on the assumption that most illegal economic activity is reflected in the use of cash. Therefore, changes in this ratio, which measures the use of cash, can be used to estimate the level of illegal economic activity. Using this method, Edgar Feige has estimated that between 18% and 23% of U.S. income goes unreported (Feige, 1989).

As important as providing a more inclusive measure of the informal economy in the United States, the GCR presents a more robust and dynamic indicator. Only in examining the variance in the informal economy from year to year can the independent variable, the informal economy size, be assessed. Feige's method of informal economy estimation using the GCR allows this causal analysis.

Determinants of the Informal Economy

The absolute size of the informal economy changes over time as does its size relative to the formal economy. What drives this change? The Feige and Cebula study provides interesting hypotheses. First and foremost, one would expect compliance with tax laws to be a function of enforcement. That is, as enforce activities,

Table 17.1 Regression Predictors of Taxation Noncompliance

Variable\Estimation	1960–2008	1970–2008	1980–2008
Average tax rate	.43**	.56***	.42*
Tax Reform Act	−3.56***	−3.65***	−3.59***
Unemployment	1.77***	1.79***	1.59***
Per capita income	.0039***	.0039***	.0038***
Dissatisfaction with government	192	.345#	.172
Audit	−.73#	−.968*	−1.24*
Interest rate	.388***	.365***	.446***
R_2	.91	.86	.81
$AdjR_2$	.88	.82	.74

*** Indicates statistical significance at the 1% level; **indicates statistical significance at the 2.5% level; *indicates statistical significance at the 5% level; and # indicates statistical significance at the 10% level.

audits, increase, compliance increases. Also positively associated with noncompliance, it would seem as the tax rate. One would expect those in higher tax brackets to engage in noncompliance at a higher rate than lower tax bracket individuals. Also positively associated with noncompliance, it is hypothesized, are unemployment rates and per capita GDP. In the negative correlation column, one would expect satisfaction with government, a regularly measured variable, to be inversely related to compliance. What follows in Table 17.1 are the results unearthed in the Feige and Cebula (2011) study.

Most striking in the findings of Feige and Cebula is that taxation noncompliance is strongly associated with capacity. As per capita income and resultant tax rates increase, so too does tax evasion; as unemployment diminishes capacity, tax evasion rises. The relationship between income and unemployment and evasion is highly significant (.001) in all three periods assessed. Note that the relationship between income/tax rate and noncompliance and between unemployment and noncompliance, though capacity related, is fundamentally different. Increases in income are associated with higher taxation rates, which provide greater incentive for evasion. Unemployment simply reduces household income and seemingly therefore the ability and willingness to pay appropriate income taxes. The strong relationship between interest rates and compliance is also capacity functional. The negative impact of audit frequency upon noncompliance is not as strong as intuited. There is no significant relationship in the longest interval and only one of .05 significance for the two others. However, the variable of the passage and implementation of the Tax Reform Act of 1986 is highly significant in all measured intervals. This suggests that the perception of tax fairness and a belief that the tax payers are accountable is associated with compliance. Also counterintuitive is the relationship between tax rates and compliance. As predicted, the relationship is positive, that is, the higher the rate, the greater the rate of noncompliance, but it is not as significant as capacity relationships. Finally, the notion that higher levels of dissatisfaction with government lead to higher levels of tax noncompliance is not supported by this study.

Although the dependent variable in the Feige and Cebula study includes illegal gains, it is not likely that most of the independent variables measured have much of an impact upon this segment of the informal economy. Capacity measures have not been linked positively to criminal behavior in other studies and may even suppress the relationships here analyzed. Enforcement activities in the form of audits of course do in some cases detect criminal activity and would act to suppress it, thereby reinforcing the reported negative relationship. There is no intuitive reason to suspect relationships between tax rates or dissatisfaction with governments as predictors of criminal activity that generates income.

The Relative Size of the U.S. Informal Economy

Tables 17.2 and 17.3 present the size of the informal economies of European countries (Table 17.2) and selected, highly developed non-European countries (Table 17.3) for a 10-year period ending in 2013 (Schneider, 2013). All these estimates are based upon the exhaustive work of Friedrich Schneider of

Table 17.2 Size of the Shadow Economy of 27 European Countries over 2003–2013 (in % of off. GDP)

	Year										
Country	**2003**	**2004**	**2005**	**2006**	**2007**	**2008**	**2009**	**2010**	**2011**	**2012**	**2013**
Austria	10.8	11	10.3	9.7	9.4	8.1	8.47	8.2	7.9	7.6	7.5
Belgium	21.4	20.7	20.1	19.2	18.3	17.5	17.8	17.4	17.1	16.8	16.4
Bulgaria	35.9	35.3	34.4	34	32.7	32.1	32.5	32.6	32.3	31.9	31.2
Cyprus	28.7	28.3	28.1	27.9	26.5	26	26.5	26.2	26	25.6	25.2
Czech Republic	19.5	19.1	18.5	18.1	17	16.6	16.9	16.7	16.4	16.0	15.5
Denmark	17.4	17.1	16.5	15.4	14.8	13.9	14.3	14	13.8	13.4	13.0
Estonia	30.7	30.8	30.2	29.6	29.5	29	29.6	29.3	28.6	28.2	27.6
Finland	17.6	17.2	16.6	15.3	14.5	13.8	14.2	14	13.7	13.3	13.0
France	14.7	14.3	13.8	12.4	11.8	11.1	11.6	11.3	11	10.8	9.9
Germany	17.1	16.1	15.4	15	14.7	14.2	14.6	13.9	13.7	13.3	13.0
Greece	28.2	28.1	27.6	26.2	25.1	24.3	25	25.4	24.3	24.0	23.6
Hungary	25	24.7	24.5	24.4	23.7	23	23.5	23.3	22.8	22.5	22.1
Ireland	15.4	15.2	14.8	13.4	12.7	12.2	13.1	13	12.8	12.7	12.2
Italy	26.1	25.2	24.4	23.2	22.3	21.4	22	21.8	21.2	21.6	21.1
Latvia	30.4	30	29.5	29	27.5	26.5	27.1	27.3	26.5	26.1	25.5
Lithuania	32	31.7	31.1	30.6	29.7	29.1	29.6	29.7	29.0	28.5	28.0
Luxemburg (Grand-Duché)	9.8	9.8	9.9	10	9.4	8.5	8.8	8.4	8.2	8.2	8.0
Malta	26.7	26.7	26.9	27.2	26.4	25.8	25.9	26	25.8	25.3	24.3
Netherlands	12.7	12.5	12	10.9	10.1	9.6	10.2	10	9.8	9.5	9.1
Poland	27.7	27.4	27.1	26.8	26	25.3	25.9	25.4	25	24.4	23.8
Portugal	22.2	21.7	21.2	20.1	19.2	18.7	19.5	19.2	19.4	19.4	19.0
Romania	33.6	32.5	32.2	31.4	30.2	29.4	29.4	29.8	29.6	29.1	28.4
Slovenia	26.7	26.5	26	25.8	24.7	24	24.6	24.3	24.1	23.6	23.1
Spain	22.2	21.9	21.3	20.2	19.3	18.4	19.5	19.4	19.2	19.2	18.6
Slovakia	18.4	18.2	17.6	17.3	16.8	16	16.8	16.4	16	15.5	15.0
Sweden	18.6	18.1	17.5	16.2	15.6	14.9	15.4	15	14.7	14.3	13.9
United Kingdom	12.2	12.3	12	11.1	10.6	10.1	10.9	10.7	10.5	10.1	9.7
27 EU countries/ average (unweighted)	**22.3**		**21.9**	**21.5**	**20.8**	**19.9**	**19.2**	**19.8**	**19.6**	**19.2**	**18.9**

the Johannes Kepler University in Austria. For all countries, Schneider's estimates calibrate a slight decline, in Europe from 22.3% to 18.9% and in the non-European states from 12.15% to 8.6%. Estimates of the U.S. informal economy decline during the period from 8.5% to 6.6%. It is only a speculation based upon the relationships in the U.S. economy, but the decline in the informal economy may be related to the declining interest and income levels associated with the international recession. That is, when income levels do not advance or even decline, the incentive for tax evasion diminishes. Of course, periods of economic decline are often paired with spikes in the crime rate. This did not occur in the United States during this recession and also did not occur across most other countries assessed with the possible exception of property crime where there was a slight increase in Europe. Another pattern that seems to hold across the European set of countries is that the informal economies are much higher in the

Table 17.3 Size of the Shadow Economy of Five Highly Developed Non-European Countries over 2003–2013 (in % of off. GDP)

Country/Year	2003	2004	2005	2006	2007	2008	2009	2010	2011	2012	2013
Australia	13.7	13.2	12.6	11.4	11.7	10.6	10.9	10.3	10.1	9.8	9.4
Canada	15.3	15.1	14.3	13.2	12.6	12	12.6	12.2	11.9	11.5	10.8
Japan	11	10.7	10.3	9.4	9	8.8	9.5	9.2	9	8.8	8.1
New Zealand	12.3	12.2	11.7	10.4	9.8	9.4	9.9	9.6	9.3	8.8	8.0
United States	8.5	8.4	8.2	7.5	7.2	7	7.6	7.2	7	7.0	6.6
Other OECD countries/ unweighted average	12.16	11.92	11.42	10.38	10.06	9.56	10.1	9.7	9.46	9.18	8.6

east than the west. For example, the United Kingdom ranges from 12.2% to 9.7% and Germany from 17.1% to 13%, but Poland ranges from 27.7% to 23.8% and Slovenia from 26.7% to 23.1%. This pattern may be related to higher taxation rates in the east as well as higher levels of unemployment. Note that the difference from low to high shadow economies is quite high; the difference between the lowest and highest state approaches a fourfold difference.

According to Schneider's study, the size of the U.S. informal economy is relatively small. It should be noted that Schneider's estimates, which are based upon the size of the informal economy relative to the GDP, are roughly similar to Feige and Cebula's, which report the size as a percentage of gross national income. The size of the U.S. informal economy may be smaller due to a lower U.S. tax rate compared to European countries, generally higher employment levels, and a relatively effective auditing bureaucracy, the U.S. IRS. The decline in the U.S. internal economy during this period as previously noted may be related to declining interest rates and the lack of income growth during the worldwide recession. IRS audits actually decline throughout this period and therefore do not suggest a decline.

Conclusion

The informal economy in the United States appears to be a diminishing share of total income and\the GDP. It constitutes approximately one-fifth of reported income levels and less than 10% of the GDP. Its size is related to overall economic health of the economy and the intensity of tax law enforcement. The impact of both organized and unorganized crime upon the informal economy is more idiosyncratic. Relative to other developed economies, the size of the U.S. informal economy is smaller but seems to respond to the same macrophenomenon. Projecting forward, economic recovery in the United States may have offsetting impacts upon the size of the informal economy. Rising employment levels are associated with decreases but higher taxation levels due to rising incomes and resultant tax rates are associated with increases. Increase interest rates are likewise associated with increases. Given the pressure upon the IRS due to partisan posturing, it is difficult to imagine a more robust regiment of taxation enforcement, a phenomenon that could lead to informal economy increases. It follows that the most likely result will be a slightly expanding informal economy in the United States in the near term.

Even though the informal economy in the United States is relatively small, its size and prospect for growth should be concerning. Given the lower levels of taxation in the United States, erosion of the tax base has great incidence upon vital governmental activity and debt levels. Closing the gap between the formal and informal economy would mean getting more government service at little or no additional cost to most tax payers. Importantly, the dynamic of the informal economy is delegitimizing and destabilizing the public sector at a time when the U.S. polity is strained by significant cultural and political cleavages. Strategies to close the gap would allay both economic and political tensions.

References

Feige, E. (1989). *The Underground Economies: Tax Evasion and Information Distortion*, Cambridge University Press, Cambridge, UK.

Feige, E. and Cebula, R. (2011). America's unreported economy: Measuring the size, growth and determinants of income tax evasion in the U.S., September, MPRA Paper No. 34781. http://mpra.ub.uni-muenchen.de/34781/.

Feige, E. and Cebula, R. (2011). America's unreported economy: Measuring the size, growth and determinants of income tax evasion in the U.S., September, MPRA Paper No. 34781. http://mpra.ub.uni-muenchen.de/34781/:16. (Accessed September 2011.)

Schneider, F. Size and development of the shadow economy of 31 European and 5 other OECD countries from 2003 to 2013: A further decline. http://www.econ.jkn.at/schneider. (Accessed June 2014.)

Slemrod, J. (2007). Cheating ourselves: The economics of tax evasion, *Journal of Economic Perspectives*, 21(1), 26.

18. Human Factors and Compliance

A Depth-Psychological Perspective on White and Blue Collar Crimes

Christian Felsenreich

Introduction

As most of the chapters in this book vividly illustrate, the informal economy, corruption, fraud, and organized crime do not emerge "out of nothing." There is always a context that is the cultural medium for all white and blue collar crime activities. While it is standard today to analyze the sociological backgrounds to these crimes, it is still not very usual to take a psychological perspective and even more unusual to bring psychotherapeutic findings into consideration. But it is, as this writer tries to show, this very micro level—the understanding of the inner drivers of the people involved—that could be of much help to get a deeper understanding of criminal schemes and their influence on people's relationships and society. It is an approach focusing on the so-called human factors, where, based on a humanistic worldview and the findings of depth psychology, the inner deficits of both the leaders and the followers, the power systems and their hierarchic realities and group dynamics are made visible. An approach that innovative risk managements of high risk environments for many decades has already followed. Analogies can be drawn with the new compliance management systems urgently needed in organizations.

Impressions from the Courtroom*

* The author has personally witnessed the judicial processing.

There is no better place to study the personalities and the relationship between the proponents of criminal acts as in the judicial processing of large corruption cases. Not only do offenses come to light, but the psychological dynamics that lead to fraud, bribery, and the emergence of economic criminal networks within organizations can be seen. Even if it is too late in the face of the damage in the present case, one can learn from it to prevent future cases.

"I was vain," says the former Austrian right wing party politician Klaus W. at the start of the fourth Telekom process,* who admits committing the offenses with which he is charged—embezzlement, a false statement in the corruption-investigation-committee, and aiding and abetting in the use of false invoices. The speaking of W. in large courtroom of the Vienna Regional Court is characterized by many emotional occupied I-messages, and it seems he speaks freely about not allowed political party financing. He reports how he felt at this or that time of the ongoing criminal acts and how the relationships developed between him and the other people involved. A general laughter goes through the ranks, when he narrates one or another anecdote in his broad dialect. Although his reports are anything but positive content because they expose the destructive force of what happened the way *how* the former MP and Tyrolean farmer accept responsibility shows very human traits. You get the feeling that someone has landed on the dock who carries a kind of openness within himself—maybe even something akin to childlike innocence. You look at him and see the stress when he talks about his misdemeanors, saying about it: "That's why I'm sitting here now."

A completely different picture is presented by his codefendant, who comes to sit next to him on the accused bench. Dr. Peter H., a longtime adviser and lobbyist of Telekom and suspected to have been a hub for dubious money flow (also in different other cases), announces that he does not understand why he should be held accountable for what he has done. Accordingly, he pleads "not guilty." In polished language and without any emotion, H. constantly takes up the inconsistencies of the accusations brought against him. One has the feeling of having a man in front of him, who is very rational, has extensive rhetorical skills, and a high persuasive power, and who is very well prepared. Someone, psychology postulates, with a pronounced effect-awareness. Here, I-messages are sent from calculus and only feelings get addressed, if this seems to promise a strategic advantage in the argument. Although H. pronounces that "seen from the perspective of today he would have done this or that differently," what remains is, he loaded none of guilt onto his shoulders. And even if his views diametrically stand opposed to the confessions of W., his message is clear: "All that had been done was legal business."

* The Telekom Austria Group is Austria's biggest telecom provider, with about 16,000 employees generating about 4 euro billion p.a. The group declined in 1998 from the governmental postal AG. It is listed on the Vienna Stock Exchange and was listed on the New York Stock Exchange. The majority owner today is America Mobil from Mexican Miliardär Carlos Slim. In the years after privatization, the company was involved in several severe corruption cases.

Lessons from High-Risk Management

Now it is not the task of a court to judge if a defendant is sympathetic or not. As well, this chapter is not about prejudging the court or speculating about guilt or nonguilt. Also, that a case of Telekom Austria that is selected is not a must. There are (unfortunately) plenty of other cases in our country from which one could derive similar considerations. The example of such judicial work-up of corrupt acts is intended to give an idea about the processes and implications that led men on the so-called inclined railways. This material is presented so that we can draw lessons to determine how organizations and systems can become more resistant against threats and errors in the future.

A useful starting point for analysis represents many years of experience in the risk management of high-safety environments. It is agreed, for example, in aviation since the 1970s, how important a proactive approach on safety is, but also the fact that an exclusively technical development of safety devices does not (necessarily) add more safety, nor do an constantly increase of new rules and regulations. This insight comes from the investigation of many aircraft incidents, showing that around 80% of accidents are primarily caused by human error. So the conclusion in aviation was to develop safety cultures, which means to intensively focus on the man himself and the man/machine and man/regulations interface.

In the theory of systemic human factors risk management, two concepts—"drift into failure" (Snook, 2000, pp. 179–201) and "normalization of deviance" (Vaughan, 1996, pp. 62–64)—are significant. Both state, that if organizations do not develop systemic perspectives to perceive external threats and employee errors, erosion will take place—practically *and* socially. "Drift into failure" means that organizations slowly move, step by step, in the direction of an unwanted event (incident or accident) or maneuver themselves by their behavior, based on (false) beliefs, misjudgments, and other negative and often self-perpetuating or reinforcing dynamics (vicious circles), in a difficult, at worst hopeless situation. "Normalization of deviance" can be seen as the social process (group dynamic) by which the involved perceive the "drift" as a normal (necessary and reasonable) process.

For the efforts and abilities to prevent such imbalances in designated high-risk industries, the term *resilience* is used. One opinion leader in the field of resilience (Eric Hollnagel et al., 2006) defines the process in his book *Resilience-Engineering* by stating, "The performance of individuals and organizations must at any time adjust to the current conditions." In other words, an organization must be able to find *proactive* answers to their *threats* (from outside) and their *errors* (from inside). In practice, this is only possible if there is a sustainable, open, and in-depth examination of those facts and realities that are perceived as unalterable constraints.

However, this entails the knowledge that necessary adaptation cannot be accomplished in the "outer world" alone (it is not enough just to change rules and regulations!). There is adaption needed, where the inner growth or personal growth of the characters that form or represent the organization is required. So it is necessary to deal with both the psychological and sociological aspects of the hierarchy, group dynamics, mass phenomena, feedback cultures, and incentive systems and with the various personality types of the people involved. This also includes a knowledge of human stress patterns, which means the subconscious drivers and the irrationality of the people when they come into stress situations. A basic premise of resilience implies, therefore, that the knowledge about threats and errors lies in the organization itself and the aim and content of resilience efforts within the meaning of the human factor is to strengthen the social and emotional competence and the relationship and conflict resolution skills of the organization and its members.

To Analyze the Human Factor: Transactional Analysis

Transactional analysis (developed by the psychiatrist Eric Berne during the late 1950s) is a depth-psychological theory, where the content described earlier is represented in a psychological model. It focuses on human relationships and helps to *analyze* people's *transactions* according their so-called ego states (Berne, 1964). Transactions mean the communication and behavior caused by thoughts and emotions between humans or groups of humans. The ego-state model parts people's psyches into the adult, child, and parent. Simplified, these 3 levels can be categorized as shown in Figure 18.1.

Transactional analysis theory postulates that effective relationships among adults, depending on whether they are in the superior or subordinate role, should be held on an *adult-to-adult* ego-state level. This does not argue against hierarchies and is not saying that both parent and child ego-state levels are negative. On the contrary, hierarchies are recognized as important and a degree of parenting (control) of the inferiors is needed for (good) managers, especially if they are in the role of supervisors. So, conversely, a good degree of *childish* trust (surrender) of followers toward the chiefs is important for functioning working relationships, but both should be integrated in the adult ego state. With integration is meant that the inherent thoughts and feelings (also the negative ones) are (allowed to be) conscious and there is on both sides awareness and a shared definition about the different professional roles. This also implies that leadership is determined through competence and not through personal ego and that leading should be mainly something giving. All this represents space for a reflexive encounter and a minimization of transferences.* Such (*really*) professional relationships can be named as *synergetic hierarchy* (Figure 18.2).

* Transference is a depth-psychological concept that postulates that we are all constantly in processes where emotions and desires originally associated with one person (e.g. parent) are sub-consciously shifted to another person (http://www.thefreedictionary.com/transference).

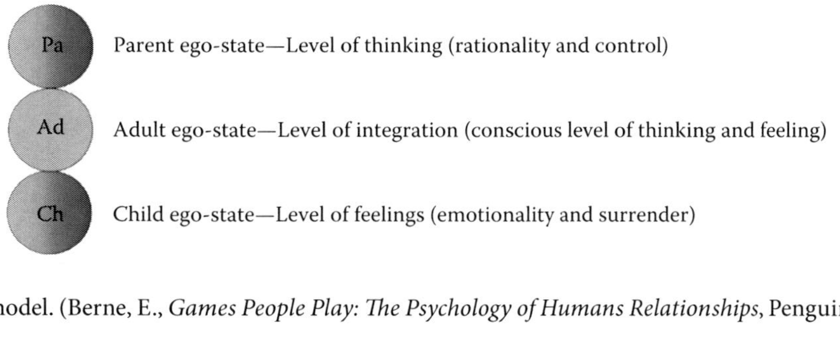

FIGURE 18.1 Ego-state-model. (Berne, E., *Games People Play: The Psychology of Humans Relationships*, Penguin Books, New York, 1964.)

Chapter 18

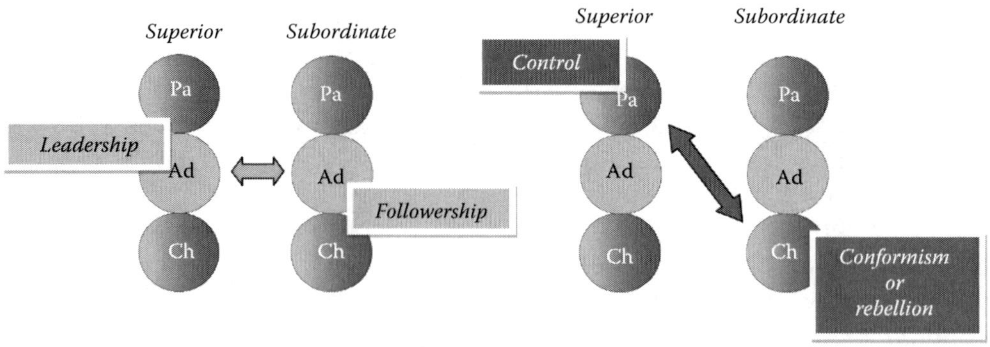

FIGURE 18.2 Synergetic hierarchy versus steep hierarchy showed on the basis of transactional analyses. (Felsenreich, C. About: Loyalty and resilience—Why a new view on human error should focus on the dark sides of basically positive human attitudes. Master thesis in Human Factors and System Safety. Lund/Sweden: Lund University/School of Aviation, 2008.)

Steep hierarchy is highly determined through the presence of transferences and no space for reflexive behavior. The superior has the (boundless) power and control over "his" subordinate(s). The latter are forced to act, conform, or rebel against the leader and the system. It needs an enormous amount of one's personal "rebellious"* means (inner and outer), *not* conflict-avoiding power, to not conform in a steep hierarchical system. The consequences for the so-called whistle-blowers are horrendous. The German psychotherapist and author Heinz Peter Röhr (1999, pp. 165–166) states, "One has not only the boss as opponent but the whole followers system." Based on the transferences, a group dynamic settles in where conformists, fulfilling the will of superiors, are not fighting against the problem but against the *whistle-blowers* who point out the problem, which in turn is the social base for the "normalization of deviance," and that is indeed *the* drama for systems. Step by step, they get rid of their ability to reflect their own actions.

A self-reflective culture is determined through people who ask nonconformist questions, otherwise it gets pseudoreflective, and a "drift into failure" is a logical consequence. The drivers for all these dramas are deeply engendered into the society and so into the *collective subconscious*. They can be seen generally in the interactions and relationships of *normal* low-rank people (hirers, employees, electors, fans, etc.) toward their high-rank leaders (owners, managers, politicians, stars, etc.). Depth psychologist Erich Fromm (1968, pp. 76–77) lastingly explains the core of these often ambivalent but in their base, stable relationships. It is the powerful attraction *normal* people feel toward those with omnipotent self-pictures and the tendency of the first to place boundless trust into the *excellence* of the latter. The modern world, with its increasing speed and complexity, additionally creates instability. This makes the renaissance of the strong dualistic *transference* surfaces *hero* (strong leader, rescuer, role-model, etc.) and *antihero* (whistle-blower, culprit and victim, scapegoat, etc.) explicable. Members of the first group become transferred, by hopes and dreams, into "superfather figures," while the latter are transferred by frustrations, anger, and hatred (sourced from subconscious anxieties) into *losers*.

What is the individual process to build up a superfather figure personality? This can also be answered through the theories of transactional analyses. The major exponent, Thomas Harris (1967, p. 1ff), explains convincingly about the importance of the "I'm OK—you're OK" so-called life positions as a basis for functioning (balanced) *adult-to-adult* relationships. This is what should be, but Harris states that the majority of humans have a tendency to lack self-esteem, which is pictured in "I'm *not* OK—you're OK" life positions. This shows up through thoughts and feelings that others are better, smarter, prettier, more successful, etc. This can be painful on a personal level, induces transferences out of the everlasting child position, and creates a demand for *heroes*, but would by itself be harmless because the ascriptions to the outer world are hope induced and so positive. What is terribly problematic is the interaction of the minority of humans with a huge drive to find persons to fulfill the roles of the *heroes*, who have an opposite life position internalized as, "I'm OK—you're *not* OK."

Transactional analyses state that it is a very basic decision to develop an OK or a not OK view of relationships to others. By this, it is meant that it gets *decided* by the very small child subconsciously and is linked to whether

* With rebellious is meant that the rebel's driver is not to plunge the leader but to focus the wealth (the safety) of the whole organization—what is for sure idealistic (there is always also egoism involved).

the child gets treated well or not. For those grown-ups with the latter *decision* (the one traumatized) it is then not possible to transfer the libido (which basically means positive feelings) toward others. This can be seen as a collective revenge for past suffering and as compensative act to never reexperience those (painful) dependencies of childhood anymore. Extremely pictured, only the "I" stays existent. The "you" is only focused if it supports the interests of the "I." The drama is that trust gets lost and that no real relationships are feasible anymore. This is then named an "antisocial (life) script".*

An antisocial script is strongly shown in the narcissistic personality (or personality disorder). One of the opinion leaders in the field of personality disorders, Professor of Psychiatry and Director of the New York Presbyterian Hospital Otto F. Kernberg (2004, pp. 76–80), describes people with a severe narcissistic personality as ones showing a remarkable lack of empathy and (deeper) emotional interest toward others. This chronicle inner emptiness induces an unleashed will to act superior, as an everlasting search for an ego boost that never gets filled or satisfied. The paradox of a basically blown up ego but the need for ongoing ego boosts is significant. Out of this conversion, narcissistic personalities gain their power out of competition and not out of solidarity. With remarkable self-confidence and without any sense of indebtedness, they assert a right to command and rip others off. Under an often smart and handsome façade, there is something cold and inexorable.

* Building up a personality (or a personality disorder) is a pretty complex act. Basically, it can be said that an antisocial script (as every other life script) is "produced" as a reaction toward the social environment (e.g., through frustration pictured in Maslow's Pyramid), but it can also be seen as something learned (e.g., through a socialization in a feudalistic surrounding, a strong spiritual worldview [Indian caste system] or a Mafia-Context).

Based on this disconnection of real emotions, narcissistic personalities are mostly free of fear but also free of compassion. Emotions are substituted by images. Those images make it happen to act *flexible* in various directions, even if the contradictions are striking. Inconsistencies are seen as challenges accompanied by mottos like "Every path of super minds is (or was) contradicted by an ignoramus." Out of these drivers, narcissistic personalities can be remarkably convincing in selling (whatever) questionable contents (demagogic features). On their everlasting quest for "the big feeling," they are following (whatever) superlative aims (richness, fame, etc.) and are totally goal-oriented. People, even if they were longtime followers or "friends," get scarified if they are not needed anymore or standing in the way. One hundred percent loyalty is required. Criticism is strictly prohibited.

It is common sense that a lot of those features are highly desired by organizations. Leaders, with strength and without fear (with an expanded self-esteem), being goal-oriented, acting rational (without mawkishness), and having everything under control, are mainly connoted positive. Those are the ones ready to execute "sharp decisions," which is seen as a state of professionalism and which is mostly defined as a need for innovative changes. So, it is on first sight a paradox that what is detected from a psychological perspective as deficits is seen in the (real) world as strength. While (humanistic) psychology is acknowledging that narcissism as a personal style can have innovative power and people who are driven by (unnatural) superlative pretensions who follow their *fantastic* ideas can bring positive progress into the world, it states that "even more often they do not." Narcissists not only tend, powered by their megalomania and their annex to the superlative, to be set up to commit white collar crimes, they also, by their actions, prepare the field for blue collar crime activities.

Noncompliance from a Depth-Psychological Perspective

"The rot starts at the top" is not an insignificant saying. While it is often announced that a lack of structure is the major reason for whatever malfunctions in social systems almost always steep hierarchies, the existence of superfather figures, the repression of subordinates, and a missing space for reflection played a significant role in the greatest disasters in human history, as can be seen in war scenarios and the "masters" behind them. The analysis of the majority of crime cases in organizations shows the same picture. Chiefs acted with limitless control, making whistle-blowing practically impossible. Basically, in such systems, whistle-blowers never get into positions where they have something to say anyway (conformist followers are the ones getting credit), and if they are in higher positions their (inner and outer) conflicts get so strong that they resign, get fired, or quit out of their own will. *Compliance* in organizations can be seen in the same way as psychotherapy classifies (functioning) family systems. If the parents are showing enough mental stability and grown-up behavior to fulfill their roles as the ones guiding their children with respect and balanced control, the relationship between parents and children will be positive, stress situations will be handled constructively, problems will be solved, and there is a high chance that everyone will be satisfied in the system. In other words, there are rules that structure and limit the encounters, and those rules are accepted by both sides. Transactional analyses state that, according to the position in the system (adult or child), a good amount of both (positive) qualities—nourishing *and* freedom—exist (Figure 18.3).

While in organizations only adults are physically present, unfortunately on a psychological level this cannot be claimed. As already mentioned, we live in a world where a mass of inner hurt children tries to live out their dramas. *Noncompliance* arises therefore from the inability to act or react as a grown-up (adult), especially when stress situations emerge. By stress is meant both internal stress based on constraints, fears, self-esteem issues, and negative belief sets, as well as the stress from nonfunctioning relationships. This easily forms vicious circles in which subordinates, because of their rebellious inner child (e.g., rebellion against injustice) or their needy inner child (e.g., lacking attention or simply to survive), behave in a noncompliant manner, while elites tend to evolve a hubris that also leads (through their controlling parent ego) to breaking the rules. Thus simplified, it can be said that blue collar crime is based on powerlessness and white collar crime is based on power and its abuse.

Also of interest are the seeming interdependencies of blue and white collar crimes. When pretentious leaders, through their unleashed power, engage in unjust behavior and set unfair goals and competition levels that intimidate and frustrate people until at last they destroy the sense of human sociality by the corruption of values, what should the so-called little man learn from this? That he should not gain an advantage, when he gets a chance, when he hears every day about how "the ones up there" at a completely incomprehensible height "make money" and leave no stone unturned to rotate laws (keyword lobbying) so that tomorrow they come to even better *deals*? And if those whose corrupt practices come to light only with great difficulty and often even against the interests of justice stand in front of a court and get away relatively unscathed, should he behave compliantly? He must be stupid to do so!

This is a very negative kind of role modeling, where effectively the following motto settles in—"If I (or we) do not take it, the others take it," which at last corrupts top-down whole company structures and with the organizations the state structure. All this makes the devil's circle visible and understandable with its ongoing and self-preserving loss of trust and lack of reflexiveness, where antisocial behavior becomes normative. From this (humanistic) perspective, it is appropriate to conclude that a "drift into antisociality" is involved when it comes to a "drift into failure." It can be said that the trail to understand failures in organizations leads automatically to deeper social issues. In other words, organizational misbalances *are* social misbalances.

The legislation philosopher Ernst-Wolfgang Böckenförde (2011) states, "the free, secularized state lives from preconditions he himself cannot

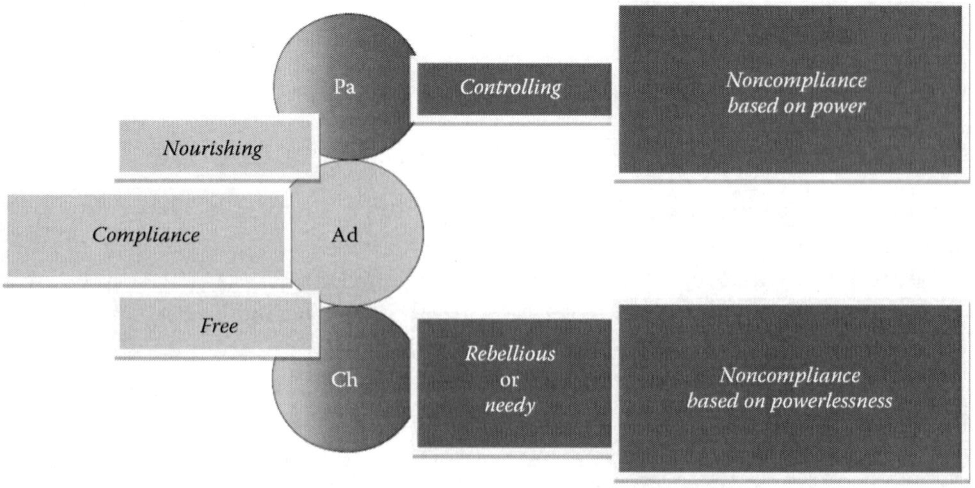

FIGURE 18.3 Compliance typology on the basis of transaction analyses. (From Felsenreich, C., Der Faktor Mensch in Compliance Praxis edition 3/2013, LexisNexis, Wien, Austria, 2013.)

guarantee," which means that already the only strategic respecting of statutes without any ethical motivation erodes at last the whole democratic structure of a civil society. So, the serious questions expanding the theme of compliance are: "How long can democratic state structures with all their increasing debts and decreasing power of their citizens (who are endangered to lose their incomes) represent a counterpart against the spread of huge and financially strong international corporations who only follow their own interests? What can be done against a new feudalistic power system, where people do not even get repressed directly, but seduced to self-exploitation?"

Unfortunately, the more unstable the times get, the more people call for strong leaders, which in turn increases the problem. The general tendencies can be seen in an EU-wide survey of the University Bielefeld (Germany) in 2011. About one-third of the Germans wished for authoritarian types of government, in Great Britain and France more than 40%, and in Portugal and Poland more than 60%. This alarming result pictures the increasing hope of people (out of their inner child) that the problems they (or we) are in today will be managed if a strong leader (superfather figure) will get the *chance* to reign.

The major difference between dysfunctional families and organizations up to state structures is that real children are definitely only victims. They are helplessly exposed to the system, unable to escape, and even if they rebelliously oppose, they are chanceless. They are innocent, while it would be an obligation for the *children* in the repressed adults to stand up and stop their dependencies. They should *grow* and develop. But *how* should they do this, when they never had learned it. And from whom, if the ones being in the lead and holding the power have no interest in helping them and, more than that, are interested in having the projections from which they achieve their power stay as they are.

Back to the Courtroom

In the Telekom Austria case(s), the theory described earlier can be seen dramatically in practice. It is a masterpiece of a systemic problem, where the "drift into failure" and the "normalization of deviance" can be lastingly studied. So speaks the involved ex-telecom manager Gernot S., who now acts as a witness for the prosecution to escape a condemnation, again and again about the *system Telekom*, a system in which those involved got used to all those deviant behaviors, were selected to perform and support them on the basis of their personalities, or had been removed if they resisted being "part of the game."

The corruption scandals in Austria that were exposed in the early 21st century involved close ties between politicians and business leaders. They resulted in a drastic decline in the citizenry's confidence in government. As noted by Mayr (2011:1) "entrepreneurs have allegedly received multi-million commissions for non-existent services." The Telekom Austria scandal and other scandals involving government and business officials have been compared to the activities of "robber barons" of past generations. The former Telekom Austria executive placed on trial for his part in a market manipulation scandal, Rudolph Fischer, stated that "he had okayed the first 500,000 euro ($669,000) payment but had not known it would be delivered in cash in a plastic bag at a popular Vienna market." He stated, "I know it was a mistake, I'm sorry," as he plead partially guilty to a charge of corruption. (Prodhan, 2013:1). Mayr (2011:2) notes, "since the turn of the millennium, so much seems certain, a band of modern-day robber barons with close links to the government, working out of offices and law firms in the center of Vienna, swindled the state out of billions of euros." While the supporters of the governmental constellation of those days insisted that they conducted numerous, long overdue reforms, the opponents saw it as a time of very negative impact on the integrity and stability of the state and society. The fact is that numerous interventions of these times are now being brought to court as corruption cases. It appears that this period, worldwide, was a time of boosting corruptive power, as the financial crises and the following economic crises that still challenge the world show.

Without any excessive negativity, it can be said that the Telekom Austria showed structures of organized crime. Suspected criminal acts were (and up to now are) price manipulation, illegal campaign contributions to FPÖ and BZÖ, donations to organizations part of four parties, influencing contract awards, questionable football sponsorship, and unclear corporate takeovers. The Telekom IV process that is focused on in this writing relates to the charge of illegal party financing for the BZÖ election campaign of 2006. One of the suspected masterminds in many other corruption cases, the party-free but ÖVP- and

BZÖ-close former finance minister Karl-Heinz G., was "only" accused of getting an exclusive flight for a private golf trip to Spain paid by Telekom in 2004 (by the way, the bill for the business jet was also paid by the consulting agency of Dr. Peter H. his golf mate). Three Telekom board members the national BZÖ manager a advertising entrepreneur and a former spokesman for the justice minister had to defend themselves in front of court.

The steep hierarchies and their exponents in the system politics and organizations are the next puzzle stones in understanding the incidents at Telekom. The way *how* W. described in front of court the relationship to his former party chief Dr. Jörg H. pictures W.'s role in this (steep hierarchical) system and how this system functioned (or better, not functioned). The charismatic (highly narcissistic) former country deputy of Carinthia, who was one of the major figures in the most costly criminal case in Austria ever (the Hypo Alpe Adria scandal that led Carinthia in the insolvency and loaded a debt of approximately 20 billion euros on Austrian taxpayers' shoulders), died in 2008 in a mysterious car accident. W.'s personality style let him now with deep homage, and sweeping euphoria full of melancholy reporting: "Jörg reigned absolutely!" All this draws a picture of the wishes of a needy child towards a superfather figure full of associated transferences. Additionally the way W. talks about his first contact with Dr. H. supports this perception of W.'s personal drama. W. stated that, "Dr. H. has contacted *me personally*—such an important person!"

While W., as an former MP, is (for the outside world) already in a position of committing white collar crime, in his inner self he is not. He projects wishes onto big father figures, in the hope that their shining brings also light into his life. A conformist follower, who sees his chance to succeed in fulfilling the wishes of the ones he worships, he is not a leader but a child who denies to take responsibility in front of the powerful leaders he calls friends who now get punished from another authority (from the parental forces in court) for their wrongdoings. He has big self-doubts and he is feeling them. In the words of depth psychology, he shows lastingly "I am not OK—you are OK" patterns. Also, his "fishing for compliments" from the auditorium at court can be classified as a need for acknowledgment. While this is not saying that W. could not cause large harm or even should not be held accountable for what he had done (he is an adult and not child), one can come to the conclusion that, under other circumstances, he would have not shown (such) corruptive actions. So, in his depth, W. shows a typical blue collar crime activist behavior.

In contrast, H. presents his deep "I am OK—you are not OK" attitudes. Even under the pressure that appearance in court puts on him, he stays in the role to control the scenery. He shows deep inner confidence, trying hard to be smarter than "the others." He does not speak with his codefendants in the breaks. He does not try to get into coalition with the others. He fights for himself alone (as probably he had always done in his life). He believes in his strength and the fact that he is someone special who does not need others. He shows a lot of signs of having deep self-image deficits, which in the opposite to W. he is not feeling, but subconsciously compensates by working hard and using all his analytical intelligence to be (and stay) in his role of power. He is acting as an gray eminence and is so a true representative of white collar crime.

The great influence of H. is indeed interesting because he (H. was *only* a consultant) held no de facto power position at Telekom. There must have been an identification of the (real) power holders (Telekom—as political bosses) toward him. H. must have enjoyed great confidence from the highest ranks. Because criminal offenses were involved, the authorities may have developed over time a dependency (inescapable alliances) on the mastermind who was the one capable of enforcing their personal interests in power, influence, and money. This initially strengthened the relationships, but now, here in court, the fragility and the inability of those involved to take deeper (adult) relationships become visible. Here reigns the motto "every man for himself."

The Telekom IV trial ended on the night of September 13, 2013 with guilty verdicts against Dr. Peter H. (2½ years of imprisonment) and Klaus W. (2 years on probation and 3 months of imprisonment). Not to anyone's surprise, W. accepted the punishment, while H. announced his appeal. "This I will not tolerate," he said in an interview shortly after the judgment, stating, "See, my problem is, that the real guilty one is the witness for the prosecution Gernot S., who now messes me in the process, to protect himself and his friend Klaus W. But as everyone knows, the court always protects the key witnesses." While the ex-Telekom manager Gernot S. indeed holds an interesting group dynamic position (what is he now—whistleblower, offender, and/or betrayer who reveals his accomplice?) the reaction from Dr. H. is standard for one with an "I am OK—you are not OK" life position. In such stress situations, the decompensative force of an unleashed parental role (wanting everlasting control) becomes visible. It is (paradox) a life drama of a person not being able to take (an adult) responsibility for his own behavior. It shows the interconnection to the child ego state by his (very childish–rebellious/defiant) announcement, "the others are to blame."

The media (still) describes H.'s career with the superlative write-ups *PR-Guru* and *Star Lobbyist*, something that H. probably likes. What he perhaps does not like is that they report about his new life as a *dropout*. After all the judicial proceedings, he began a new life in his villa on a picturesque beach in Brazil. He probably does not like that the media publicizes the bankruptcy of all his consulting firms, that he is allegedly penniless, and had to apply for procedural help for his court proceedings against his former "friends." H. tries to sue former finance minister Karl-Heinz G., who also was an owner's representative of Telekom at the time H. gained 25 million euros in consulting fees, and consulting partner Walter M., with whom he made about 10 million euros in the so-called BUWOG affair, where again Karl-Heinz G. is suspected to have pulled the strings. Involved in the dispute is 32 million euros. Besides the impression that the term "friendship" in this ambiance seems like a joke, it confirms the validity of the existence of antisocial life scripts in these activities. In any case, it would fit well into the picture if H. would try to escape the further process or the execution of the judgment. Wouldn't be Brazil a nice option Probably the money is already there!

Conclusion

It is almost always the same. Supposedly great men leave shambles and the little men have to pay the bill. As the variety of far-reaching criminal offenses in business and politics and the generated harm sums show, it seems more important than ever to use a new form of intelligent risk management that includes classifying many more organizations as high-risk environments. One of the core statements of human factor–based risk management is that the knowledge about (all kinds of) malfunctions in organizations is present in the organizations themselves. In other words, there are always enough people in huge companies as in other social systems up to state structures who have enough insight (personally and practically) to "pull the ripcord" if this is necessary. The reason why they stay silent and/or chanceless has to be found in the steep hierarchies, without space for "real" reflection, that make effective whistle-blowing impossible. The goal must be the implementation of safety cultures that proactively deal with the human factor. This involves forcing self-regulative power and *not* (only) to maximize outside regulation. A modern compliance management system must, in addition to its legal expertise, develop an expertise in psychological and psychodynamic phenomena. From the perspective of this writing, this is how to understand white and blue collar crimes in depth and how to protect the members of a democratic or civil power–based society from the damage created by the informal economy, fraud, and corruption.

References

Newspapers and Periodicals

Böckenförde, E.W. Verheerende Wirkung auf die Rechtskultur. Interview by Werth, W. ORFNews. February 10, 2011. online. Retrieved February 10, 2011 from http://oel.orf.at/artikel/ 269234/.

EU-Studie: Jeder Dritte wünscht sich "starken Mann". March 11, 2011. ORF-News online. Retrieved March 11, 2011 from http://www.orf.at/stories/2046991/.

Felsenreich, C. Der Faktor Mensch in Compliance Praxis edition March 2013. Wien, Austria: LexisNexis.

Mayr, W. (2011). Corruption scandals in Austria: A web on sleaze in elegant Vienna, in Spiegel online, October 13:1–4. Retrieved August 10, 2015 from http://www.spiegel.de/international/europe/corruption-scandals-in-austria-a-web-of-sleaze-in-elegant-Vienna-a-79///3.htm.

Möchel, K. Star-Lobbyist wurde zum Aussteiger in Brasilien. June 27, 2014, pp. 1, 9. KURIER print.

Nikbakhsh, M. and Kramar-Schmid, U. Exklusiv: Telekom zahlte 25 Millionen an Grasser-Freund Hochegger. January 29, 2011. PROFIL online. Retrieved September 28, 2014 from http://www.profil.at/home/exklusiv-telekom-25-millionen-grasser-freund-hochegger-287585.

Peter Hochegger: Ich kämpfe um meinen Ruf. Interview. September 14, 2013. oe24 online. Retrieved August 29, 2014 from http://www.oe24.at/oesterreich/politik/Hochegger-ueber-das-Schock-Urteil/116002117.

Prodhan, G. (2013). Ex-Telekom Austria exec tell court he's sorry for share scandal, in Reuters online, February 11:1–2. Retrieved August 10, 2015 from http://www/reuters/com/article/2013/02/11austria-corruption-telekom-idUSL5NOB85RO20130211.

profil.at/articles/1104/560/296767_s8/exklusiv-telekom-25-millionen-grasser-freund-hochegger.

TA-Prozess: Kronzeuge Schieszler belastet Hochegger. August 5, 2013. ORF-News online. Retrieved August 6, 2013 from http://www.orf.at/stories/2193643/.

Telekom Austria zahlte 2004 Golf-Rückflug für Grasser. August 24, 2014. ORF-News online. Retrieved August 24, 2014 from http://www.orf.at/#/stories/2243003/.

Verheerende Wirkung auf die Rechtskultur. Interview with Ernst-Wolfgang Böckenförde. February 10, 2011. Werth, W. ORF-News online. Retrieved February 10, 2011 from http://oe1.orf.at/artikel/ 269234/.

Books and Papers

Berne, E. (1964). *Games People Play: The Psychology of Humans Relationships*. New York: Penguin Books.

Felsenreich, C. (2008). About: Loyalty and resilience—Why a new view on human error should focus on the dark sides of basically positive human attitudes. Master thesis in Human Factors and System Safety. Lund/Sweden: Lund University/School of Aviation.

Felsenreich, C. and Kriechbaum, K. (2008). *Politik-analyse, politik therapie. Interaktives fehlermanagement*. Wien, Austria: Kriechbaum-Verlag.

Freud, S. (1921). Massenpsychologie und Ich-analyse. Leipzig-Wien-Zürich: Internationaler Psychoanalytischer Verlag.

Fromm, E. (1964). *The Heart of Man: Its Genius for Good and Evil*. New York: Harper & Row.

Harris, T. (1967). *I'm O.K.—You're O.K.: A Practical Guide to Transactional Analyses*. New York: Harper & Row.

Hollnagel, E., Woods, D., and Leveson, N. (eds.) (2006). *Resilience Engineering: Concepts and Precepts*. Hampshire, UK: Ashgate.

Kernberg, O. (2004). *Aggressivity, Narcissism and Self-Destructiveness in the Psychotherapeutic Relationship: New Developments in the Psychopathology and Psychotherapy of Severe Personality Disorders*. New Haven, CT/London, UK: Yale University Press.

Röhr, H. (1999). *Narzissmus: Das innere gefängnis*. München, Germany: dtv.

Snook, S. (2000). *Friendly Fire: The Accidental Shoot Down of U.S. Black Hawks over Northern Iraq*. Princeton, NJ: Princeton University Press.

Vaughan, D. (1996). *The Challenger Launch Decision: Risky Technology, Culture and Deviance at NASA*. Chicago, IL: The University of Chicago Press.

19. Conclusion and Future Perspectives

Maximilian Edelbacher, Peter C. Kratcoski, and Bojan Dobovšek

Birth of an Idea

The decision to write a book on the informal (shadow) economy and its relationship with corruption, fraud, organized crime, was made by the editors after they attended several professional conferences and presented papers on such topics as organized crime, financial crime, corruption, fraud, and terrorism. These conferences were the European Society of Criminology in Ljubljana, the European Society of Criminology meeting in Bilbao, the International Police Executive Symposium in Budapest, the meeting of the Academic Council on the United Nations System in Vienna, and the Society for Police and Criminal Psychology held in Ottawa, Canada. Several of the authors of the chapters in this book also attended these conferences and presented papers on the subjects mentioned above. The relationship of the informal economy to corruption, fraud, and organized crime became evident as the formal and informal discussions and correspondence by several of the presenters continued after the close of the professional meetings. The work group's interest in these topics was heightened when the great financial crisis of 2008 almost crippled the financial security of many nations throughout the world. It later became clear that this crisis might have been avoided if there were more controls on the financial institutions and if these financial institutions had less opportunity to engage in the types of criminal activity, such as fraud and corruption, that increased their profits but tended to weaken the security of the financial system.

The connection between the financial security of a nation and crime was not always apparent, even to those who were considered experts in financial matters. For example, Edelbacher notes that at a symposium that focused on the effects and dangers of catastrophes, and the need to establish *early warning* systems to prevent the crisis that might follow from such catastrophic events as a flood, tsunami, not one participant except Christian Felsenreich and himself mentioned the financial crisis and how to develop a method to stop financial crises.

As others became interested in the subject of financial crimes and how to prevent such crimes, several professors and police practitioners, who had either completed research or written on the subject, presented several papers at professional meetings on various facets of financial crime and its relationship to financial security. For example, a round table discussion on financial crimes was conducted at the European Society of *Criminology* Meeting in Ljubljana, and panel presentations on this topic took place at the European Society of Criminology meeting in Bilbao, the International Police Executive Symposium in Budapest, the Academic Council on the United Nations System in Vienna, and the Society for Police and Criminal Psychology held in Ottawa. In addition, several of the participants of the sessions mentioned earlier decided to write chapters for a book on the topic of the effects of financial crimes on the global economy. These discussions led to a book edited by Maximilian Edelbacher, Peter Kratcoski, and Michael Thiel, titled *Financial Crime: A Threat to the Global Economy*, was published in 2012.

Several of the authors in the book emphasized how criminal organizations, such as the Italian Mafia, were able to infiltrate legitimate businesses as well as launder their illegally gained money and invest it into legitimate businesses. The idea to continue the work and to expand it to include the relationship of organized crime, white collar crime, fraud, and corruption with the informal economy was offered by Bojan Dobovšek. He as well as the other coeditors, contacted potential contributors and motivated them to write on their research or experiences dealing with the informal economy and crime. Based on his own research, Dobovšek concluded that the relationship between organized crime, fraud, corruption, and white collar crime was strong at the present time and this relationship was having the same negative effect on the global formal economy as it did before the economic crisis of 2008. Since the link between the informal economy and various types of crimes was of great interest to those practitioners and academics who had participated in the conferences and symposiums mentioned about, Maximilan Edelbacher, Peter Kratcoski, and Bojan Dobovšek, approached Dilip Das, the editor of the International Police Executive Symposium Co-Publications with CRC Press Advances in Police Theory and Practice Series, with a proposal for CRC Press to publish an edited book titled *Corruption, Fraud, Organized Crime, and the Shadow Economy*. The proposal was accepted by the criminal justice editor of CRC Press.

The first part of the book includes chapters that provide information on the definitions associated with the concept *informal economy*; how the formal and informal economies are related; how the informal economy is related to criminal activity, in particular organized crime, financial crime, fraud, and corruption; and how the informal economy is manifested in different societies and under different circumstances and the methods governments and law enforcement agencies use to curtail criminal activity associated with the informal economy. The later chapters provide specific illustrations of how the cultures, values of ethnic groups, nationalities, and governments have traditionally responded to crimes associated with the informal economy.

In Chapter 1, the introductory chapter, the authors identify several concepts that have been used to delineate the characteristics of the informal economy. Such terms as the *shadow economy*, *underground economy*, *second economy*, *gray economy*, *black market*, and others have been used to identify and describe the informal economy. None of the concepts fully describes the essence of the informal economy. Several are too general in scope and others, such as the "black market," are too specific. It appears that the definition of the concept *informal economy* tends to encompass all of the other definitions used to refer to the unrecorded portion of the overall economy of a nation, and thus it was chosen for this book.

The concept *organized crime* also has many meanings. In the past, it was associated exclusively with crime syndicates, such as the Mafia. However, the research findings and writings of a number of scholars, such as Sutherland, revealed that the concept *organized crime* should include many forms of white collar crime, including corporate crime and financial crime.

It is also mentioned by several of the authors that, while the effects of the crimes generally associated with the informal economy, such as bribery, fraud, various types of smuggling, money laundering, and corruption generally have a negative effect on an economy, the dirty money earned from such criminal activities can help stimulate the economy in a country in which the economic situation is very bad. In the earlier part of the economic growth of such countries as Thailand, Singapore, and Hong Kong, it was the investments of illegally gained money that helped stimulate the economic growth of these countries.

The informal economy is emerging worldwide as an antipode to the formal economy. Perhaps only partially visible and parallel to the current social and economic life of European cities, it is romantic and appealing to tourists. Aspects of it can be found in the streets and squares of the cities, with venders selling flowers in the streets and in restaurants, with its links to drugs and prostitution, with low paying jobs and opportunities for immigrants, with the sale of stolen goods, the so-called black market, and with young people, tourists, and students who spend money on the goods and services connected to both the formal and the informal economy (Shapeland, 2003). The informal economy can be seen in three different forms of formal policy. These are the financial, economic order (formal economic), social order (state and urban policy), and the criminal justice system. In some areas, there are no clear dividing lines between the formal and informal economies. Work-related activities, which are usually performed by students, young adults entering the labor force, migrants, those working in the tourist-related occupations such as hospitality and construction work, generally receive low pay. In some cases, the employer pays taxes and health insurance (formal economy), and in other cases, the employer's contribution for health and other employee benefits, such as unemployment insurance, is not paid (informal economy). Thus, there are at least two different definitions (dimensions) of the informal economy that must be considered in any analysis of the relationship of the informal economy and crime. The economic definition defines the informal sector as a sector that does not contribute to the national tax revenue (formal economy), and the legal definition defines the criminal activities (forbidden) related to the informal economy. Politicians provide a third definition, often referred to as the slippery slope, that is, the attempts of the government officials to hide the "gray areas" of the informal economy under the carpet, using the rationale that it is necessary to do so to assure the economic and social stability of the country. Examples of this third dimension can be found in the manner in which the governments of various countries, responded to the practices of large banks and investment agencies that were either borderline criminal or definitely in violation of criminal laws. In some instances, the U.S. Congress actually appeared to be assisting the banks and investment firms. There have been attempts to integrate these definitions by using a 3D analysis of the informal economy, that is the "white economy," the part of the economic activity that is protected from taxes for the reasons mentioned earlier, the "gray" economy, the part providing work and services "off the record" or "under the carpet" and the "black" illegal economic activity. However, the fiscal and economic factors that define the differences in the economic definition and that try to distinguish whether a particular activity falls in the formal or informal sector are not necessarily in step with the social and political factors that influence the decision whether an offense is punishable or not, as defined in criminal law. The differences between the formal and informal sectors of the economy are based on the historical development of the culture, time and space, and legal system of a particular country. Thus, the definitions of "formal" and "informal economy" may differ in various countries of Europe, Asia, South America, and North America. For example, in an analysis of research completed on the relationship between human trafficking and the informal economy in Belgium, income received from the "black market" and fraud did not appear in the assessment of the national economy, so it was regrouped in the informal economic sector of the national economy.

Since the activities that define the informal economy are more heterogeneous than those of the underground economy, the informal economy concept has become an artificial construct that exists primarily because of the efforts of countries to regulate the taxation of such economies (Shapland, 2013).

Paoli (2003), describes the informal economy as being essentially connected to the formal economy, since without a formal economy, which is the national regulatory framework for economic activities, there would not be an informal economy. The ideal market economy, without regulation and no distinction between formal and informal, loses it meaning. The essence of the informal economy, therefore, is the relationship between government and economic activity. The government originates and regulates taxes and determines what sources of income are subject to taxation. For example, it took a U.S. Supreme Court ruling to determine that income derived from illegal sources was still subject to federal income taxation. Given the fact that the boundaries of the informal economy are regularly crossed by both legitimate and illegitimate organizations, it can be confirmed that some criminal organizations are able to be active simultaneously and continuously in both the formal and informal sectors of the economy.

Many economists believe that an informal economy is necessary for the survival of the formal economy in some developing countries, since economic enterprises operating in the formal economy find it difficult to survive because of the poor economic policies of the government as well as the inept leadership and corruption of the leaders of government. The high tax burden placed on legitimate entrepreneurs tempts these entrepreneurs to acquire services through the informal economy, which includes "black" and informal employment (Shapeland and Ponsaers, 2009). With a large portion of the national economy being based on the informal economy, a country can adjust its economy, and begin to become part of a modern society that is grounded in economic and political globalization. However, if the economy becomes too much supported by the informal economy and tax evasion, this dependence on the informal economy becomes a serious threat to the individual and society (Dobovšek and Pirnat, 2008).

The Informal Economy and Organized Crime

Chapter 2, written by Dobovšek and Slak, focuses on the link between the informal economy and organized crime. They introduce the complex issue of informal economy from a criminological standpoint. It is interesting to follow their analysis of deviant behavior, which each of us may have a slight tendency to commit. The so-called bad tax morale is a feature that can be observed by nearly all citizens. "Bad tax morale" defined as the construction of financial instruments by enterprises to avoid taxes, is being used by international companies and by criminal organizations as a standard cheating model to overcome tax authorities all over the world. This model is as popular in Austria as in Germany, Serbia, or the United States. Dobovšek and Slak show that legitimate economic actors try to shape their business on the one hand through lobbying influencing political groups and powerful individuals, and on the other hand by engaging in informal practices as well. Some of these informal practices are not different from those practiced by criminal organizations. The shadow economy is influenced, and its extension is dependent on a number of factors, such as the increase of taxes and social security payments, quality of state institutions, the tax morale, and the public sector services.

In Chapter 3, Schneider shares the findings of his more than 25 years of research on shadow economy, organized crime, and corruption. Schneider et al. (2012) conducted an empirical investigation of the financial flow of the money gained from organized crime and tax fraud in developed countries that infiltrates the official economic system. They found that, the growth of the world economy was quite high and improved the economic well-being all over the globe, but this development was accompanied by an increase in the proceeds from organized crime and an increase of tax and financial fraud during the last 20 years. They noted that, "In absolute terms the worldwide money laundered increased by 36% from 1996 to 2005 and by 33% from 2005 to 2009. The key focus lies on drugs: in the year 2000 it is estimated that laundered money was $0.6 trillion USD and this amount doubled in the year 2009 to $1.2 trillion USD." In the research, it was found that drugs were the greatest source of illegal money, with 50% of the total coming from drugs, followed by counterfeiting (39%), human trafficking (5%), and oil (2%). The classic criminal component accounts for only 27%–31% of the total amount of dirty money. Thus, it is clear that capital flight and tax fraud accounts for the largest proportion of the dirty money (Schneider et al., 2012). From this short summary of the work of Schneider and his coresearchers, it is clear how dangerous the activities of organized crime are to the economies of nations throughout the world. From their preliminary findings, it was determined as follows: First, the necessity for money laundering by organized criminals is obvious, since many illegal (criminal) transactions are done by cash. The cash from criminal activities must be laundered in order to have some "legal" funds for investment or consumption in the legal world. Second, to get an estimate of the extent and range of illegal financial activity in transnational crime over time is very difficult. Although, the estimates of the money that is laundered from several types of crimes exceeds several billions of dollars, the estimates are likely to have a wide margin of error. However, it gives a clear indication of how important money laundering and the turnover of transnational crime are. Third, tax fraud and/or illegal cross border capital flows are by far the biggest and highest share of all illegal transactions, quite often 66% of all illegal capital flows or proceeds (Schneider nd Enste 2013).

The contribution of Schneider is a real eye-opener. The statistics and numbers of the informal economy in relation to the legal economy show the dangers that it poses for democratic, vulnerable societies. Schneider concludes that international co-operation by law enforcement and justice systems is a must and a significant challenge for international organizations, governments, and authorities.

In Chapter 4, on the multidimensional Mafia strategy, Antinori explains the new business strategy of the Mafia organizations in Italy and the development of the economic Mafia system. He reports that the Mafia has moved its activities more and more from violence to becoming involved in various aspects of the informal economy and corrupt activities. Antinori, quoting from the former judge Giovanni Falcone, who was killed by the Mafia in 1992, gives the judge's description of Mafia activities by stating, "First their money arrives, then they come with their own methods." A wiretapped talk from November 9, 1989, between two Napoleon members of Camorra during the "Fall of the Berlin Wall" is typical for a Mafia-like organization's behavior. One of the speakers stated, "Go to East Berlin, you must buy everything, everything, everything, buy discos, bars, pizzerias, everything, everything, everything." Antinori continues, "The infiltrative mafia strategy is characterized by the segmentation, as evidenced by the fact that among the confiscated enterprises for mafia crimes: 48.5% is constituted by limited liability companies, 27.3% by individuals, while only 3.5% by joint-stock company" (http://www.sosimpresa.it/24_xii-rapporto-sos-impresa.html).

Violence is only used if there is no other possibility to influence and motivate individuals to act in the way the Mafia prefers. Corruption is the most used tool to influence and motivate opposition characters to change their minds and to create a climate of Mafia-friendly decisions. The success rate of the new Mafia proves the efficiency of its strategy. Antinori cited the example of the Mafia gaining control of soil moving and waste dumping to show the effect very clearly. Antonio Maria Costa, the former executive director of the United Nations Office on Drugs and Crime (UNO in Vienna until 2010), said in his speech at the Royal Institute of International Affairs in 2012, "With the outbreak of the financial crisis—and in the middle of a cash crisis—too many banks are open to the money laundering coming from illegal and criminal activities" (Antinori, 2012). This is described exactly in the book, *Financial Crimes: A Threat to Global Security. as a Global Threat* (Edelbacher, Kratcoski, and Thiel, 2012). For example, in Austria the largest financial institution, Bank Austria, was sold to the Italian Bank UniCredit, the largest financial institution of Italy. Criminal statistics of the Ministry of the Interior, Department for Money Laundering, show that about 40% of all suspicious transactions reported were from the former Eastern Bloc countries, like Russia or Ukraine. The four big players of the Austrian financial institutions expanded into the Eastern countries very much after the "Fall of the Iron Curtain." Today, they are confronted with enormous problems. Out of the transferees, a lot were from suspicious sources. There is evidence that a high percentage of the money comes from criminal groups—Mafia-like organizations and oligarchs who launder their suspicious income through Austrian banks. This is very often discovered when law enforcement investigations in organized crime cases follow the flow of the money, but it is difficult to prove the illegality, because virtually no investigation assistance is provided by law enforcement and the justice system of these countries.

Chapter 5, written by Kratcoski describes the connection between the informal economy, white collar crime, and corruption. The primary focus of this chapter is the effects organized crime and financial crimes have on the national economy and the security of the United States, although these effects can threaten the economy of any country. He uses several examples of the everyday world familiar to each of us and links them together with examples of the business world and organized crime, maintaining that nothing has changed in the relationship of the business world and organized criminals since the time of Al Capone. He states, "No doubt almost every adult in the United States either contributes to the informal economy in some way, or at least knows who has contributed. As adults, our experiences with the informal economy may be related to having an electrician, plumber, or carpenter complete a job 'under the table,' that is, no record of the work in terms of the amount earned is filed with the tax collection authorities." He continues, "The California Department of Insurance (2014, p. 1) notes that, 'Underground economy' is a term that refers to those individuals and businesses that deal with cash and/or use other schemes to conceal their activities and their true tax liability from government licensing, regulatory and taxing agencies." Feige, maintains that, "The underground economy causes a loss of hundreds of billions of dollars in tax revenue each year" (Feige, 2009, p. 7). The 9/11 Commission Report of 2002 stated that criminal activities such as price fixing, corruption of officials, Ponzi schemes, insider trading, money laundering, and racketeering were shown to be connected to the to the financing of terrorist activities and posed a threat to national security. The government began a concerted effort to prevent and control financial crime activity by targeting terrorist money, identifying terrorist financiers, and freezing their assets.

The RICO (1970) Racketeer Influenced Corruption Organizations (RICO) Act of 1970 and the USA PATRIOT Act of 2001 built the legal basis for investigating organized crime and all forms of racketeering. Kratcoski explains the links between the informal economy, organized crime, and white collar crime by analyzing the financial crisis of 2007/2008. Many regulations that were enacted after the world crisis of 1929/30 had been abolished in the 1990s, and have to be reestablished by the U.S. Securities and Exchange Commission in 2010. The Dodd-Frank Wall Street Reform Act and Consumer Protection Act were passed by the U.S. Congress as a reaction to the financial crisis of 2007/08. The purpose of this Act was to "promote the financial stability of the United States by improving accountability and transparency in the financial system, to end 'too big to fail' institutions, to protect the American taxpayer by bailouts, to protect consumers from abusive financial services practices, and for other purposes" (H.R. 473//:www.sec.gov/). Kratcoski concludes, "Regardless of the enhanced efforts to combat financial crimes and other crimes related to the informal or shadow economy, there is still a lack of commitment because of the large number of people who either engage in criminal activities, know someone who engages in criminal activities relating to the informal economy, or benefit from such acts."

In Chapter 6, written by Thiel, he elaborates on the relationship of the insurance industry to the informal economy. He offers two basic possibilities. The person seeking to be insured can be the main actor in an insurance scheme by overestimating the risk he takes. If an overrated risk is taken by an insurer, this may attract criminals, who see this as an opportunity to defraud the insurance company. In the second area, the insurance business is a capital investment, a multibillion Euro market. A transaction for investment may be suspicious, but nothing specific has been reported, even though the potential for criminal involvement exists. Both insurer and the person insured can be victims of fraud actions. All forms of fraud have been perpetrated by CEOs themselves and by customers reporting faked damages, exaggerating the loss size of an actual damage, or causing damage deliberately. Other fraud activities in the shadow economy include pretend sickness to obtain insurance benefits and other forms of cheating.

Gottschalk, in Chapter 7, discusses the role of lawyers as defenders of white collar criminals. He offers insights on the issue of the fights between prosecutors and defendants attorneys. He reports that law enforcement agencies and prosecutors are very often not prepared to counteract the strategies used by attorneys who defend high level white collar criminals. Organized white collar criminals very often have better access to the legal infrastructure for the professional advice of legal experts in the fields of law and tax regulations. They can afford to engage the best lawyers in these areas, and consequently are well informed about the limitations of laws, and of official state authorities, the justice system, and law enforcement bodies. In some instances, the resources of law enforcement agencies and prosecution services are much smaller than those of criminal organizations. Lawyers defending white collar criminals use the limitations and legal restrictions of the law to develop excellent defense strategies. The burden of proof can be so heavy that law enforcement agencies and tax authorities cannot gather enough evidence to convict white collar criminals. Through legislation, including the RICO Act in the United States and the anti-Mafia regulations in Italy, the burden of proof needed to convict a defendant has been reduced. For example, the RICO Act allows the prosecution of an individual on the basis of belonging to a criminal organization (RICO, 1970), but in general, the human rights standards of the European Human Right Convention seem to favor the criminals, and white collar criminals in particular. The presumption of innocence very often seems to be much stronger than the evidence of criminal activity.

In Chapter 8, written by Potz, Sporer, Zorgoi, and Burbeck, the authors elaborate on the possibility of using the *falsified prospect theory*. In researching the effects of corruption on Foreign Direct Investments (FDI) in China and Russia, they discovered that, on the one hand, both countries are notorious for being rather corrupt, based on the Transparency International interpretation, but, on the other hand, it is not really clear if corruption in these countries should be understood as a rather disturbing factor, the so-called "grabbing hand," or as a supporting factor, the so-called "helping hand." In China, as well as in Russia, investors are confronted with rather high levels of corruption when entering the market, but no valid generalization about the impact of corruption on foreign direct investment can be concluded.

In Chapter 9 that follows, Meissnitzer examines the dangers involved with social fraud. Social fraud becomes very popular in a mobile world where employees and entrepreneurs act in a global market. Very often control mechanisms fail in such an environment. The European Union members were confronted with this problem when new, economically poor countries sought admission to the Union. The market is immediately open for cheating activities when the ineffective or nonexistent control mechanisms of the poorer countries clash with the control methods in place in the more prosperous countries in the union. Criminal exploitation of human beings used as cheap labor is increasing. In Austria, 10 years ago, a so-called "construction Mafia" was established. Although the tax authorities seized 40 million euros, the construction Mafia still found a few loopholes. They were responsible for an alleged 800 million to 1 billion euros in damages. The members of the construction Mafia tended to be associated with defrauding the social security and welfare system in Austria. About 7500 persons employed by 20 letterbox companies had to pay a registration fee to be registered in the social security system. The Austrian financial police estimated the average number of bogus registrations of inactive persons to be around 25% of all registrations by letterbox companies. Since Austria has a high standard of social welfare offered to employees, the motivation to commit fraud is very strong. Evidence showed that pregnant women were offered the opportunity to give birth in Austrian hospitals, as well as access to maternity benefits and in-hand cash by the illegal agents of the construction Mafia. Meissnitzer also notes that persons registered as employees in a letterbox company not only work in construction, but also in the transport sector, agriculture, forestry, gastronomy, security, business, and in the meat and other industries. The construction Mafia makes enormous profits with a low risk of being exposed. The employer simply sees the opportunity to reduce labor costs and tax loads. In 2005, the Austrian government tried to repress this fraud scheme by the passage of the Social Fraud Act. As a result, eight major groups controlling more than 200 letterbox companies were eliminated, but this legal approach was not enough to tackle the entire problem, and still a number of shortcomings are evident. The law does not provide for an actual chain liability, which helps the criminals to avoid investigation consequences.

Perspectives on the Informal Economy in Specific Countries

In Chapter 10, Edelbacher relates his experiences and involvement at the Vienna Liaison Office of the Academic Council on the United Nations System, specialized in fighting organized crime, white collar crime, and corruption. This former police chief of the Major Crime Bureau in Vienna describes how the Federal Police of Austria were confronted with a dramatic increase in the amount of crime from 1991 to 1994, after the "Fall of the Iron Curtain." People were victimized by thefts and burglaries. The insurance industry also experienced an increase on fraudulent claims. Then, in 1996 and 1997, Mafia groups from the south and east poured into Austria and established their business. The criminal organizations succeeded in many fields, but they did not succeed in corrupting the Austrian law enforcement system, even though they tried to do so. It took many years for before the security system adapted to the new challenges, but eventually crime prevention became much more important and people became aware that, to combat crime, they had to increase their own levels of security by using measures to protect their homes, property, and personal integrity.

In Chapter 11, Simonović and Bošković describe the basis factors of the shadow economy as the "Achilles heel of the state." They say, "The Shadow Economy is a response to weak functioning of authority (government) and state in the sense of their incapability to enforce laws and regulations. High unemployment rates, low quality of public services, low tax-related morale and the tolerant attitude and stand of the citizens toward the shadow economy are the main causes." Both authors elaborate on the fact that the sanctions of the international community against Serbia brought about widespread corruption. In a short period of time, the sanctions provided opportunities to a group of individuals who gained their wealth on the basis of the shadow economy by smuggling and corruption and who managed to develop wealth, political power, influence, and excellent international ties in foreign trade. Their wealth and power have their roots in the shadow economy, money laundering, organized crime, and corruption. Lack of political will, lack of expertise and trust in the official institutions, heavy burden of taxes, low salaries, inappropriate tax policies, insufficiently restrictive laws, inadequate law enforcement, and numerous weaknesses in the work inspectorates are factors pushing the shadow economy and favoring organized crime, corruption, and fraud. As described by the two authors, the Republic of Serbia suffered extremely on the one hand by the sanctions of the international society and on the other hand by the continuous changes of the legislative environment, often inconsistent and selective application of law, unstable economic and political environment that generated a symbiosis of shadow economy, corruption, and organized crime. It is pointed out that "The more shadow or black economy in a society exists, the higher degree of corruption and vice versa is the outcome."

In Chapter 12, written by Xiangxia, titled "The Relationship of the Shadow Economy and Corruption in China," the author contributes to our understanding of how the informal economy is manifested in China. She traces the relevant links of the informal economy to organized crime, especially corruption. She writes, "Since last year (2013), the Chinese government has been making great efforts to combat corruption. China is one of the largest countries in the world and in 2013 its GDP was approximately $9.3 trillion USD" (Online News, retrieved on May 16, 2014 from http://www.guancha.cn/economy/2014 01 20 200873 s.shtmI). Even though there appeared to be a decrease in the percentage of increase in the amount of corruption when 1993 is compared to 2003, nevertheless there was an increase for each year. Thus, it is conclusive that the amount of corruption has increased each year, especially in the economically well-developed areas of China. Corruption and the shadow economy are much more active in the developed areas than in northwest China where the economic development is much lower than it is in central and eastern China. The greatest power is held by the national public officers and civil servants and some of these officials tend to build ties with criminal organizations and also engage in corruption. In conclusion, the author feels that the Chinese government has a long and difficult fight before it can control corruption and the shadow economy that is grounded in corruption.

In Chapter 13, Yokoyama shares his knowledge about Japan's experiences with organized crime and its relationship with the shadow economy and corruption in his chapter on organized criminal gangs in Japan. He contributes a historical-based description of the development of organized criminal groups originally known as Yakuza, a name accepted by the public and used by the media, which translates as "hooligan" or a "worthless scamp" (Yokoyama, 1999, p. 135). Around 1960 the police advocated that they be called Boryokudan, which means a violent group. The gang members were categorized as Bakuto (gamblers), Tekiua (peddlers or stallkeepers), and Gurentai (street hooligans). For a long period of time, these criminal organized groups based their income on gambling, black market activities, illegal economic activities, and violence by strong arm protection. Later, they changed to trafficking and selling drugs, especially methamphetamine stimulant drugs, trafficking weapons, the construction business, loan-giving, and money laundering. The Japanese criminal organizations gained power and influence through their underground network and tried to ally themselves with right-wing or conservative political parties. Corruption was rampant. Young people admired the luxurious life style of the members of the criminal organizations, and therefore it was not a problem to enlist them for the dirty jobs. To cope with the organized crime phenomenon, new laws were passed, and the Public Safety Commission began to issue stop orders to curtail their violent demands.

In Chapter 14, Cofan, from Romania, describes the so-called outsiders of societies who created big business in the field of the shadow economy. For centuries, the ethnic groups of Sinties and Romas who are not willing to integrate into any state have existed in Asia, America, and Europe. They prefer to stay and live on their own, they like a free life, to be mobile, and to run their own business. They are called "gypsies." This is the name of the ethnic group, native to northwestern India. Beginning in the fifth century they migrated to Iran and the Mediterranean Asia and in the ninth century to the Byzantine Empire. From there they have entered southeastern and central Europe and north of Africa in the tenth to fourteenth centuries. Today, the United States, Canada, the European Union are confronted with enormous problems from these groups. They are an economic power based primarily on income out of the shadow economy, and also disturb societies by their mobility and tendency toward criminality.

Another example of organized criminal activity in the shadow economy is apparent in the activities of the "Hells Angels." In Chapter 15, Gottschalk writes: "A distinction must be made between noncriminalized and criminalized bikers. The one group of Hells Angels can be described as a criminal matrix organization. As shadows of the real world, criminal bikers participate in an organized shadow economy. Some of the profit is kept in the shadow economy for consumption. Some of the profit is laundered into the legal economy for investments in tattoo studios, construction companies, restaurants, hotels, and other enterprises, both nationally and internationally. Hells Angels make money in prostitution, drug manufacturing, dealing and smuggling, extortion, auto theft, weapons dealing, and human trafficking. The business of Hells Angels in Norway is organized from seven chapters across the country. The leaders of them are a special brand of entrepreneurs who consider the law in society as not valid either for themselves or for their business activities. Hells Angels are involved in a number of black markets. Goods and services are traded illegally."

In Chapter 16, Eman, Furdi, Hacin, and Dobovšek discuss the gray economy, corruption, and organized crime in Slovenia. In their chapter, they report what changed in Slovenia after the financial crisis of 2008 and why people slowly drifted into using shadow and/or illegal services. Since Slovenia became an independent state, it has experienced a complex development, due to changes in the socioeconomic field. As a result of political instability, economic deregulation, frequent migrations and insecurities in the labor market, the gray economy, corruption and organized crime increased. Dobovšek and his team analyzed these developments in Slovenia, using statistical data and applying the crime mapping methodology, especially in the regions of Ljubana and Maribor. They state, "By the beginning of the economic crisis, the economic turndown, rising unemployment, lower disposable income, and insecurity, people drifted much more into the shadow economy. The changes in the socioeconomic field changed individual human values." Pečar (1996) states that crime always reflects the general social conditions, and organized crime, corruption, and the gay economy are no exceptions. In today's neoliberal society, because of the decreasing social transfers and a low tax morality, governments have enormous problems in balancing their yearly budget. According to the Shadow Economy Report in Europe, the gray economy in 2013 was worth more than 2.15 million euros and caused tremendous problems to national governments that tried to balance their budgets by avoiding tax increases and benefit cuts that would hamper economic recovery (Schneider, 2013, p. 3). Schneider also emphasizes four major factors of the gray economy: savings, lack of guilty conscience, low risk of detection, and easy participation.

Dobovšek and his team continue, "Another threat is corruption: Dimc (2012, pp. 20–22) states that independent international indicators, unlike national ones, point to the fact that the level of corruption in Slovenia is stagnating or that it is not increasing. The extent of damage caused by corruption in the Republic of Slovenia ranges between 1.5 and 2 percent of GDP, which amounts to between 531 and 708 million Euros. In the framework of Transparency International's Corruption Perception Index, which indicates the experts' perception of corruption in the public sector and politics, Slovenia is ranked 43rd in 2013 (it held 37th place in 2012)." This is a development similar to what occurred in Austria. In both countries the level of corruption increased, accompanied by sensational corruption cases. The last election in Slovenia showed that people want a political change, as there were several new political parties elected to parliament. This seems to be a better sign of a changing political culture than in Austria, because there the traditional parties in the government still do not show an earnest political will to change their behavior. Minority groups are too weak to push them in a better direction.

In Chapter 17, Baker informs us about the size, determinants, and comparisons of the informal economy in the United States, providing a political science view of this issue. He states, "No area is as finely calibrated as the economy. Employment, production, and money supply are specified in multiple ways and are measured in quarterly, monthly, weekly, and in some cases daily intervals. The simplest definition of the informal economy is the difference between actual individual and corporate income and reported income levels. This difference is a result of underreporting income and/or overstating deductions. Following Edgar Feige (1989), the level of illegal economic activity is estimated between 18% and 23% of U.S. income that goes unreported. Compared to other countries, the informal economy in the U.S. is relatively small. The dynamic of the informal economy is delegitimizing and destabilizing the public sector at a time when the U.S. polity is strained by significant cultural and political cleavages. Strategies to close the gap would allay both economic and political tensions."

In Chapter 18, written by Felsenreich, the human risk factor is investigated. He asks, "How can human nature be analyzed and calculated to establish a risk-management that will protect the members of a democratic society against the damage of the informal economy, fraud and corruption?" An individual risk profile could help to calculate the personal risk that may be involved by selecting an individual for special leadership and management positions. Everybody can be at risk to becoming active in informal economy, fraud, and corruption.

Summary: The Informal Economy and Crime in the Future

After reviewing the materials provided by the authors in their chapters, it is apparent that the matter of the informal economy and its relationship to the formal economy, organized crime, financial crime, corruption, and fraud is very complex. Its extent and influence on the welfare of the each country is dependent on a number of factors. In some countries, involvement in the informal economy is deeply rooted in the culture and traditions and is not regarded as illegal or criminal; in others, the citizens are aware of its illegality but still take part in it. In new democracies, the citizens may be aware that the underground economy is politically controlled or influenced by organized crime, but they view it as a necessary evil in the evolution of their economy. In countries with well-established democracies, banks and corporations have been implicated in schemes to defraud both the government and average citizens. In other countries, including Italy and Romania, ethnic groups operate openly outside the law and victimize the citizens who do not have the power to control them.

These differing situations make it very difficult to propose solutions that will help control the functioning of the underground economy in the future and reduce its effect on the economies of the countries it threatens. Legislative solutions have been attempted, with mixed results. Law enforcement efforts to identify the perpetrators behind the illegal activities are constantly being made, but the problem often goes beyond local situations and is fed and controlled by globally organized criminal organizations. Its control will require individualized strategies for each nation to address the specific situations and circumstances occurring in that country. In addition, solutions must involve continued and expanded assistance from Interpol and the United Nations.

References

Antinori, A. (2011). Organized crime, the mafia, white collar crime and corruption. In *Financial Crimes: A Threat to Global Security*, M. Edelbacher, P. Kratcoski, and M. Theil (eds.). Boca Raton, FL: CRC Press, pp. 145–160.

California Department of Insurance. (2014). *Fraud Investigation.* http://www.edd.ca.gov/payroll_taxes/underground_economy_operations.htm (Accessed June 15, 2014.)

Dimc, M. (2012). Korupcija. In *Nacionalni system integritete v Sloveniji*, V.S. Habic (ur). Ljubljana, Solvenia: Narodna in university knjiznica, pp. 20–22.

Feige, E. (2009). The underground economy and the currency enigma. *Public Finance* [*Finances Publiques*], 49(Suppl.): 119–136.

Paoli, L. (2003). The informal economy and organized crime. In *The Informal Economy: Threat and Opportunity in the City*, J. Shapeland, H. Albrecht, J. Ditton, and T. Godefroy (eds.). Freiburg im Breisgau, Germany: Luscrim, pp. 133–173.

Pečar, J. (1996). Podjetniska kriminaliteta. *Revija za kriminalistiko in kriminologijo* 47(30): 203–212.

Shapland, J. (2003). Looking at opportunities in the informal economy of cities. In *The Informal Economy: Threat and Opportunity in the City*, J. Shapland, H. Albrecht, J. Ditton, and T. Godefroy (eds.). Freiburg im Breisgau, Germany: luscrim, pp. 1–25.

Shapland, J. and Ponsaers, P. (eds.) (2009). *The Informal Economy and Connections with Organized Crime*. The Hague, the Netherlands: Bju Legal Publishers.

Schneider, F. (2013). The financial flows of transnational crime and tax fraud in central European countries: What do we (not) know? *Public Finance Review/Special Issue: The Shadow Economy, Tax Evasion and Money Laundering,* 41(5), 677–707.

Schneider, F. and Enste, H. (2013). *The Shadow Economy and International Survey*. Cambridge, UK: Cambridge University Press.

Yokoyama, M. (1999), Trends of organized crime by Boryokudan in Japan. In S. Einstein and M. Amir (eds.) *Organized Crime: Uncertainties and Dilemmas.* Chicago, IL: The Office of International Criminal Justice, the University of Illinois at Chicago, pp. 135–154.

Index

E

F

G

H

I

J

K

L

M

Y